The Best Test Preparation for the

AP
Chemistry Exam

9th Edition

Updated and Edited by

Kevin R. Reel
The Westminster Schools
Atlanta, GA

Philip E. Dumas, Ph.D.
Chairperson of Chemistry Department
College of New Jersey, Ewing, NJ

Ronald M. Fikar, Ph.D.
Research Associate
Rutgers University, New Brunswick, NJ

Jerry W. Samples, Ph.D.
Associate Professor of Civil and
Mechanical Engineering
United States Military Academy
West Point, NY

Jay Templin, Ed.D.
Assistant Professor of Biology
Widener University, Wilmington, DE

William Uhland
Research Scientist
Cytogen Corporation, Princeton, NJ

Research & Education Association, Inc.
Visit our website at
www.rea.com

Research & Education Association
61 Ethel Road West
Piscataway, New Jersey 08854
E-mail: info@rea.com

The Best Test Preparation for the
AP CHEMISTRY EXAM

Printed in the United States of America

Library of Congress Control Number 2006922707

International Standard Book Number 0-7386-0221-3

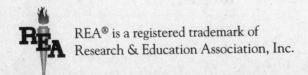

CONTENTS

ABOUT OUR AUTHOR

Kevin R. Reel has been in science education for over 25 years and has taught AP Chemistry for 12 years. He has written numerous articles for academic journals and has contributed to many textbooks in chemistry, health, and environmental science. He earned his BA and MS from Stanford University, and is currently the high school principal at The Westminster Schools in Atlanta, Georgia.

ABOUT RESEARCH & EDUCATION ASSOCIATION

Founded in 1959, Research & Education Association is dedicated to publishing the finest and most effective educational materials—including software, study guides, and test preps—for students in middle school, high school, college, graduate school, and beyond. Today, REA's wide-ranging catalog is a leading resource for teachers, students, and professionals. We invite you to visit us at *www.rea.com* to find out how "REA is making the world smarter."

ACKNOWLEDGMENTS

In addition to our authors, we would like to thank Larry B. Kling, Vice President, Editorial, for supervising development; Pam Weston, Vice President, Publishing, for setting the quality standards for production integrity and managing the publication to completion; Christine Reilley, Senior Editor, for preflight editorial review; Diane Goldschmidt, Associate Editor, for post-production quality assurance; Jeff LoBalbo, Senior Graphic Artist, for his graphic arts contributions and post-production file mapping; Christine Saul, Senior Graphic Artist, for cover design; Rob Coover for his editorial contributions; Patricia Van Arnum for technical and editorial review; and Wende Solano for typesetting the manuscript.

AP CHEMISTRY STUDY SCHEDULE

The following study schedule allows for thorough preparation for the AP Chemistry Examination. Although it is designed for six weeks, it can be condensed into a three-week course by collapsing each two-week period into a single week. Be sure to set aside at least two hours each day to study. Bear in mind that the more time you spend studying, the more prepared and relaxed you will feel on the day of the exam.

Week	Activity
1	Read and study Chapter 1, which will introduce you to the AP Chemistry Examination. Carefully read and study the Chemistry Review included in Chapters 2–5 of this book.
2 & 3	Carefully read and study the Chemistry Review included in Chapters 6–14 of this book.
4	Take Practice Tests 1 and 2 in this book. After scoring your exam, carefully review all incorrect answer explanations. If any particular subjects seem difficult, review them by referring back to the appropriate section of the Chemistry Review.
5	Take Practice Tests 3 and 4, and after scoring your exam, carefully review all incorrect answer explanations. If any particular subjects seem difficult, review them by referring back to the appropriate section of the Chemistry Review.
6	Take Practice Tests 5 and 6. After scoring them, review all incorrect answer explanations. Study any areas in which you consider yourself to be weak by using the Chemistry Review and any other reliable sources you have on hand. Review our practice tests again to be sure you understand the problems that you originally answered incorrectly.

Excelling on the AP Chemistry Exam

Chapter 1

EXCELLING ON THE AP CHEMISTRY EXAM

ABOUT THE EXAMINATION

The Advanced Placement Chemistry Examination is offered each May at participating schools and testing centers throughout the world. The Advanced Placement Program is designed to allow high school students to pursue college-level studies while attending high school. Participating colleges, in turn, grant credit and/or advanced placement to students who do well on the examinations.

The Advanced Placement Chemistry course is designed to be the equivalent of a college introductory chemistry course, often taken by chemistry majors in their first year of college. Since the test covers a broad range of topics, no student is expected to answer all of the questions correctly. (Consequently, it is important for students to not feel defeated when confronting a question that appears unanswerable.)

The examination follows the outline, published by the College Board, that appears below. The exam is divided into two 90-minute sections. The first section is composed of 75 multiple-choice questions designed to test recall of a broad range of concepts and calculations. The score students earn on the multiple-choice test composes 45% of the total score. Calculators are not permitted on the multiple-choice portion of the exam, although simple arithmetic may be needed to answer some questions.

The second section is a free-response exam and constitutes 55% of the final grade. Calculators are allowed on Part A, during which the student has 40 minutes to complete two problems. Calculators are not allowed on Part B, during which students have 50 minutes to complete chemical reaction questions and three essay questions. Most hand-held calculators are allowed in the examination. However, calculators with typewriter-style (QWERTY) keypads are not allowed. If you are unsure if your calculator is permitted, check with your teachers or Educational Testing Service.

A detailed outline of the topics on the examination and specific strategies for both portions of the Advanced Placement Chemistry examination follow.

DETAILED OUTLINE OF THE EXAMINATION

The following is an outline of the general breadth of topics that the College Board identifies as being on the AP Chemistry Examination.

I. **Structure of Matter (20% of the AP test)**

    A.   Atomic theory and structure

        1. Evidence for atomic theory

        2. Atomic mass

        3. Atomic number, mass number, isotopes

        4. Electron energy levels, quantum numbers, atomic orbitals

        5. Periodic relationships: atomic radii, ionization energy, electron affinity, oxidation states.

    B.   Chemical Bonding

        1. Binding forces

            a. Types of forces: ionic, covalent, network covalent, metallic, hydrogen bonding, van der Waals.

            b. Relationships to states, structure, and properties of matter.

            c. Polarity of bonds, electronegativities.

        2. Molecular Models

            a. Lewis structures

            b. Hybridization of orbitals, resonance, sigma and pi bonds.

            c. VSEPR (valence shell electron pair repulsion)

   3. Geometry of molecules and ions, structural isomerism of simple organic molecules and coordination compounds; dipole moments of molecules, relation of properties to structure.

C.   Nuclear chemistry: nuclear equations, half-lives, and radioactivity; chemical applications.

II.   States of Matter (20% of the AP test)

A.   Gases

   1. Laws of ideal gases

      a. Equation of state for an ideal gas

      b. Partial pressures

   2. Kinetic-molecular theory

      a. Interpretation of ideal gas laws on the basis of theory

      b. Avogadro's hypothesis and the mole concept

      c. Dependence of kinetic energy on temperature

      d. Deviations in the ideal gas laws

B.   Liquids and Solids

   1. Liquids and solids from the kinetic-molecular viewpoint

   2. Phase diagrams

   3. Changes of state, including critical points and triple points

   4. Structure of solids; lattice energies

C.   Solutions

   1. Types of solutions and factors affecting solubility

   2. Methods of expressing concentration

   3. Raoult's law and colligative properties; osmosis

   4. Behavior of non-ideal solutions

III.   Reactions (35-40% of the AP test)

A.   Reaction types

   1. Acid-base reactions, concepts of Arrhenius, Brønsted-Lowry, and Lewis; coordination complexes, amphoterism.

2. Precipitation reactions

3. Oxidation-reduction reactions

    a. Oxidation number

    b. The role of the electron in oxidation-reduction

    c. Electrochemistry: electrolytic and galvanic cells; Faraday's laws; standard half-cell potentials; Nernst equation; prediction of the direction of redox reactions

B.   Stoichiometry

1. Ionic and molecular species present in chemical systems; net ionic reactions

2. Balancing of equations, including oxidation-reduction reactions

3. Mass and volume relations with emphasis on the mole concept, including empirical formulas and limiting reactants

C.   Equilibrium

1. Concept of dynamic equilibrium, physical and chemical; Le Chatelier's principle; equilibrium constants

2. Quantitative treatment

    a. Equilibrium constants for gaseous reactions: K_p, K_c

    b. Equilibrium constants for reactions in solution

        i.   Constants for acids and bases; pK; pH

        ii. Solubility product constants and their application to precipitation and dissolution of slightly soluble compounds

        iii. Common ion effect; buffers; hydrolysis

D.   Kinetics

1. Concept of reaction rate

2. Use of experimental data and graphical analysis to determine reaction order, rate constants, and rate laws

3. Effect of temperature on reaction rates

4. Energy of activation; the role of catalysts

     5. Relationship between the rate-determining step and mechanism of reaction

  E. Thermodynamics

     1. State functions

     2. First law: change in enthalpy; heat of formation; heat of reaction; Hess's law; heats of vaporization and fusion; calorimetry

     3. Second law: entropy; free energy of formation; free energy of reaction; dependence of change in free energy of enthalpy and entropy changes

     4. Relationship between change in free energy, equilibrium constants, and electrode potentials

IV. Descriptive Chemistry (10-15% of the AP test)

  A. Chemical reactivity and products of chemical reactions

  B. Relationships in the periodic table; horizontal, vertical, and diagonal with examples of alkali metals, alkaline earth metals, halogens, and the first series of transition metals

  C. Introduction to organic chemistry: hydrocarbons and functional groups (structure, nomenclature, chemical properties)

V. Laboratory (5-10% of the AP test)

  A. Making observations of chemical reactions

  B. Recording data

  C. Calculating and interpreting results based on observed quantitative data

  D. Effectively communicating experimental results, including error analysis

MULTIPLE-CHOICE STRATEGIES

Format and Scoring

Each correct answer in the multiple-choice section earns one point, while each wrong answer causes one-quarter (1/4) point to be taken off the score earned on this section. Omitted questions receive neither credit nor deduction.

The multiple-choice section is subtly broken into two subsections, Part A and Part B. Part A questions give information and a set of answers that can be used for three to five questions. Part B presents standard multiple-choice questions that provide information, and then offer five options for answers, options (A) through (E).

Strategies

The following strategies will help you study for and take the multiple-choice section of the AP Chemistry examination.

- To prepare for the multiple-choice section, use the content review in this book. If you know each item in this content review, you will get a great score on your multiple-choice section. After studying the content review, use the practice exams to test your knowledge. When you miss a problem, go back to the content review to be sure that you understand the material.

- When taking the exam, keep a one-question-per-minute pace and go directly through the test. Quite often, easy questions toward the end of the multiple-choice test are not answered because students do not get to them. Mark the unanswered questions that you skip on your answer sheet, so you may easily return to them. Always be sure that you fill in the bubble that corresponds to the question that you are answering.

- Once you have answered most of the multiple-choice questions during the initial 60-minute pass-through of the exam, you now have 30 minutes to answer the tougher or more time-consuming questions. Once again, start at the beginning; try not to skip around. You will probably find that you are more warmed up; some of these answers will now come to you and you will wonder why you skipped the question during the first pass-through of the exam.

- For questions you don't know, it is worth guessing IF you can eliminate at least two possible answers. If you can't eliminate at least two answers, then leave the answer blank; the odds are stacked against you to get the question correct. Answers for conceptual questions that contain extreme words like "never" or "always" are likely candidates for elimination. Once you guess on an answer, move on and forget about the question. Studies show that students tend to change guesses from right answers to wrong answers more often than the other way around. Trust your intuition on these.

FREE-RESPONSE STRATEGIES

OVERVIEW OF SECTION II

- You will be given 40 minutes for Part A and 50 minutes for Part B, for a total of 90 minutes for Section II.

- In Part A, you will complete two problems, each with multiple parts (usually a through e). The first question involves equilibrium topics.

- In Part B, you will answer a group of reaction questions, and then three essays. The first essay covers a laboratory topic, the second essay covers a general topic, such as periodic trends. For the last essay, you have a choice to answer one of two options.

- Clearly demonstrate the steps you use to arrive at your answers. The curve for the test is steep, so partial credit can make the difference between a very good score and a poor score.

- Pay attention to significant figures.

- Be sure to write your answers in the space provided following each question.

- Data necessary for the solution of the problems may be found in the tables at the beginning of the test. Be familiar with the type of information that is available on this data sheet. An example of the data sheet can be found with the practice examinations in this book.

PART A, QUESTION 1

Format and Scoring

In the first question of Part A, you will be given one equilibrium question with multiple parts. The equilibrium question may focus on gaseous systems, the solubility product constant, the base dissociation constant, or the acid dissociation constant. This part of the free-response test is worth 20 percent of the free response section of the test.

Strategy

This is the most predictable section of the AP Chemistry examination, and it can sometimes be the most difficult. However, if a student is comfortable with all the topics mentioned under "What to Study," then this section will feel easy.

Nine points are distributed over the different parts of this question. Usually, the distribution of these points is easily understood by normal student intuition. For example, when given past Part A questions, current students are just as successful as experienced teachers in guessing how College Board readers will distribute points. In other words, if it seems important to you, the student, put it down to be sure that you earn credit.

A few pointers will maximize the grade that you earn on this section:

- Always show your work. Even if you can't answer the question, write down the formula that you think would be involved. You may still get two of the three points for that question without ever solving the problem. When the average score is about 4.5 points out of 9 points, picking up two-thirds of the available points still puts you in the top half.

- Include units and the correct number of significant digits in your answer when appropriate. A general rule of thumb is to use three significant figures if you don't know what is expected of you. Forgetting the units of the answers may cost a point for each of the four parts of the question.

- Graders typically do not count off more than once for any mistake. Therefore, if you make a mistake in Part A, and then carrying that answer forward to solve Part B also leads to an incorrect answer for B, even though you were otherwise correct, they might still give you full credit. However, this is unlikely to happen if you don't show your work, so, once again, SHOW YOUR WORK.

- Circle or underline your answer so the reader can find it. This seems like a funny thing to get in the way, but it does happen that a student works out the correct answer and the reader simply isn't sure which answer the student intends to submit.

- Practice equilibrium problems in this book and your text. In particular, be sure that you know how to find the pH of different types of solutions.

Examples of Past Questions

- A acid dissociation reaction, along with the corresponding K_a, is given.

Question a: Write the equilibrium expression for the reaction.

Question b: Determine the pH of a 0.1 M solution of the acid.

Question c: Titrate the weak acid with a strong base and determine the resulting pH.

Question d: Calculate the pH of the solution at the equivalence point.

Question e: Use the Henderson-Hasselbach equation to determine the pH of a buffer involving the weak acid.

Question f: Given the pK_a of several indicators, determine the best indicator to use when titrating this particular weak acid.

- The percent ionization was given for a reaction in which a weak base is added to water.

    Question a: Write the equilibrium expression for the reaction.

    Question b: Calculate the K_b from the percent ionization of the weak base in water.

    Question c: Calculate the pH that results when some of the weak base is titrated with a given number of moles of strong acid.

    Question d: Combine one of the above equations with another equation, such as K_w, to calculate the K_a of the conjugate acid of the weak base.

- A reaction that involves gases in the reactants and/or products, and the corresponding equilibrium constant, is given.

    Question a: Write the equilibrium expression for the equilibrium constant.

    Question b: Given partial pressures under non-equilibrium conditions, determine Q and the direction of the reaction.

    Question c: If K_p were originally given, calculate K_c.

    Question d: Given other equilibrium constants for related reactions, use the combination of constants and reactions to calculate the equilibrium constant for a new reaction.

- A reaction that involves the dissolving of a slightly soluble salt, and its corresponding K_{sp}, is given.

  Question a: Write the equilibrium expression for a dissolving process.

  Question b: Determine the molar solubility of one of the ions involved in the solubility reaction.

  Question c: Determine the molar solubility of one of the ions under conditions in which the other ion is already present (common ion effect), as it would be for hydroxide ions if the pH were not neutral.

  Question d: Given a volume and concentration of two solutions which, when combined, cause the precipitation reaction to occur, determine whether or not the precipitation will take place.

  Question e: Determine the quantity of precipitate that formed under one of the previous conditions.

What to Study

- Be sure to study Chapter 10 in this review book.

- Understand Le Chatelier's principle; in particular how a shift in reaction concentration can affect the direction of the reaction.

- Know well the chapter on equilibrium. In particular, be sure that you understand the following about weak acid/base systems since most of these questions will involved acids and bases.

  1. Determining the pH of a weak acid or basic solution.

  2. Determining the pH of a buffer solution.

  3. Determining the pH of a the solution that results from a partial titration—particularly adding a weak acid and strong base together, or adding a weak base and strong acid together.

- Understand the reactions associated with different types of equilibrium constants, and how those equilibrium constants might be related to one another. (For example, how to convert between K_w, K_a, and K_b; or how to convert between K_p and K_c.)

- Gaseous equilibrium may involve equilibrium vapor pressure, so be sure to study the chapter on the phases of matter (Chapter 6).

- Solubility product constant problems, including the following:

    1. Determine the molar solubility knowing the K_{sp}, and visa versa.

    2. Determine the molar solubility at various pH levels using the common ion effect, or in a buffered solution.

    3. Determine whether or not a precipitate will form when two solutions are combined.

- Relate the equilibrium constant to other values, such as cell voltage, the reaction quotient, or free energy.

- Understand the relationship between equilibrium constants and multiple reactions.

PART A, QUESTIONS 2-3

Format and Scoring

For your next question, you must solve your choice of one of two problems. The first problem is often a stoicheometry problem that involves some other important topic, such as partial pressures, limiting reactants, free energy, and oxidation-reduction, for example. The second type of problem usually involves calculations from more than one topic regarding reactions, such as thermodynamics, calorimetry, kinetics, oxidation-reduction (voltaic or electrolytic cell), or colligative properties. Like the equilibrium question, students can earn up to nine points on this section. Also like the equilibrium question, this section is worth 20 percent of the free-response section of the test. Remember, partial credit is available for writing formulas and correct set-up, even if you can't reach the correct solution. Quite often, one of the points is attributed to getting the units correct, so just writing the correct formula and the units of the answer may earn two-thirds of the points for a problem. This is a lot of points given the fact that the average score on this problem is typically about 50% (about 4.5 out of 9 points).

Strategies

All the same problem-solving hints mentioned about the Part A problem apply to this problem as well. Show your work. Write correct formulas even if you can't solve the problem. Include units in your answer. Take significant figures into consideration.

Examples of Past Problems

- The mass of two reactants in an oxidation-reduction reaction is given.

    Question a: Identify the limiting reactant; show all calculations.

    Question b: Determine the concentration of one of the products in solution.

    Question c: Determine the standard electrode potential for the galvanic cell based on this reaction.

    Question d: Given a similar oxidation-reduction reaction, determine the change in free energy for the reaction under standard conditions.

    Question e: Given non-standard concentrations, calculate the electric potential for the cell.

- The molecular formula of a small hydrocarbon molecule is given.

    Question a: Write the balanced equation for the combustion of the hydrocarbon molecule.

    Question b: Determine the volume of gas that would be collected at a specific temperature and pressure if a given mass of the organic molecule were completely combusted.

    Question c: The amount of heat given off during the above question is given; calculate the molar change in enthalpy for the reaction.

    Question d: The hydrocarbon molecule is a gas at room temperature; compare its effusion rate with that of another gas of known molar mass.

    Question e: The structure of the hydrocarbon is given; write a structure for an isomer of the hydrocarbon.

- The percent composition is given for a gaseous hydrocarbon.

    Question a: Determine the empirical formula.

    Question b: Determine the molar mass, given the density of the gas at a given temperature and pressure.

Question c: Compare the effusion rate of this gas with that of another, given the molar mass of the second gas.

Question d: The gas reacts in a confined chamber at a given temperature and pressure; calculate the number of moles of gas produced.

Question e: Heats of formation of water and carbon dioxide are given; calculate the heat of formation for the hydrocarbon gas.

Question f: With the heat of formation known, calculate the maximum amount of temperature change of a bomb calorimeter with a given heat capacity.

- The mass of an oxide is combined with a given volume of gas at a specific temperature and pressure.

Question a: Determine the number of moles of gas available for the reaction.

Question b: Determine the limiting reactant for the reaction.

Question c: Determine the amount of one of the products formed during the reaction.

Question d: Another reaction is given, which occurs entirely in solution. Calculate the mass of product formed given the concentrations of the reactants.

Question e: One of the products is a strong acid. Determine the pH of the solution when the reaction is complete.

- A chemical reaction is given, along with a chart of initial concentrations of each reactant and the initial reaction rate that corresponds to the concentrations, for each of four different experiments.

Question a: Determine the order of the reaction with respect to each reactant.

Question b: Write the rate law for the overall reaction.

Question c: Calculate the value and units for the specific rate constant.

Question d: The reaction is an oxidation-reduction reaction; calculate the standard cell potential given the reduction potential for each half reaction.

Question e: Determine the total number of electrons transferred in the reaction.

What to Study

• Be sure to study the calculations involved with the following chapters in this review book; each chapter has examples that simulated the kind of questions you will find on these problems:

  − Chapter 5: Gases

  − Chapter 7: Solutions

  − Chapter 9: Stoichiometry

  − Chapter 11: Kinetics

  − Chapter 12: Thermodynamics

PART B, QUESTION 4

Format and Scoring

In the first question of Part B, you will be given eight sets of chemical reactants written in words. You must write the unbalanced net ionic equation (reactants and products) for five of the eight reactions. For example:

Question: Solutions of ammonia and nitric acid are mixed.

Answer: $NH_3 + H^+ \rightarrow NH_4^+$

You will be given a periodic table and a table of standard reduction potentials, but no other information. A calculator is not allowed or needed on this section.

There are 15 points available for this set of questions, and this section is worth 15 percent of the points on the Free-Response section of the test. You will earn one point for each set of correct reactants and two points for each set of correct products. Partial credit is given. According to the outcome of past tests released by the College Board, the average score is five points out of the 15 available (three points per reaction.) All you need to do to earn the average score is write the correct reactants for five of the reactions. However, this review will give you a set of steps so that it shouldn't be difficult to earn most, if not all, the 15 available points.

Strategy

The most effective strategy in succeeding on Part C is to first recognize the formulas for the reactants. Once the reactant formulas are written down, you can relax knowing that you have earned the average score and you have barely started answering the question. Second, you need to recognize that most of the reactions that will be given to you will be one of four easily recognizable types of reactions that are summarized below. The following steps will help you succeed on Part C of the AP test.

1.   **Write down the formulas for as many reactants as you can.**

If you don't know the formula, eliminate that question and move on to another one.

2.   **Is it a precipitation reaction?**

If you know the solubility rules, identifying these reactions and writing the resulting net ionic equations should be straightforward. Remember to not include spectator ions in the net ionic reaction. Only those ions that come together to form the insoluble inorganic compound should be written.

Question: Solutions of silver nitrate and potassium iodide are mixed.

Answer: $Ag^+ + I^- \rightarrow AgI$

Question: A solution of lead nitrate is added to a solution of ammonium sulfide.

Answer: $Pb^{++} + S^{--} \rightarrow PbS$

3.   **Is it an acid-base reaction?**

Remember that most acid-base reactions simply move a proton from one reactant to another.

a.   **Does a strong acid neutralize a strong base?**

The net ionic reaction for this type of acid-base neutralization is always the same.

Question: Strong hydrochloric acid is added to a solution of sodium hydroxide.

Answer: $H^+ + OH^- \rightarrow H_2O$

b.   **Does a strong acid neutralize a weak base?**

The net ionic equation should depict a proton combining with the basic molecule.

Question: Strong hydrochloric acid is added to an ammonia solution.

Answer: $H^+ + NH_3 \rightarrow NH_4^+$

c. **Does a strong base react with a weak acid?**

A proton from the weak acid combines with the hydroxide ion to form an anion and water.

Question: Solutions of sodium hydroxide and acetic acid are mixed.

Answer: $HC_2H_3O_2 + OH^- \rightarrow C_2H_3O_2^- + H_2O$

d. **Does a weak acid react with a weak base?**

Keep an eye out for Lewis acid-base reactions, in which the acid accepts an electron pair from and combines with a weak base.

Question: Solutions of boron trifluoride and ammonia are mixed.

Answer: $BF_3 + NH_3 \rightarrow BF_3NH_3$

e. **Is a coordination-complex formed?**

This is another example of a Lewis acid-base reaction, where a transition metal serves as an electron-pair acceptor (Lewis acid). You would recognize this if a transition metal is placed in a solution with soluble ammonia, cyanide, hydroxide, or thiocyanate ions. You may combine the metal with as many polyatomic anions as you wish; just be sure that the total charge on the ion is correct. The charge on the metallic atom does not change.

Question: A solution of iron (III) chloride is added to a solution of potassium thiocyanate.

Answer: $Fe^{3+} + SCN^- \rightarrow FeSCN^{2+}$

4. **Is it an oxidation-reduction reaction?**

One element increases in oxidation state while another is reduced in oxidation state.

a. **Are two uncombined elements coming together?**

Combine the two elements to form a compound with reasonable oxidation states for each element.

Question: Magnesium metal is burned in oxygen gas.

Answer: $Mg + O_2 \rightarrow MgO$

b. **Is a carbon compound combusting with oxygen?**

An alkane, alkene, or alkyne is oxidized by oxygen gas to form carbon dioxide and water.

Question: Butane gas ignites in the presence of oxygen gas.

Answer: $C_4H_{10} + O_2 \rightarrow CO_2 + H_2O$

c. **Is a single reactant decomposing?**

Decomposition usually occurs because an uncommon oxidation state in one element gives way to a more common oxidation state.

Question: Hydrogen peroxide solution is exposed to bright light.

Answer: $H_2O_2 \rightarrow O_2 + H_2O$

d. **Is a solid transition metal placed in a solution of metallic ions?**

Use the chart of standard reduction potentials. The change with the highest reduction potential is reduced in charge. Voltaic or galvanic cells are an example of this type of reaction.

Question: Copper metal is placed in a solution of silver nitrate.

Answer: $Cu + Ag^+ \rightarrow Cu^{++} + Ag$

e. **Does an electrical current pass through a solution?**

If so, this reaction takes place in an electrolytic cell. Only a limited number of possible reactions are possible.

Question: An electrical current runs between two electrodes in molten sodium chloride.

Answer: $NaCl \rightarrow Na + Cl_2$

f. Is a solid metal placed into an acid?

The metal is oxidized, and hydrogen gas is formed. Remember, water can also be an acid; check to be sure the dissociation of water on the reduction potential chart shows a higher tendency to be reduced, such as the case with calcium in water.

Question: Magnesium metal is placed into a weak solution of hydrochloric acid.

Answer: $Mg + H^+ \rightarrow Mg^{++} + H_2$

5.   **Be sure that reactions in solution are written as net ionic reactions.** Also, since you will not be given any points for balancing the reaction or writing the phases down, don't waste time doing either of these.

6.   **Be absolutely clear about which reactions that you want graded.** It helps to circle the final net ionic reaction you wish graded simply to draw the graders attention to your answer. If you do not do this, the grader may simply attribute points to the first five reactions you have written anything near, whether or not you intended that question to be graded or not.

Summary of Steps

1.   **Write down the formulas for as many reactants as you can.**

2.   **Is it a precipitation reaction?**

3.   **Is it an acid-base reaction?**

4.   **Is it an oxidation-reduction reaction?**

5.   **Be sure that reactions in solution are written as net ionic reactions.**

6.   **Be absolutely clear about which reactions that you want graded.**

What to Study

•   Use the Periodic Chart to discern common oxidation states in Chapter 2

•   Memorize the strong acids and strong bases in Chapter 7.

- Memorize the solubility rules in Chapter 7.

- Know how to write net ionic reactions as outlined in Chapter 8.

- Understand the different types of reactions from Chapter 8.

- Know the names of common ions in Chapter 13.

- Know the names of organic compounds identified in Chapter 13.

- Practice answering Part C questions in the ten-minute time limit.

PART B, QUESTION 5

Format, Scoring, and Strategy

- Question 5 is a multiple-part question that addresses one of the recommended laboratory activities, as outlined in Chapter 14 of this review book.

- Question 5 is worth 15% of the total score on the Free-Response section of the AP Chemistry Exam.

- This question may involve the reading of graphs, laboratory data, decisions about what to measure, and the interpretation of data.

- The best way to prepare for this question is to be absolutely sure to fully understand each example problem in Chapter 14 of this review book. Then study the concepts in each chapter in this book that refer to each respective laboratory.

- Questions in the recent past have focused on qualitative analysis, Beer's law, oxidation-reduction reactions, acid-base titrations, and calorimetry.

PART B, QUESTION 6

Format, Scoring, and Strategy

- Question 6 is a multiple-part question that covers some general aspect of chemistry.

- This question is worth 15% of the total score on the Free-Response section of the AP Chemistry Exam.

- Questions from exams in the recent past have focused on the chemistry of everyday events, building and understanding a galvanic cell, the relationship between ionization energies and electron configuration, and the relationship between structure and physical properties.

PART B, QUESTIONS 7-8

Format, Scoring, and Strategy

- Questions 7-8 are considered "essay" questions, in which you may write sentence-long or multiple-sentence answers for each of four or five parts.

- You are given the choice to answer either Question 7 OR Question 8.

- This essay will count a maximum of 15% of the total score of the Free-Response section of the AP Chemistry Examination.

- Read both questions entirely before you choose which question you will answer.

- After you choose which question you will answer and re-read the question to be sure that you know what is being asked of you.

- Be sure that your answer is clearly identified on your answer sheet, and is clearly separate from any scratch work or preparatory outline you might jot down on the page.

- Keep your answers direct; try not to include extraneous information that does not support your answer.

- This section requires a conceptual understanding of the material, and any topic in the College Board outline might be used. Topics will vary widely. Past topics have included: equilibrium, Dalton's law, structure and bonding, chemical explanations for common events, the relationship between physical properties and structure, electron configuration rationale for differences in periodic properties, radioactive decay, thermodynamics, hybridization, and kinetics.

Atomic Theory and Structure

Chapter 2

ATOMIC THEORY AND STRUCTURE

EVIDENCE FOR ATOMIC THEORY

DALTON

• John Dalton performed chemical reactions and carefully measured the masses of reactants and products.

• Dalton proposed that all matter is composed of subunits call **atoms**. Atoms had different identities, called **elements**. Elements combined together in definite ratios to form **compounds**.

• Atoms are never created or destroyed during chemical reactions.

THOMPSON

• J.J. Thompson observed the deflection of particles in a cathode ray tube.

• Concluded that atoms are composed of positive and negative charges.

• He called negative charges **electrons**, and he suggested that the positive charges were distributed in islands throughout the atom, like raisins in raisin bread. Some people at the time called this the "plum pudding" model of the atom.

MILLIKAN

• Robert Millikan used oil drops falling in an electric field of known strength to calculate the charge-to-mass ratio of electrons and to surmise the charge contained by a single electron.

RUTHERFORD

- Ernest Rutherford fired alpha particles (that he knew to be positively charged) through thin, gold foil.

- Rutherford measured the resulting scatter patterns of the alpha particles after they hit the foil. He found that most of the alpha particles moved right through the foil, or were deflected slightly. However, some alpha particles were deflected at large angles, as though they had collided with a heavier object and bounced back.

- He concluded that the positive charge and mass of the atom were concentrated at the center of the atom, and that the rest of the atom is mostly empty space. This directly countered Thompson's "plum pudding" model.

PLANCK

- Max Planck determined that electromagnetic energy is quantized, or composed of discrete bundles, expressed by the equation below.

ENERGY AND ELECTROMAGNETIC RADIATION

$$E = h\,v$$

or, since $c = v\,\lambda$,

$$E = \frac{h\,c}{\lambda}$$

E = Energy of the photon, J

h = Planck's constant, 6.63×10^{-34} J • sec

v = frequency of light, sec^{-1}

λ = wavelength of light, m

c = speed of light, 3.00×10^{8} m / sec

BOHR

- Niels Bohr applied the idea of quantized energy to show that electrons exist around the nucleus at a fixed radius.

- Electrons with higher energy exist farther from the nucleus.

- The Bohr model is only accurate for atoms and ions with one electron. It was clear that a more complex model was needed to explain atoms with multiple electrons.

- Electrons give off energy in the form of electromagnetic radiation when they move from a higher level, or excited state, to a lower level. The energy represented by the light, using Planck's equation, represents the difference between the two energy levels of the electron.

- Electrons are restricted to specific energy levels around the nucleus, expressed by the equation below.

ENERGY LEVEL OF AN ELECTRON

$$E_n = \frac{-2.18 \times 10^{-18} \text{ J}}{n^2}$$

E = Energy of the electron, J

n = Electron energy level (principal quantum number)

DeBROGILE

- Louis deBrogile identified the wave characteristics of matter by combining Einstein's relationship between mass and energy ($E = mc^2$) and the relationship between velocity and the wavelength of light ($E = hv$).

- This shows that all particles with momentum have a corresponding wave nature.

DeBROGILE WAVELENGTH OF PARTICLES

$$\lambda = \frac{h}{mv}$$

λ = wavelength associated with particle, m

m = mass of particle, kg

h = Planck's constant, 6.63×10^{-34} J • sec

v = velocity of particle, m/sec

mv = momentum of particle, kg m /sec

HEISENBERG

- Werner Heisenberg, in the early 20th century, said that it is impossible to simultaneously know both the position and momentum of an electron.

- For small particles, such as electrons, this uncertainty suggests that we need a wave model, rather than a Newtonian model, to understand their behavior.

SCHRODINGER

- Erwin Schrodinger, in the early 20th century, attributed a wave function to electrons.

- The wave function describes the probability of where an electron might exist. The regions of high probability are called **orbitals**, even though they are more like clouds than orbits.

- The orbital of each electron is described in Schrodinger's equation, which is beyond the scope of an AP Chemistry course. These orbitals can be described as s, p, d, or f orbitals, as used in electron configurations described later in this chapter.

ATOMIC MASS, ATOMIC NUMBER, ISOTOPES

ATOMIC MASS

- The mass of an atom consists of the cumulative mass of all the particles in the atom, which includes protons, neutrons, and electrons.

- The mass of the electrons is insignificant relative to the mass of protons or neutrons. Therefore, the atomic mass is calculated by adding up the masses of the protons and neutrons.

- Example:

  A helium atom consists of two protons and two electrons. It would have an atomic mass of 4 amu. (atomic mass units, or the mass of one proton or neutron.) It is depicted as helium-4.

ATOMIC NUMBER

- The atom number is composed of the total nuclear charge, or number of protons in the nucleus of the atom.

- The atomic number is also the number of electrons surrounding the nucleus of a neutral atom.

- The atomic number is the smaller of the two numbers that exist for each element on the periodic table.

- Example:

  An atom of the element, carbon-14, has a atomic number of 6. Therefore, it has 6 protons in its nucleus, and 6 electrons around the nucleus when it is neutral.

ISOTOPES

- Atoms with the same number of protons but different number of neutrons are **isotopes** of one another.

- Example:

  Carbon-12 and carbon-14 are the same element (carbon), which is defined as having 6 protons. The difference in the mass numbers indicate that carbon-12 has 6 neutrons, while carbon-14 has 8 neutrons.

AVERAGE MASS NUMBER

• In nature, elements naturally occur as a combination of more than one isotope.

• The average mass number takes into account the relative frequencies of the different isotopes.

• The average mass number is also called the **atomic weight**.

• This number is also the **molar mass** of the element, or the mass in grams of one mole of atoms.

• This is the larger number that exists on the periodic table of elements.

• The atomic weight is probably closest in value to the most commonly existing isotope.

Example:

Naturally occurring lead (Pb) exists as a combination of four isotopes, Pb-204, Pb-206, Pb-207, and Pb-208. Given the natural abundance of each isotope describe in the following chart, calculate the average mass number of lead.

Pb-204	1.42%
Pb-206	24.10%
Pb-207	22.10%
Pb-208	52.40%

Solution:

Multiply the frequency, expressed as a fraction, by the mass of each isotope. Then add the contributions of each isotope together to get the total average mass.

$(0.0142)(204) + (0.241)(206) + (0.221)(207) + (0.524)(208) =$ **207.2**

ELECTRONS

• Schrodinger's equation describes the location and shape taken by each **electron cloud** in an atom.

• Each electron can be described by a set of four quantum numbers. The **Pauli Exclusion Principle** states that no two electrons can occupy the same exact energy level, or have the same set of four quantum numbers.

- There are three ways to model the location of electrons in atoms: quantum numbers, orbital notation, and electron configurations.

- The **quantum numbers** are like an address that describes the general distance from the nucleus, the type of orbital filled, the orientation of that orbital, and the "spin" direction on each electron in each orbital.

- **Orbital notation** identifies where each electron exists in each orbital. In this model, it is clear whether or not electrons have parallel spin.

- **Electron configurations** identify the number of electrons in each type of orbital at each energy level.

- According to the **Aufbau Principle**, electrons exist first at the lowest possible energy level, unless energy has put them into an excited state.

- **Hund's Rule** states that electrons enter orbitals of equal energy singly with the same spin (*i.e.*, unpaired) before they become paired.

QUANTUM NUMBERS

Every electron in an atom can be uniquely described with a different combination of the four quantum numbers described below. Each combination of quantum numbers describes a unique level of energy contained by the electron. Each of the four numbers represents a different trait of the electron.

Principal Quantum Number: n

- **Principal quantum number** represents the shell an electron occupies.

- Shells are also called **energy levels**.

- Shells can have possible values of n = 1,2...7.

- Indicates the approximate distance to the nucleus and relative energy. Therefore, electrons with higher values of *n* are further from the nucleus and have higher energy.

Angular Momentum Quantum Number: l

- **Angular momentum quantum number** represents the subshell the electron occupies.

- This number describes the shape of an electron's orbital. Possible shapes include the following:

    When n = 1, l = 0 (meaning there is one possible type of orbital, *s*)

    When n = 2, l = 0 (*s* orbital) or *l* = 1 (*p* orbital)

    When n = 3, l = 0 (*s* orbital), *l* = 1 (*p* orbital), or *l* = 2 (*d* orbital)

    When n ≥ 4, l = 0 (*s* orbital), *l* = 1 (*p* orbital), *l* = 2 (*d* orbital), or *l* = 3 (*f* orbital)

Magnetic Quantum Number: m_l

- **Magnetic quantum number** represents the orbital position.

- Possible values range from –l...0...+l for all possible values of n.

    When l = 0, m_l = 0 (there is one value, representing one possible *s* orbital)

    When l = 1, m_l = –1, 0, 1 (there are three possible *p* orbitals)

    When l = 2, m_l = –2, –1, 0, 1, 2 (there are five possible *d* orbitals)

    When l = 3, m_l = -3, –2, –1, 0, 1, 2, 3 (there are seven possible *f* orbitals)

- The orbital with the most negative number is filled first.

MAGNETIC SPIN QUANTUM NUMBER: M_s

- Each orbital can contain as many as two electrons, one with a positive spin (+1/2) and one with a negative spin (–1/2).

- The first ground state electron in each orbital takes the +1/2 value.

$_{17}Cl$ = ●)2)8)7 ← valence electrons

nucleus

ATOMIC ORBITALS AND ELECTRON CONFIGURATIONS

Table — Electron Arrangements

Main Levels n = 1	n = 2			n = 3	Summary
Sublevels s ($l = 0$)	s ($l = 0$)	p ($l = 1$)		s ($l = 0$)	
H ↑					$1s^1$
He ↑↓					$1s^2$
Li ↑↓	↑				$1s^22s^1$
Be ↑↓	↑↓				$1s^22s^2$
B ↑↓	↑↓	↑ ○ ○			$1s^22s^22p^1$
C ↑↓	↑↓	↑ ↑ ○			$1s^22s^22p^2$
N ↑↓	↑↓	↑ ↑ ↑			$1s^22s^22p^3$
O ↑↓	↑↓	↑↓ ↑ ↑			$1s^22s^22p^4$
F ↑↓	↑↓	↑↓ ↑↓ ↑			$1s^22s^22p^5$
Ne ↑↓	↑↓	↑↓ ↑↓ ↑↓			$1s^22s^22p^6$

PARAMAGNETISM AND DIMAGNETISM

- **Dimagnetic** elements have paired electrons in each orbital. To have this situation, all subshells are filled. These elements are not affected by magnetic fields.

- **Paramagnetic** elements have an unpaired electron in at least one orbital. The unpaired electron creates a magnetic field in the atom that responds to external magnetic fields.

- **Molecular orbitals** also create dimagnetism and paramagnetism.

PERIODIC TRENDS

ATOMIC RADII

- Moving from left to right across a period, atomic radius decreases.

- Moving down a group from top to bottom, atomic radius increases.

- Cations have small radii than their corresponding neutral atoms.

- Anions have larger radii than their corresponding neutral atoms.

IONIZATION ENERGY

- Moving from left to right across a period, ionization energy increases.

- Moving down a group from top to bottom, ionization energy decreases.

- More energy is needed for each succeeding ionization.

- Significantly more energy is needed to break a full shell of electrons.

- Elements with low ionization energies are more easily oxidized.

ELECTRON AFFINITY

- Moving from left to right across a period, electron-affinity energy given off increases.

- Moving down a group from top to bottom, electron-affinity energy given off does not change appreciably.

ELECTRONEGATIVITY

- Moving from left to right across a period, electronegativity increases.

- Moving down a group from top to bottom, electronegativity decreases.

Bonding

Chapter 3

BONDING

BONDS BETWEEN ATOMS

IONIC ATTRACTIONS

- **Ionic attractions** occur between elements—usually a combination of metal and non-metal atoms—that have a difference in electronegativity greater than 2.0.

- In an ionic attraction, an electron leaves the less electronegative atom—creating a positive charge, and migrates to the more electronegative atom—creating a negative charge. The unlike charges that result create an attraction between the two atoms.

- Ionic attraction follows Coulomb's Law. The strength of attraction is directly proportional to the amount of charge and inversely proportional to the square of the distance between the two charges.

- Ionic attractions satisfy the valence shells of the elements involved in the attraction. The metal loses electrons to have a filled shell. The non-metal gains electrons to have a filled shell.

COVALENT BONDS

- **Covalent bonds** occur between elements—usually non-metals—that have a difference in electronegativity between 0 – 2.1.

- In covalent bonds, electrons are shared between two atoms. The attraction is created from the attraction between the opposite magnetic fields created by the two electrons in the bond. The number of covalent bonds that a non-metal may form equals eight minus the group number of the element.

- **Double and triple bonds.** Electrons in a covalent bond satisfy the valence shell octets of both elements in the bond. The first covalent bond between two non-metals is a **sigma bond** (σ), where the electrons are paired along the axis between the two atoms. Any additional covalent bonds between non-metals are **pi bonds** (π), where the electrons are paired through the sideways overlap of p-orbitals above and below the inter-nuclear axis. For example, a double bond consists of one sigma and one pi bond. Sigma bonds are much stronger than pi bonds, and therefore are more difficult to break.

- **Nonpolar covalent bonds** form when the difference in electronegativity of the two atoms is negligible (< 0.4). Electrons in the bond are shared equally. Typical examples of nonpolar bonds are those between diatomic molecules of the same element, such as F_2 or Cl_2.

- **Polar covalent bonds** form when the difference in electronegativity of the two atoms is between $0.5 - 2.1$. In a polar covalent bond, the element with the greater electronegativity takes on a slightly negative charge ($\varsigma-$), and the element with the lesser electronegativity takes on a slightly positive charge ($\varsigma+$). In effect, the electrons in the bond are closer to the element with greater electronegativity.

  Example:

$$\varsigma + \overset{(2.1)}{H} - \overset{(3.5)}{O} \ \varsigma -$$

- A **dipole moment** exists in a polar covalent bond that points to the more electronegative atom. Dipole moments add together like vectors to create a total dipole moment on the molecule, as described in this chapter under "Structure and Physical Properties."

  Example:

$$\varsigma + \overset{(2.1)}{H} - \overset{(3.5)}{O} \ \varsigma -$$

$$\longmapsto$$

NETWORK COVALENT

- Network covalent crystals are groups of non-metal atoms held together by covalent bonds. A commonly-cited example is a diamond, which is a network covalent crystal of carbon atoms.

- Network covalent crystals tend to have very high melting and boiling points, and a very high amount of energy is needed to break apart the crystal.

METALLIC ATTRACTION

- Metals are the elements on the periodic table to the left of the stairs.

- Outer electrons of metals are delocalized and may be associated with one atom or another.

- Delocalized electrons give metals many of their physical properties: luster (because easily excited electrons give off photons as they return to the ground state), and electrical and thermal conductivity (because electrons move easily from atom to atom).

- Metallic bonding is created because all the metallic atoms share their outer electrons in a manner that are thought of as an "electron sea." The electrons are delocalized and move freely between the outer energy levels of the different atoms. This delocalization of electrons promotes electrical and thermal conductivity. Metals also demonstrate malleability and ductility.

MOLECULAR MODELS

Covalent bonding can be modeled in a number of different ways, with each type of model having its own strengths and weaknesses.

LEWIS STRUCTURES

- **Lewis structures** model the valence electrons that are involved in covalent bonding.

- The group number on the period table gives the number of valence electrons available for bonding. Normally, the "octet rule" must be satisfied to combine other atoms with a central atom, that is, the combination of the central atom's valence electrons and the electrons from other atoms bonded to the central atom should equal eight to create a stable Lewis structure.

- **Resonance structures** are an attempt to model delocalized electrons, or electrons that are shared between multiple bonds. For example, to allow the octet of sulfur in the sulfur dioxide molecule to be satisfied, it would show a double bond to one oxygen and not the other. However, the bonds to both oxygen atoms are equal, and demonstrate a bond length and strength somewhere between a single and a double bond. Therefore, the correct structure would be something between the following two resonance structures:

$$:S = O \quad \leftrightarrow \quad :S - O$$
$$| \qquad\qquad\qquad ||$$
$$O \qquad\qquad\qquad O$$

- Lewis structures are limited because they do not adequately depict delocalized electrons (except through resonance structures), the difference between sigma and pi bonds, or explain the concept of expanded octets.

HYBRIDIZATION, VSEPR, AND BOND GEOMETRY

- **Hybridization** refers to the process of electrons mixing traits of different atomic orbitals to create bonding orbitals. The hybridization model helps explain the difference in bond strength between sigma and pi bonds and correctly predicts the geometry of molecules. The following chart (on page 41) details the relationship between the number of electrons around a central atom, its hybridization, and the geometry of the molecule.

- **VSEPR**, or *valence shell electron-pair repulsion*, dictates that electron pairs will repel one another, thus creating a molecular geometry where each electron pair is as far as possible from every other electron pair. Unbonded pairs are slightly more repellant than other pairs. VSEPR theory gives a good explanation for the geometry found in the chart (on page 41).

- **Expanded octets** are created when highly electronegative atoms bond to large central atoms and there is space to allow either five or six electron pairs around the central atom. Expanded octets require d-electrons to participate in hybridization (see chart on page 41).

Table — Summary of Hybridization

Number of Bonds	Number of Unused e pairs	Type of Hybrid Orbital	Angle between Bonded Atoms	Geometry	Example
2	0	sp	180°	Linear	BeF_2
3	0	sp^2	120°	Trigonal planar	BF_3
4	0	sp^3	109.5°	Tetrahedral	CH_4
3	1	sp^3	90° to 109.5°	Pyramidal	NH_3
2	2	sp^3	90° to 109.5°	Angular	H_2O
6	0	sp^3d^2	90°	octahedral	SF_6

ISOMERS

- **Isomers** are molecules that have the same formula but different structure—or arrangement of the atoms. Two isomers will have different physical and chemical properties, which will depend on how the atoms are arranged and the intermolecular forces that are created as a result.

  Example: below are the two structural isomers of butane, each with the same formula, but different structures.

  n-butane: $CH_3 — CH_2 — CH_2 — CH_3$

  isobutene: $CH_3 — \overset{\displaystyle CH_3}{\underset{\displaystyle CH_3}{\overset{|}{\underset{|}{CH}}}} — CH_3$

ATTRACTIONS BETWEEN MOLECULES

VAN DER WAALS FORCES

- **Van der Waals forces** are sometimes referred to as dispersion forces, or "instantaneous dipoles." These forces are created by the chance movement of electrons in a system of atoms bonded together.

- The strength of attraction is proportional to the number of electrons in the molecule. These forces are weak relative to polar intermolecular forces, and only become apparent if there are many electrons, or if the molecules come very close together.

POLARITY

- A **polar intermolecular attraction** can exist between two polar molecules. The slightly positive end of one molecule forms an electrostatic attraction to the slightly negative end of another molecule.

- A **hydrogen bond** occurs when a hydrogen atom is involved with a polar intermolecular attraction to a more electronegative atom.

- Polar intermolecular attractions are much stronger than van der Waals forces.

STRUCTURE AND PHYSICAL PROPERTIES

- **Physical properties are related to the forces between atoms and molecules in a crystal.** Hardness of crystal, melting point, and boiling point are all a measure of the strength of inter-atomic or intermolecular attraction holding the crystal together. Stronger attractions result in lower vapor pressures.

- **Network covalent crystals** have the strongest attraction holding atoms together. The have the highest melting points and are the hardest of all crystals.

- **Ionic crystals** have strong electrostatic forces holding atoms together. They tend to have high melting and boiling points, and are poor conductors in the solid phase (because the electrons are in fixed positions). However, when ionic crystals are in the aqueous phase, they are good conductors because the charge is mobile.

- **Nonpolar molecules** held together predominantly with van der Waals forces are soft crystals, easily deformed, and vaporize easily. They have much lower melting and boiling points than polar compounds of similar molar mass. Nonpolar molecules are poor conductors, and tend to be more volatile because of their high vapor pressure.

- **Polar molecules** have intermolecular attractions that are weaker than ionic forces, but much stronger than nonpolar dispersion forces. The melting and boiling points of polar compounds depend on the strength of the dipole moment of the two compounds. The stronger the cumulative dipole moment, the greater the intermolecular attraction and the higher the melting and boiling point.

• **Hydrogen bonds** are the strongest polar intermolecular attraction because the hydrogen atom has only one electron. When that electron leaves, the exposed proton of the hydrogen nucleus is strongly attracted to the slightly negative charge of the other molecule. Consequently, polar molecules with hydrogen bonds have higher melting and boiling points than polar molecules of similar molar mass that do not have hydrogen bonds.

• **Summary of strength of attraction:**

Covalent > ionic > metallic > polar intermolecular > nonpolar inter-molecular

Example: if a covalent attraction needs to be broken to melt a solid, it will take more energy than if an ionic attraction needs to be broken, which will take more energy than a metallic attraction, and so on.

Nuclear Chemistry

Chapter 4

NUCLEAR CHEMISTRY

NUCLEAR REACTIONS AND EQUATIONS

ALPHA DECAY

- Nucleus emits a package of two protons and two neutrons, called an alpha particle (α), which is equivalent to the nucleus of a helium atom.

- Usually occurs with elements that have a mass number greater than 60.

- Alpha decay causes the mass number and atomic number to both decrease by two.

- Example:

$$^{238}_{92}U \rightarrow \alpha \text{ particle } (^{4}_{2}He) + {}^{234}_{90}Th$$

BETA DECAY

- Nucleus emits a beta particle (β-) that degrades into an electron as it passes out of the atom.

- Usually occurs with elements that have a mass number greater than its atomic weight.

- Beta decay causes the mass number to remain the same, but increases the atomic number by one. Beta decay converts a neutron into a proton.

- Example:

$$^{234}_{90}Th \rightarrow \beta^- \text{ particle } (^{0}_{-1}e) + {}^{234}_{91}Pa$$

POSITRON DECAY

- Nucleus emits a particle that degrades into a positron as it passes out of the atom.

- Usually occurs with elements that have a mass number less than its atomic weight.

- Positron decay causes the mass number to remain the same, but decreases the atomic number by one. Positron decay converts a proton into a neutron and a positron.

- Example:

$$^{13}_{7}N \rightarrow \, ^{0}_{+1}e + \, ^{13}_{6}C$$

ELECTRON CAPTURE

- Nucleus captures a low energy electron.

- Usually occurs with isotopes that have a mass number less than its atomic weight.

- Electron capture causes the mass number to remain the same, but decreases the atomic number by one. Electron capture converts a proton into a neutron.

- Example:

$$^{0}_{-1}e + \, ^{18}_{9}F \rightarrow \, ^{18}_{8}O$$

GAMMA RADIATION

- Gamma rays (γ) are high-frequency, high-energy, electromagnetic radiation that are usually given off in combination with alpha and beta decay.

- Gamma decay can occur from a nucleus when it undergoes a transformation from a higher energy state to a lower energy state. The resulting atom may or may not be radioactive.

- Gamma rays are photons, which do not have mass or charge.

RATE OF DECAY; HALF-LIFE

• Half-life is the time it takes for 50% of an isotope to decay.

• Nuclear decay represents a "first-order" reaction that depends on the amount of material and the rate constant.

• $T_{1/2} = \dfrac{0.693}{k}$

where k is the decay constant.

• Example:

Strontium-85 has a half-life of 65.2 days. How long will it take for 20 grams of strontium-85 to decay into five grams of strontium-85?

Solution:

It takes two half-lives to decrease the amount of strontium-85 from 20 grams to 5 grams. 2×65.2 days $= 130.4$ days.

NUCLEAR STABILITY AND RADIOACTIVITY

• When the average atomic weight of an element is greater than an unstable isotope's mass number, the nucleus of the isotope will increase the neutron:proton ratio through positron emission or electron capture.

• When the average atomic weight of an element is less than an unstable isotope's mass number, the nucleus of the isotope will decrease the neutron:proton ratio through beta decay.

• Radiation is measured in **rads**, or radiation absorbed dose. 100 rads equals 1.0 joule of energy absorbed by 1.0 kg of tissue. **Rems** are another radiation dose unit, and are equal to the number rads multiplied by the potency of the particular type of radiation to cause biological damage. Below is a chart that outlines the relationship between some general doses and different levels of biological damage.

Dose (mrem)	Cause	Effect
3 mrem	5-hour flight	none
7 mrem/yr	building materials	none
50 mrem/yr	cosmic radiation	none
50 mrem	diagnostic x-ray	none
200 mrem/yr	Typical annual dose	none
700 mrem	brain scan	none
1000 mrem/yr	Safety threshold	none
10,000 mrem/yr		cancer risk
25,000-50,000		decrease in white blood cells
350,000 – 500,000		risk immediate death, half die in 30 days

Gases

Chapter 5

GASES

IDEAL GAS LAWS

- **Ideal gases** are gases that behave according to an approximation that makes the following assumptions:

  1. The volume of the gas molecule is negligible compared to the space between the molecules.

  2. There is negligible intermolecular attraction between gas molecules.

- The ideal gas approximation is most accurate for gases at low pressure and high temperature.

- Under ideal conditions, the following laws hold true.

BOYLE'S LAW

- **Boyle's law** states that the volume of a gas is inversely proportional to pressure, when temperature is constant.

- This can be summarized by the expression,

$$\boxed{P_1 V_1 = P_2 V_2}$$

Example: A 4.0-liter elastic weather balloon travels from sea level, at 1.0 atm pressure, to a higher altitude, where the pressure is 0.20 atm. What is the new volume of the balloon?

Solution:

$$V_2 = \frac{P_1 V_1}{P_2} = \frac{1.0 \text{ atm} \times 4.0 \text{L}}{0.20 \text{ atm}} = 20.0 \text{ L}$$

CHARLES'S LAW

*   **Charles's law** states that the volume of a given amount of gas is directly proportional to temperature, when pressure is constant.

*   This can be summarized by the expression,

$$\boxed{V_1 T_2 = V_2 T_1}$$

Example:

A gas occupies 2.0 L at 300 K. What is the volume of the gas at 200 K, assuming that the pressure is constant?

Solution:

$$V_2 = \frac{V_1 T_2}{T_1} = \frac{2.0 \text{ L} \times 200 \text{ K}}{300 \text{ K}} = 1.3 \text{ L}$$

LAWS OF GAY-LUSSAC

*   The **law of Gay-Lussac** states that at constant volume, the pressure exerted by a given mass of gas varies directly with the absolute temperature.

*   This can be summarized by the expression,

$$\boxed{P_1 T_2 = P_2 T_1}$$

Example:

A gas in a rigid container exerts 6.0 atm at 300 K. What is the pressure that the gas exerts at 500K?

Solution:

$$P_2 = \frac{P_1 T_2}{T_1} = \frac{6.0 \text{ atm} \times 500 \text{ K}}{300 \text{ K}} = 10 \text{ atm}$$

*   Guy-Lussac's **law of combining volumes** states that when reactions take place in a gaseous state at constant temperature and pressure, the volume of reactants and products can be expressed as the ratios given by the stoicheometric coefficients in the balanced reaction.

DALTON'S LAW

- **Dalton's law** states that the total pressure exerted by a mixture of gases is equal to the sum of the partial pressures of the gases in the mixture.

$$P_{total} = P_1 + P_2 + P_3 + \ldots$$

- Dalton's law comes into play when a gas is collected over water, where the total pressure measured is equal to the pressure exerted by the collected gas plus the water vapor pressure at the temperature of the system.

Example:

A sample of methane gas is collected over water at an ambient pressure of 0.972 atm. The vapor pressure of water at this temperature is 0.243 atm. What is the pressure exerted by the methane?

Solution:

$$P_{total} = P_{water} + P_{methane}$$

$$P_{methane} = P_{total} - P_{water} = 0.972 \text{ atm} - 0.025 \text{ atm} = 0.947 \text{ atm}$$

- Partial pressures of individual gases in a gas mixture are proportional to the mole fraction of the gas in the mixture, which can be summarized by the following expression.

$$P_{gas\ a}\ n_{total} = P_{total}\ n_{gas\ a}$$

Example:

A rigid container with a combination of nitrogen and oxygen gas is at a pressure of 2.4 atm. If the mole fraction of nitrogen gas is 0.16, what is the partial pressure exerted by the nitrogen gas?

Solution:

$$P_{nitrogen} = \frac{P_{total}\ n_{nitrogen}}{n_{total}} = \frac{2.4 \text{ atm} \times 0.16 \text{ moles nitrogen}}{1.0 \text{ total moles}} = 0.38 \text{ atm}$$

AVOGADRO'S LAW

- **Avogadro's law** states that under conditions of constant temperature and pressure, the volume of a gas is proportional to the number of moles of gas present. This law can be summarized by the expression,

$$V_1 \, n_2 = V_2 \, n_1$$

Example:

For the reaction,

$$N_2 \, (g) + 3 \, H_2 \, (g) \leftrightarrow 2 \, NH_3 \, (g)$$

What volume of hydrogen gas combines completely with 2 liters of nitrogen gas, assuming constant temperature and pressure?

Solution:

$$V_2 = \frac{V_1 n_2}{n_1} = \frac{2.0 \, L \times 3 \, moles}{1 \, mole} = 6.0 \, L$$

COMBINED IDEAL GAS LAW

• All of the above laws can be combined to show that the pressure times volume, divided by number of gas mole and temperature, equal a constant ratio, which is usually expressed by the ideal gas law in the following manner.

IDEAL GAS LAW
$PV = nRT$
P = Pressure of the gas, atm
V = Volume of the gas, L
n = number of gas moles, mol
R = Ideal gas constant, 0.082 L atm / K mol
T = Absolute temperature, K

Example:

What is the pressure exerted by 3.0 moles of gas at 200 K in a 2.0-liter container?

Solution:

$$P = \frac{nRT}{V} = \frac{(3.0 \text{ mole} \times 0.082 \text{ L atm} \times 200 \text{ K})}{(2.0 \text{ L}) \qquad \text{K mol}} = 24.6 \text{ atm}$$

- **Standard temperature and pressure** is 273 K and 1.0 atm. (This is not to be confused with the temperature of a system under thermodynamically standard conditions, which is 298 K and 1.0 atm.)

- 1.0 mole of gas at STP occupies a volume of 22.4 L, regardless of the identity of the gas.

- The ideal gas law can be rewritten in terms of the molar mass of a gas and its density using the following equation.

IDEAL GAS LAW AND DENSITY

P (mm) = dRT

P   =   Pressure of the gas, atm

mm =   molar mass of gas molecule, g/mol

d   =   density of the gas, g/L

R   =   Ideal gas constant, 0.082 L atm / K mol

T   =   Absolute temperature, K

Example:

A gas sample with a density of 1.67 g/L exerts a pressure of 2.0 atm at a temperature of 299 K. What is the molar mass of the gas?

Solution:

$$\text{Molar mass} = \frac{dRT}{P} = \frac{(1.67 \text{ g}) (0.082 \text{ L atm}) (299 \text{ K})}{\text{L} \qquad \text{K mol} \; 2.0 \text{ atm}} = 20.5 \text{ g/mol}$$

Example:

Compare the density of hydrogen gas with that of water vapor, at constant temperature and pressure.

Solution:

$$(mm)_{hydrogen} \times d_{water} = (mm)_{water} \times d_{hydrogen}$$

$$\frac{d_{water}}{d_{hydrogen}} = \frac{(mm)_{water}}{(mm)_{hydrogen}} = \frac{18}{2} = 9$$

Therefore, water vapor is nine times more dense than hydrogen gas at any given temperature and pressure.

KINETIC THEORY

KINETIC MOLECULAR THEORY

•   Kinetic molecular theory states the following:

1.   Gases are composed of tiny particles that are in continuous, random motion.

2.   The volume occupied by the atoms and/or molecules in a gas is negligibly small. A gas is mostly empty space.

3.   The molecules collide with one another in perfectly elastic collisions (no net loss in energy).

4.   There are no attractive forces between particles; they move independently of each other.

5.   The average kinetic energy of all the molecules of gas is directly proportional to the absolute temperature of the gas.

•   All gases at the same temperature will have the same kinetic energy.

GRAHAM'S LAW

•   Graham's law is a result of the kinetic theory of matter, since two different gases at the same temperature and pressure, gas a and gas b, will both have the same kinetic energy.

$$\frac{1}{2} m_a v_a^2 = \frac{1}{2} m_b v_b^2$$

- **Effusion** is the process by which a gas escapes from one chamber to another by moving through a small hole. The rate of effusion is proportional to the velocity of the gas.

- **Graham's law of effusion** follows the format of the equation for kinetic energy. The law tells us that gas molecules of smaller molar mass move faster than gas molecules of larger molar mass, and that the faster moving molecule undergoes effusion faster.

GRAHAM'S LAW OF EFFUSION

$$\frac{r_a{}^2}{r_b{}^2} = \frac{M_b}{M_a}$$

r_a = rate of effusion of gas a

r_b = rate of effusion of gas b

M_a = molar mass of gas a, g/mol

M_b = molar mass of gas b, g/mol

Example:

A mixture of helium and carbon dioxide form a mixture in a rigid container. A small leak is created in the container; how much faster will the helium exit the container than the carbon dioxide?

Solution:

$$\frac{M_{carbon\ dioxide}}{M_{helium}} = \frac{r_{helium}{}^2}{r_{carbon\ dioxide}{}^2} = \frac{44}{4} = 11$$

Therefore, helium leaves the container $(11)^{\frac{1}{2}}$ or 3.3 times faster than carbon dioxide.

DEVIATIONS FROM IDEAL GAS LAWS

- Real (non-ideal) gases occur when the volume of the molecule is significant relative to the space between the molecules, or there is significant intermolecular attraction between molecules.

- If the volume of the space occupied by the molecules becomes significant, the measured volume of the gas will be larger than the volume calculated using the ideal gas law.

- If the intermolecular attraction between gas molecules becomes significant, the measured pressure of the gas will be less than the pressured calculated using the ideal gas law.

- Most gases are ideal under normal temperatures and pressures. However, under high pressures or low temperatures (when gas molecules come closer together) gases will be more likely to demonstrate real behavior.

- Real gases follow the van der Waals equation, listed below. The values for *a* and *b* are unique for each gas molecule.

VAN DER WAALS EQUATION FOR REAL GASES

$$\left(P + \frac{n^2 a}{V^2}\right)(V - nb) = nRT$$

P = Pressure of the real gas, atm

V = Volume of the gas molecules + space between molecules, L

n = number of gas moles, mol

R = Ideal gas constant, 0.082 L atm / K mol

T = Absolute temperature, K

a = intermolecular attraction constant for the gas

b = space occupied by one mole of gas molecules

Liquids and Solids

Chapter 6

LIQUIDS AND SOLIDS

PHASE DIAGRAMS

- A **phase diagram** shows the state of a substance (solid, liquid, or gas) at any given temperature and pressure.

- The lines on the diagram indicate those places where a substance exists simultaneously in both phases.

- The **critical point** is that temperature and pressure above which a substance must exist as a gas.

- The **triple point** is that temperature and pressure at which the substance may exist in all three phases: solid, liquid, and gas.

- The **vapor pressure curve** defines the boundary between the liquid phase and the gas phase on the phase diagram. The vapor pressure curve determines the partial pressure of gas that can be in the vapor phase at any given temperature.

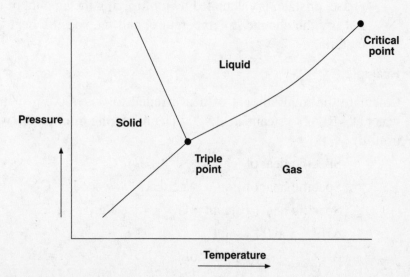

PHASE CHANGES

• Phase changes are caused by changes in pressure or temperature.

• Phase change involves a change in enthalpy (ΔH) that is unique for each substance and each change.

Change of phase	Name of change	ΔH for change
Solid to liquid	Melting (fusion)	$\Delta H > 0$
Liquid to solid	Freezing	$\Delta H < 0$
Liquid to gas	Vaporization	$\Delta H > 0$
Gas to liquid	Condensation	$\Delta H < 0$
Solid to gas	Sublimation	$\Delta H > 0$
Gas to solid	Deposition	$\Delta H < 0$

• A **heating curve** is a temperature vs. time graph when heat is added at a constant rate, or a temperature vs. heat added graph. A heating curve in reverse is called a **cooling curve**. The heating curve for water is shown on page 65. Two procedures are used to calculate the heat added or subtracted in a heating or cooling curve.

   – Heat required to change state is calculated by multiplying the change in enthalpy for the change (such as melting or freezing) by the amount of material.

   – Heat required to increase the temperature of the material in one phase, or state, is calculated by multiplying the amount of material, by the change in temperature, and the specific heat of the material.

Example:

Calculate the total amount of heat needed to raise 20.0 g of frozen water at −10 °C to steam at 115 °C. The following information will be useful:

$\quad$ Specific heat of ice = C_{ice} = 2.1 J/g °C

$\quad$ Specific heat of liquid water = C_{water} = 4.2 J/g °C

$\quad$ Specific heat of steam = C_{steam} = 1.8 J/g °C

$\quad$ ΔH_{fusion} = 6.0 kJ /mol

$\quad$ $\Delta H_{vaporization}$ = 40.7 kJ/mol

Solution:

The answer equals the sum of the heats of the following processes.

Heat needed to raise ice to melting point =

$$20 \text{ g} \times \frac{2.1 \text{ J}}{\text{g } °C} \times 10 \text{ }°C = 420 \text{ J}$$

Heat needed to melt ice =

$$20.0 \text{ g} \times \frac{1.0 \text{ mol}}{18.0 \text{ g}} \times \frac{6.0 \text{ kJ}}{\text{mol}} = 6.66 \text{ kJ}$$

Heat needed to raise water to boiling point =

$$20 \text{ g} \times \frac{4.2 \text{ J}}{\text{g } °C} \times 100° \text{ C} = 8400 \text{ J}$$

Heat needed to boil water =

$$20 \text{ g} \times \frac{1.0 \text{ mol}}{18.0 \text{ g}} \times \frac{40.7 \text{ kJ}}{\text{mol}} = 45.2 \text{ kJ}$$

Heat needed to raise steam to final temperature =

$$20 \text{ g} \times \frac{1.8 \text{ J}}{\text{g } °C} \times 15° \text{ C} = 540 \text{ J}$$

Total heat needed = 0.420 kJ + 6.66 kJ + 8.40 kJ + 45.2 kJ + 0.54 kJ = <u>61.22 kJ</u>

Typical Heating Curve

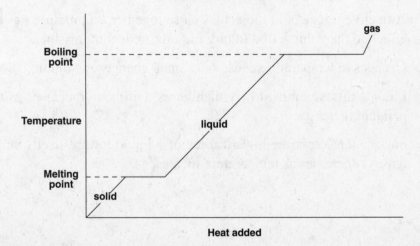

- The **normal melting point** is the temperature that corresponds to the solid-liquid equilibrium at 1.0 atm pressure.

- The **normal boiling point** is the temperature that corresponds to the liquid-gas equilibrium at 1.0 atm pressure.

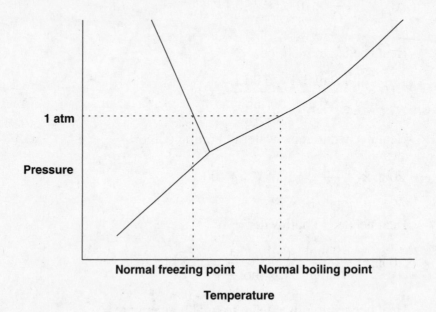

PROPERTIES OF LIQUIDS

- Liquids are composed of molecules that are constantly and randomly moving with respect to one another.

- Liquids maintain a definite volume, but their shape depends on the contour of the container holding them.

- Attractive forces hold molecules close together, so pressure has little effect on the volume of a liquid. Liquids are incompressible.

- Changes in temperature cause only small changes in volume.

- Liquids diffuse more slowly than gases. Diffusion increases as temperature increases.

- Surface tension is the inward force of a liquid toward itself. Surface tension decreases as temperature increases.

PROPERTIES OF SOLIDS

• Solids retain their shape and volume when transferred from one container to another.

• Solids are virtually incompressible.

• The attractive forces between atoms, molecules, or ions in a solid are relatively strong. The particles are held in a fixed position relative to one another.

• **Crystalline solids** are composed of structural units bounded by a specific geometric pattern and have sharp melting points. Table salt (NaCl) is a crystalline solid. The following are different configurations of atoms in crystals.

   1. A **unit cell** is the smallest repeating unit in a crystalline solid.

   2. **Simple cubic** unit cells have one atom at each of the corners of the cube. One-eighth of each of the eight atoms atom is inside the cube, so a simple cubic contains a total of one atom per unit cell.

   3. **Face-centered crystal** is a simple cubic unit cell, with one additional atom shared between two unit cells on each face of the cube. There are a total of three atoms per unit cell.

   4. **Body-centered crystal** is a simple cubic unit cell, with one additional atom in the center of the cube. There are a total of two atoms per unit cell.

• **Amorphous solids** do not display a specific geometry and do not have a sharp melting point. Glass is an amorphous solid.

Solutions

Chapter 7

SOLUTIONS

SOLUBILITY

SOLUTION PROCESS

- **Solvation** is the interaction of solvent molecules with solute molecules (or ions) to form loosely bonded aggregates of both solvent and solute. The attraction between solute and solvent must be greater than the force that holds the solute together in order for the solute to dissolve.

- **Hydration** describes the solvation process when water is the solvent.

- **Miscible** solutions occur when one substance is soluble in all proportions with another substance.

FACTORS THAT AFFECT SOLUBILITY

Concentration

- A **saturated solution** occurs when a solid solute is in equilibrium with dissolved solute.

- The **solubility** of a solute is the molar concentration of dissolved solute at saturation.

- **Supersaturated solutions** contain more solute that required for saturation.

Temperature

- The solubility of solids in liquids increases with increasing temperature when the $\Delta H_{solvation}$ is exothermic.

- The solubility of solids in liquids decreases with increasing temperature when the $\Delta H_{solvation}$ is endothermic.

- For gases in liquids, the solubility usually decreases with increasing temperature.

Pressure: Henry's Law

- While pressure does not appreciably affect the solubility of liquids or solids in liquids, Henry's law determines how much the solubility of gases in liquids increases when the partial pressure of the same gas above the liquid increases.

- Henry's law states that the amount of gas that can dissolve in a liquid is directly proportional to the partial pressure of the gas above the liquid.

- Henry's law is most accurately obeyed for gases that do not dissociate or react with the liquid.

HENRY'S LAW

$$P = kC$$

P = Partial pressure of the gas above the solution, atm

k = Henry's law constant, L atm /mol

C = Molar concentration of gas in solution, mol/L

Example:

The partial pressure of carbon dioxide at sea level is 0.0004 atm. The Henry's law constant for carbon dioxide is 32.0 L atm/mol at 25 °C. What is the molar concentration of carbon dioxide in a glass of water at sea level?

Solution:

$$C = \frac{P}{k} = \frac{0.0004 \text{ atm mol}}{32.0 \text{ L atm}} = 1.25 \times 10^{-5} \text{ M}$$

SOLUTION CONCENTRATIONS

MOLARITY

$$\text{Molarity (M)} = \frac{\text{Moles Solute}}{\text{Liters Solution}}$$

Example:

What is the molarity of a solution when 10.0 g of HCl is completely dissolved in dissolved water to make 500 mL of solution? What is the pH of the solution?

Solution:

$$0.55 \text{ M HCl} = 10.0 \text{ g HCl} \times \frac{1 \text{ mole}}{36.45 \text{ g}} \times \frac{1}{0.5 \text{ L}}$$

pH $0.26 = -\log [0.55]$

- pH is defined as the negative log of the molar hydrogen ion concentration. This means that the pH is the negative of the exponent to which ten is raised for the molar hydrogen ion, or hydronium ion concentration.

$$\text{pH} = -\log [\text{H}^+]$$

Examples:

$[\text{H}^+]$	pH
1×10^{-1}	1
1×10^{-2}	2
1×10^{-8}	8
1×10^{-10}	10
1×10^{-14}	14

MOLALITY

$$\text{Molality} = \frac{\text{Moles Solute}}{\text{Kilograms Solvent}}$$

Example:

What is the molality of the solution that is created when 10.0 g of NaCl is added to 800 g of water?

Solution:

$$0.214 \text{ molal} = 10.0 \text{ g solute} \times \frac{1 \text{ mole solute}}{58.45 \text{ g NaCl}} \times \frac{1}{0.8 \text{ kg solvent}}$$

MOLE FRACTION

$$\boxed{\text{mole fraction} = \frac{\text{moles solute}}{\text{total solution moles}}}$$

Example:

1.00 g ethanol is mixed with 100.0 g pure water. What is the mole fraction of the ethanol?

Solution:

$$0.0217 \text{ moles ethanol} = 1.000 \text{ g ethanol} \times \frac{1.0 \text{ mol ethanol}}{46.07 \text{ g ethanol}}$$

$$5.555 \text{ moles water} = 100.0 \text{ g water} \times \frac{1.0 \text{ mole water}}{18.00 \text{ g water}}$$

$$\text{Ethanol mole fraction} = \frac{\text{moles ethanol}}{\text{mol water} + \text{mol ethanol}} =$$

$$\frac{0.0217}{5.5772} = 0.00389$$

COLLIGATIVE PROPERTIES

RAOULT'S LAW

- **Raoult's law** describes how the vapor pressure curve of a solvent is depressed when a solute dissolve in the solvent.

- A depressed vapor pressure curve also causes other colligative properties to change, such as boiling and freezing points, and osmotic pressure.

RAOULT'S LAW

$$P = XP^O$$

P = vapor pressure of solution, atm

P^O = vapor pressure of pure solvent, atm

X = mole fraction of solvent

Example:

What is the vapor pressure of an aqueous solution that is created when 400.0 g of glucose are dissolved in 500.0 g of water at 25 °C? (The vapor pressure of pure water at 25 °C is 0.031 atm.) The molecular weight of glucose is 180 g/mol.

Solution:

$$\text{Moles glucose} = \frac{400.0 \text{ g glucose} \times \text{mol}}{180 \text{ g glucose}} = 2.22 \text{ moles glucose}$$

$$\text{Moles water} = \frac{500.0 \text{ g water} \times \text{mol}}{18 \text{ g water}} = 27.77 \text{ moles water}$$

$$\text{Moles fraction of water} = \frac{\text{moles water}}{\text{Total moles}} = \frac{27.77}{29.99} = 0.93$$

Vapor pressure of solution = XP^O = (0.93) (0.031 atm) = <u>0.028 atm</u>

Example:

20.0 g of an unknown is dissolved in 125 g of pure water, and shows a vapor pressure of 0.030 atm at 25 °C. What is the molar mass of the unknown?

Solution:

$$\text{mole fraction of water} = \frac{P_{solution}}{P_{pure\ water}} = \frac{\text{moles water}}{\text{mol water} + \text{mole unknown}}$$

moles unknown = 0.33 moles

$$\text{unknown molar mass} = \frac{20.0 \text{ g}}{0.33 \text{ mol}} = 60.6 \text{ g/mol}$$

BOILING POINT ELEVATION

- For colligative properties, the change in the property is directly proportional to the moles of particles dissolved in the solute.

- The Van't Hoff factor takes into account dissociation that may occur when a solute dissolves. When one mole of dissolved solute creates one mole of particles in solution (as in a non-electrolyte), then the Van't Hoff factor would be 1.0. When two moles of particles are put into solution for every mole of solute dissolved, such as with NaCl in water, then the Van't Hoff factor would be 2.0.

BOILING POINT ELEVATION

$$\Delta T = k_b m i$$

ΔT = Change in solvent boiling point, °C

k_b = molal boiling point constant of the solvent, °C kg/mol

m = molality of solute, mol/kg

i = Van't Hoff factor of solute

Example:

Compare the effects of 10.0 g sucrose (158.0 g/mol) with 10.0 of magnesium chloride (95.2 g/mol) in changing the boiling point of 100.0 g of water. (The molal boiling point constant of water is 0.51 °C kg/mol.)

Solution:

Note that the Van't Hoff factor for sucrose is 1.0, since it is a non-electrolyte. However, the Van't Hoff factor for magnesium chloride is 3.0, since it completely dissociates in water.

$$\Delta T \text{ due to sucrose} = \frac{0.51\ °C\ kg}{mol} \times \frac{10.0\ g\ sucrose\ mol}{158.0\ g \times 0.10\ kg\ solvent} \times$$

$$1.0 = 0.3\ °C$$

$$\Delta T \text{ due to } MgCl_2 = \frac{0.51 \text{ °C kg}}{\text{mol}} \times \frac{10.0 \text{ g } MgCl_2 \text{ mol}}{95.2 \text{ g} \times 0.10 \text{ kg solvent}} \times$$

$$3.0 = 1.6 \text{ °C}$$

The sucrose raises the boiling point by 0.3 °C, whereas the magnesium chloride raises the boiling point by 1.6 °C.

FREEZING POINT DEPRESSION

FREEZING POINT DEPRESSION

$$\Delta T = k_f mi$$

ΔT = Change in solvent freezing point, °C

k_f = molal freezing point constant of the solvent, °C kg/mol

m = molality of solute, mol/kg

i = Van't Hoff factor of solute

Example:

Enough magnesium chloride is placed on a cold wet road to create a 2.5 molal solution with the water on the road. At what temperature will ice form on the road? (The molal freezing point constant for water is 1.86 °C kg/mol.

Solution: The Van't Hoff factor for magnesium chloride is 3.0 since it completely dissolves in water; K_f = 1.86 °C kg/mol and m = 2.5 mol/kg.

$$\Delta T = k_f mi = \frac{1.86 \text{ °C kg}}{\text{mol}} \times \frac{2.5 \text{ mol}}{\text{kg}} \times 3.0 = 14 \text{ °C}$$

Since the freezing point of pure water is 0.0 °C, then the freezing point of the solution created by the magnesium chloride is −14 °C.

OSMOTIC PRESSURE

OSMOTIC PRESSURE

$$\pi V = nRTi$$

π = osmotic pressure, atm

V = volume of the solution, L

n = moles of solute, mol

R = ideal gas constant, 0.082 L atm / K mol

T = temperature, K

i = Van't Hoff factor of the solute

Example:

Exactly one gram (1.000 g) of an unknown protein was dissolved in enough pure water to make 500 mL of solution. The resulting osmotic pressure exerted by the solution was 0.002 atm at 298 K. What is the molar mass of the protein? (Assume that the protein is an non-electrolyte.)

Solution:

$$\text{Molar mass} = \frac{\text{mass solute} \times R\,T}{\pi\,V} =$$

$$\frac{1.000\text{ g} \times 0.082\text{ L atm} \times 298\text{ K}}{0.002\text{ atm} \times \text{K mol} \times 0.5\text{ L}} = 24{,}436\text{ g/mol}$$

NONIDEAL SOLUTIONS

- **Ideal solutions** follow Raoult's Law. The vapor pressure of a solution is directly proportional to the mole fraction of the solvent in the solution.

- **Nonideal solutions** experience a vapor pressure that is different from that predicted by Raoult's Law.

- **Negative deviations** from Raoult's Law occur when there is a stronger solute-solvent attraction, such as hydrogen bonding, that prevents solvent molecules from escaping into the vapor phase. Negative deviations also occur when the $\Delta H_{solution}$ is large and exothermic.

- **Positive deviations** from Raoult's Law occur when both the solute and solvent are very volatile, and also when $\Delta H_{solution}$ is large and endothermic.

Reaction Types

Chapter 8

REACTION TYPES

ACID-BASE REACTIONS

*   **Arrhenius Theory** states that acids are substances that ionize in water to donate protons (H^+), and bases produce hydroxide ions (OH^-) when put into water.

    Example:

    Arrhenius acid: $HC_2H_3O_2 \rightarrow C_2H_3O_2^- + H^+$

    Arrhenius base: $NH_3 + H_2O \rightarrow NH_4^+ + OH^-$

*   **Brønsted-Lowry Theory** states that acids donate protons—like an Arrhenius acid—and bases accept protons. Simply put, a proton moves from one compound to another. Each compound in a conjugate acid-base pair are different from each other by the existence of a proton.

    Example:

    $HC_2H_3O_2 + OH^- \rightarrow C_2H_3O_2^- + H_2O$

*   **Lewis Theory** defines an acid as an electron-pair acceptor and a base is an electron-pair donor. The Lewis definition of acid-base reactions allow the inclusion of reactions that may not involve protons, such as the formation of coordination complexes.

    Example:

    $BF_3 + NH_3 \rightarrow BF_3NH_3$

*   **Neutralization** is the process where an Arrhenius acid and base is combined to form a salt and water.

    Example:

    $HCl + NaOH \rightarrow H_2O + NaCl$

- **Amphoteric** compounds can act as either acids or bases.

  Example:

  $Al(OH)_3 + OH^- \rightarrow [Al(OH)_4]^-$

  $Al(OH)_3 + 3\ H^+ \rightarrow Al^{3+} + 3\ H_2O$

PRECIPITATION REACTIONS

- Precipitation reactions occur when soluble reactants are mixed together to form an insoluble product, according to the solubility rules below.

  Example:

  $Pb^{2+}\ (aq) + 2\ I^-\ (aq) \rightarrow PbI_2\ (s)$

- Precipitation reactions are best written as **net ionic reactions**, where only the ions that combine to form the precipitate are shown. All other ions that remain dissolved in solution are **spectator ions**.

  Example:

  Full equation: $Pb(NO_3)_2\ (aq) + 2\ KI\ (aq) \rightarrow PbI_2\ (s) + 2\ KNO_3\ (aq)$

  Net ionic reaction: $Pb^{2+}\ (aq) + 2\ I^-\ (aq) \rightarrow PbI_2\ (s)$

SOLUBILITY RULES FOR IONS IN SOLUTION

- All compounds with IA metals and ammonium are **soluble**.

- All **nitrates are soluble**.

- All **chlorates and perchlorates are soluble**.

- All **acetates are soluble**.

- All **halides are soluble**, EXCEPT those that combine with Ag^+, Pb^{2+}, and Hg_2^{2+}

- All **sulfates are soluble**, EXCEPT those that combine with Ag^+, Pb^{2+}, and Hg_2^{2+}, Ca^{2+}, Sr^{2+}, Ba^{2+}.

- All **hydroxides are insoluble**, EXCEPT those with IA metals, ammonium, Ca^{2+}, Sr^{2+}, Ba^{2+}.

- All **carbonates are insoluble**, EXCEPT those that contain IA metals and ammonium.

- All **phosphates are insoluble**, EXCEPT those that contain IA metals and ammonium.

- All **sulfites are insoluble**, EXCEPT those that contain IA metals and ammonium.

- All **chromates are insoluble**, EXCEPT those that contain IA metals and ammonium.

- All **sulfides are insoluble**, EXCEPT those that contain IA metals, IIA metals, and ammonium.

OXIDATION-REDUCTION REACTIONS

- **Oxidation** occurs when an atom increases control over an electron, or shows an increase in oxidation state. The oxidized species causes some other compound to be reduced, and is therefore called the **reducing agent**.

- **Reduction** occurs when an atom decreases control over an electron, or shows a reduced oxidation state. The reduced species causes some other compound to be oxidized, and is therefore called the **oxidizing agent**.

- Oxidation-reduction reactions can be either spontaneous (and occur without an input of energy) or non-spontaneous (occur only with the input of energy).

- The number of electrons lost in oxidation always equal the number of electrons gained in reduction.

- When the oxidation and reduction half-reactions are physically separated, oxidation occurs at the **anode**, reduction occurs at the **cathode**.

- "**Leo** the lion says **ger**" means

  Loss of **e**lectrons, **o**xidation; **g**ain of **e**lectrons, **r**eduction.

OXIDATION STATES

- **Oxidation state** is a term that is used interchangeably with the term, **oxidation number**.

- Assigning oxidation numbers can help determine which compound is oxidized, and which compound is reduced. An increase in oxidation number during a reaction indicates oxidation; a decrease in oxidation number shows reduction.

- Oxidation numbers can help balance oxidation-reduction reactions (see the Stoichiometry chapter regarding balancing oxidation-reduction reactions.)

- Rules for assigning oxidation numbers:

    1. The total oxidation number of any element, ion, or compound equals the charge on that element, ion, or compound.

    2. Except in the case of hydrides, hydrogen has an oxidation state of +1 when combined with other atoms.

    3. Except in peroxides, oxygen has an oxidation state of -2 when combined with other atoms.

    4. IA, IIA, and VIIA elements tend to take the oxidation state of their most common ion when combined with other atoms.

TYPES OF OXIDATION-REDUCTION REACTIONS

- **Two uncombined elements come together**

    Example: $Mg + O_2 \rightarrow MgO$

- **Combustion with oxygen**

    Example: $C_4H_{10} + O_2 \rightarrow CO_2 + H_2O$

- **Decomposition of a single reactant**

    Example: $H_2O_2 \rightarrow O_2 + H_2O$

- **A solid transition metal is placed in a solution of metallic ions.** Use the chart of standard reduction potentials. The change with the highest reduction potential is reduced in charge. Voltaic or galvanic cells are an example of this type of reaction; see the next section.

    Example: $Cu + Ag^+ \rightarrow Cu^{++} + Ag$

- **Electrolytic cells**

    Example: $NaCl\ (l) \rightarrow Na\ (l) + Cl_2\ (g)$

- **A solid metal is added to an acid**

    The metal is oxidized and hydrogen gas is formed. Remember, water can also be an acid; check to be sure the dissociation of water on the reduction potential chart shows a higher tendency to be reduced, such as the case with calcium in water.

    Example: $Mg + H^+ \rightarrow Mg^{++} + H_2$

VOLTAIC (GALVANIC) CELLS

- **Voltaic, or galvanic cells** convert chemical energy into electrical energy by isolating the oxidation and reduction half-reactions.

- The **electromotive force** is the force with which the electrons flow through an external wire from the negative electrode to the positive electrode.

- **Oxidation occurs at the anode**, which is negatively charged for voltaic cells.

- **Reduction occurs at the cathode**, which is positively charged for voltaic cells.

- The greater the tendency for the two half-reactions to occur spontaneously, the greater the cell potential voltage, or E_{cell}, which is measured in volts (V).

- Cells are identified short-hand by the oxidation half-reaction first.

  Example:

  The short-hand notation for the reaction, $Cu + Ag^+ \rightarrow Cu^{++} + Ag$, is

  $Cu /Cu^{++} // Ag^+/Ag$.

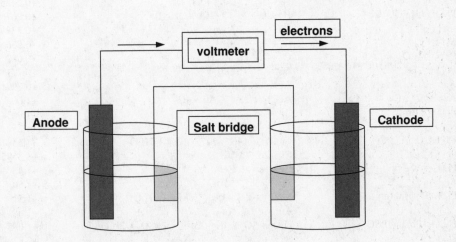

Table — Standard Electrode Potentials in Aqueous Solutions at 25°C.

Electrode	Electrode Reaction	$E°_{red}$
Acid Solutions		
Li I Li$^+$	Li$^+$ + e$^-$ $\rightarrow$ Li	−3.045
K I K$^+$	K$^+$ + e$^-$ $\rightarrow$ K	−2.925
Ba I Ba^{2+}	Ba^{2+} + 2e$^-$ $\rightarrow$ Ba	−2.906
Ca I Ca^{2+}	Ca^{2+} + 2e$^-$ $\rightarrow$ Ca	−2.87
Na I Na$^+$	Na$^+$ + e$^-$ $\rightarrow$ Na	−2.714
La I La^{3+}	La^{3+} + 3e$^-$ $\rightarrow$ La	−2.52
Mg I Mg^{2+}	Mg^{2+} + 2e$^-$ $\rightarrow$ Mg	−2.363
Th I Th^{4+}	Th^{4+} + 4e$^-$ $\rightarrow$ Th	−1.90
U I U^{3+}	U^{3+} + 3e$^-$ $\rightarrow$ U	−1.80
Al I Al^{3+}	Al^{3+} + 3e$^-$ $\rightarrow$ Al	−1.66
Mn I Mn^{2+}	Mn^{2+} + 2e$^-$ $\rightarrow$ Mn	−1.180
V I V^{2+}	V^{2+} + 2e$^-$ $\rightarrow$ V	−1.18
Zn I Zn^{2+}	Zn^{2+} + 2e$^-$ $\rightarrow$ Zn	−0.763
Tl I Tl I I I$^-$	Tl I (s) + e$^-$ $\rightarrow$ Tl + I$^-$	−0.753
Cr I Cr^{3+}	Cr^{3+} + 3e$^-$ $\rightarrow$ Cr	−0.744
Tl I TlBr I Br$^-$	TlBr(s) + e$^-$ $\rightarrow$ Tl + Br$^-$	−0.658
Pt I U^{3+}, U^{4+}	U^{4+} + e$^-$ $\rightarrow$ U^{3+}	−0.61
Fe I Fe^{2+}	Fe^{2+} + 2e$^-$ $\rightarrow$ Fe	−0.440
Cd I Cd^{2+}	Cd^{2+} + 2e$^-$ $\rightarrow$ Cd	−0.403
Pb I PbSO$_4$ I SO$_4$$^{2-}$	PbSO$_4$ + 2e$^-$ $\rightarrow$ Pb + SO$_4$$^{2-}$	−0.359
Tl I Tl$^+$	Tl$^+$ + e$^-$ $\rightarrow$ Tl	−0.3363
Ag I AgI I I$^-$	AG I + e$^-$ $\rightarrow$ Ag + I$^-$	−0.152
Pb I Pb^{2+}	Pb^{2+} + 2e$^-$ $\rightarrow$ Pb	−0.126
Pt I D$_2$ I D$^+$	2D$^+$ + 2e$^-$ $\rightarrow$ D$_2$	−0.0034
Pt I H$_2$ I H$^+$	2H$^+$ + 2e$^-$ $\rightarrow$ H$_2$	−0.0000
Ag I AgBr I Br$^-$	AgBr + e$^-$ $\rightarrow$ Ag + Br$^-$	+0.071
Ag I AgCl I Cl$^-$	AgCl + e$^-$ $\rightarrow$ Ag + Cl$^-$	+0.2225
Pt I Hg I Hg$_2$Cl$_2$ I Cl$^-$	Hg$_2$Cl$_2$ + 2e$^-$ $\rightarrow$ 2Cl$^-$ + 2Hg(l)	+0.2676
Cu I Cu^{2+}	Cu^{2+} + 2e$^-$ $\rightarrow$ Cu	+0.337
Pt I I$_2$ I I$^-$	I$_2$$^-$ + 2e$^-$ $\rightarrow$ 3I$^-$	+0.536
Pt I O$_2$ I H$_2$O$_2$	O$_2$ + 2H$^+$ 2e$^-$ $\rightarrow$ H$_2$O$_2$	+0.682
Pt I Fe^{2+}, Fe^{3+}	Fe^{3+} + e$^-$ $\rightarrow$ Fe^{2+}	+0.771
Ag I Ag$^+$	Ag$^+$ + e$^-$ $\rightarrow$ Ag	+0.7991
Au I AuCl$_4$$^-$, Cl$^-$	AuCl$_4$$^-$ + 3e$^-$ $\rightarrow$ Au + 4Cl$^-$	+1.00
Pt I Br$_2$ I Br$^-$	Br$_2$ + 2e$^-$ $\rightarrow$ 2Br$^-$	+1.065
Pt I Tl$^+$, Tl^{3+}	Tl^{3+} + 2e$^-$ $\rightarrow$ Tl$^+$	+1.25
Pt I H$^+$, Cr$_2$O$_7$$^{2-}$, Cr^{3+}	Cr$_2$O$_7$$^{2-}$ + 14H$^+$ 6e$^-$ $\rightarrow$ 2Cr^{3+} + 7H$_2$O	+1.33
Pt I Cl$_2$ I Cl$^-$	Cl$_2$ + 2e$^-$ $\rightarrow$ 2Cl$^-$	+1.3595
Pt I Ce^{4+}, Ce^{3+}	Ce^{4+} + e$^-$ $\rightarrow$ Ce^{3+}	+1.45
Au I Au^{3+}	Au^{3+} + 3e$^-$ $\rightarrow$ Au	+1.50
Pt I Mn^{2+}, MnO$_4$$^-$	MnO$_4$$^-$ + 8H$^+$ + 5e$^-$ $\rightarrow$ Mn^2 + 4H$_2$O	+1.51
Au I Au$^+$	Au$^+$ + e$^-$ $\rightarrow$ Au	+1.68
PbSO$_4$ I PbO$_2$ I H$_2$SO$_4$	PbO$_2$ + SO$_4$ + 4H$^+$ + 2e$^-$ $\rightarrow$ PbSO$_4$ + 2H$_2$O	+1.685
Pt I F$_2$, F$^-$	F$_2$(g) + 2e$^-$ $\rightarrow$ 2F$^-$	+2.87
Basic Solutions		
Pt I SO$_3$$^{2-}$, SO$_4$$^{2-}$	SO$_4$$^{2-}$ + H$_2$O + 2e$^-$ $\rightarrow$ SO$_3$$^{2-}$ + 2OH$^-$	−0.93
Pt I H$_2$ I OH$^-$	2H$_2$O + 2e$^-$ $\rightarrow$ H$_2$ + 2OH$^-$	−0.828
Ag I Ag(NH$_3$)$_2$$^+$, NH$_3$(aq)	Ag(NH$_3$)$_2$ + e$^-$ $\rightarrow$ Ag + 2NH$_3$ (aq)	+0.373
Pt I O$_2$ I OH$^-$	O$_2$ + 2H$_2$O + 4e$^-$ $\rightarrow$ 4OH$^-$	+0.401
Pt I MnO$_2$ I MnO$_4$$^-$	MnO$_4$$^-$ + 2H$_2$O + 3e$^-$ $\rightarrow$ MnO$_2$ + 4OH$^-$	+0.588

Calculating Cell Voltage

Example:

Find the standard cell voltage for the reaction, $Cu + Ag^+ \rightarrow Cu^{++} + Ag$.

Solution:

1. Break the reaction into the oxidation and reduction half reactions.

    Oxidation: $Cu \rightarrow Cu^{++} + 2e^-$

    Reduction: $e^- + Ag^+ \rightarrow Ag$

2. Use the chart of standard reduction potentials to find the reduction potential ($E^°_{red}$) for each half reaction. Since $E^°_{ox} = - E^°_{red}$, then reverse the sign of the reduction potential for the oxidation half-reaction, then add the two potentials together for the total cell potential under standard conditions. (Note that the oxidation or reduction potentials are not multiplied by the stoicheometric coefficient, as would be heats of reaction or entropies.)

Oxidation:	Cu	$\rightarrow Cu^{++} + 2e^-$	$E^°_{ox} = -0.34$ V
Reduction:	$e^- + Ag^+$	$\rightarrow Ag$	$E^°_{red} = 0.80$ V

    Total reaction: $Cu + Ag^+ \rightarrow Cu^{++} + Ag$ $\quad E^°_{total} = 0.46$ V

NERNST EQUATION

*   **The Nernst equation** is used to calculate the cell voltage under non-standard conditions.

THE NERNST EQUATION

$$E_{cell} = E^°_{cell} - RT/nF \ln Q$$

$$E_{cell} = E^°_{cell} - 0.06/n \ln Q$$

E_{cell}	=	cell voltage under non-standard conditions, Volts
$E^°_{cell}$	=	cell voltage under standard conditions, Volts
R	=	Ideal gas constant, 8.31 V C / mol K
T	=	absolute temperature, K
n	=	moles of electrons transferred in the reaction, mol
F	=	Faraday's constant, 96,486 C / mol
Q	=	reaction quotient for the reduction half-reaction

Example:

What is the total cell voltage for the reaction, $Cu + Ag^+ \rightarrow Cu^{++} + Ag$, when $[Ag^+] = 0.10$ M and $[Cu^{++}] = 2.0$ M? Use equilibrium principles to explain the difference between this cell potential and the cell potential at standard conditions.

Solution:

$$E_{cell} = E°_{cell} - 0.06/n \ln Q = (0.46) - [0.06/2 \ln (2.0/0.10)] = 0.34 \text{ V}$$

The cell is non-standard in that the concentrations of the product are above 1.0 M and the concentrations of the reactant are below 1.0 M. The law of mass action suggests that the reaction will be less likely to go in a forward direction, and so will have less cell potential in the forward direction.

ELECTROLYTIC CELLS

- **Electrolytic cells** use electrons from a power source to force an otherwise non-spontaneous oxidation-reduction reaction to occur.

- The cathode is negatively charged, and the anode is positively charged. Oxidation takes place at the anode, and reduction takes place at the cathode.

- The AP Chemistry exam will require knowledge of two aspects of electrolytic cells: knowledge of the *type of reactions* that occur at the cathode and anode, and knowledge of *how much* reactant will be used up with a given amount of electrical charge.

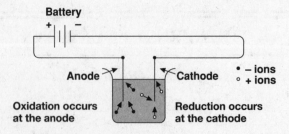

ELECTRICAL REACTIONS
In electrolytic cells, electrical energy is converted into chemical energy

- The following table summarizes the types of reactions that occur in an electrolytic cell. Examine the reactants that are available; the highest priority half-reaction will occur at each electrode. For example, if both water and chloride ions are available, the chloride ions will be oxidized and used up before water is oxidized.

Oxidation Reactions at the Anode	Reduction Reactions at the Cathode
First priority: halogen ions form gases. $$eg: Cl^- (aq) \rightarrow Cl_2 (g)$$ Second priority: water ionizes to form gas. $$eg: H_2O (l) \rightarrow 2H^+ + O_2 (g)$$	First priority: transition metal ions form solid. $$eg: Cu^+ (aq) \rightarrow Cu (s)$$ Second priority: water ions form gases. $$eg: 2H_2O (l) \rightarrow 2OH^- (aq) + H_2 (g)$$ Third priority: molten metal ions form solid. $$eg: Na^+ (l) \rightarrow Na (s)$$

Examples

Determine what material will be produced at the cathode and anode when each of the following are placed in an electrolytic cell.

1. NaCl (aq) (Answer: H_2 (g) at the cathode, Cl_2 (g) at the anode.)

2. NaCl (l) (Answer: Na (s) at the cathode, Cl_2 (g) at the anode.)

3. $Cu(NO_3)_2$ (aq) (Answer: Cu (s) at the cathode, O_2 (g) at. the anode.)

FARADAY'S LAW

• Faraday's Law connects the amount of charge at an electrolytic electrode to the number of moles of electrons involved.

FARADAY'S LAW

1.0 Faraday (F) = 1.0 mole electrons = 96,486 Coulombs

• Faraday's Law can be used along with the following definition of charge to solve a number of different types of questions that might be found on the AP Chemistry test, particularly in the Multiple Choice section.

CURRENT, CHARGE, AND TIME

$$I = \frac{q}{t}$$

I = Current, expressed in amperes, A

q = Charge, expressed in coulombs, C

t = Time, expressed in seconds, sec

Example:

A current of 4.0 A passes for 30 seconds through an electrolytic cell that contains a aqueous solution of silver nitrate. What mass of silver will be deposited at the cathode in that time?

Solution:

$$0.13 \text{ g Ag} = 4.0 \text{ A} \times 30 \text{ sec} \times \frac{C}{A \text{ sec}} \times \frac{1.0 \text{ mol e}^-}{96,485 \text{ C}} \times$$

$$\frac{107.868 \text{ g AG}}{1.0 \text{ mol e}^-}$$

Stoichiometry

Chapter 9

STOICHIOMETRY

BALANCING CHEMICAL EQUATIONS

- Balanced chemical reactions are an artifact of the Law of Conservation of Mass. Matter is neither created nor destroyed during a chemical change.

- The same number of like atoms must exist both as reactants and products.

- To balance reactions, alter only the coefficients; do not change the formula.

- In general when balancing reactions, balance the hydrogen and oxygen atoms last.

- If there is a change in oxidation number that is not a combustion reaction, go to the next section, "Balancing Oxidation-Reduction reactions."

- When faced with an unbalanced reaction that involves the combustion of a hydrocarbon, look for the following:

  1. First match the number of carbons in the hydrocarbon in the reactants by adjusting the coefficient of carbon dioxide in the product.

     Example:

     $$\underline{C}_3H_8 + O_2 \rightarrow \underline{3C}O_2 + H_2O$$

     Three carbon atoms on both sides.

  2. Then balance the hydrogen atoms by adding a coefficient to water in the product so that the hydrogen atoms equal the number of hydrogen atoms in the reactant hydrocarbon.

Example:

$$C_3\underline{H_8} + 5O_2 \rightarrow 3CO_2 + \underline{\mathbf{4H_2}}O$$

Eight hydrogen atoms on both sides.

3. Finally, add up the oxygen atoms in the products (carbon dioxide and water) and adjust the coefficient for the oxygen molecule in the reactants so that all oxygen atoms balance.

Example:

$$C_3H_8 + \underline{\mathbf{5O_2}} \rightarrow \underline{\mathbf{3CO_2}} + \underline{\mathbf{4}}H_2\underline{O}$$

Ten oxygen atoms on both sides.

BALANCING OXIDATION-REDUCTION REACTIONS

- Balancing oxidation-reduction reactions requires balancing both mass and charge. Not only must the same number of each kind of atom exist on both sides of the yield sign, but the number of electrons lost in oxidation must equal the number of electrons gained during reduction.

- Balancing oxidation-reduction reactions is NOT trial-and-error, as some might tell you. There is a well established method that allows you to get the right answer the first time, every time.

  1. Establish oxidation numbers for each atom.

  2. Create two "half reactions"; one that shows the atoms oxidized, the other shows the reduced atoms.

  3. Show how many electrons are given up in the oxidation half-reaction, and how many electrons are used in the reduction half-reaction.

  4. Multiply the coefficients of each species in one or both half-reaction so that the number of electrons lost in oxidation equals the number of electrons gained in reduction.

  5. Balance mass of elements that do not change in oxidation state.

  6. Recombine half reactions.

  BIG hints:

  1. Try to balance the major common ions that do not have an atom that changes in oxidation state, such as the nitrate ion, as an entire unit.

2. If the reaction occurs in an acidic solution, balance oxygen before the hydrogen. Then add the number of water molecules on the other side to balance the oxygen. Balance the remaining hydrogen atoms by adding H^+ to one side of the equation.

3. In basic solution, balance as though in an acidic solution, then "neutralize" each H^+ by adding an equal number of OH^- ions to both sides.

Example:

Balance the following reaction in terms of both mass and charge. The reaction occurs in an acidic solution.

$Fe(NO_3)_2 + HNO_3 + KMnO_4 \rightarrow Fe(NO_3)_3 + Mn(NO_3)_2 + H_2O + KNO_3$

Solution:

1. **Establish oxidation numbers for each atom.**

    For now, don't worry about atoms or polyatomic ions that do not change in oxidation state.

    $$\underset{+2}{Fe(NO_3)_2} + HNO_3 + \underset{+7}{KMnO_4} \rightarrow \underset{+3}{Fe(NO_3)_3} + \underset{+2}{Mn(NO_3)_2} +$$

    $H_2O + KNO_3$

2. **Create two "half reactions"; one that shows the atoms oxidized, the other showing the reduced atoms.**

3. **Show how many electrons are given up in the oxidation half-reaction, and how many electrons are used in the reduction half-reaction.**

    Oxidation: $Fe^{+2} \rightarrow Fe^{+3} + 1e^-$

    Reduction: $5e^- + Mn^{7+} \rightarrow Mn^{2+}$

4. **Multiply the coefficients of each species in one or both half-reaction so that the number of electrons lost in oxidation equals the number of electrons gained in reduction.**

    Oxidation: $\underline{5}Fe^{+2} \rightarrow \underline{5}Fe^{+3} + \underline{5}e^-$

    Reduction: $\underline{5}e^- + Mn^{7+} \rightarrow Mn^{2+}$

5. **Recombine half reactions.**

6.   **Balance mass of elements that do not change in oxidation state.**

   Hints:

   * **You may want to balance polyatomic atoms as a single unit.**

   * **Be sure to not change the coefficients of the atoms that change in oxidation state.**

   * **If the reaction occurs in an acidic solution, balance oxygen before the hydrogen. Then add the number of water molecules on the other side to balance the oxygen. Balance the remaining hydrogen atoms by adding H^+ to one side of the equation.**

$5 \text{ Fe(NO}_3)_2 + 8 \text{ HNO}_3 + \text{KMnO}_4 \rightarrow 5 \text{ Fe(NO}_3)_3 + \text{Mn(NO}_3)_2 + 4 \text{ H}_2\text{O} + \text{KNO}_3$

MOLE CONVERSIONS

•   The factor-label method is useful in solving mole conversions.

•   Conversion factors are ratios in which the numerator is equal, by definition, to the denominator. For example, if there are 12 inches to 1 foot, then that definition can be written as either

$$\frac{12 \text{ inches}}{1 \text{ foot}} \quad \text{or} \quad \frac{1 \text{ foot}}{12 \text{ inches}}$$

in such a manner that will cancel out units of given information and result in units of the answer.

•   The numbers used should all be significant figures, and the answer should contain no more significant figures than the least number of significant figures of the conversions and given information.

PARTICLES

•   There are 6.02×10^{23} (Avogadro's number) particles in a mole. This can be used to determine the number of particles in a mole of atoms or molecules.

Example:

How many atoms are in 0.2 moles of atoms?

Solution:

$$0.2 \;\cancel{\text{mol atoms}}\; \times \; \frac{6.02 \times 10^{23} \text{ atoms}}{1.0 \;\cancel{\text{mol atoms}}} = 1.2 \times 10^{22} \text{ atoms}$$

MASS

- Atomic and molecular weights can be used to convert moles to grams, and vice versa.

  Example:

  What is the mass of 4.20 moles of carbon atoms?

  Solution:

$$4.20 \;\cancel{\text{mol atoms}}\; \times \; \frac{12.011 \text{ grams carbon}}{1.0 \;\cancel{\text{mol atoms}}} = 50.45 \text{ grams carbon}$$

GASES

- While stoichiometry problems can result in answers in moles, the ideal gas law can be used to convert that number of moles to some unknown variable in the ideal gas law equation.

- At STP (standard temperature and pressure), 1.0 mole of gas occupies 22.4 liters. This can be used as a conversion factor in solving stoichiometric equations.

  Example:

  What is the volume of 8.26 moles of gas at STP?

  Solution:

$$8.26 \;\cancel{\text{moles gas}}\; \times \; \frac{22.4 \text{ liters gas}}{1.0 \;\cancel{\text{moles gas}}} = 185 \text{ liters gas}$$

SOLUTIONS

- Stoichiometric problems that involve solutions usually require a molar solution conversion at some point to get the answer, where

$$\textbf{Molarity} = \textbf{M} = \frac{\textbf{moles solute}}{\textbf{Liters solution}}$$

Example:

How many moles of glucose exist in 1.4 liters of a 0.20-molar solution of glucose?

Solution:

$$1.4 \ \cancel{\text{liter solution}} \ \times \ \frac{0.20 \ \text{moles glucose}}{1.0 \ \cancel{\text{liter solution}}} = 0.28 \ \text{moles glucose}$$

STOICHIOMETRY PROBLEMS

- Stoichiometry problems refer to a type of question in which the student is given an amount of reactant or product in a chemical reaction, and then asked to find the corresponding amount of reactant or product.

- Stoichiometry problems can all be solved using the following steps.

  1. Balance the reaction

  2. Write down the units of the answer next to an equals sign "=".

  3. On the other side of an equals sign, write down the number and units of the given information.

  4. Use a ratio to convert the given information into moles.

  5. For the next ratio, use the balanced reaction to relate the number of moles of the given substance to the number of moles of the substance in the answer.

  6. Convert the number of moles of the substance in the answer to the actual units of the answer. Be sure that your answer has the correct units, and the same units as those that remain on the other side of the equals sign after the other units are canceled.

  Example:

  In the reaction,

  $$N_2 \ (g) + H_2 \ (g) \rightarrow NH_3 \ (g)$$

  What mass of ammonia will be produced when 10.0 grams of nitrogen gas reacts completely?

  Solution:

  1. Balance the reaction

  $$N_2 \ (g) + 3 \ H_2 \ (g) \rightarrow 2 \ NH_3 \ (g)$$

2. Write down the units of the answer next to an equals sign "=".

x grams NH_3 =

3. On the other side of an equals sign, write down the number and units of the given information.

x grams NH_3 = 10.0 grams N_2

4. Use a ratio to convert the given information into moles.

$$\text{X grams } NH_3 = 10.0 \text{ g } N_2 \times \frac{1 \text{ mol } N_2}{28.0 \text{ g } N_2}$$

5. For the next ratio, use the balanced reaction to relate the number of moles of the given substance to the number of moles of the substance in the answer.

$$\text{x grams } NH_3 = 10.0 \text{ } \cancel{\text{g } N_2} \times \frac{1 \text{ mol } N_2}{28.0 \text{ } \cancel{\text{g } N_2}} \times \frac{2 \text{ mol } NH_3}{1 \text{ mol } N_2}$$

6. Convert the number of moles of the substance in the answer to the actual units of the answer. Be sure that your answer has the correct units, and the same units as those that remain on the other side of the equals sign after the other units are canceled.

$$12.15 \text{ grams } NH_3 = 10.0 \text{ } \cancel{\text{g } N_2} \times \frac{1 \text{ } \cancel{\text{mol } N_2}}{28.0 \text{ } \cancel{\text{g } N_2}} \times \frac{2 \text{ } \cancel{\text{mol } NH_3}}{1 \text{ } \cancel{\text{mol } N_2}}$$

$$\times \frac{17.01 \text{ g NH3}}{1 \text{ } \cancel{\text{mol } NH_3}}$$

Example that involves numbers of particles:

What number of hydrogen molecules react with 2.0 moles of nitrogen gas in the reaction,

$N_2 \, (g) + 3 \, H_2 \, (g) \leftrightarrow 2 \, NH_3 \, (g)$

Solution:

$$2.0 \text{ mol } N_2 \times \frac{3 \text{ mol } H_2}{1 \text{ mol } N_2} \times \frac{6.02 \times 10^{23} \text{ molecules}}{1 \text{ mol } H_2 \text{ molecules}} =$$

3.6×10^{24} molecules

Example that involves mass:

What mass of hydrogen gas is used to completely react with 2.0 mol of nitrogen gas in the reaction,

N_2 (g) + 3 H_2 (g) 2 NH_3 (g) ?

Solution:

$$2.0 \text{ mol } N_2 \times \frac{3 \text{ mol } H_2}{1 \text{ mol } N_2} \times \frac{2.016 \text{ grams } H_2}{1 \text{ mol } H_2} = 12.1 \text{ grams } H_2$$

Example that involves a gas:

What volume of ammonia gas is produced at STP when 12.6 g of hydrogen gas reacts completely in the following reaction,

N_2 (g) + 3 H_2 (g) $\leftrightarrow$ 2 NH_3 (g) ?

Solution:

$$12.6 \text{ g } H_2 \times \frac{1 \text{ mol } H_2}{2.016 \text{ g } H_2} \times \frac{2 \text{ mol } NH_3}{3 \text{ mol } H_2} \times \frac{22.4 \text{ liters } NH_3}{1 \text{ mol } NH_3}$$

$$= 93.3 \text{ liters } NH_3$$

Example that involves a solution:

What volume of 0.10 M HCl is needed to completely neutralize 0.20 moles of sodium acetate in the following reaction,

$H_2O + C_2H_3O_2^-$ (aq) $\leftrightarrow$ $HC_2H_3O_2$ (aq) + OH^- (aq) ?

Solution:

$$0.20 \text{ mol } C_2H_3O_2^- \times \frac{1 \text{ mol HCl}}{1 \text{ mole } C_2H_3O_2^-} \times \frac{1.0 \text{ liter solution}}{0.10 \text{ mol HCl}}$$

$$= 2.0 \text{ liter solution}$$

LIMITING REACTANTS

* Limiting reactant problems are stoichiometric questions that ask you to calculate the amount of product created when given a specific amount of more than one reactant.

* Limiting reactant problems are solved like any other stoichiometric problem. However, you must go through the stoichiometric calculation with both sets of given information.

- The limiting reactant is the reactant that runs out first as the chemical reaction proceeds. Therefore, it is the reactant that produces the least amount of product.

Example:

In the following reaction, a 12.8 L sample of CO at 2.0 atm and 300 K is combined with 6.33 g of Fe_2O_3. How many liters of carbon dioxide are formed at the same temperature, and which is the limiting reactant?

$$Fe_2O_3 \ (s) + 3 \ CO \ (g) \rightarrow 2 \ Fe \ (s) + 3 \ CO_2 \ (g)$$

Solution:

(i) $12.8 \text{ L CO} \times \dfrac{3 \text{ L CO}_2}{3 \text{ L CO}} = 12.8 \text{ L CO}_2$

(ii) $6.33 \text{ g Fe}_2\text{O}_3 \times \dfrac{1 \text{ mol Fe}_2\text{O}_3}{159.7 \text{ g Fe}_2\text{O}_3} \times \dfrac{3 \text{ mol CO}_2}{1 \text{ mol Fe}_2\text{O}_3} \times$

$\dfrac{(.082 \text{ L atm})(300 \text{ K})}{2.0 \text{ atm K mol}} = 1.46 \text{ L CO}_2$

Therefore, iron oxide is the limiting reactant and 1.46 L of carbon dioxide is formed.

EMPIRICAL FORMULAS AND PERCENT COMPOSITION

- The empirical formula is the simplest ratio of atoms in a molecule. The empirical formula may or may not be the same as the molecular formula. The molar mass is the information that is needed to convert from the empirical formula to the molecular formula.

- Mass-mole conversions are necessary in finding empirical formulas from experimental data using the following steps.

  1. Change the "%" to grams by assuming that you have 100 grams of material.

  2. Convert from mass into grams for all atoms involved.

  3. Divide the moles of each atom by the value that represents the smallest number of moles of atoms.

Example:

(a) What is the empirical formula of the hydrocarbon that contains 85.7% carbon?

(b) Vapor pressure calculations determine the molar mass of the compound to be 28.0 g/mol. What is the molecular formula of the compound?

Solution:

(a) $85.7 \text{ g C} \times \dfrac{1.0 \text{ mol C}}{12.011 \text{ g C}} = 7.135 \text{ mol C}$

$14.3 \text{ g H} \times \dfrac{1.0 \text{ mol H}}{1.008 \text{ g H}} = 14.186 \text{ mol H}$

Empirical formula: $C_{7.135}H_{14.186}$, or CH_2

(b) Since the molar mass is twice the mass of the empirical formula, then the molecular formula is twice the empirical formula; C_2H_4.

Equilibrium

Chapter 10

EQUILIBRIUM

LE CHATELIER'S PRINCIPLE

- **Le Chatelier's principle** states that when a system at equilibrium is disturbed by a change in pressure, temperature, or the amount (concentration) of product or reactant, the reaction will shift to minimize the change and establish a new equilibrium.

- **Change in concentration:** Adding products to a reaction at equilibrium will shift the reaction to produce reactants; adding reactants to a reaction at equilibrium will shift the reaction to produce products. See the section on the reaction quotient, Q, below.

- **Change in temperature:** An increase in temperature causes the equilibrium to shift to use up the added heat. For example, when heat is added to an exothermic reaction, it will shift to the left to use up the heat. An endothermic reaction will shift to the right to use up heat when heat is added.

- **Change in pressure:** An increase in pressure causes an equilibrium to shift in the direction that produces the fewest number of gas moles. For example, in the reaction that dissolves a gas into a liquid, increasing the pressure on the system will cause the equilibrium to shift to produce more dissolved gas.

- **Addition of a catalyst or an inert gas** will not cause an equilibrium to shift; the amounts of reactants and products would remain unchanged.

EQUILIBRIUM CONSTANTS

- Equilibrium constants are ratios.

  For the reaction, **aA + bB $\leftrightarrow$ cC + dD,**

The ratio of the product concentrations, raised to their stoichiometric coefficients, to the reactant concentrations, raised to their stoichiometric coefficients, is the equilibrium constant, K_{eq}. This is also called the **law of mass action**.

$$K_{eq} = \frac{[C]^c \, [D]^d}{[A]^a \, [B]^b}$$

- Pure substances, such as water or solids, do not show up in the equilibrium expression; only molar solutions or, as with K_p, gaseous pressures.

- The **equilibrium constant for a multi-step process** is equal to the product of the equilibrium constants for each step.

  Example: For a set of three reactions that add to equal a total reaction,

  $$K_{total} = K_1 \times K_2 \times K_3$$

- The **equilibrium constant for a reverse reaction** is the inverse of the equilibrium constant for a forward reaction.

  Example:

  $$K_{reverse} = \frac{1}{K_{forward}}$$

- There are different equilibrium constants for different types of reactions.

Type of Reaction	Equilibrium Constant
Reaction in solution; reactants and products expressed as a concentration in moles/liter.	K_c
Gaseous reaction, reactants and products expressed in units of pressure. $N_2\,(g) + 3\,H_2\,(g) \leftrightarrow 2\,NH_3\,(g)$	K_p
The dissociation of water $H_2O \leftrightarrow H^+\,(aq) + OH^-\,(aq)$	K_w

Type of Reaction	Equilibrium Constant
Reactions that produce a proton (H^+) from a Bronsted-Lowry acid. eg: $HC_2H_3O_2\ (aq) \leftrightarrow H^+\ (aq) + C_2H_3O_2^-\ (aq)$	K_a
Reactions that produce a hydroxide ion (OH^-) from a Brønsted-Lowry base. eg: $H_2O + C_2H_3O_2^-\ (aq) \leftrightarrow HC_2H_3O_2\ (aq) + OH^-\ (aq)$	K_b
Reactions that produce dissolved ions in aqueous solution from a solid. eg: $PbI_2\ (s) \leftrightarrow Pb^{2+}\ (aq) + 2\ I^-\ (aq)$	K_{sp}

REACTION QUOTIENT, Q

- The reaction quotient, Q, can be used to calculate the direction and degree to which a reaction will shift when new products or reactants are added (Le Chatelier's principle).

- The reaction quotient for a reaction is found using the same ratio as the equilibrium constant, but at non-equilibrium conditions.

For the reaction, **aA + bB $\leftrightarrow$ cC + dD**

$$Q = \frac{[C]^c\ [D]^d}{[A]^a\ [B]^b}$$

- If the reaction quotient is greater than the equilibrium expression, there are more products than there would be at equilibrium. By Le Chatelier's principle, the reaction will shift toward equilibrium by using products and producing more reactants.

When Q > K, reaction proceeds to the left toward reactants.

When Q < K, reaction proceeds to the right toward products.

When Q = K, reaction is at equilibrium.

Example:

In the following reaction,

$N_2\ (g) + 3\ H_2\ (g) \leftrightarrow 2\ NH_3\ (g)$

The K_c is 5.9×10^{-2}. The molar concentrations of each reactant and product are: $[N_2] = 0.40$ M, $[H_2] = 0.80$ M, and $[NH_3] = 0.20$ M. Which direction will the reaction go as it begins to establish equilibrium?

Solution:

$$Q = \frac{(.20)^2}{(.4)(.8)^3} = 0.195$$

$Q > K$, Therefore the reaction goes to the left (toward the reactants).

EQUILIBRIUM CONSTANTS FOR GASEOUS REACTIONS

- Concentrations of reactants and products in the gas phase may be expressed in units of molarity (moles/liter) or partial pressures (atm, Pa, mmHg).

- The ideal gas law ($P = NRT$) is used to convert between the equilibrium constant expressed in gas moles/liter (K_c) to the equilibrium constant expressed in gas pressures (K_p); see below.

- The equilibrium expression for K_p only contains those species that are in the gas phase. For example, the K_p for the vaporization of water from liquid is simply the equilibrium vapor pressure of water.

GAS EQUILIBRIUM CONSTANT

$$K_p = K_c \, (RT)^{\Delta n}$$

K_p = Equilibrium constant, partial pressures

K_c = Equilibrium constant, molar concentrations

R = ideal gas constant, 0.082 L atm / K mol

T = Absolute temperature, K

Δn = (Moles of gas in products) – (Moles of gas in reactants)

Example:

The value of K_p is 8.3×10^{-3} at 700 K for the reaction,

$N_2\ (g) + 3\ H_2S\ (g) \leftrightarrow 2\ NH_4HS\ (g)$

What is the value of K_c?

Solution:

$$\frac{K_p}{(RT)^{\Delta n}} = K_c \quad \text{where} \quad n = 1$$

$$\frac{K_p}{(R)(T)} = K_c = (8.3 \times 10^{-3})/(0.082)\,(700) = 1.46 \times 10^{-4}$$

EQUILIBRIUM CONSTANTS FOR REACTIONS IN SOLUTION

THE DISSOCIATION OF WEAK ACIDS AND BASES

- The water dissociation constant, $K_w = 10^{-14} = K_a K_b = [H^+]\,[OH^-]$. This relationship can be used to freely convert between all these concentrations and equilibrium constants.

- Equilibrium constants, K_a and K_b, can be used to calculate the pH of a weak acid or base solution.

Example:

What is the pH of a 0.10 molar solution of acetic acid, $HC_2H_3O_2$, which has a $K_a = 1.8 \times 10^{-5}$?

Solution:

1. Write the equation of the reaction that occurs when the weak acid or base is put in water, and its corresponding equilibrium expression.

   $HC_2H_3O_2\ (aq) \leftrightarrow H^+\ (aq) + C_2H_3O_2^-\ (aq)$

   $$K_a = \frac{[H]^+\,[C_2H_3O_2^-]}{[HC_2H_3O_2]}$$

2. When the weak acid is placed in water, some number of moles/liter (x) will dissociate. For each mole of weak acid that dissociates, one mole of the proton and one mole of the weak base will be formed.

$$HC_2H_3O_2\ (aq) \leftrightarrow H^+\ (aq) + C_2H_3O_2^-\ (aq)$$

Before equilibrium: 0.10M   0   0

After equilibrium: 0.10 – x   x   x

3. Write the equilibrium expression in terms of the number of dissociated moles, x, which also happens to be the molar concentration of protons.

$$K_a = \frac{(x^2)}{(0.10 - x)} = 1.8 \times 10^{-5}$$

4. Assume that the amount of x that dissociates is small relative to the amount of weak acid, so neglect the x portion of the denominator while solving the x in the numerator. (Hint: this works when there is a small level of dissociation. To not make this assumption would require the quadratic equation to solve; however, you will not be required to use the quadratic equation on the AP Chemistry Examination.)

$$x^2 = 1.8 \times 10^{-5} \times 0.10$$

$$x = \sqrt{1.8 \times 10^{-6}} = [H^+]$$

$$[H^+] = 1.34 \times 10^{-3}$$

$$pH = -\log [H^+]$$

$$pH = -\log [1.3 \times 10^{-3}]$$

$$pH = 2.87$$

TITRATION OF WEAK ACIDS AND BASES

*   **To find the pH of a solution as a result of the titration of a weak acid or base,** you use the same general process that you used to find the pH of a weak acid or base, but you insert a step that uses up reactants before you apply the appropriate equilibrium expression. This is a very important type of question in part A of the free response portion of the AP examination!

Example:

What is the pH that results when 10 ml of 0.2 M sodium hydroxide solution is added to 50 mL of a 0.10 M solution of acetic acid, $HC_2H_3O_2$? The K_a of acetic acid is 1.8×10^{-5}.

Solution:

1. Write the equation of the reaction that occurs when the weak acid reacts with the strong base put in water, and its corresponding equilibrium expression.

$$HC_2H_3O_2 + OH^- \leftrightarrow H_2O + C_2H_3O_2^-$$

$$K = \frac{1}{K_b} = \frac{[C_2H_3O_2^-]}{[OH^-][HC_2H_3O_2]}$$

2. Convert all volumes and concentrations to moles, then run the reaction mole-for-mole. Do not worry about applying the equilibrium expression at this time.

$$HC_2H_3O_2 \quad + \quad OH^- \quad \leftrightarrow \quad H_2O \quad + \quad C_2H_3O_2^-$$

Before reaction: 0.005 mol   0.002 mol   0 mol

After reaction: 0.003 mol   0 mol   0.002 mol

3. Use the equilibrium expression that relates the remaining weak acid and its conjugate base with H^+; from this, you can find the pH. (You can also use the equilibrium expression of the reaction that is given, solve for $[OH^-]$, and use K_w to convert your answer to $[H^+]$; but the answer for pH will end up being the same.)

$$K_a = \frac{[H^+][C_2H_3O_2^-]}{[HC_2H_3O_2]}$$

$$[H^+] = \frac{K_a[C_2H_3O_2^-]}{[HC_2H_3O_2]} = \frac{(1.8 \times 10^{-5})(0.002 \text{ mol})}{(0.003 \text{ mol})}$$

$$[H^+] = 1.2 \times 10^{-5}; \text{ pH} = -\log[H^+]$$

$$\text{pH} = 4.92$$

•   **If the number of moles of hydroxide ions exceeds the amount of weak acid,** the pH may be found by using K_w to convert your answer to $[H^+]$; then find the pH directly.

Example:

What is the pH that results when 30 mL of 0.2 M sodium hydroxide solution is added to 50 mL of a 0.10 M solution of acetic acid, $HC_2H_3O_2$?

Solution:

1. Write the equation of the reaction that occurs when the weak acid reacts to the strong base put in water, and its corresponding equilibrium expression.

$$HC_2H_3O_2 + OH^- \leftrightarrow H_2O + C_2H_3O_2^-$$

2. Convert all volumes and concentrations to moles, then run the reaction mole-for-mole. Do not worry about applying the equilibrium expression at this time.

	$HC_2H_3O_2$	+	OH^-	$\leftrightarrow$	H_2O	+	$C_2H_3O_2^-$
Before reaction:	0.005 mol		0.006 mol				0 mol
After reaction:	0 mol		0.001 mol				0.00t mol

3. With the hydroxide ion leftover, K_w is the equilibrium expression that should be used to calculate $[H^+]$; from this, you can find the pH. Don't forget to put the remaining hydroxide moles in the total liters of solution to get the final molarity.

$$K_w = [H^+][OH^-]$$

$$[H^+] = K_w [OH^-] = (1.0 \times 10^{-14})(0.001 \text{ mol}/0.08 \text{ liter})$$

$$[H^+] = 1.25 \times 10^{-16}; \text{ pH} = -\log [H^+]$$

$$\text{pH} = 15.9$$

SOLUBILITY PRODUCT CONSTANTS

*   The solubility product constant (K_{sp}) refers to the product of the molar concentration of soluble ions that exists at the saturation point of the solution.

* K_{sp} refers to ionic compounds that are considered soluble. However, to some degree, some miniscule amount of ions dissolve from "insoluble" compounds. The K_{sp} can tell you the degree to which those ions have dissolved.

*   There are two types of problems you will see that involve K_{sp}:

    1. Find the molar solubility of a compound from K_{sp}, or visa versa.

    2. Determine whether or not a precipitate will form when two solutions are added together.

*   The molar solubility of a compound can be calculated from K_{sp} in the following example.

Example:

The K_{sp} for $BaCO_3$ is 2.58×10^{-9}. How many moles of barium carbonate can dissolve in 1.0 liter of solution?

Solution:

$x^2 = 2.58 \times 10^{-9}$

$x = 5.08 \times 10^{-5}$

- You can find the K_{sp} from the molar solubility in the following example.

Example:

The molar solubility for CuS is 9.2×10^{-23} M. What is the solubility product constant for copper sulfide?

Solution:

$K_{sp} = (x)^2 = (9.2 \times 10^{-23})^2$

$K_{sp} = 8.5 \times 10^{-45}$

- The following example shows how to determine whether a precipitate will form when two solutions are mixed together.

Example:

10.0 mL of 1.0×10^{-4} M lead nitrate solution is mixed with 500 mL of 1.0×10^{-5} M potassium iodide solution. Will a precipitate form? (The K_{sp} for lead iodide is 1.8×10^{-8}.)

Solution:

First, calculate the new molar concentrations of the lead and iodide ions; then plug those concentrations into the K_{sp} expression to find Q. Finally compare Q with the K_{sp}. If $Q < K_{sp}$, then no precipitate will form.

$[Pb^{2+}] = (0.010 \text{ L}) (1.0 \times 10^{-4} \text{ M}) / 0.510 \text{ L} = 1.96 \times 10^{-6}$ M

$[I^-] = (0.50 \text{ L}) (1.0 \times 10^{-5} \text{ M}) / 0.510 \text{ L} = 9.80 \times 10^{-6}$ M

$Q = [Pb^{2+}] [I^-]^2 = (1.96 \times 10^{-6}) (9.80 \times 10^{-6})^2 = 1.88 \times 10^{-16}$

Since $Q < K_{sp}$, then no precipitate will form.

COMMON ION EFFECT

- The common ion effect occurs when the ion of one equilibrium exists also in another equilibrium. One concentration satisfies both equilibria.

- The following example shows how to calculate the molar solubility of a compound in a solution where a common ion is already dissolved in the solution.

Example:

The K_{sp} for $Mg(OH)_2$ is 8.9×10^{-12}. What is the molar solubility of magnesium hydroxide in a solution that is pH 4 ?

Solution:

$K_{sp} = [Mg^{2+}] [OH^-]^2$ (where $[OH^-] = 10^{-10}$ M)

molar solubility $= [Mg^{2+}] = K_{sp} / 10^{-20} = 8.9 \times 10^8$ M
(very soluble)

BUFFERS

- A buffer is an aqueous combination of a weak acid and its conjugate base, or a weak base and its conjugate acid.

- A buffer solution resists a change in pH when new H+ or OH^- ions are added. The H^+ ions react with the weak base to form water; the OH^- ions react with the weak acid to form water.

- Maximum buffer capacity occurs when $pH = pK_a$ for the weak acid. However, the buffering capacity will be exhausted if either the weak acid or the weak base are used up.

- Buffers are best described by the Henderson-Hasselbach equation, which is derived by solving for $[H^+]$ in the equilibrium expression, then taking the negative log of each side of the equation.

THE HENDERSON-HASSELBACH EQUATION

$$pH = pK_a + \log \frac{[A^-]}{[HA]}$$

$[A^-]$ = molar concentration of conjugate base

$[HA]$ = molar concentration of weak acid

pH = pH of the solution

pK_a = $- \log K_a$ of the weak acid

Example:

What is the pH of the buffer solution created by combining 100 mL of 0.2 M acetic acid and 400 mL of 0.10 M sodium acetate? ($K_a = 1.8 \times 10^{-5}$)

Solution:

$$[H^+] = \frac{K_a[HC_2H_3O_2]}{[C_2H_3O_2^-]} = \frac{(1.8 \times 10^{-5})(.1 \text{ L})(.2 \text{ M}/.5 \text{ L})}{(.4 \text{ L})(.1 \text{ M}/.5 \text{ L})} =$$

$9.0 \times 10^{-6} \text{ M} = [H^+]$

$pH = -\log [H^+]$

$pH = -\log [9.0 \times 10^{-6}]$

$pH = 5.0$

Kinetics

Chapter 11

KINETICS

REACTION RATE

- Kinetics determines the speed of a reaction, and is dependent on the mechanism by which reactants turn into products.

- Reaction rate is based on the rate of appearance of a product or disappearance of a reactant, and is expressed as a change in concentration over time.

- Reaction rates are determined experimentally by measuring concentrations.

- Reaction rates increase by increasing concentration or by increasing the temperature.

- Reaction rates may also increase by increasing the surface area of the reactant—which is the same as increasing the concentration of possible participants in the reaction, or by adding a catalyst.

REACTION RATE

$$\text{rate of reaction} = \frac{\Delta \text{ concentration}}{\Delta \text{ time}} = k \text{ [reactants]}^{x}$$

k	= rate constant
[reactants]	= molar concentrations of reactants, mol/L
x	= reaction order

RATE LAW AND REACTION ORDER

• The **rate law** describes the rate of the reaction as a function of a rate constant, which is dependent on the temperature and the concentrations of the reactants.

• All rate laws take the form, **rate = k [reactants]^x**, where k is the rate constant, [reactants] refers to the molar concentration of reactants, and the exponent, x, is the reaction **order**.

• For all **single step reactions**, the rate law for that particular step can be surmised from the balanced equation for that step because the rate of the forward reaction is proportional to the concentration of available reactants.

Example:

Total reaction (single step): A → B + C   rate = k [A]
                                             (first order)

Or

Total reaction (single step): A + A → B   rate = k [A]^2
                                             (second order)

Or

Total reaction (single step): A + B → C   rate = k [A] [B]
                                           (second order overall)

• It cannot be assumed that a reaction involves only a single step. Therefore, the rate law (and determination of the order of reaction with respect to each reactant) can only be determined experimentally.

Example:

Use the experimental data on the following table to determine the rate law for the reaction,

A + B → C

Trial	[A]	[B]	Initial rate of formation of C (M/sec)
1	0.10	0.40	0.02
2	0.10	0.80	0.04
3	0.20	0.80	0.16

Solution:

When doubling [B] between the first and second trial (holding [A] constant), the reaction rate also doubles. Therefore, the rate of the reaction is *first order* with respect to [B]. When doubling [A] between the second and third trial (holding [B] constant), the reaction rate quadruples. Therefore, the rate changes as a square of a change in [A]; the reaction rate is *second order* with respect to [A]. The overall rate law of the reaction is the combination of the two orders: rate = k [A]^2 [B].

• The integrated rate laws for the different orders of reaction can be used to calculate the concentrations of reactants at specific times. The following chart summarizes the integrated rate laws, straight line plots, and method of calculating half-life for the different reaction orders.

	Zero Order Reactions	**First Order Reactions**	**Second Order Reactions**
Rate law	k	k [A]	k [A]^2
Integrated rate law	[A] = -kt + [A$_{initial}$]	ln[A] = -kt + ln[A$_{initial}$]	$\dfrac{1}{A} = kt + \dfrac{1}{[A_{initial}]}$
Plot for straight line	[A] vs. t	ln [A] vs. t	$\dfrac{1}{[A]}$ vs. t
k and slope of line	Slope = $-k$	Slope = -k	Slope = k
Half-life	[A$_{initial}$] / 2k	0.693 / k	1 / k [A$_{initial}$]

KINETICS AND EQUILIBRIUM

• Equilibrium occurs when the rate of the forward reaction equals the rate of the reverse reaction.

• The relationship between the equilibrium constant, K, and the rate constants, k_f and k_r, can be found by setting the rate law of the forward reaction equal to the rate law of the reverse reaction, then isolating the concentrations on one side of the equation and the rate constants on the other.

KINETICS AND EQUILIBRIUM

At equilibrium, $k_{forward}$ [reactants]^y = $k_{reverse}$ [products]^x

$$K_{eq} = \frac{k_{forward}}{k_{reverse}} = \frac{[products]^x}{[reactants]^y}$$

TEMPERATURE AND REACTION RATES

- Reaction rate depends on temperature, since molecules at greater temperature have greater kinetic energy and collide both more frequently and with greater force.

- When collisions occur with sufficient energy, or the **activation energy**, then a reaction will occur.

- The rate constant (which is proportional to reaction rate) is different at different temperatures. The rate constant will double (approximately) for every 10 K increase in temperature.

TEMPERATURE, RATE CONSTANT, AND ACTIVATION ENERGY

$$\ln k = \frac{-Ea}{RT} + \ln [A]$$

Where:

k = rate constant (proportional to reaction rate)

Ea = Activation energy, J

[A] = molar concentration of reactant, A, mol/L

R = Ideal gas constant, 8.31 J/K mol

T = temperature, K

ACTIVATION ENERGY AND CATALYSTS

- The **activation energy** is the amount of energy needed to cause a reaction to occur.

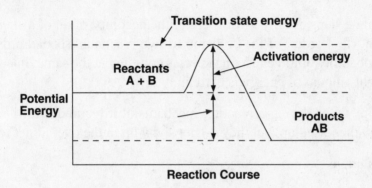

$$\Delta E = \Sigma\, E \text{ products} - \Sigma\, E \text{ reactants}$$

- **Catalysts** increase the rate of a reaction by facilitating a faster pathway, or mechanism, without itself being used up during the reaction. Therefore, catalysts do not appear in a balanced chemical equation.

- The new mechanism of reaction created by a catalyst has a lower activation energy.

- In living systems, catalysts are frequently used to speed up reactions that –without the catalyst—might be too slow to be useful for the organism.

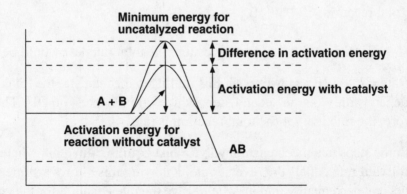

REACTION MECHANISMS

- Most chemical reactions involve more than one step. The combination of steps is called the **mechanism** of reaction, and must add to yield the total reaction.

- Single steps usually involve either the decomposition of a single reactant (first order) or the collision of two reactants (second order). The probability of three reacting species colliding at the same time with the right amount of energy is extremely low.

- Sometimes during a reaction mechanism, **intermediates** are formed and then used up; but they do not show up in the overall net reaction.

  Example:

  Step one: A $\rightarrow$ C + X

  Step two: B + X $\rightarrow$ D

  Total reaction: A + B $\rightarrow$ C + D

- The slowest step in the set of reactions in a mechanism determines the overall rate of the reaction, so it is called the **rate-determining step**.

  Example:

  Step one: A $\rightarrow$ C

  Step two: B $\rightarrow$ D   slow step (rate-determining step)

  Total reaction: A + B $\rightarrow$ C + D

  If the total reaction were a single step, the total rate law would be

  Rate = k [A] [B]. However, in this multistep mechanism, the total rate depends only on the second step, which only depends on [B]. Therefore, the rate law for the total reaction is rate = k [B].

- Some steps in a mechanism involve a **fast equilibrium step**, where the forward rate equals the reverse rate. Knowing this allows a student to generate an equality that may help solve the rate equation for the entire mechanism.

Example:

Step one: A   → C + X   fast equilibrium

Step two: B + X → D   slow step (rate
                                                determining step)

Total reaction: A + B → C + D

The total rate depends only on the second slow step, which depends on both [B] and [X] (Rate = k [B] [X]). However, the rate law cannot be expressed in terms of a concentration that doesn't show up in the total reaction (X). The fast equilibrium step allows you to express [X] in terms of reactants that actually show up in the total reaction, since in a fast equilibrium, the rate of the forward reaction equals the rate of the reverse reaction.

$k_{forward}$ [A] = $k_{reverse}$ [X] [C] in a fast equilibrium

Solving for [X]:

$$[X] = \frac{k_{forward}\,[A]}{k_{reverse}\,[C]} = \frac{k[A]}{[C]}$$

Substituting back in for [X] in the original rate equation, Rate = k [B] [X], gives you the rate law for the total reaction,

rate = k [A] [B] / [C].

• You will probably be asked to determine whether or not an experimentally derived rate law is consistent with a particular reaction mechanism. Use the rate-determining step and the fast equilibrium step principles to derive a rate law that matches the mechanism. (This is probably more difficult than what you might expect to see on the AP test because of the fractional exponent.)

Example:

Derive the rate law for the following mechanism for the production of phosgene gas from chlorine and carbon monoxide.

Step one: Cl_2 ↔ 2 Cl   fast equilibrium

Step two: Cl   + CO ↔ COCl   fast equilibrium

Step three   COCl + Cl   → $COCl_2$ slow step

Total reaction: Cl_2 + CO → $COCl_2$

Solution:

1. Overall rate of reaction = rate of slow step = k [COCl] [Cl$_2$]

2. Remove the intermediate in the rate law by using the fast equilibrium.

    [COCl] = k [CO] [Cl$_2$]$^{1/2}$

3. Rate of overall reaction = k [COCl] [Cl$_2$]$^{3/2}$

Thermodynamics

Chapter 12

THERMODYNAMICS

STATE FUNCTIONS

WHAT ARE STATE FUNCTIONS?

- The state of a system is defined by conditions of pressure, temperature, and number of moles of a substance.

- State functions depend only on initial and final states of a system. Thermodynamics deals with initial and final states.

- State functions are not dependent on how one gets from the initial state to the final state. The mechanism of getting from one state to another is represented by the kinetics of a reaction.

TYPES OF STATE FUNCTIONS

- Entropy (S), enthalpy (H), and free energy (G) are state functions.

- **Entropy** is a measure of disorder, measured in J/K.

- **Enthalpy** is energy released or absorbed by the reaction, measured in J.

- **Free energy** is the energy available to do work, measured in J.

- Most thermodynamics at this level deals with changes in entropy, enthalpy, and free energy between an initial state and a final state. (ΔS, ΔH, and ΔG, respectively.)

STANDARD STATE CONDITIONS

- Standard state conditions for state functions are indicated by a "°".

Example: $\Delta S°$ represents the standard change in entropy; $\Delta H°$ represents the standard change in enthalpy, and $\Delta G°$ represents the standard change in free energy.

• Standard conditions are a very specific set of conditions, which include

1. Gases are at 1 atmosphere pressure.

2. Liquids and solids are pure.

3. Solutions are at 1molar concentration.

4. The temperature is 25° C, or 298 K.

• Do not confuse thermodynamic standard conditions, where the temperature is 298 K, with standard temperature and pressure (STP) for gases, where the temperature is 273 K.

FIRST LAW AND ENTHALPY

FIRST LAW OF THERMODYNAMICS

• **The first law of thermodynamics** is commonly referred to as the law of Conservation of Energy.

• More specifically, the first law states that the change in internal energy is equal to the difference between the energy supplied to the system as heat and the energy removed from the system as work performed on the surroundings.

FIRST LAW OF THERMODYNAMICS

$$\Delta E = q - w$$

where

$$w = -P\Delta V$$

ΔE = Change in total energy, or internal energy of the system

q = Heat added to the system

w = Work done by the system on the surroundings

P = Pressure of the system

ΔV = Change in volume of the system

Example:

An ideal gas absorbs 100 L atm of heat energy, which expands against a pressure of 8.0 atm. The total energy of the system is –20.0 L atm. How much does the volume change during the expansion?

Solution:

$$\Delta E = q - w = q + (P\Delta V)$$

$$\Delta V = \frac{E - q}{P} = \frac{-20.1 \text{ L atm} - 100 \text{ L atm}}{8.0 \text{ atm}} = 15 \text{ L}$$

ENTHALPY

- **Enthalpy** is a state function.

- The **enthalpy change** in a reaction (ΔH) is the difference between the enthalpy of contained in the products and the enthalpy contained in the reactants.

- **Exothermic reactions** give off heat energy, $\Delta H_{reaction} < 0$. The products of the reaction have less enthalpy than the reactants.

- **Endothermic reactions** take in heat energy, $\Delta H_{reaction} > 0$. The products of the reaction have more enthalpy than the reactants.

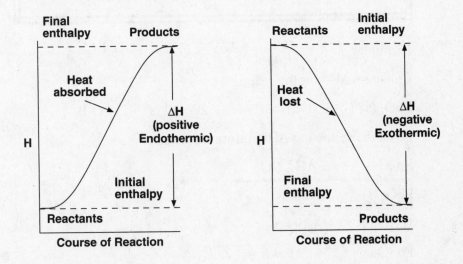

ENTHALPY CHANGE DURING A REACTION

$$\Delta H_{reaction} = \Sigma H_{products} - \Sigma H_{reactants}$$

HEATS OF FORMATION, HEATS OF REACTION

- The **standard heat of formation** ($\Delta H°_f$) is the change of enthalpy for the reaction that forms a compound from its pure elements under standard conditions.

- The standard heat of formation ($\Delta H°_f$) for a pure element at standard conditions is zero.

- Standard heats of formation can be used to estimate the $\Delta H°$ of any reaction

$\Delta H°$ AND HEATS OF FORMATION

$$\Delta H° = \Sigma H°_f \text{ (products)} - \Sigma H°_f \text{ (reactants)}$$

Example:

Calculate $\Delta H°$ for the reaction,

$$PbO_2 \text{ (s)} + 2H_2SO_4(l) + Pb(s) \rightarrow 2PbSO_4(s) + 2H_2O(l)$$

given the following $\Delta H°f$ information.

Species	$\Delta H°_f$ (kJ)
PbO_2 (s)	−66.3
$H_2SO_4(l)$	−194.5
$PbSO_4(s)$	−219.9
$H_2O(l)$	−68.3

Solution:

$\Delta H°_{reaction} = \Sigma H°_f (\text{products}) - \Sigma H°_f (\text{reactants})$

$\Delta H°_{reaction} = [(2 \times -219.9) + (2 \times -68.3)] - [(-66.3) + (2 \times -194.5)]$

$\Delta H°_{reaction} = -121.1 \text{ kJ}$

HESS' LAW

- Hess' Law states the $\Delta H°$ of a reaction that is composed of multiple steps is equal to the sum of the $\Delta H°$ from each step. Hess' law is an offshoot of the first law of thermodynamics because energy must be conserved in order for the sum of the energies of component reactions to be equal to the energy of the total reaction.

Example:

REACTION	$\Delta H_{reaction}$ (kJ/mol)
1. $N_2 (g) + O_2 (g) \rightarrow 2 NO$	$\Delta H_1 = 180$
2. $2NO(g) + O_2 (g) \rightarrow 2 NO_2$	$\Delta H_2 = -112$
total $N_2 (g) + O_2 (g) \rightarrow 2 NO_2$	$\Delta H_{total} = 68$

BOND ENERGIES

- **Bond energies** are the amount of energy given off when bonds are formed, or the amount of energy used when bonds are broken.

- Bond energies deal with reactants and products in their gaseous state under standard conditions.

- Breaking bonds is an exothermic process; making bonds is an endothermic process.

- Heats of reaction can be estimated by finding the difference between the bond energies of the bonds made and the bond energies of the bonds broken.

- Bond energies used in this way to find heats of reaction is an example of Hess' Law.

ΔH° AND BOND ENERGIES

$$\Delta H°_{reaction} = \Sigma H°_{bond\ energies}\ \textbf{(bonds broken)} -$$

$$\Sigma H°_{bond\ energies}\ \textbf{(bonds made)}$$

Example:

Use the following table of bond energies to approximate the change in enthalpy when one mole of propane undergoes complete combustion, according to this reaction.

$$C_3H_8 + 5O_2 \rightarrow 3CO_2 + 4H_2O$$

Bond	$\Delta H°_{bond}$ (kJ/mol)
C – H	413
C – C	347
O – H	467
C = O	794
O = O	495

Solution:

$$\Delta H°_{reaction} = \Sigma H°_{bond}\ \text{(bonds broken)} - \Sigma H°_{bond}\ \text{(bonds made)}$$

Bond broken	Bonds made
$8 \times$ C – H	$8 \times$ O – H
$1 \times$ C – C	$6 \times$ C= O
$5 \times$ O = O	

$$\Delta H°_{reaction} = [(347) + (8 \times 413) + (5 \times 495)] - [(6 \times 794) + (8 \times 467)]$$

$$\Delta H°_{reaction} = -2374\ kJ$$

CALORIMETRY

- **Calorimetry** is the laboratory measurement of heats of reaction. The measured change in temperature of the calorimeter identifies how much heat is either absorbed or contributed to the reaction inside it.

- The heat given off by the reaction equals the heat absorbed by the calorimeter. Likewise, the heat absorbed by the reaction equals the heat given off by the calorimeter.

- **Coffee cup calorimeters** assume that all the heat of a reaction is absorbed by water in the calorimeter.

- **Bomb calorimeters** contain materials other than water that absorb the heat from the reaction. For bomb calorimeters, the heat absorbed equals the specific heat capacity of the calorimeter (in J/°C) multiplied by the change in the temperature of the calorimeter (ΔT).

CALORIMETRY

Coffee cup: $\Delta H_{reaction} = -q = -mc\Delta T$

Bomb: $\Delta H_{reaction} = -q = -C\Delta T$

q	= heat added to (or subtracted from) calorimeter, J
m	= mass of water in calorimeter, g
c	= specific heat of water in calorimeter, J/ g °C
ΔT	= temperature change of calorimeter, in °C
$\Delta H_{reaction}$	= heat given off (or absorbed) by the reaction, J
C	= heat capacity of the bomb calorimeter, J/°C

- Measured heats of reaction can be compared to heats of reaction that are estimated using heats of formation or bond energies.

Example:

A bomb calorimeter with a heat capacity of 10.8 J/°C is used to find the heat of combustion for a molecule. If the calorimeter increases in temperature by 82 °C during the reaction, what is the measured heat of combustion for the reaction?

Solution:

$\Delta H_{reaction} = -q = -C\Delta T$

$\Delta H_{reaction} = -10.8 \text{ J/°C} \times 82 \text{ °C} = -8856 \text{ J}$

SECOND LAW, ENTROPY, AND FREE ENERGY

ENTROPY AND THE SECOND LAW OF THERMODYNAMICS

- **Entropy** is a measure of disorder, and carries the units of J/K.

- Entropy is a state function. The change in entropy of a reaction (ΔS) is the difference between the entropy contained in the products and the entropy contained in the reactants.

$\Delta S°$ FOR A REACTION (SYSTEM)

$$\Delta S° = \Sigma \, S° \text{ (products)} - \Sigma S° \text{ (reactants)}$$

- The **second law of thermodynamics** states that the entropy of the universe increases during a spontaneous reaction.

- The change in entropy of the universe is defined as the ΔS of the system (or the reaction) + the ΔS of the surroundings.

ENTROPY, ENTHALPY, AND FREE ENERGY

- The entropy of the universe is defined as the $\Delta S_{system} + \Delta S_{surroundings}$, which must increase in a spontaneous reaction, according to the second law of thermodynamics.

  - $\Delta S_{surroundings} = -\Delta H / T$, therefore

  - $\Delta S_{system} + \Delta S_{surroundings}$ can be rewritten as $\Delta S_{system} - \Delta H / T$, which must increase in a spontaneous reaction.

  - Multiplying by $-1/T$, $\Delta H - T\Delta S_{system}$ must then increase in a spontaneous reaction.

- $\Delta H - T\Delta S_{system}$ is defined as free energy, ΔG, which is the amount of work that a reaction is able to do.

- Therefore, for spontaneous processes, $\Delta G < 0$.

FREE ENERGY

$$\Delta G^\circ = \Delta H^\circ - T\Delta S^\circ$$

ΔG° = standard free energy change of reaction, J

ΔH° = standard enthalpy change of reaction, J

T = temperature, K

ΔS° = standard entropy change of reaction, J/K

CONDITIONS OF REACTION SPONTANEITY

ΔH°	T	ΔS°	ΔG°	Spontaneous?
<0	Low	>0	<0	Yes
<0	High	>0	<0	Yes
>0	Low	<0	>0	No
>0	High	<0	>0	No
>0	Low	>0	>0	No
>0	High	>0	<0	Yes
<0	Low	<0	<0	Yes
<0	High	<0	>0	No

FREE ENERGY OF REACTION

Free Energy of Formation

- The free energy of formation of a substance is the ΔG° for the reaction that forms the substance from uncombined elements as they exist under standard conditions.

- The free energy is the maximum amount of heat that can be devoted to performing work by a reaction.

Example:

Use the following table of free energies to calculate the free energy for the combustion of one mole of ethanol.

$$2\ C_2H_5OH\ (l) + 6O_2\ (g) \rightarrow 4CO_2\ (g) + 6H_2O\ (g)$$

Species	ΔG_f° (kJ/mol)
$C_2H_5OH\ (l)$	$\Delta G_f = -175$
$O_2\ (g)$	$\Delta G_f = 0$
$CO_2\ (g)$	$\Delta G_f = -394$
$H_2O\ (g)$	$\Delta G_f = -229$

Solution:

$$\Delta G^{\circ}_{reaction} = \Sigma \Delta G^{\circ}_f\ (products) - \Sigma \Delta G^{\circ}_f\ (reactants)$$

$$\Delta G^{\circ}_{reaction} = [(4 \times -394) + (6 \times -229)] - (-175)$$

$$\Delta G^{\circ}_{reaction} = -2775\ kJ$$

Hess' Law and Free Energies

- Hess' law works with free energies as well as enthalpies.

- The ΔG° of a reaction that is composed of multiple steps is equal to the sum of the ΔG° from each step.

	REACTION			$\Delta G_{reaction}$ (kJ/mol)
1.	$N_2\ (g)\ +\ 2\ O_2\ (g)$	$\rightarrow$	$2\ NO_2\ (g)$	$\Delta G_1\ =\ 104$
2.	$2\ NO_2\ (g)\ +$	$\rightarrow$	$2\ N_2O_4\ (l)$	$\Delta G_2\ =\ 90$
total	$N_2\ (g)\ +\ 2\ O_2\ (g)$	$\rightarrow$	$2\ N_2O_4\ (l)$	$\Delta G_{total} = 194$

ΔG°, K, AND E°

FREE ENERGY, EQUILIBRIUM, CELL VOLTAGE

$$\Delta G° = -nFE°_{total} = -RT \ln K$$

$\Delta G°$ = standard free energy change of reaction at equilibrium, J

n = number of moles of electrons transferred in the reaction, mol

F = One faraday, 96,486 coulombs/mol electrons

$E°_{total}$ = Standard cell voltage, V

R = Ideal gas constant, 8.31 J / mol-K

T = temperature, K

K = equilibrium constant

Example:

Given the following thermodynamic data, calculate $\Delta G°$, equilibrium constant, and $E°_{total}$ for the reaction that turns iron metal into rust ($Fe_2O_2(s)$) under standard conditions.

Species	$\Delta H°_f$ (kJ)	S° (J/ K mol)
Fe_2O_3 (s)	−826	90
O_2 (g)	0	205
Fe (s)	0	28

Solutions:

(i) Find $\Delta H°$ for the reaction, $2Fe(s) + 3/2 \, O_2 \, (g) \rightarrow Fe_2O_3 \, (s)$

$\Delta H°_{reaction} = \Sigma H°f \, (\text{products}) - \Sigma H°f \, (\text{reactants}) = -826 \text{ kJ}$

(ii) Find $\Delta S°$ for the reaction, $2Fe(s) + 3/2\ O_2\ (g) \rightarrow Fe_2O_3\ (s)$

$\Delta S° = \Sigma\ S°$ (products) - $\Sigma\ S°$ (reactants)

$\Delta S° = (90) - [(1.5 \times 205) + (2 \times 28)] = -273.5 = 274$ J/K mol

(iii) Find $\Delta G°$ for the reaction, $2Fe(s) + 3/2\ O_2\ (g) \rightarrow Fe_2O_3\ (s)$

$\Delta G° = \Delta H° - T\Delta S° = -826 - (298)(-0.274) = -744$ kJ

(iv) Find $E°_{total}$ from $\Delta G°$

$\Delta G° = -nFE°_{total}$

$E°_{total} = \dfrac{\Delta G°}{nF} = 744{,}000\ \text{J} / (3)(98{,}486\ \text{C}) = 2.52$ V

(v) Find K from $\Delta G°$

$\Delta G° = -RT \ln K$

$\ln K = -\Delta G°/RT$

$K = e^{-\Delta G°/RT}$ (a very large number!)

Descriptive Chemistry

Chapter 13

DESCRIPTIVE CHEMISTRY

PRODUCTS OF CHEMICAL REACTIONS

PRECIPITATION REACTIONS

If you know the solubility rules, identifying these reactions and writing the resulting net ionic equations should be straightforward. Remember to not include spectator ions in the net ionic reaction. Only those ions that come together to form the insoluble inorganic compound should be written.

Question: Solutions of silver nitrate and potassium iodide are mixed.

Answer: $Ag^+ + I^- \rightarrow AgI$

ACID-BASE REACTIONS

Remember that most acid-base reactions simply move a proton from one reactant to another.

1. **A strong acid neutralizes a strong base**

The net ionic reaction for this type of acid-base neutralization is always the same. Students should memorize the strong acids and bases.

Question: Strong hydrochloric acid is added to a solution of sodium hydroxide.

Answer: $H^+ + OH^- \rightarrow H_2O$

2. **A strong acid neutralizes a weak base**

The net ionic equation should depict a proton combining with the basic molecule.

Question: Strong hydrochloric acid is added to an ammonia solution.

Answer: $H^+ + NH_3 \rightarrow NH_4^+$

3. **A strong base reacts with a weak acid**

A proton from the weak acid combines with the hydroxide ion to form an anion and water.

Question: Solutions of sodium hydroxide and acetic acid are mixed.

Answer: $HC_2H_3O_2 + OH^- \rightarrow C_2H_3O_2^- + H_2O$

4. **A weak acid reacts with a weak base**

Keep any eye out for Lewis acid-base reactions, in which the acid accepts an electron pair from and combines with a weak base.

Question: Solutions of boron trifluoride and ammonia are mixed.

Answer: $BF_3 + NH_3 \rightarrow BF_3NH_3$

5. **A coordination-complex formed**

This is another example of a Lewis acid-base reaction, where the metal serves as an electron-acceptor. You would recognize this if a transition metal is placed in a solution with soluble ammonia, cyanide, hydroxide, or thiocyanate ions. You may combine the metal with as many polyatomic anions as you wish; just be sure that the total charge on the ion is correct. The oxidation state of the metallic atom does not change.

Question: A solution of iron (III) nitrate is added to a solution of potassium thiocyanate.

Answer: $Fe^{3+} + SCN^- \rightarrow FeSCN^{2+}$

OXIDATION-REDUCTION REACTIONS

One element increases in oxidation state while another is reduced in oxidation state.

1. **Two uncombined elements come together**

Combine the two elements to form a compound with reasonable oxidation states for each element.

Question: Magnesium metal is burned in oxygen gas.

Answer: $Mg + O_2 \rightarrow MgO$

2.   A carbon compound combusts with oxygen

An alkane, alkene, or alkyne is oxidized by oxygen gas to form carbon dioxide and water.

Question: Butane gas ignites in the presence of oxygen gas.

Answer: $C_4H_{10} + O_2 \rightarrow CO_2 + H_2O$

3.   A single reactant decomposes

Decomposition usually occurs because an uncommon oxidation state in one element gives way to a more common oxidation state.

Question: Hydrogen peroxide solution is exposed to bright light.

Answer: $H_2O_2 \rightarrow O_2 + H_2O$

4.   A solid transition metal is placed in a solution of metallic ions

Use the chart of standard reduction potentials. The change with the highest reduction potential is reduced in charge. Voltaic or galvanic cells are an example of this type of reaction.

Question: Copper metal is placed in a solution of silver nitrate.

Answer: $Cu + Ag^+ \rightarrow Cu^{++} + Ag$

5.   An electrical current pass through a solution

If so, this reaction takes place in an electrolytic cell. Only a limited number of possible reactions are possible.

Question: An electrical current runs between two electrodes in molten sodium chloride.

Answer: $NaCl \rightarrow Na + Cl_2$

6.   A solid metal is placed into an acidic solution

The metal is oxidized and hydrogen gas is formed. Remember, water can also be an acid; check to be sure the dissociation of water on the reduction potential chart shows a higher tendency to be reduced, such as the case with calcium in water.

Question: Magnesium metal is placed into a weak solution of hydrochloric acid.

Answer: $Mg + H^+ \rightarrow Mg^{++} + H_2$

RELATIONSHIPS IN THE PERIODIC TABLE

ATOMIC RADII

- Moving from left to right across a period, atomic radius decreases.

- Moving down a group, atomic radius increases.

- Cations have small radii than their corresponding neutral atoms.

- Anions have larger radii than their corresponding neutral atoms.

IONIZATION ENERGY

- Moving from left to right across a period, ionization energy increases.

- Moving down a group, ionization energy decreases.

- More energy is needed for each succeeding ionization.

- Significantly more energy is needed to break a full shell of electrons.

- Elements with low ionization energies are more easily oxidized.

ELECTRON AFFINITY

- Moving from left to right across a period, electron-affinity energy given off increases.

- Moving down a group, electron-affinity energy given off does not change appreciably.

ELECTRONEGATIVITY

- Moving from left to right across a period, electronegativity increases.

- Moving down a group, electronegativity decreases.

REACTIVITY OF THE MAIN GROUPS

- **Group IA** elements are the most reactive of the metals. The outer "s" electron is loosely held and easily removed—and more easily removed for larger elements. Group IA elements react violently with water and are so reactive that they are never found naturally in an uncombined state. Hydroxides of IA elements are strong bases; increased size of the IA element will increase the base strength of the element's hydroxide.

- **Group IIA** are also very reactive and do not tend to be found uncombined in nature. They react slowly with oxygen to form oxides and with water to form hydroxides.

- **Transition metals** all react very slowly with oxygen or water, and some, do not react at all. The metals with lower reactivity can exist in uncombined in nature, and therefore were some of the first metals discovered by ancient civilizations.

- The lightest of the **IIIA** group are non-metallic, while the remaining are all metals. Group IIIA elements are all mildly reactive. For example, aluminum resists combining with oxygen or reacting with water at normal temperatures, but it will react with hydrochloric acid.

- The first element of the **Group IVA** elements (carbon) is a non-metal. It is followed by two metalloids (silicon and germanium), and then by two metals (tin and lead). The first three elements are semi-conductors and fairly reactive.

- **Group VA** consists of two non-metals, two metalloids, and a metal. The more reactive of these elements combine readily with oxygen and some of the more reactive metals.

- **Group VIA** elements easily gain electrons, such as oxygen, with this ability decreasing with the larger elements.

- **Group VIIA** elements gain electrons most easily, with the most highly reactive element being the smallest in this group (fluorine).

- **Group VIIIA** are the inert gases and, because they have a full outer shell of electrons, do not combine easily with other elements. For example, the smaller inert gases exist as monoatomic gases. The largest in this group can combine with other elements, but only with highly electronegative elements (such as fluorine and chlorine) in coordinate covalent bonds.

INORGANIC COMPOUNDS

NAMING INORGANIC COMPOUNDS

- Monoatomic cations take the name of the element. *E.g.*, "sodium" for Na^+.

- Cations with multiple possible oxidations states should have the oxidation state listed with a Roman numeral. *E.g.*, Tin (IV) oxide for SnO_2

- Monoatomic anions take the name of the element, but ends with "ide". *E.g.*, "fluoride" for F^-.

- Name the cation first, then the anion. *E.g.*, "sodium fluoride".

- Use Greek prefixes for multiple ions. mono-, di-, tri-, tetra-, penta-, hexa- hepta-, octa-, etc. *E.g.*, dinitrogen pentoxide for N_2O5.

- Be sure to memorize the common cations and anions on the following charts.

COMMON CATIONS

Name	Formula
Hydrogen	H^+
Lithium	Li^+
Sodium	Na^+
Potassium	K^+
Cesium	Cs^+
Beryllium	Be^{2+}
Magnesium	Mg^{2+}
Calcium	Ca^{2+}
Barium	Ba^{2+}
Aluminum	Al^{3+}
Iron II / III	Fe^{2+} / Fe^{3+}
Copper I / II	Cu^+ / Cu^{2+}
Tin II / IV	Sn^{2+} / Sn^{4+}
Lead II / IV	Pb^{2+} / Pb^{4+}
Mercury I / II	Hg^+ / Hg^{2+}
Ammonium	NH^{4+}

COMMON ANIONS

Name	Formula
Hydride	H^-
Fluoride	F^-
Chloride	Cl^-
Oxide	O^{2-}
Sulfide	S^{2-}
Nitride	N^{3-}
Phosphide	P^{3-}
Carbonate	CO_3^{2-}
Bicarbonate	HCO_3^-
Hypochlorite	ClO^-
Chlorite	ClO_2^-
Chorate	ClO_3^-
Perchlorate	ClO_4^-
Iodite	IO_2^-
Iodate	IO_3^-
Acetate	$C_2H_3O_2^-$
Permanganate	MnO_4^-
Dichromate	$Cr_2O_7^-$
Chromate	CrO_4^-
Peroxide	O_2^{2-}
Nitrite	NO_2^-
Nitrate	NO_3^-
Sulfite	SO_3^{2-}
Sulfate	SO_4^{2-}
Hydrogen sulfate	HSO_4^-
Hydroxide	OH^-
Cyanide	CN^-
Phosphate	PO_4^{3-}
Hydrogen phosphate	HPO_4^{2-}
Dihydrogen phosphate	H_2PO^{4-}

ORGANIC MOLECULES

- There is very little organic chemistry on the AP Chemistry Examination.

- Most of the organic content has focused on an awareness of the basic alkane formula and isomerism, the difference between pi and sigma bonding, and the most common functional groups.

- The reactions of some of the functional groups, such as carboxylic acids in acid-base reactions or alkane combustion, are discussed in other places. (See "Products of Chemical Reactions" earlier in this chapter.)

ALKANES

Alkane	Formula
Methane	CH_4
Ethane	C_2H_6
Propane	C_3H_8
Butane	C_4H_{10}
Pentane	C_5H_{12}
Hexane	C_6H_{14}
Heptane	C_7H_{16}
Octane	C_8H_{18}
Nonane	C_9H_{20}
Decane	$C_{10}H_{22}$

ALKENES AND ALKYNES

- **Alkenes** are hydrocarbons that contain a double bond between at least two carbons. Alkenes have the general formula, C_nH_{2n}.

- **Alkynes** are hydrocarbons that contain a triple bond between at least two carbons. Alkynes have the general formula, C_nH_{2n-2}.

- The first covalent bond between two non-metals is a **sigma bond** (σ), where the electrons are paired along the axis between the two atoms.

- Any additional covalent bonds between non-metals are **pi bonds** (π), where the electrons are paired through overlap of p-orbitals above and below the inter-nuclear axis. For example, a double bond consists of one sigma and one pi bond. A triple bond consists of one sigma and two pi bonds.

- Sigma bonds are much stronger than pi bonds, and therefore have much higher bond energies and are more difficult to break.

ORGANIC FUNCTIONAL GROUPS

Functional Group	General formula	Example
Halohydrocarbon	$R-\overset{\displaystyle H}{\underset{\displaystyle H}{\overset{\displaystyle \mid}{\underset{\displaystyle \mid}{C}}}}-Cl$	Carbon tetrachloride
Alcohol	$R-\overset{\displaystyle H}{\underset{\displaystyle H}{\overset{\displaystyle \mid}{\underset{\displaystyle \mid}{C}}}}-OH$	Ethanol
Ether	$R-\overset{\displaystyle H}{\underset{\displaystyle H}{\overset{\displaystyle \mid}{\underset{\displaystyle \mid}{C}}}}-O-\overset{\displaystyle H}{\underset{\displaystyle H}{\overset{\displaystyle \mid}{\underset{\displaystyle \mid}{C}}}}-R$	Diethyl ether
Aldehyde	$R-\overset{\displaystyle H}{\underset{\displaystyle O}{\overset{\displaystyle \mid}{\underset{\displaystyle \parallel}{C}}}}-H$	Formaldehyde
Ketone	$R-\overset{\displaystyle H}{\underset{\displaystyle O}{\overset{\displaystyle \mid}{\underset{\displaystyle \parallel}{C}}}}-R$	Methyl ethyl ketone
Carboxylic acid	$R-\underset{\displaystyle O}{\underset{\displaystyle \parallel}{C}}-OH$	Acetic acid
Ester	$R-\underset{\displaystyle O}{\underset{\displaystyle \parallel}{C}}-O-\overset{\displaystyle H}{\underset{\displaystyle H}{\overset{\displaystyle \mid}{\underset{\displaystyle \mid}{C}}}}-R$	Diphenyl ester

Laboratories

Chapter 14

LABORATORIES

LABORATORY SAFETY

• Always wear goggles when working with pure chemicals and flames.

• Don't put chemicals in your mouth or eyes, either on purpose or otherwise. That means do not touch your eyes or mouth when you are in the laboratory.

• Always ventilate your work area well.

• Heat substances slowly; be sure to point heating glassware away from you or others.

• When diluting acid, "do it like you should and add the acid to the water."

LABORATORY MEASUREMENTS

• Remember that you can have only one uncertain digit in the data that you record. For example, an uncertain digit would be a guessed number between two lines on a graduated cylinder. A thorough set of laboratory measurements will include +/- values, which create a range of acceptable error for every measurement.

• When measuring mass, be sure to allow objects to return to room temperature before weighing. Don't forget to subtract the mass of the weigh paper or container when recording the mass of a compound.

• When measuring the volume of a liquid in a graduated cylinder, be sure to look at the number the corresponds to the bottom of the meniscus.

• Don't forget to take into account the partial pressure of water when collecting a gas over water, as with a eudiometer tube.

- Be sure to help others after you achieve accurate measurements by not contaminating stock chemicals and solutions. Always put the chemical into a clean container. Don't touch the tip of a dropper touch surfaces other than the stock solution.

- When recording data, be sure to do so on a lab sheet or bound book that will be available to you, your lab partner, and your teacher. Be sure that the conditions of the measurement are clearly identified on your data sheet.

- Consider the type of error that is most reasonably created by any given measurement. For example, when using a coffee-cup calorimeter to measure the heat of an exothermic reaction, there is a high probability that some heat will escape into the surroundings, thereby resulting in a measured value that is less than the expected value. In this case, there is no chance that heat would move from the surroundings to the reaction.

- The following traits can be measured by the corresponding methods.

  1. Concentration: titration, spectrophotometer

  2. Mass: balance

  3. Volume: volumetric flask, graduated cylinder, buret, eudiometer, pipette

  4. Volts: voltmeter

  5. Amps: ammeter

  6. pH: litmus paper, pH electrode

EXAMPLE PROBLEMS FOR THE RECOMMENDED EXPERIMENTS

Each of the following experiments are recommended by the College Board for AP Chemistry courses. While the sample problem listed here is not the only example of the experiment, they represent the most common types of calculations involved in the experiment and the common questions that are asked in Problem 6 (Part B) of the Free-Response section of the AP Chemistry exam.

1. Determination of the formula of a compound

Example problem:

A student cuts a 5.30 g magnesium ribbon into small pieces, then began to heat it in a 14.20 g crucible. Over time, the magnesium ignited and burned to form a white, grayish and powdery substance. After the crucible cooled, the student measured the mass of the crucible that contained the powder and found it to be 22.70 g.

(a) What is the mass of the powder in the crucible?

22.7 g – 14.20 g = <u>8.50 g powder</u> (5.30 g Mg and 3.20 g O)

(b) What is the formula of the oxide formed?

$$\text{Moles of Mg} = 5.30 \text{ g Mg} \times \frac{1 \text{ mol MG}}{24.3 \text{ g MG}} = 0.218 \text{ mol Mg}$$

$$\text{Moles of O added} = 3.20 \text{ g O} \times \frac{1 \text{ mol O}}{15.99 \text{ g O}} = 0.200 \text{ mol O}$$

Formula: <u>MgO</u>

(c) What is the mass percent of oxygen in the compound?

$$\frac{3.20 \text{ g O}}{8.50 \text{ g MgO}} \times 100\% = \underline{37.6\% \text{ oxygen}}$$

(d) What is the most likely source of error in the experiment, and how do these results demonstrate that error?

It is more likely that some of the magnesium did NOT combine with oxygen in an incomplete reaction, and therefore demonstrate slightly fewer moles of oxygen than magnesium, rather than the other way around. The experimental observations demonstrate this type of error (0.200 mol O vs. 0.218 mol Mg).

2. Determination of the percentage of water in a hydrate

Example problem:

A student obtained 4.23 g of blue-colored hydrate of copper sulfate from the teacher, and then heated the substance in a 16.80 g crucible over moderate heat for several minutes. Over time, the entire substance appeared to turn white, at which time the student removed the crucible from the heat. The student measured the mass of the crucible and substance together and found it to be 19.50 g.

(a) What mass of water was removed from the hydrate?

19.50 g total – 16.80 g crucible = 2.70 g anhydrate

4.23 g hydrate - 2.70 g anhydrate = 1.53 g water

(b) How many moles of water were removed from the hydrate?

$$1.53 \text{ g water} \times \frac{1.0 \text{ mole water}}{18.00 \text{ g water}} = 0.085 \text{ moles water}$$

(c) How many moles of the anhydrous copper sulfate were left in the container after heating?

$$2.70 \text{ g CuSO}_4 \times \frac{1.0 \text{ mole CuSO}_4}{159.61 \text{ g CuSO}_4} = 0.017 \text{ moles CuSO}_4$$

(d) What is the formula of the hydrate of copper sulfate?

Since 0.085 mol water is five times 0.017 moles copper sulfate, the formula of the hydrate is $CuSO_4 \bullet 5H_2O$.

(e) What is the percentage of water in the hydrate?

$$\frac{5 \times 18.00 \text{ g water}}{249.61 \text{ g CuSO}_4 \bullet 5H_2O} \times 100\% = 36.0\%$$

(f) What type of error would be created if the student did not heat the copper sulfate long enough and not remove all the water?

If less than the entire amount of water were removed, the student would have attributed a greater amount of the original mass to copper sulfate, and less to water. The student would probably end up concluding that coefficient for water would have been some integer less than 5.

3. **Determination of the molar mass by vapor density**

Example problem:

A student in a laboratory at sea level puts 5.00 g of a volatile liquid in a flask that has a single hole stopper in it that is immersed in a boiling water bath at 373 K. At the point where the last small bit of the liquid evaporates, the flask is plunged into cold water and 0.789 g of the volatile liquid re-condenses. Afterward, the flask is cleaned out and the interior volume of the flask is found to be 287 mL.

(a) What is the pressure at which the volatile liquid both evaporated and condensed? (1.0 atm)

(b) Use the vapor pressure of the volatile liquid to determine its molar mass.

$$\text{Molar mass} = \frac{gRT}{PV} = \frac{0.789 \text{ g}}{1.0 \text{ atm}} \times \frac{0.082 \text{ L atm}}{\text{K mol}} \times \frac{373 \text{ K}}{0.287 \text{ L}}$$

$$= 84.16 \text{ g / mol}$$

(c) The volatile liquid is found to be 14.37% hydrogen and 85.63% carbon. What is the empirical formula of the volatile liquid?

$$14.37 \text{ g H} \times \frac{1.0 \text{ mol H}}{1.008 \text{ g H}} = 14.26 \text{ mol H}$$

$$85.63 \text{ g C} \times \frac{1.0 \text{ mol C}}{12.011 \text{ g C}} = 7.129 \text{ mol C}$$

Empirical formula: CH_2

(d) What is the molecular formula of the compound?

Since the molar mass of the empirical formula is one-sixth the molar mass of the experimentally determined molar mass, then the molecular formula is six times the empirical formula, or C_6H_{12}.

4. **Determination of the molar mass by freezing point depression**

Example problem:

A student is given a 3.80 g sample of an unknown non-electrolyte solid and asked to find its molar mass by freezing point depression. The student decides to use 40.00 g of benzene as a solvent, which has a melting point of 5.5 °C and molal freezing point constant of 5.12 °C kg/mol.

(a) What is the significance of the unknown solute being a non-electrolyte. How could the student have figured that property out if she hadn't been told this information?

Freezing point depression is given by the equation $\Delta T = k_f mi$; where ΔT is the amount the freezing point is depressed, k_f is the molal freezing point constant of the solvent, m is the molality of the solvent, and i is the van't Hoff factor—which refers to the degree of ionization of the solute in the solvent. If the unknown solute is a non-electrolyte, then it is not ionized and $i = 1.0$.

(b) Describe how the student should find the freezing point of the unknown/solvent mixture using graphical means.

The student should place the solution in a test tube and immerse the tube in ice, then measure and record the temperature at regular intervals of time. When the temperature values are plotted vs. time, the slope of the resulting best-fit line will decrease sharply, and then change abruptly. The new melting point of the solution is that temperature which corresponds to the point where the slope of the cooling curve abruptly changes.

(c) The student measures the ΔT to be 3.2 °C. What is the molality of the solution that contains the unknown?

$$m = \frac{\Delta T}{k_f i} = \frac{3.2\ °C\ mol}{5.12\ °C\ kg} = 0.625\ molal$$

(d) How many moles of the unknown were in the test solution?

$$0.025\ moles\ unknown = \frac{0.625\ moles\ unknown}{kg\ solvent} \times$$

$$0.0400\ kg\ solvent$$

(e) What is the molar mass of the unknown substance?

$$molar\ mass = \frac{grams\ of\ unknown}{moles\ of\ unknown} = \frac{3.80\ g\ unknown}{0.025\ mol\ unknown} =$$

$$152\ g/mol$$

5. **Determination of the molar volume of a gas**

Example problem:

A 0.035 g sample of magnesium ribbon is placed in a stoppered flask that is connected to a eudometer tube, which collects gas by water displacement. When concentrated HCl is placed in the flask with the magnesium, 32.42 mL hydrogen gas is produced in the eudiometer tube.

(a) Write the balanced chemical reaction that occurs when the magnesium is combined with the HCl.

$$Mg\ (s) + 2H^+\ (aq) \rightarrow Mg^{2+}\ (aq) + H_2\ (g)$$

(b) How many moles of hydrogen gas are expected to be produced from this amount of magnesium in this reaction.

$$.00144 \text{ moles } H_2 \text{ } (g) = 0.035 \text{ g Mg} \times \frac{1 \text{ mol Mg}}{24.31 \text{ g Mg}} \times$$

$$\frac{1 \text{ mol } H_2 \text{ } (g)}{1 \text{ mole Mg}}$$

(c) How many moles of water also exists with the collected hydrogen gas in the eudiometer tube? (Vapor pressure of water at 22 °C = 0.030 atm.)

$$n = \frac{PV}{RT} = \frac{0.030 \text{ atm (K mol)}}{0.082 \text{ L atm}} \times \frac{0.03242 \text{ L}}{295 \text{ K}} =$$

$$4.02 \times 10^{-5} \text{ mol water}$$

(d) What is the mole fraction for the water vapor that exists in the eudiometer tube?

$$\text{Mole fraction} = \frac{\text{moles water}}{\text{total moles}} = \frac{\text{pressure water}}{\text{total pressure}} = 0.03$$

(e) What is the percent error between the number of moles of hydrogen gas actually produced at 1.0 atm and 22 °C and the expected yield of hydrogen gas?

$$0.0013 \text{ moles } H_2 = \frac{PV}{RT} = \frac{(1.0 - 0.03) \text{ atm (K mol)}}{0.082 \text{ L atm}} \times \frac{.03242 \text{ L}}{295 \text{ K}}$$

$$\frac{0.00144 - 0.00130}{0.00144} \times 100\% = 9.7\% \text{ error}$$

6. Standardization of a solution using a primary standard

Example:

A student wishes to use a known concentration of $KMnO_4$ for an oxidation titration in Experiment #8 below. However, to do this experiment, the student must know exactly the concentration of a stock solution of $KMnO_4$ that is in the storeroom. She carefully mixes a solution of 0.10-molar oxalic acid to react with the $KMnO_4$ in the following reaction.

$$5 \text{ } H_2C_2O_4 + 2MnO_4^- + 3 \text{ } H_2SO_4 \rightarrow 2 \text{ } MnSO_4 + 10 \text{ } CO_2 + 8 \text{ } H_2O$$

(a) How does the student know when the oxalic acid uses up all the permanganate ion in the sample?

The permanganate ion is a deep purple color. When the ion is used up, the solution in the beaker will be clear.

(b) Is the oxalic acid oxidized or reduced?

During the reaction the carbon atom in the oxalic acid molecule goes from an oxidation state of +3 to an oxidation state of +4. Since the oxidation state of the carbon increases during the reaction, then the carbon in the oxalic acid is oxidized.

(c) 50 mL of the oxalic acid solution is require to completely react with 100 mL of the permanganate solution. What is the concentration of the permanganate solution?

$$\frac{0.050 \text{ L } H_2C_2O_4 \text{ solution}}{0.100 \text{ L } MnO_4 \text{ solution}} \times \frac{0.10 \text{ moles } H_2C_2O_4}{\text{L } H_2C_2O_4 \text{ solution}} \times$$

$$\frac{2 \text{ moles } MnO_4^-}{5 \text{ moles } H_2C_2O_4} = 0.02 \text{ M } MnO_4^-$$

7. Determination of concentration by acid-base titration, including a weak acid or weak base.

Example:

A student wishes to find the concentration of acetic acid ($K_a = 1.8 \times 10^{-5}$) by titrating it with a standardized solution of 0.10 M NaOH in the following reaction,

$$HC_2H_3O_2 + OH^- \leftrightarrow H_2O + C_2H_3O_2^-$$

(a) Will the equivalence point be an acidic or basic pH? Give an explanation for your answer.

When the equivalence point is reached (moles acid = moles base) the pH will be basic. Inspection of the titration equation indicates that the only species left at the equivalence point are water and the acetate ion. Water is neutral, and the acetate ion—being the conjugate base of a weak acid—is basic. Therefore, at the equivalence point, only neutral or basic species remain in the solution.

(b) It takes 40 mL of 0.10 M NaOH added to a 100 mL acid solution of unknown concentration to reach the equivalence point. What is the concentration of the weak acid?

At the equivalence point, the moles of acid in the solution equal the moles of base in the solution,

moles acid = moles base, or

$$\text{Molarity}_{acid} \times \text{Volume}_{acid} = \text{Molarity}_{base} \times \text{Volume}_{base}$$

$$\text{Molarity}_{acid} = \frac{\text{Molarity}_{base} \times \text{Volume}_{base}}{\text{Volume}_{acid}}$$

$$\text{Molarity}_{acid} = 0.10 \text{ M} \times 0.040 \text{ L} / 0.100 \text{ L} = 0.04 \text{ M}$$

(c)   What is the pH at the equivalence point?

To answer this question, you need to run the reaction, mole for mole, then apply the appropriate equilibrium constant to find the [H+], and then find the pH.

	$HC_2H_3O_2$	+	OH^-	$\leftrightarrow$	H_2O	+	$C_2H_3O_2^-$
Before reaction:	0.004 mol		0.004 mol				0 mol
After reaction:	0 mol		0 mol				0.004 mol
After equilibrium	x mol		x mol				0.004 – x mol

$$K = \frac{1}{K_b} = \frac{K_a}{K_w} = \frac{1.8 \times 10^{-5}}{1.0 \times 10^{-14}} = 1.8 \times 10^9 = \frac{[C_2H_3O_2^-]}{[OH^-][HC_2H_3O_2]} =$$

$$\frac{0.004 \text{ mol}/.140 \text{ L}}{x^2} = 1.8 \times 10^9; \text{ solving for x};$$

$$x = [OH^-] = 3.98 \times 10^{-6}$$

$$[H^+] = 2.5 \times 10^{-9}; pH = -\log [H^+]; \text{ so}$$

$$pH = 8.6$$

8.   Determination of a concentration by oxidation-reduction titration

Example problem:

A student wishes to analyze an ore sample for Fe^{2+} content. To do this she crushes the ore sample, then soaks it in concentrated HCl to dissolve the Fe^{2+}; then she oxidizes the Fe^{2+} ion to Fe^{3+} using a standardized solution of potassium permanganate.

(a) Write the balanced oxidation-reduction reaction that the student will undergo in this titration.

$$5Fe^{2+} + 8H+ + MnO_4^- \rightarrow 5Fe^{3+} + Mn^{2+} + 4H_2O$$

(b) To analyze the sample, the student creates a standardized solution of potassium permanganate by combining 3.20 g of KMnO4 with enough water to yield 200 mL of solution. What is the molar concentration of the standardized solution?

$$\frac{3.20 \text{ g KMnO}_4}{0.200 \text{ L sln}} \times \frac{1.0 \text{ mole KMnO}_4}{158.04 \text{ g KMnO}_4} = 0.10 \text{ M KMnO}_4$$

(c) How does the student know when she reaches the end point, when all the iron (II) has been converted into iron (III)?

As long as there is iron (II) in the solution that is analyzed, the otherwise dark purple permanganate ion will be used up and turn clear. However, when the iron (II) has been used up—such as at the end point—an additional permanganate ion added will remain unreacted and the sample solution will turn purple.

(d) A 10.00 gram sample of the ore is crushed and titrated with the standardized solution. It takes 6.32 mL of the standardized solution to reach the end point. How many moles of iron (II) are in the sample that was analyzed?

$$0.00632 \text{ L KMnO}_4 \text{ sln} \times \frac{0.10 \text{ mole KMnO}_4}{\text{liters KMnO}_4 \text{ sln}} \times$$

$$\frac{5 \text{ mol Fe}^{2+}}{1 \text{ mole KMnO}_4} = .0032 \text{ moles Fe}^{2+}$$

(e) What is the mass percent of iron (II) in the sample?

$$0.0032 \text{ mol Fe}^{2+} \times \frac{55.85 \text{ g Fe}^{2+}}{1 \text{ mol Fe}^2} \times \frac{1}{10.00 \text{ g total}}$$

$$\times 100\% = 1.8\% \text{ Fe}^{2+}$$

9. **Determination of mass and mole relationships in a chemical reaction**

This experiment can easily be done separately, or in conjunction with some of the other recommended experiments. For example, the mass-mole questions could easily accompany the first experiment with magnesium.

Example:

A student cuts a 2.80 g magnesium ribbon into small pieces, then began to heat it in a 14.20 g crucible. Over time, the magnesium ignited and burned to form a white, grayish and powdery substance. After the crucible cooled, the student measured the mass of the crucible that contained the powder and found it to be 18.73 g.

(a)   What is the mass of the powder in the crucible?

   18.73 g – 14.20 g = 4.53 g powder (2.80 g Mg and 1.73 g O)

(b)   How many moles of magnesium were in the crucible when the reaction began?

$$\text{Moles of Mg} = 2.80 \text{ g Mg} \times \frac{1 \text{ mol Mg}}{24.3 \text{ g Mg}} = 0.115 \text{ mol Mg}$$

(c)   Approximately how many moles of oxygen were added to the magnesium during the reaction?

$$\text{Moles of O added} = 1.73 \text{ g O} \times \frac{1 \text{ mol O}}{15.99 \text{ g O}} = 0.108 \text{ mol O}$$

10.   Determination of the equilibrium constant for a chemical reaction

Example problem:

A student is given a solution of acetic acid and is asked to find the equilibrium constant for the following equilibrium.

$HC_2H_3O_2 \, (aq) \rightarrow H+ \, (aq) + C_2H_3O_2^- (aq)$

(a)   Describe how the student can use this information and a pH meter to find the K_a of acetic acid.

The student can make a standardized solution of acetic acid, then measure its pH. The pH can tell the student how much the acetic acid has dissociated. From the amount dissociated, the student can determine the concentrations of all species after equilibrium, and then calculate the equilibrium constant using the relationship:

$$K_a = \frac{[H^+]\,[C_2H_3O_2^-]}{[HC_2H_3O_2]}$$

(b) Calculate the initial concentration (before equilibrium is established) of the sample of acetic acid if 2.0 mL of an initial 12.0 M stock solution is diluted to make 400 mL of solution. The concentration is the molarity of the solution. The relationship between molarity and volume of a given solution can be expressed as:

$$(Molarity_{initial\ sln})(Volume_{initial\ sln}) = (Molarity_{diluted\ sln})(Volume_{diluted\ sln})$$

Since molarity is expressed as moles of solute/liters of solution, we must use liters to express the volume and therefore have:

$$(12.0\ M)\ (0.00200\ L) = (Molarity_{diluted\ sln})\ (0.400)$$

$$Molarity_{diluted\ sln} = (12)\ (.0200)/0.400 = .06\ M$$

(c) After equilibrium is established, the student measures the pH to be 2.98. What is the dissociation constant (K_a) for this reaction?

$$HC_2H_3O_2\ (aq) \leftrightarrow H+\ (aq)\ +\ C_2H_3O_2^-\ (aq)$$

Equilibrium concentrations: 0.06M $10^{-2.98}$ $10^{-2.98}$

Plugging into the equilibrium expression:

$$K_a = \frac{[H^+]\,[C_2H_3O_2^-]}{[HC_2H_3O_2]} = \frac{(10^{-2.98})^2}{(0.06)} = 1.8 \times 10^{-5}$$

(d) What is a reasonable approximation for the standard free energy, $\Delta G°$, for this reaction?

$$\Delta G° = -RT\ \ln\ K = -(8.31\ J\ /\ K\ mol)\ (300\ K)\ \ln\ 1.8 \times 10^{-5} = 27,000\ J$$

11. **Determination of appropriate indicators for various acid-base titrations. Determining pH.**

This experiment is often done in conjunction with the titration of acids and bases. In particular, it helps students to understand which indicators to use for which kind of titration.

Example:

A student is given the following indicators, all of which change color at the end-point listed.

Indicator	Endpoint pH
Methyl orange	5
Methyl red	5
Bromothymol blue	7
Phenolphthalein	9
Thymol blue	9

A student is assigned to find the appropriate indicator for each of the following titrations. Calculate the pH of the end point of each titration and decide which indicator to use.

Titration #1: Titration of 20 mL of hydrochloric acid using a standard solution of sodium hydroxide, in which it takes 60 mL of 0.10 M sodium hydroxide solution to reach the end point.

Titration #2: Titration of 100 mL of a solution acetic acid using a standard solution of sodium hydroxide, in which it takes 40 mL of 0.10 M sodium hydroxide solution to reach the end point. The ionization constant for acetic acid is 1.8×10^{-5}.

Titration #3: Titration of 40 mL of ammonia solution using a standard solution of hydrochloric acid, in which it takes 20 mL of 0.20 M hydrochloric acid to reach the end point. The K_b for ammonia is 1.8×10^{-5}.

Titration #1:

$H+ + OH^- \leftrightarrow H_2O$

When the moles of base added equal the moles of acid (the end point) then the remaining species in the solution is simply water, so the solution would be neutral, or pH 7. Bromothymol blue would be the best indicator.

Titration #2:

$$HC_2H_3O_2 \quad + \quad OH^- \quad \leftrightarrow \quad H_2O \quad + \quad C_2H_3O_2^-$$

At the end point, the acid and base are used up and the acetate ion and water remain. The pH can be calculated using equilibrium principles.

After reaction:	0 mol	0 mol	0.004 mol
After equilibrium	x mol	x mol	0.004 − x mol

$$K = \frac{1}{K_b} = \frac{K_a}{K_w} = \frac{1.8 \times 10^{-6}}{1.0 \times 10^{-14}} = 1.8 \times 10^8 =$$

$$\frac{[C_2H_3O_2^-]}{[OH^-][HC_2H_3O_2]} = \frac{0.004 \text{ mol}/.140 \text{ L}}{x^2}$$

$x = [OH^-] = 1.26 \times 10^{-5}$

$[H^+] = 7.9 \times 10^{-10}$; $pH = -\log [H^+]$

$pH = 8.6$

Therefore, phenolphthalein or thymol blue would be the best indicator.

Titration #3:

$$NH_3 \quad + \quad H^+ \quad \leftrightarrow \quad NH_4^+$$

After reaction:	0 mol	0 mol	0.004 mol
After equilibrium	x mol	x mol	0.004 – x mol

$$K = \frac{1}{K_a} = \frac{K_b}{K_w} = \frac{1.8 \times 10^{-5}}{1.0 \times 10^{-14}} = 1.8 \times 10^8 = \frac{[NH_4^+]}{[H^+][NH_3]} =$$

$$\frac{0.004 \text{ mol}/.060 \text{ L}}{x^2}$$

$x = [H^+] = 1.26 \times 10^{-5}$

$pH = 4.7$

Either methyl orange or methyl red would be the correct indicator to use for this titration.

12. **Determination of the rate of a reaction and its order**

Example:

A student runs an experiment that measures the rate of reaction between iodine and acetone at varied concentrations, according to the following reaction:

$$C_3H_6O + I_2 \rightarrow C_3H_6OI + H^+ + I^-$$

The student measures the time it takes for the iodine to disappear when varying the concentrations in the following four trials.

[acetone] (M)	[H⁺] (M)	[I₂] (M)	rate of reaction (M/sec)
0.100	0.100	0.100	2.6×10^{-7}
0.100	0.100	0.200	2.6×10^{-7}
0.100	0.200	0.400	5.2×10^{-6}
0.200	0.200	0.400	1.0×10^{-5}

(a) Determine the order of the reaction with respect to each chemical species tested.

The reaction is first order with respect to acetone and H^+, and zero order with respect to iodine.

(b) What is the rate equation for this reaction?

Rate = k [C₃H₆O] [H⁺]

(c) What is the value and units for the rate constant, k?

2.6×10^{-5} L / M sec

13. **Determination of the enthalpy change associated with a reaction.**

Example:

A student wishes to calculate the molar heat of combustion of butane, and is given only a beaker, a thermometer, and a small disposable cigarette lighter.

(a) Design an experiment and determine what needs to be measured in order to find the molar heat of combustion of butane.

The student can use the butane in the lighter to heat water and measure the temperature change in the water. Weighing the lighter before and after the reaction will allow the student to calculate the number of moles of butane used. Multiplying the change in temperature of the water by the mass of the water, by its specific heat (4.18 J/g°C), will tell the student how much heat was absorbed by the water. This type of "coffee cup calorimetry" is crude, but gives a reasonable approximation of an enthalpy of combustion.

(b) The student weighs the lighter to be 8.72 grams before starting. The lighter is found to only weigh 6.88 g after the student held the lighter open for several minutes under the beaker that contained 400 g of water. During this time, the temperature of the water rose by 22.4 °C.

(i) How many moles of butane were used up?

$$1.84 \text{ g butane} \times \frac{1 \text{ mol butane}}{58.0 \text{ g butane}} =$$

0.0317 moles butane used up

(ii) How much heat was absorbed by the water?

$$q = mc\Delta T = 400 \text{ g} \times 4.18 \text{ J/g°C} \times 22.4 \text{ °C} = 3.75 \times 10^4 \text{ J}$$

(iii) What is the molar heat of combustion for butane that can be calculated from these measurements?

$$\frac{3.75 \times 10^4 \text{ J}}{0.0317 \text{ mol}} = 1.18 \times 10^6 \text{ J/mol} = 1.18 \times 10^3 \text{ kJ/mol}$$

(d) What is the most typical type of error that this student will get in her measurement, and in which direction will this error push the results?

Typically, not all the heat emitted by the reaction will go into raising the temperature of the water; some will be lost to the surroundings. This will result in a measured value that is significantly less kJ/mol than the expected value.

14. **Separation and qualitative analysis of anions and cations**

Example problem:

A student is given four flasks, labeled A through D, that contain soluble solutions of silver nitrate, barium nitrate, nickel nitrate, and lead nitrate. However, the student does not know which solution is in which flask. The student is also given three flasks with solutions of known identity: 1.0 M solutions of sodium chloride, potassium sulfate, and sodium hydroxide, respectively.

(a) When a sample from flask A is mixed with the sodium chloride and potassium sulfate solutions separately, both mixtures result in a cloudy white precipitate. What is the composition of flask A? Write the net ionic reactions for the precipitation reactions that occur.

$Pb^{2+} + 2Cl^- \rightarrow PbCl_2 \ (s)$

$Pb^{2+} + SO_4^{2-} \rightarrow PbSO_4 \ (s)$

The flask contains a solution of lead nitrate.

(b) When a sample from flask B is mixed with the sodium chloride and potassium sulfate solutions separately, only the mixture with potassium sulfate yields a precipitate, which is white. What is the composition of flask B? Write the net ionic reaction for the precipitation reaction that occurs.

$$Ba^{2+} + SO_4^{2-} \rightarrow BaSO_4 \, (s)$$

The flask contains a solution of barium nitrate.

(c) A sample from flask C, when mixed with the sodium chloride and potassium sulfate, does not yield a precipitate in either case. However, a combination of a sample from flask C and sodium hydroxide yields a green precipitate. What is the composition of flask C? Write the net ionic reaction for the precipitation reaction that occurs.

$$Ni^{2+} + 2OH^- \rightarrow Ni(OH)_2 \, (s)$$

The flask contains a solution of nickel nitrate.

(d) A sample from flask D when mixed with sodium chloride yields a white precipitate. However no precipitate forms when a sample from flask D is mixed with potassium sulfate. What is the composition of flask D? Write the net ionic reaction for the precipitation reaction that occurs.

$$Ag^+ + Cl^- \rightarrow AgCl \, (s)$$

The flask contains a solution of silver nitrate.

(e) Which of the above precipitates formed in the above reactions will most likely dissolve upon the addition of concentrated HCl; why?

The nickel hydroxide precipitate will dissolve because the hydroxide ions will combine with the protons from the HCl to form water.

15. **Synthesis of a coordination compound and its chemical analysis**

A number of different coordination compounds can by form in the laboratory. One of the frequently synthesized coordination compounds is the formation of iron thiocynate in the following reaction,

$$Fe^{3+} + SCN^- \rightarrow FeSCN^{2+}$$

The formation of the product is quickly evident as a blood-red/orange solution with no precipitate, which absorbs light at 445 nm.

16. Analytical gravimetric determination

Example:

A student is given 2.482 grams of a powdered mixture that contains both $MgCl_2$ and $CaCO_3$. She is then to find the mass percent of the magnesium chloride in the mixture. To begin the analysis, the student dissolves the solid in strong acid, and then precipitates one of the compounds with lead nitrate.

(a)   What will happen to the calcium carbonate when the acid is added to the mixture?

The acid will dissolve the calcium carbonate; carbon dioxide gas will be emitted, leaving the dissolved calcium in solution.

(b)   What will be the precipitate when the lead nitrate is added to the solution. Given the dependence on this reaction, which strong acid should NOT be used in the first step?

The soluble lead ions will combine with the chloride ions to form insoluble lead chloride. For this reason, HCl should NOT be used in the first step. It would add chloride ions and result in an inaccurately high value for the percent of magnesium chloride in the mixture.

(c)   When the lead nitrate is added, 5.280 g of precipitate is formed. What is the mass percent of magnesium chloride in the original mixture?

$$5.280 \text{ g PbCl}_2 \times \frac{1 \text{ mol PbCl}_2}{278.1 \text{ g PbCl}_2} \times \frac{2 \text{ mol Cl}}{1 \text{ mol PbCl}_2} \times$$

$$\frac{1 \text{ mol MgCl}_2}{2 \text{ mol Cl}} \times \frac{95.21 \text{ g MgCl}_2}{1 \text{ mol MgCl}_2} = 1.807 \text{ grams MgCl}_2$$

Mass percent $= 1.807 \text{ g} / 2.482 \text{ g} \times 100\% = \underline{72.8\% \text{ MgCl}_2}$

(d)   What would be the maximum volume of gas collected during the first step if the surrounding temperature and pressure were 300 K and 0.92 atm, respectively?

0.675 g of calcium carbonate remain.

$$0.675 \text{ g CaCo}_3 \times \frac{1 \text{ mol CaCO}_3}{100.09 \text{ g CaCO}_3} \times \frac{1 \text{ mol CO}_2}{1 \text{ mol CaCO}_3} =$$

0.0067 mol CO_2

$$V = \frac{nRT}{P} = \frac{(0.0067 \text{ mol}) (0.082 \text{ L atm}) (300 \text{ K})}{(0.92 \text{ atm}) \text{ K mol}} =$$

$\underline{0.179 \text{ L } CO_2}$

17. Colorimetric or spectrophotometric analysis

In 2004, the College Board added Beer's Law to the list of equations on the AP Chemistry test. Beer's Law makes it possible to use a spectrophotometer to measure the concentration of colored solutions, and is most useful in experiments where concentrations are measured, such as kinetics, equilibrium, or quantitative analysis of colored ions in solution. Beer's Law is described by the following relationship.

BEER'S LAW

$$A = \varepsilon l c$$

A = Absorbance of light by the solution. For example, when A = 0, no light is absorbed. When A = 1, 1% of the light is absorbed. When A = 2, 99% of the light is absorbed. The amount of light that is absorbed depends on the following three factors.

ε = molar absorptivity (sometimes called the *extinction coefficient*) which varies with the wavelength of light and the material used.

l = length of the light path that moves through the solution.

c = molar concentration of the solution

Beer's Law is used along with the following two-step process to have a spectrophotometer determine the concentration of an unknown solution.

1. Determine the optimal wavelength for the solution you are studying. This can be done by measuring the absorbance of a standard solution over the entire wavelength spectrum of the spectrophotometer. The wavelength where the solution shows the highest absorbance is the *optimal wavelength*, and should be used for the next step.

Example:

A student generated the following data by using a spectrophotometer to analyze the absorbance of a 0.10 M solution of $CoCl_2$. What is the optimal wavelength to set up a calibration curve? (Answer: 500 nm)

Wavelength (nm)	Absorbance
400	0.01
420	0.10
440	0.20
460	0.32
480	0.42
500	0.58
520	0.42
540	0.32
560	0.16
580	0.04
600	0.02

2. Establish a calibration curve by measuring the absorbance of various known concentrations of the solution at the optimal wavelength. Use the resulting A vs. concentration curve to interpolate the concentration of the unknown solutions in the study.

Example:

A student measures the absorbance of various concentrations of cobalt chloride solution (at 500 nm) and obtains the following data.

Concentration (M)	Absorbance
0.020	0.11
0.040	0.22
0.060	0.33
0.080	0.44
0.100	0.55

What is the concentration of a solution for which the absorbance is measured to be 0.38?

Answer:

Remember that there is a linear relationship between absorbance and concentration (Beer's Law). Therefore, if the measured value of 0.38 is half-way between the standardized points of 0.33 and 0.44, then the concentration of the unknown solution is half-way between the respective standard concentrations of 0.060 M and 0.080 M, or 0.07 M.

18. Separation by Chromatography

Chromatography is a useful technique in qualitative identification of an unknown compound in comparison with a known compound. For example, in laboratory #22, students are asked to synthesize acetyl-salicylic acid, or common aspirin. Chromatography gives a student the ability to test whether or not the synthesis reaction worked by developing the product on a chromatography plate along side known compounds, such as the reactants in the reaction and a known sample of acetylsalicylic acid.

The student can create a quantitative comparison by measuring the R_f value associated with each spot that has developed on the chromatography plate. The value is found in the following manner:

$$R_f = \frac{\text{distance covered by solvent front}}{\text{distance covered by sample}}$$

Chromatography is a useful method of separation because the process can easily separate different substances through minute differences in their physical properties. This is possible because different compounds demonstrate varied attraction to either the *stationary phase*—which is the thin layer of silica gel on the surface of a glass or plastic plate, and the *mobile phase*—which is the solvent that migrates up the plate via capillary action. Compounds that are more attracted to the mobile phase than the stationary phase will have a high Rf value. Conversely, compounds that are more attracted to the stationary phase than the mobile phase will have a low Rf value.

19. Preparation and properties of buffer solutions

Example:

(a)   Describe briefly how buffers work. Use specific chemical reactions with the acetic acid/acetate system to show how it minimizes a change in pH when either a strong acid or a strong base is added to the system.

A buffer is a combination of a weak acid and its conjugate base. When this combination exists, any additional protons added to the solution would react with the conjugate base to form water, and little change in pH results.

eg: $C_2H_3O_2^- + H+ \rightarrow H_2O$

Likewise, any additional hydroxide ions added to the solution would react with the weak acid to form water, and little change in the pH results, except with the very slight increase in pH due to the addition of the conjugate base.

eg: $HC_2H_3O_2 + OH^- \rightarrow H_2O + C_2H_3O_2^-$

(b)   Use the Henderson-Hasselbach equation to describe why the ideal buffer pH for a buffer system equals the pK_a of the weak acid.

The Henderson-Hasselbach equation shows the relationship between the pK_a and the pH, at different concentrations of the weak acid and the conjugate base.

$$pH = pK_a + \log \frac{[A^-]}{[HA]}$$

The maximum buffering ability exists when the buffer system is equally equipped to neutralize added acid or base, or where the molar concentration of the weak acid equals the concentration of its conjugate base, (where the [A–] / [HA] ratio equals 1.0.) When [A-] / [HA] = 1.0, then the log of that ratio equals zero, and the $pH = pK_a$ of the acid.

(c)   Design an experiment to test the buffering ability of a buffer system. Be sure to identify what variable(s) you would keep constant, and what variable(s) you would change.

One way to test buffering ability is to test different buffer systems. Another type of test would be to look at buffering capability when the members of the buffer are at different concentrations. For each of the different systems you would test, you would use an appropriate indicator that would change color when the buffer is exhausted, and then keep adding a measured amount of acid (or base) until the system reaches its end point. A comparison of the amount of acid (or base) added would give a measure of the system's ability to buffer changes in pH.

(d) Given a 350 mL of a 0.20 M solution of acetic acid, what mass of solid sodium acetate would you add to the solution to achieve the maximum buffering ability of the solution?

$$0.350 \text{ L acid soln.} \times \frac{0.2 \text{ mol acid}}{1 \text{ L acid soln}} \times \frac{1 \text{ mol acetate}}{1 \text{ mol acid}} \times$$

$$\frac{82.0 \text{ g NaC}_2\text{H}_3\text{O}_2}{1 \text{ mol acetate}} = 5.74 \text{ g}$$

20. Determination of electrochemical series

Example:

(a) In the following picture, identify the following components of a galvanic cell.

   i.   voltmeter

   ii. anode

   iii. cathode

   iv. salt bridge

(b) Where does reduction take place? (at the cathode)

(c) The solution in the beaker on the right is 1.0 M $AgNO_3$, and the electrode in that beaker is solid silver (Ag). Use the chart of standard reduction potentials to calculate the total cell potential when the beaker on the left is filled with each of the following solutions, separately; and the electrode is composed of the corresponding solid metal.

   i.   1.0 M $Al(NO_3)_3$ (2.46 Volts)

   ii. 1.0 M $Zn(NO_3)_2$ (1.56 Volts)

   iii. 1.0 M $Fe(NO_3)_2$ (1.24 Volts)

   iv. 0.001 M $Cu(NO_3)_2$ (0.44 Volts)

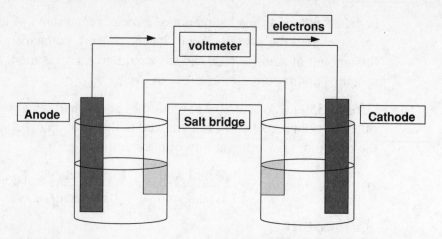

21. **Measurements using electrochemical cells and electroplating**

Example:

Two carbon rods, each with a mass of 8.000 g, are put into a 100.0 mL solution of 2.0 M $CuSO_4$. Electrodes from the two poles of a power source are placed at each electrode and the power is turned on for 20 minutes. An ammeter indicates that the current is 2.0 A for the entire time.

(a) What is the reaction at the cathode?

$Cu^{2+}(aq) + 2 e^- \rightarrow Cu\ (s)$

(b) What is the reaction at the anode?

$2H_2O(l) \rightarrow 4H^+(aq) + O_2\ (g) + 4\ e^-$

(c) What is occurring to the pH of the solution as the experiment proceeds?

Protons are being formed, so the pH decreases as the experiment proceeds.

(d) How many moles of electrons were delivered to the cathode during the experiment?

$$2.00\ A \times 20.0\ min \times \frac{60\ sec}{min} \times \frac{C}{A\ sec} \times \frac{1\ mole\ e^-}{96,486\ C} =$$

<u>0.0249 mol e⁻</u>

(e) What is the predicted new mass of the cathode when it is dried and re-weighed after the experiment?

$$0.0249 \text{ mol electrons} \times \frac{1 \text{ mole copper}}{2 \text{ moles electrons}} \times 63.55 \text{ g Cu} =$$

$\underline{0.7911 \text{ g Cu}}$

Final mass electrode = initial mass + mass Cu added = $\underline{8.7911 \text{ g}}$

(f) What is the $[Cu^{2+}]$ of the solution after the experiment is complete?

Moles Cu^{2+} before the reaction = $0.100 \text{ L} \times 2.0 \text{ moles} = 0.200$ moles

Moles Cu^{2+} after the reaction = $0.200 \text{ mol} - 0.0125 = 0.1875$ moles

$[Cu^{2+}] = 0.1875 \text{ moles} / 0.10 \text{ L} = 1.875 \text{ M}$

22. Synthesis, purification, and analysis of an organic compound

This laboratory usually entails performing a chemical reaction, purifying the product, and then measuring the physical properties of the product to confirm that the desired chemical change has taken place. One of the most common reactions used in high school for organic synthesis is the hydrolysis reaction.

In a hydrolysis reaction, a strong acid, such as concentrated sulfuric acid, can be used to remove water from two molecules and convert the combination of an alcohol and a carboxylic acid into an ester. For example,

$$C-O \boxed{H+HO} -C- \quad \rightarrow \quad C-O-C-$$
$$\qquad\qquad\quad \| \qquad\qquad\qquad\qquad\qquad \|$$
$$\qquad\qquad\quad O \qquad\qquad\qquad\qquad\qquad O$$

This is often done with salicylic acid and acetic acid to form acetylsalicylic acid, or aspirin. Aspirin is less water soluble than both salicylic acid and acetic acid. So the product can be washed with a less polar solvent, the the solvent can be evaporated to yield the product.

Another way to analyze the product is using thin-layer chromatography. A student can dissolve both a sample of known acetylsalicylic acid and a sample of the product of the reaction that you ran in a mixture of solvents, such as toluene/ethyl formate/formic acid. Two plates can be spotted with each of the solutions, then allowed to develop. A student can compare the R_f value of the reaction product with the R_f value of the known solution of acetylsalicylic acid to confirm whether or not the reaction yielded the intended product.

Practice
Exam 1

AP Chemistry

Practice Exam 1

Section I

TIME: 90 minutes
75 questions
45% of the entire test

(Answer sheets appear in the back of this book.)

DIRECTIONS: Each set of lettered choices below refers to the numbered questions or statements immediately following it. Select the one lettered choice that best answers each question. A choice may be used once, more than once, or not at all in each set.

Part A

Questions 1 - 4

    (A) K

    (B) Ca

    (C) Cr

    (D) Fe

    (E) Cu

1.   Does <u>not</u> form monatomic ions of 2^+ charge

2.   Forms the oxide ion $M_2O^{2-}_7$, in which M represents the metal

3.   Is found in nature in its metallic state

4.   Is an important construction material

Questions 5 - 7

    (A) HF

    (B) H_2O

    (C) NH_3

    (D) CH_4

    (E) $NaBH_4$

5.   Is an organic molecule

6.   Is a strong reducing agent

7.   Forms a basic solution when mixed with water

Questions 8 - 10

    (A) covalent bonding

    (B) ionic bonding

    (C) hydrogen bonding

    (D) π bonding

    (E) metallic bonding

8.   Involves electron transfer from one atom to another

9.   Does NOT occur in an aqueous solution of CH_3CO_2Na

10.   Is responsible for the relatively high boiling point of water

Questions 11 - 13

$$A\ (aq) + 2B\ (aq) \rightarrow C\ (aq)$$

The rate law for the reaction above is:

$$\text{rate} = k\ [B]^2$$

11.   What is the order of the reaction with respect to B?

    (A) 0   (D) 3

    (B) 1   (E) 4

    (C) 2

12. What will happen to the rate of the reaction if the amount of A in the solution is doubled?

(A) The rate will double.

(B) The rate will halve.

(C) The rate will be four times bigger.

(D) The rate will be four times smaller.

(E) It will have no effect.

13. The rate constant k is expressed in which units?

(A) L/mol·sec   (D) sec^{-1}

(B) mol/L·sec   (E) sec^{-2}

(C) mol^2/L^2·sec

Questions 14 - 17

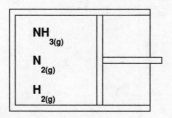

Three gases are in equilibrium in a closed chamber sealed with a piston. The equilibrium expression is:

$$2\,NH_3\,(g) \leftrightarrow N_2\,(g) + 3H_2\,(g)$$

(A) The mole fraction of N_2 increases.

(B) The mole fraction of N_2 decreases.

(C) The mole fraction of N_2 remains the same.

(D) The mole fraction of N_2 increases and then decreases.

(E) The reaction is endothermic, and we add heat.

Which of the above occurs in each of the following cases?

14. The piston is pushed into the chamber.

15. More H_2 is added as the piston is adjusted to maintain constant pressure.

16. The chamber is heated while the piston is held steady.

17. A catalyst is added while the piston is held steady.

Answer questions 18 - 21 using the phase diagram below:

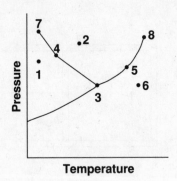

18. At which point can all three phases coexist at equilibrium?

    (A) 3   (D) 7

    (B) 4   (E) 8

    (C) 5

19. At which point can only the solid phase exist?

    (A) 1   (D) 5

    (B) 2   (E) 6

    (C) 3

20. Which is the critical point?

    (A) 2   (D) 7

    (B) 5   (E) 8

    (C) 6

21. At which point can only the solid and liquid phases coexist?

    (A) 3   (D) 1

    (B) 4   (E) 2

    (C) 5

Questions 22 - 24

    (A) tetrahedral

    (B) square planar

    (C) linear

    (D) trigonal planar

    (E) octahedral

22. Which of the molecular geometries is typical of sp^3 bonding?

23. Which of the molecular geometries is typical of sp^2 bonding?

24. Which of the following molecular geometries is typical of sp bonding?

Part B

DIRECTIONS: The following questions consist of questions or incomplete statements followed by five answers or completions. Select the best answer in each case.

25. A deuterium nucleus contains how many protons and neutrons?

	protons	neutrons
(A)	1	0
(B)	2	0
(C)	1	1
(D)	1	2
(E)	2	2

26. $\_MnO_4^- + \_H^+ + \_Fe^{2+} \rightarrow \_Fe^{3+} + \_Mn^{2+} + \_H_2O$

When the skeleton equation above is balanced and all coefficients reduced to their lowest whole-number terms, what is the coefficient for H^+?

(A) 4
(B) 6
(C) 8

(D) 9
(E) 10

27. Which of the following elements has the highest ionization energy?

(A) Ne
(B) Cl
(C) Si

(D) Na
(E) Li

28. Which of the following elements is the <u>least</u> electronegative?

    (A) Al   (D) Na

    (B) Br   (E) Li

    (C) F

29. A sample of hydrogen gas is in a closed container, at 1.0 atmosphere pressure and 27°C. If the sample is heated to 127°C, the pressure will be approximately which of the following?

    (A) 4.0 atm   (D) .67 atm

    (B) 1.3 atm   (E) .25 atm

    (C) .75 atm

30. Which of the following structures represents 1,1-dibromoethane?

```
          Br   H
          |    |
    (A) Br - C – C - H
          |    |
          H    H
```

```
          Br    Br
          |     |
    (B) H - C – C - H
          |     |
          H     H
```

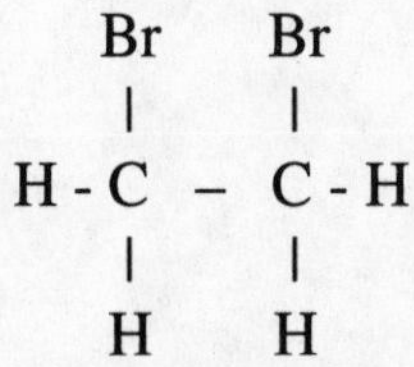

    (C) $CH_3 - CH_2 - Br - CH_2 - CH_3$

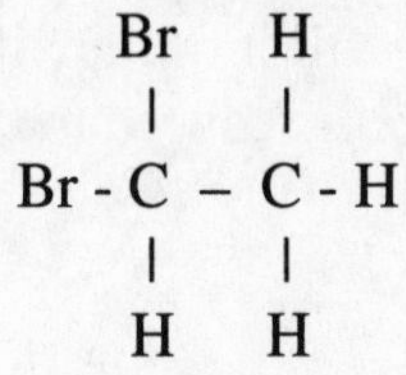

    (D) Br–C $\equiv$ C–Br

```
    (E) Br        H
          \      /
            C = C
          /      \
        Br         H
```

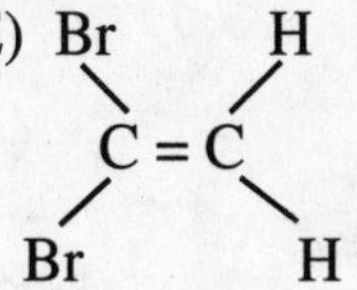

31. What is the pH of a 1.0M solution of formic acid if the K_a is 1.77×10^{-4}?

    (A) $\log\left[\dfrac{1.77 \times 10^{-4}}{H^+}\right]$

    (D) $-\log\left[\left(1.77 \times 10^{-4}\right)^{\frac{1}{2}}\right]$

    (B) $\log[A^-]$

    (E) 0

    (C) $\log[(1.77 \times 10^{-4})]$

32. The most probable oxidation number for the element with atomic number 53 is:

    (A) –5

    (D) +5

    (B) –1

    (E) +7

    (C) +1

33. A gas takes up 4.0 L at STP. What volume will it occupy if the temperature increases by 100 K and the pressure is reduced to 0.2 atm?

    (A) 0.0365 L

    (D) 14.6 L

    (B) 0.731 L

    (E) 27.3 L

    (C) 2.95 L

34. Which of the following is <u>incorrect</u>?

    (A) 1 liter = 1000 cm³

    (D) 1 liter = 1 meter³

    (B) 1 meter = 100 cm

    (E) 1 milliliter = 10^{-6} meter³

    (C) 1 milliliter = 1 cm³

35. Hydrolysis of sodium acetate yields

    (A) a strong acid and a strong base

    (B) a weak acid and a weak base

    (C) a strong acid and a weak base

(D) a weak acid and a strong base

(E) water

36. The oxidation state of manganese in $KMnO_4$ is

(A) +1   (D) +4

(B) +2   (E) +7

(C) +3

37. Identify the conjugate base of acetic acid in the following reaction:

$$HC_2H_3O_2 + OH^- \leftrightarrow H_2O + C_2H_3O_2^-$$

(A) $HC_2H_3O_2$

(B) OH^-

(C) H_2O

(D) $C_2H_3O_2^-$

(E) $H_2C_2H_3O_2$

38. The following three kinetic experiments are for the reaction in which A and B react to form the product, C. What is the order of the reaction with respect to the reactant, B?

Trial	[A]	[B]	Initial rate of formation of C (M/sec)
1	0.10	0.20	0.02
2	0.10	0.40	0.08
3	0.20	0.40	0.16

(A) First order

(B) Second order

(C) Third order

(D) Fourth order

(E) Zero order

39. Which of the following is true of an electrochemical cell?

    (A) the cathode is the site of reduction

    (B) the anode is negatively charged

    (C) the cell voltage is independent of concentration

    (D) charge is carried from one electrode to the other by metal atoms passing through the solution

    (E) the cathode is the site of oxidation

40. How many grams of He occupy a volume of 11.2 liters at STP?

    (A) 1 g   (D) 6 g

    (B) 2 g   (E) 8 g

    (C) 4 g

41. What is the hydronium ion concentration of an HCl solution at pH 3?

    (A) 0.001 M   (D) 0.3 M

    (B) 0.003 M   (E) 3 M

    (C) 0.1 M

42. How many grams of Na are present in 30 g of NaOH?

    (A) 10 g   (D) 20 g

    (B) 15 g   (E) 22 g

    (C) 17 g

43. What is the approximate density of fluorine gas at STP?

    (A) 0.8 g/L   (D) 2.0 g/L

    (B) 1.0 g/L   (E) 2.3 g/L

    (C) 1.7 g/L

44. How much water must be evaporated from 500 ml of 1M NaOH to make it 5 M?

   (A) 100 mL   (D) 300 mL

   (B) 200 mL   (E) 400 mL

   (C) 250 mL

45. Which of the following methods is best suited to separate a 500 ml sample of two miscible liquids whose boiling points differ by approximately 60°?

   (A) distillation

   (B) fractional distillation

   (C) paper chromatography

   (D) use of a separatory funnel

   (E) spectroscopy

46. 20 liters of NO gas react with excess oxygen. How many liters of NO_2 gas are produced if the NO gas reacts completely?

   (A) 5 liters   (D) 40 liters

   (B) 10 liters   (E) 50 liters

   (C) 20 liters

47. What is the molar concentration of I^- in 1 liter of a saturated water solution of PbI_2 if the K_{sp} of lead iodide is 1.4×10^{-8}?

   (A) 3.0×10^{-3} (D) 2.4×10^{-3}

   (B) 1.2×10^{-4} (E) 1.4×10^{-8}

   (C) 5.9×10^{-5}

48. What is the density of a diatomic gas whose gram-molecular weight is 80 g at STP?

   (A) 1.9 g/L   (D) 4.3 g/L

   (B) 2.8 g/L   (E) 5.0 g/L

   (C) 3.6 g/L

49. How many liters of H_2 can be produced by the decomposition of 3 moles of NH_3 at STP?

   (A) 4.5 L   (D) 96 L

   (B) 27 L   (E) 101 L

   (C) 67.2 L

50. If a reaction causes an ion in solution to precipitate in elemental form, then this reaction is best described as being

   (A) exothermic   (D) acid-base

   (B) endothermic   (E) oxidation-reduction

   (C) photochemical

51. Which of the following best describes the hybridization usually found in Group IIIA elements?

   (A) s   (D) sp^3

   (B) sp   (E) sp^3d^2

   (C) sp^2

52. The electron configuration $1s^2 2s^2 2p^6 3s^2 3p^4$ is that of

   (A) O   (D) Cl^-

   (B) S   (E) Ar

   (C) P^+

$$H$$
$$|$$
53. The functional group $R-C=O$ indicates a(n)

(A) alcohol   (D) ether

(B) aldehyde   (E) ketone

(C) ester

54. An atom, $_A^B X$, undergoes nuclear radioactive decay by emitting two beta particles and an alpha particle. The atom's new identity is given by

(A) $_{A+2}^{Y-2} X$ (D) $_A^{B-4} Y$

(B) $_{A+2}^{Y-2} Y$ (E) $_A^{B-4} X$

(C) $_{A-4}^{B-2} X$

55. A 0.5 molal solution could be prepared by dissolving 20 g of NaOH in how much water?

(A) 0.5 L   (D) 1 kg

(B) 0.5 kg   (E) 2 L

(C) 1 L

56. Which statement is true for a liquid/gas mixture in equilibrium?

(A) The equilibrium constant is dependent on temperature.

(B) The amount of the gas present at equilibrium is independent of pressure.

(C) All interchange between the liquid and gas phases has ceased.

(D) The concentration of the liquid varies widely.

(E) It will move into the solid phase.

57. The equilibrium expression $K_e = [CO_2]$ applies to which of the reactions below?

 (A) $C + O_2 (g) \leftrightarrow CO_2 (g)$

 (B) $CO (g) + 1/2\, O_2 (g) \leftrightarrow CO_2 (g)$

 (C) $CaCO_3 (s) \leftrightarrow CaO (s) + CO_2 (g)$

 (D) $CO_2 (s) \leftrightarrow C (s) + O_2 (g)$

 (E) $CaO (s) + CO_2 (g) \leftrightarrow CaCO_3 (g)$

58. At the meniscus, what does the buret read?

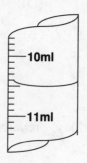

 (A) 11.45 ml   (D) 10.40 ml

 (B) 10.54 ml   (E) 10.4 ml

 (C) 10.5 ml

59. The standard electrode in electrochemistry involves the oxidation or reduction of which of the following?

 (A) gold   (D) magnesium

 (B) platinum   (E) hydrogen

 (C) copper

60. $Zn \rightarrow Zn^{2+} + 2e^-$ $\varepsilon° = +0.76V$
    $Cr^{3+} + 3e^- \rightarrow Cr$ $\varepsilon° = -0.74V$

    The annode of this cell is composed of which of the following materials?

    (A) Zn

    (B) Cr

    (C) Zn^{2+}

    (D) Cr^{3+}

    (E) water

61. The complete combustion of 1 mole of propane (C_3H_8) results in the liberation of 488.7 kcal. What is the heat of formation of propane?

    The reaction is: C_3H_8 (g) $+ 5O_2$ (g) $\rightarrow 3CO_2 + 4H_2O$

    $\Delta H_f°$ (kcal/mole): CO_2 is -94.1 and H_2O is -57.8

    (A) $+6.9$ kcal/mole

    (B) -19 kcal/mole

    (C) -24.8 kcal/mole

    (D) -63.6 kcal/mole

    (E) -143.2 kcal/mole

62. The following mechanism was suggested for the reaction between chlorine gas and carbon monoxide. If the overall order of the reaction is first order with respect to chlorine gas, which of the following statements must be true?

    Cl_2 $\leftrightarrow 2\,Cl$
    Cl $+ CO \leftrightarrow COCl$
    $COCl + Cl \leftrightarrow COCl_2$
    _____
    Cl_2 $+ CO \leftrightarrow COCl_2$

    (A) The reaction is not in equilibrium.

    (B) The first step in the mechanism must be a fast equilibrium step.

    (C) The third step in the mechanism must be the rate-determining step.

    (D) The second step in the mechanism must be the rate-determining step.

    (E) The first step in the mechanism must be the rate-determining step.

63. A reaction that occurs only when heat is added is best described as:

    (A) exothermic

    (B) endothermic

    (C) an equilibrium process

    (D) spontaneous

    (E) non-spontaneous

64. Neutral atoms of F (fluorine) have the same number of electrons as

    (A) B^{3-}

    (B) N^+

    (C) Ne^-

    (D) Na^-

    (E) Mg^{3+}

65. A reaction at equilibrium may shift toward yielding more products by

    (A) adding a catalyst

    (B) increasing the pressure

    (C) increasing the temperature

    (D) removing the products from the reaction mixture as they are formed

    (E) decreasing the reactant concentration

66. Which of the following has the smallest mass?

    (A) a hydrogen nucleus

    (B) an alpha particle

    (C) a neutron

    (D) a helium nucleus

    (E) a beta particle

67. The greatest reduction of the average kinetic energy of water molecules occurs when water is

    (A) cooled as a solid

    (B) cooled as a liquid

(C)   cooled as a gas

(D)   converted from a gas to a liquid

(E)   converted from a liquid to a solid

68.   Which of the following solid crystals has, on average, one atom per cubic unit cell?

(A)   face-centered

(B)   body-centered

(C)   rhombic

(D)   all cubic crystals

(E)   simple cubic crystals only

69.   An equation for the electrolysis of water is

$$H_2O \ (l) + 68.3 \ kcal \rightarrow H_2 \ (g) + 1/2 \ O_2 \ (g)$$

How many liters of gaseous product are produced by the addition of 273.2 kcal of electrical energy to the reaction above?

(A)   22.4 L

(B)   44.8 L

(C)   134.4 L

(D)   96.8 L

(E)   119.2 L

70.   Which of the following is propyl butanoate?

(A) $CH_3CH_2CH_2OCH_2CH_2CH_2CH_3$

(B) $CH_3CH_2\overset{\displaystyle O}{\overset{\displaystyle \|}{C}}OCH_2CH_2CH_2CH_3$

(C) $CH_3CH_2CH_2CH_2\overset{\displaystyle O}{\overset{\displaystyle \|}{C}}OCH_2CH_2CH_3$

(D) $CH_3CH_2CH_2\overset{\displaystyle O}{\overset{\displaystyle \|}{C}}OCH_2CH_2CH_3$

(E) $CH_3CH_2CH_2CH_2CH_2CH_2CH_3$

71. Which of the following is the equilibrium vapor pressure of water at 373 K?

    (A) 0.001 atm (D) 10.0 atm

    (B) 0.10 atm   (E) 100.0 atm

    (C) 1.0 atm

72. Use the following chart to determine which set of letters represents an increase in entropy.

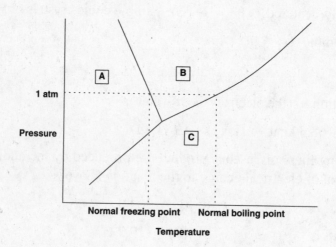

    (A) A,B,C (D) B,A,C

    (B) C,B,A (E) C,A,B

    (C) B,C,A

73. Henry's law pertains to which of the following phenomena?

    (A) The relationship between temperature and pressure, at constant pressure.

    (B) The relationship between pressure and volume, at constant temperature.

    (C) The relationship between free energy and the equilibrium constant.

    (D) The relationship between concentration and pH.

    (E) The relationship between the amount of gas dissolved in a solution and the partial pressure of the gas above the solution.

74. The following chart contains thermodynamic information about reactants and products in the combustion reaction for acetylene, C_2H_2. Which of the following quantities can be calculated from the information given in the chart?

Substance	S° (J/ K mol)	ΔH_f° (kJ/mol)
C_2H_2 (s)	201	227
CO_2 (g)	213.6	–393.5
H_2O (l)	69.96	–285.85
O_2 (g)	205.0	0

(A) The equilibrium constant for the total reaction

(B) The change in free energy for the total reaction

(C) The change in enthalpy for the entire reaction

(D) The change in entropy for the entire reaction

(E) All of the above can be calculated

75. The oxidation state of nitrogen in nitric acid (HNO_3) is

(A) +1   (D) +4

(B) +2   (E) +5

(C) +3

STOP

This is the end of Section I.

If time still remains, you may check your work only in this section.

Do not begin Section II until instructed to do so.

AP Chemistry

Practice Exam 1

Section II

TIME: 90 minutes
55% of the entire test

(Answer sheets appear in the back of this book.)

The percentages given for the parts represent the score weightings for this section of the examination. You will be given 40 minutes for Part A and 50 minutes for Part B.

You may use a calculator on Part A, but not on Part B.

Be sure to write your answers in the space provided following each question. Pay attention to significant figures.

Part A

TIME: 40 minutes
40%

YOU MAY USE A CALCULATOR ON THIS PART.

Show your work clearly for full credit.
Pay attention to significant figures in your answers.

Solve the following problem.

1. $NH_3 + H_2O \leftrightarrow NH_4^+ + OH^-$

Ammonia is a weak base that dissociates in water as shown above. At 25 °C, the base dissociation constant for NH_3, K_b, is 1.8×10^{-5}.

(a)   Write the equilibrium expression for the ionization of ammonia in water.

(b)   Determine the hydroxide ion concentration of a 0.200-molar solution of ammonia at 25 °C.

(c)   Determine the percent dissociation of a 0.200-molar solution of ammonia at 25 °C.

(d) Determine the pH of a solution prepared by adding 0.0500 mole of solid ammonium chloride to 100 milliliters of a 0.200-molar solution of ammonia.

(e) If 0.0300 mole of solid magnesium chloride is dissolved in the solution prepared in part (c) and the resulting solution is well-stirred, will a precipitate of magnesium hydroxide form? (The K_{sp} for $Mg(OH)_2$ is 1.5×10^{-11}).

Solve EITHER problem 2 or problem 3 below. Only one of these two questions will be graded.

2.   Answer parts (a) through (c) below. This question is worth 20% of the Section II score if you choose to answer it.

Solid zinc reacts in a solution of silver ions in the following reaction,

$$Zn + Ag^+ \rightarrow Zn^{++} + Ag$$

2.00 grams of Zn is added to 400 mL of 0.200 M silver nitrate.

(a)   What is the mass of silver metal that is produced when this reaction runs to completion?

(b)   Identify the limiting reactant in the previous question. Support your answer with calculations.

(c)   Determine the $E°$ for a galvanic cell that is based on this reaction.

(d)   Calculate the $\Delta G°$ for this reaction. Is this reaction spontaneous?

(e)   What will happen to the cell voltage, E, as the reaction proceeds? Use the Nernst equation to support your answer.

3.

Table 3

	Standard Heat of Formation (kJ/mol)	Absolute entropies at 25°C and 1 atm. (J/mol x K)
C(s)	0	5.69
$CO_2(g)$	−393.5	213.6
$H_2(g)$	0	130.6
$H_2O(l)$	−285.85	70
$O_2(g)$	0	205.0
$CH_4(g)$	−74.9	186.2

Using Table 3, determine:

(a) the heat of combustion of CH_4

(b) the balanced equation for the formation of CH_4 from its elements

(c) the standard entropy change $\Delta S°$ for the formation of CH_4 at 25°C

(d) the standard free energy of formation $\Delta G°$ for CH_4 at 25°C

Part B

TIME: 50 minutes

YOU MAY NOT USE A CALCULATOR ON THIS PART.

4. This question is worth 15% of Section II. Write the formulas of the reactants and products for five of the following eight reactions. Show net ionic reactions only, where appropriate. Assume the reaction takes place in aqueous solution unless otherwise specified. Do not balance the reaction.

(a) Iron wool is burned in oxygen (not an aqueous solution).

(b) Sulfur dioxide is exposed to hydrogen gas.

(c)   Tin is exposed to aqueous hydrochloric acid.

(d)   Pure hydrogen peroxide decomposes.

(e)   Manganese solid is exposed to chromium III chloride.

(f)   Tin IV oxide is exposed to hot coke.

(g)   Methane is added to water in the presence of a catalyst.

(h)   Sulfur dioxide is bubbled through nitric acid.

ANSWER BOTH OF THE FOLLOWING ESSAY QUESTIONS (15% each).

5.   Acidity of elements is related to their position on the periodic table and the number and type of other elements to which they are bonded.

    (a)   Describe the general trend of acid-base character of the oxides of the elements in the third period, beginning with sodium.

    (b)   Write two chemical reactions: one in which an acidic oxide in this period reacts with water, and one in which a basic oxide reacts with water.

    (c)   Compare the acidity of the different oxides of chlorine. What causes the variation in acidity of these oxides?

    (d)   Describe why transition metal ions will create an acidic solution when put into water.

ANSWER THE FOLLOWING LABORATORY-BASED ESSAY QUESTION.

6.   A student obtained 5.96 g of blue colored hydrate of copper sulfate from the teacher, and then heated the substance in a 17.20 g crucible over moderate heat for several minutes. Over time, the entire substance appeared to turn white, at which time the student removed the crucible from the heat. The student measured the mass of the crucible and substance together and found it to be 21.02 g.

    (a)   What mass of water was removed from the hydrate?

    (b)   How many moles of water were removed from the hydrate?

    (c)   How many moles of the anhydrous copper sulfate were left in the container after heating?

(d)   What is the formula of the hydrate of copper sulfate?

(e)   What is the percentage of water in the hydrate?

ANSWER QUESTION 7 OR QUESTION 8 BELOW. ONLY ONE OF THESE TWO QUESTIONS WILL BE GRADED. (15%)

7.   Use the following formulas to answer these questions.

XeF_4 CH_4 CH_2O

(a)   Identify the bond angles in each of the above compounds, and give an explanation for why they differ from compound to compound.

(b)   Why do "expanded octets" exist? Give a structural explanation for why more than the normal eight electrons can exist in the outer shell of the central atom.

(c)   According to the Lewis definition of acids and bases, determine whether some compounds with expanded octets are acidic or basic. Give a reason for your answer.

(d)   Give a structural reason why a difference in water solubility would exist for the above compounds.

8.   In the early part of the twentieth century, several scientists built upon each other's work to rapidly improve our understanding of atomic structure.

(a)   What experiment helped scientists determine most of the mass of the atom was concentrated in the nucleus of the atom?

(b)   What experiment conclusively shows that there is a discrete, definite energy difference between orbital locations of electrons?

(c)   What equation demonstrates the wave nature of any body that has momentum?

(d)   What equation demonstrates the conservation of mass and energy?

END OF EXAMINATION

AP Chemistry

Practice Exam 1

ANSWER KEY

Section I

1.	(A)	26.	(C)	51.	(C)
2.	(C)	27.	(A)	52.	(B)
3.	(E)	28.	(D)	53.	(B)
4.	(D)	29.	(B)	54.	(E)
5.	(D)	30.	(A)	55.	(D)
6.	(E)	31.	(D)	56.	(A)
7.	(C)	32	(B)	57.	(C)
8.	(B)	33.	(D)	58.	(B)
9.	(E)	34.	(D)	59.	(E)
10.	(C)	35.	(D)	60.	(A)
11.	(C)	36.	(E)	61.	(C)
12.	(E)	37.	(D)	62.	(E)
13.	(A)	38.	(B)	63.	(B)
14.	(B)	39.	(A)	64.	(E)
15.	(B)	40.	(B)	65.	(D)
16.	(E)	41.	(A)	66.	(E)
17.	(C)	42.	(C)	67.	(D)
18.	(A)	43.	(C)	68.	(E)
19.	(A)	44.	(E)	69.	(C)
20.	(E)	45.	(A)	70.	(D)
21.	(B)	46.	(C)	71.	(C)
22.	(A)	47.	(A)	72.	(A)
23.	(D)	48.	(C)	73.	(E)
24.	(C)	49.	(E)	74.	(E)
25.	(C)	50.	(E)	75.	(E)

DETAILED EXPLANATIONS OF ANSWERS

Practice Exam 1

Section I

1.   **(A)**   Almost all transition elements form monatomic ions of 2^+ charge, including Cr, Fe and Cu. Calcium also forms 2^+ cations by losing both of its 4s valence electrons. The valence shell of potassium (K) contains only one electron ($4s^1$). After losing this electron, potassium achieves the noble gas configuration of argon. It is then very difficult to remove another electron, hence K^{2+} ions are never found.

2.   **(C)** $Cr_2O_7^{2-}$ (dichromate ion) is a commonly encountered oxidizing agent.

3.   **(E)**   All of these metals except copper are easily oxidized to their cationic form and hence are not found in their metallic state in nature.

4.   **(D)**   Iron (Fe) is an important construction material.

5.   **(D)**   Organic chemistry is the study of carbon-based molecules. Organic molecules can be defined as those which contain carbon.

6.   **(E)**   Sodium borohydride ($NaBH_4$) and other boron compounds are used in the reduction of various organic molecules. Since boron is less electronegative than hydrogen, boron compounds can, in effect, add H^- to other molecules.

7.   **(C)**   A chemical reaction also occurs when ammonia (NH_3) dissolves in water. In aqueous solutions, ammonia acts as a base, acquiring hydrogen ions from H_2O to yield ammonium and hydroxide ions.

$$NH_3(aq) + H_2O(l) \rightleftarrows NH_4^+(aq) + OH^-(aq)$$

The production of hydroxide ions when ammonia dissolves in water gives aqueous solutions of ammonia their characteristic alkaline (basic) properties.

8. **(B)**   In ionic bonding one or more electrons are completely donated by an electropositive element such as sodium to an electronegative
element such as chlorine. The attraction between the resulting ions is electrostatic. Ionic bonding results when there is a large difference in electronegativities between two elements such as a metal and non-metal. A bond
is considered ionic if the two bonding elements differ in electronegativity
by more than 1.7.

9. **(E)**   In the sodium acetate molecule (CH_3CO_2Na) covalent, ionic,
and π bonding are represented by the structure:

$$\begin{array}{ccc} H & O & \\ | & || & \\ H-C-C-&O^-Na^+ \\ | & & \\ H & & \end{array}$$

The C-H, C-C, and C-O bonds are all covalent. In addition, the π bonding
is present in the double bond between the carbon and oxygen. The acetate
ion (CH_3COO^-), which has a negative charge, is bonded ionically to the
sodium atom, which takes on a positive charge ($Na+$). Hydrogen bonding
exists in all aqueous solutions: among water molecules and between molecules of the solute and the water. Metallic bonding is not present in this
model.

10. **(C)**   By comparison with other Group VI A compounds, we would
expect water to boil at -100 °C. Water does not boil until its temperature
reaches $+100$ °C because the water molecules must gain enough kinetic
energy to overcome hydrogen bonding, which refers to the attraction between the oxygen atom of one water molecule and the hydrogen atoms of
neighboring molecules.

$$\begin{array}{ccccc} H-O & -- & H-O & -- & H-O \\ | & & | & & | \\ H & & H & & H \end{array}$$

    – covalent bonds
    – – hydrogen bonds

This attraction is in part electrostatic, since the oxygen of a water molecule
carries a partial negative charge and the hydrogens carry a partial positive
charge.

11. **(C)**   The rate law includes the concentration of B raised to the
second power, thus it is second order in B. The rate law includes no factor

dependent on A and so it is zero order in A. The rate law is second order overall.

12. **(E)** Since A is not a factor in the rate law, changes in the concentration of A have no effect on the rate of reaction.

13. **(A)** The rate constant is the proportionality factor in kinetic equations, denoted by k. The rate is expressed in mol/L·sec and concentration of B [B] in mol/L. We can write:

$$mol/l·sec = K \, (mol/l)^2$$

which rearranges to:

$$K = l/mol·sec$$

14. **(B)** Le Chatelier's Principle applies to both questions 14 and 15. The principle states that a system perturbed from equilibrium will react in the opposite direction so as to restore equilibrium. In the first case, pushing the piston into the chamber increases the pressure of the reaction mixture. The system reacts so as to bring the pressure back down to a new equilibrium point. In the equilibrium expression for the reaction, there are two moles of gas on the left side for every four moles on the right. In order to reduce the pressure, then, the equilibrium must shift to the left. Thus, the mole fraction of N_2 decreases.

15. **(B)** In this problem the equilibrium is perturbed by an increase in the mole fraction of H_2. In order to correct this, the reaction must shift to the left until a new equilibrium point is reached. This results in a decrease in the amount of N_2 present.

16. **(E)** Several competing effects may arise from heating the chamber. One important variable is whether the reaction is exothermic or endothermic. If the reaction is endothermic, we would write:

$$2NH_3 \, (g) + heat \leftrightarrow N_2 \, (g) + 3H_2 \, (g)$$

Adding heat would drive the reaction forward in the same way that adding more NH_3 would.

17. **(C)** Catalysts affect the rates of reactions by reducing their activation energies. They do <u>not</u> affect equilibrium constants or the energy changes (free energy, enthalpy, etc.) associated with reactions.

18. **(A)**   All three phases (solid, liquid and gas) may coexist at a single pressure/temperature combination known as the triple point. This point occurs at the intersection of the solid-liquid, solid-gas and liquid-gas equilibrium curves as illustrated by point 3.

19. **(A)**   Examining a labeled phase diagram we see that the solid phase can only exist at point 1 as illustrated in the following diagram:

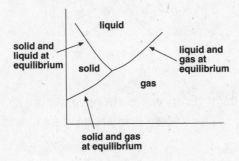

20. **(E)**   The critical point is the point above which a gas cannot change into a liquid. This means that a liquid cannot exist above this point, but at and below this point a liquid can exist. The temperature at the critical point is called the critical temperature and the pressure is called the critical pressure. The critical point in the phase diagram shown is the point 8 since above it, a gas cannot be liquefied.

21. **(B)**   Referring to the phase diagram previously given we see that the solid and liquid phases coexist on the line that contains point 4.

22. **(A)**   In sp^3 hybridization, four bonding orbitals are positioned as far from each other as possible. This requirement gives us a tetrahedral geometry:

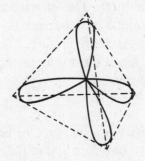

23. **(D)** In sp^2 hybridization, three bonding orbitals are positioned as far from each other as possible. This requirement yields trigonal-planar geometry:

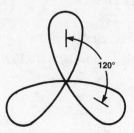

24. **(C)** In sp hybridization we are once again separating the orbitals as much as possible. The two sp orbitals are linear, and point in opposite directions.

Part B

25. **(C)** Deuterium is an isotope of hydrogen with one extra neutron. Hydrogen usually has only one proton and no neutrons in its nucleus. Deuterium has one proton and one neutron.

26. **(C)** The completely balanced reaction is:

$$MnO_4^- + 8H^+ + 5Fe^{2+} \rightarrow 5Fe^{3+} + Mn^{2+} + 4H_2O$$

27. **(A)** Ionization energy (I.E.) is the energy required to remove an electron from an elemental atom. The lowest I.E. would occur for the alkali metals (Li, Na, etc.), since by removing an electron these atoms will have a highly stable noble gas configuration. The highest I.E. would occur for noble gases (e.g. Ne), since the noble gas configuration would be destroyed by removing an electron.

28. **(D)** Electronegativity is a measure of the attraction of an atom for electrons. It increases as we move up and to the right on the periodic table (noble gases are not assigned electronegativity values). Sodium is the farthest down-left on the table of the choices given.

29. **(B)** We can use the ideal gas law, PV=nRT, where P is pressure; V is volume; n is number of gas moles; R is the universal gas constant; and T is temperature using the Kelvin temperature scale (K = 273K + degrees Celsius). Since V and n are constant, an increase in T will cause a proportional increase in P. The temperature increases from 300 K to 400 K, thus the pressure will also increase by a third from 1.0 atm to 1.3 atm. We might express this in the equation below:

$$\frac{T_1}{T_2} = \frac{P_1}{P_2}$$

30. **(A)** Dibromoethane is ethane, CH_3CH_3, with two hydrogen atoms replaced by bromine. The numbers "1,1" indicate that both bromine atoms are on the first carbon.

Thus

$$\begin{array}{ccc} & Br & H \\ & | & | \\ Br - & C - & C - H \\ & | & | \\ & H & H \end{array}$$
is the correct structure.

31. **(D)** The acid dissociation constant, K_a, applies to this reaction:

$$HA(aq) \leftrightarrow H^+(aq) + A^-(aq)$$

where

$$K_a = \frac{[H^+]\,[A^-]}{[HA]}$$

We know that $K_a = 1.77 \times 10^{-4}$ and [HA] = 1.0 M (minus a negligible amount).

$$1.77 \times 10^{-4} = \frac{[H^+]\,[A^-]}{1.0}$$

$$1.77 \times 10^{-4} = [H^+]\,[A^-]$$

since $[H^+] = [A^-]$, $1.77 \times 10^{-4} = [H^+]^2$

$$(1.77 \times 10^{-4})^{\frac{1}{2}} = [H^+]$$

pH is used to describe the hydrogen activity of a system, and mathematically is represented by the equation:

pH = $-\log [H^+]$; thus in this example,

pH = $-\log [1.77 \times 10^{-4}]^{1/2}$

32. **(B)**   53 is one short of 54, the noble gas configuration of Xenon. Element 53 would be far more likely to gain one electron, forming an ion of charge -1, than to lose electrons. Element 53 is iodine, a halogen.

33. **(D)**   Using the ideal gas law PV = nRT, where P is equal to pressure, V is equal to Volume, n is equal to number of gas moles, R is the universal gas constant and T is equal to temperature (using the Kelvin scale)

Thus $P_1V1 = nRT_1$;

Solving for n, we have $n = P_1V_1/RT_1$. Substituting $n = P_1V_1/RT_1$ into the equation for $P_2V_2 = nRT_2$ and solving for V_2, we get the expression:

$$V_2 = \frac{P_1V_1T_2}{P_2T_2}$$

At STP (standard temperature and pressure, T is 273K and pressure is 1.0 atm), and making the appropriate substitutions, we get:

$$\frac{1.0 \text{ atm} \times 4.0 \text{ L} \times 273 \text{ K}}{0.20 \text{ atm } 373 \text{ K}} = 14.6 \text{ L}$$

34. **(D)**   The correct expression would be

$$1 \text{ liter} = 1000 \text{ cm}^3 \times \left[\frac{1m}{100 \text{ cm}}\right]^3$$

$$1 \text{ liter} = 1000 \text{ cm}^3 \times \frac{1m^3}{1 \times 10^6 \text{ cm}^3}$$

$$1 \text{ liter} = 1 \times 10^{-3} \text{ m}^3$$

35. **(D)**   The hydrolysis reaction for sodium acetate proceeds as follows:

the acid dissociation

$$\overset{\displaystyle O}{\overset{\|}{CH_3CONa}} + H_2O \rightarrow \overset{\displaystyle O}{\overset{\|}{CH_3COH}} + NaOH$$

The products of the reaction are a weak acid (acetic acid) and a strong base (sodium hydroxide).

36. **(E)**   The oxidation states of the atoms of a neutral compound must add up to equal zero. For $KMnO_4$, the oxidation state of K must be +1 since it is in Group IA and the oxidation state of O must be -2 since it is in Group VIA. Thus we have:

$$1 + Mn + 4\,(-2) = 0 \text{ and } Mn = +7$$

37. **(D)**   Conjugate acid/base pairs are different from one another by only a proton. Acetic acid has a formula of $HC_2H_3O_2$; to remove a proton from it would yield the formula, $C_2H_3O_2^-$.

38. **(B)**   The rate of the reaction changes linearly as [A] is increased, which means it is first order with respect to A. However, the rate of reaction quadruples when the concentration of B is doubled, indicating that the reaction is second order with respect to B.

39. **(A)**   The cathode of an electrochemical cell is defined as the site of reduction and the anode is defined as the site of oxidation.

40. **(B)**   Since one mole of an ideal gas occupies a volume of 22.4 liters at STP we have

$$11.2 \text{ liters} \times \frac{1 \text{ mole of He}}{22.4 \text{ liters}} = 0.5 \text{ moles of He}$$

Converting to grams of He

$$0.5 \text{ moles of He} \times \frac{4 \text{ g of He}}{1 \text{ mole of He}} = 2 \text{ g of He}$$

41. **(A)**   The pH of a solution is defined as

$$pH = -\log [H^+]$$

in which $[H^+]$ is the hydronium ion concentration. Rearranging this equation, we obtain

$$[H^+] = 10^{-pH}$$

Substituting the given pH, we have $[H^+] = 10^{-3} = 0.001$.

42. **(C)**   We find that there are 23 g of sodium (its atomic weight) in 40 g of NaOH (its molecular weight). Using this as a conversion factor

$$30 \text{ g of NaOH} \times \frac{23 \text{ g of Na}}{40 \text{ g of NaOH}} = 17 \text{ g of Na}$$

Another method for determining this quantity is to convert 30 g of NaOH to moles

$$30 \text{ g of NaOH} \times \frac{1 \text{ mole of NaOH}}{40 \text{ g of NaOH}} = 0.75 \text{ mole of NaOH}$$

and calculating the weight of sodium corresponding to 0.75 mole

$$0.75 \text{ mole of Na} \times \frac{23 \text{ g of Na}}{1 \text{ mole of Na}} = 17 \text{ g of Na}$$

since one mole of Na is present in one mole of NaOH.

43. **(C)** Since one mole of an ideal gas occupies a volume of 22.4 liters at STP and fluorine is a diatomic gas (gases with the endings -gen or -ine are usually diatomic) we have

$$\frac{38 \text{ g of F}_2}{1 \text{ mole of F}_2} \times \frac{1 \text{ mole of F}_2}{22.4 \text{ liters}} = \frac{1.7 \text{ g}}{\text{liter}}$$

44. **(E)** Using the relationship

$$M_1 V_1 = M_2 V_2$$

where M is the molarity and V is the volume we have

$$(1 \text{ M}) (500 \text{ mL}) = (5 \text{ M}) (x)$$

and $x = 100 \text{ mL}$

This value gives us the volume of the final solution obtained by evaporating 500 - 100 or 400 mL of water from the initial solution.

Note that the product MV gives the number of moles of solute

$$MV = \left(\frac{\text{moles}}{\text{liter}} \right) \times \text{liter} = \text{moles}$$

45. **(A)** A simple distillation is sufficient to separate this mixture into its components. Fractional distillation would be the method of choice if the boiling points of the components were similar. Paper chromatography separates compounds by virtue of their differing amounts of interaction with the solvent used and has no use in separating this mixture. In

addition, only small quantities of testing material are reasonable for paper chromatography. A separatory funnel is used to extract a compound from one immiscible liquid to another and is not suited for this purpose. Spectroscopy is an analytical method not a separation tool.

46. **(C)** The reaction in question is

$$NO + \frac{1}{2}O_2 \rightarrow NO_2$$

or using the given coefficients

$$20\ NO + 10\ O_2 \rightarrow 20\ NO_2$$

Note that the unit of the coefficients used is liters, not moles. This does not affect the calculation since moles and liters are directly related in the case of gases (1 mole of a gas occupies 22.4 liters at STP).

47. **(A)** The solubility product of lead (II) iodide is given by

$$K_{sp} = [Pb^{2+}]\ [I^-]^2$$

where $[Pb^{2+}]$ and $[I^-]$ are the concentrations of lead ion and iodide in solution, respectively. We know that $K_{sp} = 1.4 \times 10^{-8}$ and that the concentration of iodide in solution is twice that of the lead ion from the dissociation:

$$PbI_2 \rightarrow Pb^{2+} + 2I^-$$

Setting $[Pb^{2+}] = x$, we know that $[I^-] = 2x$. Thus

$$K_{sp} = [Pb^{2+}]\ [I^-]^2 = (x)\ (2x)^2 = 1.4 \times 10^{-8}$$

Solving for x gives

$$4x^3 = 1.4 \times 10^{-8}$$

and $x = 1.5 \times 10^{-3}$

Recalling that $[I^-] = 2x$ we have

$$[I^-] = 2(1.5 \times 10^{-3}) = 3 \times 10^{-3}$$

48. **(C)** Recalling that density $= \rho = \frac{m}{v}$ gives

$$\rho = \frac{80\ g/mole}{22.4\ L/mole} = 3.6\ g/L$$

49. **(E)** The equation for the reaction is:

$$2NH_3 \rightarrow N_2 + 3H_2$$

Since 1 mole of an ideal gas occupies a volume of 22.4 L at STP (standard temperature and pressure), we have:

$$2 \text{ moles NH}_3 \rightarrow 1 \text{ mole N}_2 + 3 \text{ moles H}_2$$

$$101 \text{ L H}_2 = 3 \text{ mol NH}_3 \left(\frac{3 \text{ mol H}_2}{2 \text{ mol NH}_3} \right) \left(\frac{22.4\, 1\, \text{H}_2}{1 \text{ mol H}_2} \right)$$

50. **(E)**   The transition from ionic to elemental form involves the transfer of electrons. Such reactions are called oxidation-reduction reactions.

51. **(C)**   Boron is one of the elements in Group IIIA and has the valence electron configuration $2s^2 2p^1$. The boron atom hybridizes from its ground state. The hybrid orbitals are composed of one original s orbital and two original p orbitals. Thus the hybridization is sp^2.

52. **(B)**   The given electronic configuration indicates an atom with 16 electrons. Sulfur, atomic number 16, has 16 electrons. Oxygen, atomic number 8, has 8 electrons; P^+, atomic number 15, has 14 electrons; Cl^-, atomic number 17, has 18 electrons; and Ar, atomic number 18, has 18 electrons.

53. **(B)**

$$\overset{\displaystyle H}{\underset{|}{}}$$

The functional group $R - C = O$ represents an aldehyde. An alcohol is

indicated by $R - OH$, an ester by $R - \overset{\displaystyle O}{\overset{||}{C}} - OR^1$, an ether by

$R - O - R^1$ and a ketone by $R - \overset{\displaystyle O}{\overset{||}{C}} - R^1$.

54. **(E)**   An alpha particle is a helium nucleus, ($^4_2$He), and a beta particle is an electron. Beta particles are produced in the nucleus by the decomposition of a neutron into a proton and an electron. Thus if a beta particle is emitted, the atomic number increases by 1 while the mass number remains unchanged. For this radioactive decay, we have:

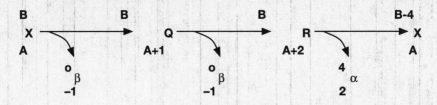

Different letters were chosen to represent the nuclei since the number of protons in the nucleus determines the atomic identity. The initial and final nuclei are represented by the same letter since they are isotopes of the same element.

55. **(D)** The molality of a solution (m) is defined as the number of moles of solute dissolved in one kilogram of solvent. The number of moles of NaOH to be used is determined to be:

$$20 \text{ g of NaOH} \times \frac{1 \text{ mole of NaOH}}{40 \text{ g of NaOH}} = 0.5 \text{ mole of NaOH}$$

Thus:

$$0.5 \text{ m} = \frac{0.5 \text{ mole of NaOH}}{\text{x kilograms of water}}$$

Rearranging

$$x = \frac{0.5}{0.5} = 1 \text{ kg of water}$$

56. **(A)** The equilibrium constant is dependent only on temperature, but the amount of each substance present at equilibrium is dependent on pressure, volume and temperature. There is still an interchange between the phases, but the same number of molecules leave and enter both phases, so the equilibrium concentrations and equilibrium constant are the same for a given pressure, volume and temperature.

57. **(C)** The equilibrium constant is defined as the product of the concentrations of the gaseous products raised to the power of their coefficients divided by the product of the gaseous reactant concentrations raised to the power of their coefficients. Only gaseous reactants and products are included in K_e since the concentrations of liquids and solids participating in the reaction are assumed to be large (as compared to those of the gases) and relatively constant. The expressions of the equilibrium constants for the reactions given are:

(A) $K_e = \dfrac{[CO_2]}{[O_2]}$

(B) $K_e = \dfrac{[CO_2]}{[CO][O_2]^{1/2}}$

(C) $K_e = [CO_2]$

(D) $K_e = \dfrac{[O_2]}{[CO_2]}$

(E) $K_e = \dfrac{1}{[CO_2]}$

58. **(B)** The buret should be read from the bottom of the meniscus (the curve in the liquid surface), providing a reading of 10.54 ml. Tenths of milliliters can be read off the scale and hundredths should be estimated. Notice that the volume measured increases going <u>down</u> the scale.

59. **(E)** The hydrogen electrode has been chosen as the standard electrode with an assigned value of $E° = 0.00V$.

60. **(A)** The anode of any electrochemical cell is defined to be the site of oxidation. Thus, since Zn is being oxidized to Zn^{2+} in this cell, it is determined to be the anode. The cathode, the site of reduction, is Cr in this cell. The solutions of the metal ions are not the anode nor the cathode but rather the electrolytic media.

61. **(C)** Recalling that the change in enthalpy for a reaction is given by the sum of the heats of formation of the reactants subtracted from the sum of the heats of formation of the products, we have

$\Delta H° = \Sigma \Delta H_f \text{ (products)} - \Sigma \Delta H_f \text{ (reactants) or}$

$-488.7 = 3(-94.1) + 4(-57.8) - (x)$

$x = 3(-94.1) + 4(-57.8) + 488.7$

$x = -24.8 \text{ kcal/mole}$

62. **(E)** The rate-determining-step determines the overall rate of the entire mechanism. The first step is the only step that uses chlorine gas. If the overall mechanism shows experimentally that the reaction rate is first order with respect to chlorine gas, then the first step of the mechanism must be the rate-determining step.

63. **(B)**   An endothermic reaction is one in which heat may be considered one of the "reactants." An exothermic reaction releases heat upon formation of the products. An equilibrium reaction may be either exothermic or endothermic. The same holds true for spontaneity; spontaneity can only be determined if one also knows the entropy change (ΔS) for the reaction.

64. **(E)**   Neutral fluorine atoms have 9 electrons as determined by their atomic number. Magnesium atoms have 12 electrons, so Mg^{3+} has 9 electrons. Boron has 5 electrons, so B^{3-} has 8 electrons (the same as oxygen). Nitrogen has 7 electrons, so N^+ has 6 electrons (the same as carbon). Neon has 10 electrons, so Ne^- has 11 electrons (the same as sodium). Sodium has 11 electrons, so Na^- has 12 electrons (the same as magnesium).

65. **(D)**   Le Chatelier's Principle may be used to predict equilibrium reactions: If a stress is placed on a system in equilibrium, the equilibrium shifts so as to counteract that stress. Hence, increasing the reactant concentration favors formation of the products while decreasing the reactant concentration favors formation of the reactants. The same holds true for altering the product concentrations. Increasing the temperature favors the reaction that absorbs heat while decreasing the temperature favors the reaction that releases heat. Increasing the pressure favors the reaction that decreases the volume of a closed system while decreasing the pressure favors the reaction resulting in an increased volume (moles of gaseous product produced are the only things counted since liquids and solids occupy a relatively small volume in comparison). However, temperature and pressure dependencies cannot be inferred from this question. The addition of a catalyst alters the reaction rate but not the position of equilibrium. The only way completion can be obtained is that we remove the products as they are formed. Now the state of the reaction becomes nonequilibrium, but it tries to come in an equilibrium state once again. This leads to formation of more products, which in turn leads to completion of the given reaction.

66. **(E)**   A beta particle is a fast electron of mass 9.11×10^{-28} g while a proton and a neutron both have a mass of 1.67×10^{-24} g. A hydrogen nucleus is a proton, and an alpha particle is a helium nucleus (two protons and two neutrons). Thus the electron (beta particle) has the smallest mass of the choices given.

67. **(D)**   Molecules in the gaseous state have by far the greatest kinetic energy. The difference in energy between the liquid and gas phases is greater than the difference in energy between the solid and liquid phases. This may readily be seen by the energy changes occurring in water; the

heat of fusion of water is 80 calories/gram while the heat of vaporization is 540 calories/gram.

68. **(E)** A simple cubic crystal is the only unit cell mentioned that has, on average, one atom per unit cell. A simple cubic unit cell has one atom in each of the eight corners of the unit cell, but only one-eighth of each of those atoms is ascribed to that particular unit cell. A face-centered unit cell has four atoms per unit cell; while a body-centered unit cell has two atoms per unit cell.

69. **(C)** 1.5 moles of gaseous product (one mole of H_2 and 0.5 mole of O_2) are produced for every 68.3 kcal of energy added to water. Since 4×68.3 kcal = 273.2 kcal, 4×1.5 or 6 moles of gaseous product are formed. Since molar volume is given as 22.4 liters at STP, 6×22.4 liters = 134.4 liters of gaseous product are evolved.

70. **(D)** The first word of the ester name is the name of the group attached to oxygen (propyl in our case). The second word is the name of the parent carboxylic acid with the suffix -ic replaced by -ate (butanoate in our case). Thus, we are looking for an ester with a propyl group attached to the oxygen of butanoic acid. This structure is

$$\overset{\displaystyle O}{\overset{\displaystyle \|}{CH_3CH_2CH_2COCH_2CH_2CH_3}}$$

$CH_3CH_2CH_2OCH_2CH_2CH_2CH_3$ has the assigned name butyl propyl ether

$$\overset{\displaystyle O}{\overset{\displaystyle \|}{CH_3CH_2COCH_2CH_2CH_2CH_3}}$$ has the assigned name butyl propanoate

$$\overset{\displaystyle O}{\overset{\displaystyle \|}{CH_3CH_2CH_2CH_2COCH_2CH_2CH_3}}$$ has the assigned name propyl pentanoate

71. **(C)** 373 K is the normal boiling point of water. By definition, the vapor pressure of any substance at its normal boiling point is 1.0 atm. The vapor pressure at the boiling point would decrease at high altitudes, but it would not be called the *normal* boiling point.

72. **(A)** The first set of letters demonstrates a substance moving from solid, to liquid, and then to gas. A substances as a solid has less entropy than it does as a liquid, and much less entropy than it does as a gas. Entropy is a state of disorder, or randomness. As a substance is heated, its increased thermal motion gives it greater disorder or entropy.

73. **(E)** Henry's law pertains to the relationship between the amount of gas dissolved in a solution and the partial pressure of the gas above the solution.

74. **(E)** All of the above can be calculated from the information given. The equilibrium constant can be calculated from the standard change in free energy, which can be calculated from the heat and entropy of reaction, which can be calculated directly from the information on the chart.

$$\Delta G^\circ = \text{-RT ln K} = \Delta H^\circ - T\Delta S^\circ$$

$$\Delta S^\circ = \Sigma\, S^\circ \text{ (products)} - \Sigma S^\circ \text{ (reactants)}$$

$$\Delta H^\circ = \Sigma H^\circ_f \text{ (products)} - \Sigma H^\circ_f \text{ (reactants)}$$

75. **(E)** The oxidation states of the element comprising a neutral compound must have a sum of zero. Thus, nitrogen in HNO_3 has an oxidation state of +5, since hydrogen and oxygen generally have oxidation states of +1 and -2, respectively.

i.e. $(1) + (x) + (-6) = 0 \quad x = 5$

Section II

Part A

1.   (a)

$$K_b = \frac{[OH^-]\,[NH_4^+]}{[NH_3]}$$

(b) $[NH_3]\,K_b = [OH^-]\,[NH_4^+] = (0.200)\,(1.8 \times 10^{-5}) = 3.6 \times 10^{-6}$

$[OH^-] = 0.0020\ M$

(c)   Percent dissociation $= 0.002/0.200 \times 100\% = 1\%$

(d)

	NH_3	+	H^+	$\leftrightarrow$	NH_4^+
Before equilibrium:	0.0200 mol		0 mol		0.0500 mol
After equilibrium:	0.0200 + x mol		x mol		0.0500 − x mol

$$[H^+] = \frac{K_a\,[NH_4^+]}{[NH_3]} = \frac{(5.5 \times 10^{-10})\,(.05\ \text{mol}/.1\ L)}{(.02\ \text{mol}/.1\ L)} = 1.4 \times 10^{-9}\ M$$

pH = 8.9

(e)

$[Mg{++}] = 0.0300\ \text{mol} / 0.10\ L = 0.300\ M$

$[OH{-}] = 1.0 \times 10^{-14} / 2.2 \times 10^{-10} = 4.5 \times 10^{-5}\ M$

Put both concentrations in the K_{sp} equation to find Q, then compare with K_{sp}.

$$Q = (0.300)\,(4.5 \times 10^{-5})^2 = 6.0 \times 10^{-10}$$

Since Q is larger than the solubility product constant, then a precipitate will form.

2.   (a)   To find out how much silver metal is produced, you must go through the stoicheometric calculation for both reactants. The reactant that produces the least will be used up first, and the amount of product that corresponds is the actual amount produced.

$$2.00 \text{ g Zn} \times \frac{1 \text{ mol Zn}}{65.38 \text{ g Zn}} \times \frac{2 \text{ mol Ag}}{1 \text{ mol Zn}} \times$$

$$\frac{107.9 \text{ g Ag}}{1 \text{ mol Ag}} = 6.60 \text{ g Ag}$$

$$0.400 \text{ L Ag solution} \times \frac{0.200 \text{ mol Ag}}{\text{L Ag solution}} \times \frac{107.9 \text{ g Ag}}{1 \text{ mol Ag}}$$

$$= 8.63 \text{ g Ag}$$

Therefore, 6.60 g Ag is produced.

(b)   Given the explanation and calculations above, zinc metal is the limiting reactant.

(c)

Oxidation:	$Zn \rightarrow Zn^{++} + 2e^-$	$E°_{ox} = 0.76 \text{ V}$
Reduction:	$e^- + Ag^+ \rightarrow Ag$	$E°_{red} = 0.80 \text{ V}$
Total reaction:	$Zn + Ag^+ \rightarrow Zn^{++} + Ag$	$E°_{total} = 1.56 \text{ V}$

The total cell potential is 1.56 V.

(d) $\Delta G° = -nFE°_{total} = -(2)(96{,}486 \text{ C})(1.56 \text{ V}) = -301{,}000 \text{ J}$ $= -301 \text{ kJ}$

Since the change in free energy is negative, then the reaction is spontaneous.

(e)   The cell voltage will decrease as the reaction continues to proceed. The Nernst equation gives the relationship between the cell potential under standard conditions and the cell potential under non-standard conditions.

$$E_{cell} = E°_{cell} - 0.06/n \ln Q$$

As products are formed, Q increases, which increases the value that is subtracted from the standard cell potential to get the new, lesser cell potential.

3.   The equation for the combustion of CH_4 is as follows:

$$CH_4 + 2O_2 \rightarrow CO_2 + 2H_2O$$

a) $\Delta H_{comb} = \Sigma H_{prod} - \Sigma H_{react} = (H_{CO_2} + H_{H_2O}) - (H_{CH_4} + H_{O_2})$

$= -393.5 + 2(-285.5) - (-74.9) = -889.6 \text{ KJ/mol} \times \text{K}$

b) $CH_4 \rightarrow 1C(s) + 2H_2 (g) \rightarrow CH_4 (g)$

c) $\Delta S = \Sigma S_{prod} - \Sigma S_{react} = (S_{CH4}) - (S_C + S_{H_2})$

$\Delta S = (1) (186.2 \text{J/mol} \times \text{K}) - (1) (5.69 \text{J/mol} \times \text{K}) - (2)$
$(130.6 \text{J/mol} \times \text{K}) = -80.7 \text{ J/mol} \times \text{K}$

d) $\Delta G = \Delta H - T\Delta S$

$= -889.6 \text{kJ/mol} - (298\text{K}) (.0807 \text{ KJ/mol} \times \text{K})$

$= 913.6 \text{kJ/mol}$

Part B

4. a) $4Fe(s) + 3O_2(g) \rightarrow 2Fe_2O_3(s)$

$Fe^0 + O_2{}^0 \rightarrow Fe^{+3}O^{-2}$

b) $SO_2 + 2H_2(g) \rightarrow S(s) + 2H_2O(g)$

$S^{+4} + H^0 \rightarrow S^0 + H^{+1}$

c) $Sn(s) + 2HCl(aq) \rightarrow SnCl_2 + H_2(g)$

$Sn^0 + H^{+1} \rightarrow Sn^{+2} + H^0$

d) $2H_2O_2(l) \rightarrow 2H_2O + O_2(g)$

$O^{-1} \qquad \rightarrow O^{-2} + O^0$

e) $3Mn (s) + 2CrCl_3 \rightarrow 2 Cr (s) + 3MnCl_2$

$Mn^0 + Cr^{+3} \rightarrow Cr^0 + Mn^{+2}$

f) $SnO_2 + 2C(s) \rightarrow Sn(l) + 2CO(g)$

$Sn^{+4} + C^0 \rightarrow Sn^0 + C^{+2}$

g) $CH_4 + H_2O \xrightarrow{\text{catalyst}} CO_2(g) + 3H_2 (g)$

$C^{-4} + H^{+1} \rightarrow C^{+4} + H^0$

h) $SO_2(g) + 2HNO_3 \rightarrow H_2SO_4(aq) + 2NO_2$

$SO^{+4} \quad N^{+5} \quad\quad \rightarrow S^{+6} \quad N^{+4}$

5.   (a)   The oxides of the elements, when placed in water, will increase in acidity moving from left to right on the periodic table. That is, the oxide of sodium, when put into water, is very basic; the oxide of magnesium less so, and so forth. On the other side of the row, the oxides of nonmetals are acidic when put into water; the oxide of chloride extremely so. (The noble gas, argon, is neglected in the discussion of this trend.)

(b)

acidic oxide: $SO_2 + H_2O \rightarrow H_2SO_3$

basic oxide: $CaO + H_2O \rightarrow Ca(OH)_2$

(c)   As more oxygen atoms are added to chlorine, the oxides become increasingly acidic. For example, HOCl is a much weaker acid than $HClO_4$. The increased number of oxygen atoms add more electronegative atoms that more strongly pull the electron from hydrogen, leaving the acidic proton.

(d)   Transition metal ions create an acidic solution when put into water because their positive charge creates enough attraction to the hydroxide ion that water will split, and form an acidic proton in the process. For example,

$Fe(H_2O)_6^{3+} (aq) \rightarrow Fe(OH)(H_2O)_5^{2+} (aq) + H^+ (aq)$

6.   (a)   21.02 g total – 17.20 g crucible = 3.82 g anhydrate

5.96 g hydrate – 3.82 g anhydrate = 2.14 g water

(b)

$2.14 \text{ g water} \times \dfrac{1.0 \text{ mole water}}{18.00 \text{ g water}} = 0.120 \text{ moles water}$

(c)

$3.82 \text{ g CuSO}_4 \times \dfrac{1.0 \text{ mole CuSO}_4}{159.61 \text{ g CuSO}_4} = 0.024 \text{ moles CuSO}_4$

(d)   Since 0.12 mol water is five times 0.024 moles copper sulfate, the formula of the hydrate is $CuSO_4 \times 5H_2O$.

(e)

$$\frac{5 \times 18.00 \text{ g water}}{249.61 \text{ g } CuSO_4 \bullet 5H_2O} \times 100\% = 36.0\%$$

7.   (a)   The bond angles in the XeF_4 are 90°. The bond angles CH_4 are 109°; and the bond angle around the carbon in the aldehyde are 120°. These differences in bond angles are based on the hybridization of the central compound, which in turn is dependent on either the number of electrons available for bonding, or the type of bonding that occurs.

For example, the carbon in CH_4 has sp^3 hybridization. Its electron pairs take on a tetrahedral shape. The carbon in CH_4O has sp^2 hybridization because of the double bond to the oxygen. Its electron pairs take on a triagonal planar shape. The xenon in XeF_4 has sp^3d^2 hybridization. Its bonded and unbonded electron pairs take on an octahedral shape, and the shape of the configuration of the atoms is square planar. These shapes are a result of the repulsion of each pair of bonded and unbonded electrons.

(b)   Expanded octets exist when a large molecule (such as Xe) is combined with a highly electronegative element (such as F). The electronegativity of one element draws into hybridization some of the electrons in the d-orbitals in the larger element, which allows for more than four bonds around the central atom.

(c)   Some expanded octet compounds can behave as Lewis bases when they have electronegative elements bonded to them, and have reactive unbonded electron pairs. (The definition of a Lewis base is an electron pair donor.)

(d)   Both XeF_4 and CH_4 are non-polar and do not dissolve with polar solvents—such as water, whereas the aldehyde is polar and mixes readily with water. The polarity of the aldehyde is a result of the difference in electronegativity between the oxygen and the other atoms, in combination with the fact that the oxygen atom is on one side of the unbalanced molecule. The other two molecules contain a symmetry that cancels out the internal dipole forces so that there is no net dipole moment on the molecules.

8.   (a)   Rutherford's alpha particle bombardment of gold foil showed that most of the atomic material was centralized in a dense nucleus. When he bombarded the foil with positively charged alpha particles, most of them went straight through the foil, or were deflected at small angles. However, some of the alpha particles were deflected at wide angles, suggesting a collision with a dense material in rare cases.

(b)   Observing the bright line spectra of excited gas molecules shows that the journey of excited electrons back to the ground state only occurs between specific energy levels. When a specific color—that corresponds to a specific energy difference—is continuously given off from an excited gas, then it is apparent that the electrons are moving between discreet energy levels.

(c)   The deBrogile equation ($\lambda = h/mv$) shows that any object with momentum also has a corresponding wavelength.

(d)   Einstein's equation ($E = mc^2$) shows that there is a corresponding energy that is associated with any mass.

▼
Practice
Exam 2

AP Chemistry

Practice Exam 2

Section I

TIME: 90 minutes
75 questions
45% of the entire test

(Answer sheets appear in the back of this book.)

DIRECTIONS: Each set of lettered choices below refers to the numbered questions or statements immediately following it. Select the one lettered choice that best answers each question. A choice may be used once, more than once, or not at all in each set.

Part A

Questions 1 – 3 refer to the valence electron dot formulas in the figure below. The letters merely identify the different atoms. They do not stand for actual known elements.

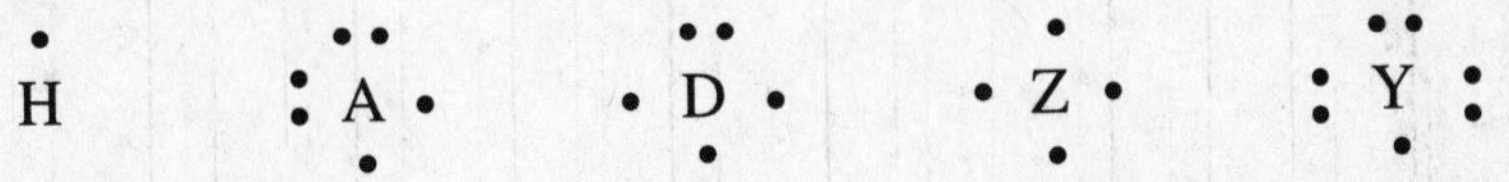

H   :A·   ·D·   ·Z·   :Y:

1.   The most active nonmetal is:

(A) A   (D) Y

(B) D   (E) Z

(C) H

2.   A likely bonding association is:

   (A) HA_2 (D) ZH_4

   (B) HD_4 (E) YZ

   (C) DH_5

3.   Element D has a valence of:

   (A) 1   (D) 5

   (B) 3   (E) 7

   (C) 4

Questions 4 - 5

   (A) Molecules are moving least rapidly and are closest together.

   (B) Water is in this state at 12 degrees Centigrade.

   (C) Mercury is in this state at room temperature.

   (D) Molecules are moving most rapidly.

   (E) Molecules maintain a definite volume but shape depends upon the contours of the container holding them.

4.   Gas

5.   Solid

6.   Plasma

Questions 7 – 9

   (A) sodium chlorate   (D) sodium hypochlorite

   (B) sodium chloride   (E) sodium perchlorate

   (C) sodium chlorite

7. NaC10

8. NaC10$_2$

9. NaC10$_3$

Questions 10 – 13

        (A) alcohol   (D) alkyne

        (B) alkane   (E) amine

        (C) alkene

10. C_2H_5OH

11. C_2H_6

12. C_2H_2

13. C_2H_4

Part B

> **DIRECTIONS:** The following questions consist of questions or incomplete statements followed by five answers or completions. Select the best answer in each case.

14. Brønsted-Lowry acid and its conjugate base?

    (A) Cu / Cu^{++}

    (B) N_2 / NH_3

    (C) $HC_2H_3O_2$ / $C_2H_3O_2^-$

    (D) $Al(OH)_3$ / $[Al(OH)_4]^-$

    (E) PbI_2 / Pb^{2+}

15. Which of the following sets of quantum numbers (listed in order of n, l, m_l, m_s) describe the highest energy valence electron of nitrogen in its ground state?

    (A) 2,0,0, +½

    (B) 2,1,1, –½

    (C) 2,1,1, +½

    (D) 2,1,–1, –½

    (E) 2,1,–1, +½

16. Given the information in this chart, which of the following answers best represents the enthalpy of combustion for hydrogen gas, in kJ/mol?

Substance	ΔH_f° (kJ/mol)
H_2 (s)	0
CO_2 (g)	–393.5
H_2O (l)	–285.85
O_2 (g)	0

    (A) 0

    (B) –393

    (C) –107

    (D) –285

    (E) +107

17. Suppose that the reaction rate of an inorganic reaction mixture at 35 degrees Centigrade is double the reaction rate at an earlier temperature setting. All other environmental factors are held constant. This earlier temperature was most likely:

    (A) 0 °C

    (B) 10 °C

    (C) 25 °C

    (D) 40 °C

    (E) 45 °C

18. For the reaction, $HCOO^- + H_2O \rightarrow HCOOH + OH^-$

    The rate expression is Rate $= k\,[HCOOH]\,[OH^-]$

    What is the overall order of this reaction?

    (A) 1   (D) 5

    (B) 2   (E) 6

    (C) 4

19. Select the indicator that changes color at a pH of 1.

    (A) congo red   (D) phenophthalein

    (B) malachite green   (E) thymol blue

    (C) methyl violet

20. Select the characteristic that is <u>not</u> a standard condition for comparing gas volumes:

    (A) Pressure – – 1 atm

    (B) Pressure – – 760 torr

    (C) Temperature – – 0 degrees Centigrade

    (D) Temperature – – 25 degrees Centigrade

    (E) Temperature – – 273 degrees Kelvin

21. A recorded Fahrenheit value in lab is 122 degrees. Its corresponding Kelvin temperature value is:

    (A) 32   (D) 273

    (B) 52   (E) 323

    (C) 152

22. Consider the balanced equation:

$$2H_2 + O_2 \rightarrow 2H_2O$$

What volume of oxygen in liters must be available at STP to allow six grams of hydrogen to react and form water?

(A) 2

(B) 11.2

(C) 16

(D) 22.4

(E) 33.6

23. Select the element with an atomic number of 19 and one electron in its valence shell:

(A) calcium

(B) chlorine

(C) hydrogen

(D) potassium

(E) sodium

24. A certain element commonly has 8 protons, 8 neutrons, and 8 electrons. Select the combination of particles that denote an isotope of this particular atom.

(A) 4 protons, 4 neutrons, 4 electrons

(B) 8 protons, 8 neutrons, 4 electrons

(C) 8 protons, 10 neutrons, 8 electrons

(D) 10 protons, 8 neutrons, 8 electrons

(E) 10 protons, 10 neutrons, 8 electrons

25. A probable compound formed from calcium and oxygen has the formula:

(A) CaO

(B) Ca_2O_2

(C) Ca_2O

(D) Ca_2O_3

(E) Ca_3O_2

26. Select the <u>incorrect</u> statement about alpha, beta, and gamma rays of radiation.

    (A) All affect a photographic plate.

    (B) Alpha rays possess charged particles.

    (C) Beta rays move most rapidly.

    (D) Beta rays lack charged particles.

    (E) Gamma rays display high frequency waves.

27. The number of valence electrons in cobalt is:

    (A) 1   (D) 4

    (B) 2   (E) 6

    (C) 3

28. Among the choices given, the atom with the largest size is:

    (A) bromine   (D) helium

    (B) chlorine   (E) iodine

    (C) fluorine

29. The final stable, disintegration product in the decay of uranium, $^{238}_{9}U$, is:

    (A) $^{210}_{83}Bi$ (D) $^{210}_{84}Po$

    (B) $^{206}_{82}Pb$ (E) $^{234}_{90}Th$

    (C) $^{210}_{82}Pb$

30. The correct ranking of alkali metals from most reactive to least reactive is:

    (A) Be–Mg–Co–Sr–Ba   (D) I–Br–Cl–F

    (B) Cs–Rb–K–Na–Li   (E) Li–Na–K–Rb–Cs

    (C) F–Cl–Br–I

31. Select the most unreactive element:

    (A) Cl   (D) S

    (B) H   (E) Xe

    (C) Na

32. Each of the following is a statement of Dalton's laws <u>except</u>:

    (A) Any gas in a mixture exerts its partial pressure.

    (B) Atoms are permanent and cannot be decomposed.

    (C) Each gas's pressure depends on other gases in a mixture.

    (D) Gases can exist in a mixture.

    (E) Substances are composed of atoms.

33. Consider the balanced equation:

    $$2KClO_3 \rightarrow 2KCl + 3O_2$$

    If 72 grams of oxygen gas are produced, the amount of potassium chlorate required in grams is:

    (A) 112   (D) 448

    (B) 224   (E) 1020

    (C) 183

34. In the following reaction, how would the equilibrium constant for the listed reaction be related to the acid ionization constant, K_a, for acetic acid?

    $$HC_2H_3O_2 + OH^- \leftrightarrow H_2O + C_2H_3O_2^-$$

    (A) K_a / K_w (D) K_a

    (B) K_w / K_a (E) $K_a K_b$

    (C) $1 / K_a$

35. An atom has an atomic mass of 45 and an atomic number of 21. Select the correct statement about its atomic structure:

    (A) The number of electrons is 24.

    (B) The number of neutrons is 21.

    (C) The number of protons is 24.

    (D) The number of electrons and neutrons is equal.

    (E) The number of protons and neutrons is unequal.

36. Boron is bombarded by alpha particles. Complete the products formed in the following equation by transmutation.

    $$_5^{11}B + {_2^4}He$$

    (A) $_6^{12}C + {_0^1}n$ (D) $_{15}^{31}P + {_0^1}n$

    (B) $_3^6L + {_0^1}n$ (E) $_{14}^{28}Si + {_1^1}H$

    (C) $_7^{14}N + {_0^1}n$

37. The least bond energy in kcals per mole is found with:

    (A) C–C   (D) H–F

    (B) H–Br   (E) O–H

    (C) H–Cl

38. The bond angles between carbon and hydrogen in methane are best labeled as:

    (A) covalent   (D) tetrahedral

    (B) ionic   (E) trihybrid

    (C) linear

39. Select the metal with the lowest melting point:

    (A) copper

    (D) phosphorous

    (B) iron

    (E) sulfur

    (C) lithium

40. HCl + NaOH → NaCl + H_2O is an example of a reaction classified as:

    (A) decomposition

    (D) single replacement

    (B) double replacement

    (E) synthesis

    (C) reversible

41. Consider this reaction under standard lab conditions:

    $FeS + 2HCl \rightarrow FeCl_2 + H_2S$

    If 22 grams of iron sulfide are completely reacted to form products, the volume of hydrogen sulfide gas produced is:

    (A) 5.6

    (D) 44.4

    (B) 11.2

    (E) 88.0

    (C) 22.4

42. Compute the quantity in grams of sucrose ($C_{12}H_{22}O_{11}$) required to make a 1M strength solution of 500 mL.

    (A) 85.5

    (D) 684

    (B) 171

    (E) 982

    (C) 342

43. Consider the following balanced equation:

    $2K + 2HCl \rightarrow 2KCl + H_2$

    The respective oxidation numbers for K, H, and Cl before and after reaction:

(A) go from 0, –1, +1 to –1, +1, 0

(B) go from 0, +1, –1 to +1, 0, –1

(C) go from 1, –1, 0 to –1, +1, –1

(D) go from 1, –1, 0 to –1, –1, 0

(E) go from 0, 0, 1 to 1, 1, –1

44. Enzymes, which are organic catalysts, always partly consist of:

(A) carbohydrates

(B) lipids

(C) nucleic acids

(D) proteins

(E) steroids

45. A correct ranking of elements in order of decreasing electronegativity is:

(A) Al–F–O–Cs–Na

(B) Cs–Na–Al–O–F

(C) F–O–Al–Na–Cs

(D) Na–F–Al–O–Cs

(E) O–Cs–Al–F–Na

46. The critical pressure of a substance is a value that is necessary to:

(A) convert a gas to a solid at its critical temperature

(B) convert a liquid to a solid at its critical temperature

(C) freeze a liquid at its critical temperature

(D) liquefy a gas at its critical temperature

(E) vaporize a liquid at its critical temperature

47. For the single-step reaction $PCl_5 \rightarrow PCl_3 + Cl_2$, the rate of the reaction is proportional to:

(A) $[Cl_2] \times [PCl_3]$

(B) $[PCl_5]$

(C) $\dfrac{[Cl_2] \times [PCl_3]}{[PCl_5]}$

(D) $\dfrac{[PCl_5]}{[Cl_3] \times [PCl_3]}$

(E) $[PCl_5 \times [PCl_3 \times [Cl_2$

48. What is the molar mass of C_2H_4O, in g/mol?

(A) 12

(B) 22

(C) 32

(D) 44

(E) 60

49. Show phases, $H_2\ (g) + S\ (s) \leftrightarrow H_2S\ (g) + energy$

$H_2 + S \leftrightarrow H_2S\ (g) + energy$

In this equilibrium, select the factor that will shift the reaction to the right:

(A) adding heat

(B) adding H_2S

(C) removing hydrogen gas

(D) removing hydrogen sulfide gas

(E) removing sulfur

50. What mass in grams of sodium hydroxide, NaOH, would be needed to create 2.0 liters of a 0.40-molar solution of NaOH?

(A) 0.8

(B) 8.0

(C) 16

(D) 19.2

(E) 32

51. Which of the following shows the highest conductivity in aqueous solution

    (A) alcohol

    (B) distilled H_2O

    (C) glucose

    (D) hydrochloric acid

    (E) sucrose

52. $HC_2H_3O_2 \leftrightarrow H^+ + C_2H_3O_2$

    Consider the above equation.

    0.5 moles/liter of acetic acid dissociates into hydrogen and acetate ions. The equilibrium concentration of the hydrogen ions is 2.9×10^{-3} moles/liter. The ionization constant for the acid is

    (A) 1.7×10^{-5}

    (B) 8×10^{-2}

    (C) 4×10^{-1}

    (D) 4×10^{-2}

    (E) 4×10^2

53. The pOH of a 1×10^{-4} M KOH solution is:

    (A) 1

    (B) 2

    (C) 4

    (D) 7

    (E) 11

54. Carbon's valence shell electron configuration can be symbolized as:

    (A) $2s^1 2p^1$

    (B) $2s^1 2p^2$

    (C) $2s^2 2p^2$

    (D) $2s^2 2p^4$

    (E) $2s^4 2p^2$

55. What is the approximate percent composition of oxygen in magnesium oxide, MgO?

    (A) 12%

    (B) 20%

    (C) 32%

    (D) 40%

    (E) 80%

56. What would be the most likely rate law for the mechanism below?

    Step one: $A + B \leftrightarrow I$ fast equilibrium
    Step two: $C + I \rightarrow D$ slow step

    Total reaction: $A + B + C \rightarrow D$

    (A)   Rate $= k\,[A]\,[B]$

    (B)   Rate $= k\,[A]\,[B]\,[C]$

    (C)   Rate $= k\,[C]$

    (D)   Rate $= k\,[C]\,[I]$

    (E)   Can't be determined from the information given

57. $\_\_H_2S + \_\_O_2 \rightarrow \_\_H_2O + \_\_SO_2$

    Balancing this equation yields the following coefficients from left to right:

    (A)   1-1-2-2   (D)   3-2-2-2

    (B)   2-3-2-2   (E)   3-2-3-2

    (C)   2-2-2-3

58. The volume in milliliters of a 0.3 M solution of NaOH needed to neutralize 3 liters of a 0.01M HCl solution is:

    (A)   .1   (D)   100

    (B)   1   (E)   1000

    (C)   10

59. The outline for a molecular sub-unit for a saturated fat molecule is depicted at:

(A)
```
            O
            ‖
      H – C
            |
      H – C – OH
            |
   HO – C – H
            |
      H – C – OH
            |
      H – C – OH
            |
      H – C – OH
            |
            H
```

(B)
```
            O
            ‖
   HO – C – C = C = C = C = C – C –
```

(C)
```
          O  H  H  H  H
          ‖  |  |  |  |
   HO – C – C –C – C – C
             |  |  |  |
             H  H  H  H
```

(D)
```
   H      H  O
    \     |  ‖
      N – C – C – OH
    /     |
   H      R
```

(E)
```
         H   H
          \ /
   H       C       H
    \     / \     /
      C       C
    /           \
   H             H
```

60. An ice cube is placed in an open glass of water at room temperature. Describe the resultant effect on its energy content and entropy.

	Energy	Entropy
(A)	decrease	decrease
(B)	increase	increase
(C)	increase	decrease
(D)	increase	remains constant
(E)	remains constant	increase

61. The K_{sp} PbCrO$_4$ is 1.0×10^{-16}. What is the molar solubility of PbCrO$_4$ in a solution with pH 4?

(A) 1.0×10^{-4} (D) 1.0×10^{-20}

(B) 1.0×10^{-8} (E) 1.0×10^{-22}

(C) 1.0×10^{-16}

62. Solid zinc oxide, ZnO, has a heat of formation of about -84 kilocalories per mole. Select the correct statement for a reaction producing 162 grams of zinc oxide.

(A) 42 kilocalories are absorbed

(B) 81 kilocalories are absorbed

(C) 81 kilocalories are released

(D) 168 kilocalories are absorbed

(E) 168 kilocalories are released

63. One mole of a substance dissolved in 1000 grams of water elevates the boiling point by .52°C and depresses the freezing point by 1.86°C. 23 grams of an alcohol, C_2H_5OH, is dissolved in a kilogram of water. At standard conditions, water's new boiling and freezing points are respectively (in °C):

(A) 100.26°, −.93°   (D) 100.52°, −1.86°

(B) .26°, −1.86°   (E) 101.04°, −1.86°

(C) .52°, −.93°

64. Select the correct solubility rule:

    (A) All ammonium salts are insoluble.

    (B) All nitrates are insoluble.

    (C) All silver salts, except $AgNO_3$ are insoluble.

    (D) All sodium salts are insoluble.

    (E) Sulfides of sodium, potassium, and magnesium are insoluble.

65. A salt formed by a neutralization reaction of a strong acid and weak base is:

    (A) HCl

    (B) NaCl

    (C) Na_2CO_3

    (D) NH_4Cl

    (E) NH_4CN

66. Substances are neither created nor destroyed, but simply changed from one form to another. This is the law of:

    (A) change of matter

    (B) conservation of energy

    (C) conservation of matter

    (D) multiple proportions

    (E) second law of thermodynamics

67. FeS_2 or "fool's gold" is also known as

    (A) hematite

    (B) lodestone

    (C) magnetite

    (D) pyrite

    (E) siderite

68. Members of a common horizontal row of the periodic table should have the same:

    (A) atomic number

    (B) atomic mass

    (C) electron number in the outer shell

    (D) number of energy shells

    (E) valence

69. The most common isotope of hydrogen has an atomic number and mass, respectively, of:

    (A) 1,0   (D) 2,1

    (B) 1,1   (E) 2,2

    (C) 1,2

70. 500 mL of a gas experiences a pressure change from 760 mm of mercury pressure to a barometric pressure of 800. If all other laboratory factors are held constant, its new volume in mL is:

    (A) 400   (D) 525

    (B) 425   (E) 595

    (C) 475

71. An atom's electron number is 11 while the number of neutrons is 12. Its atomic mass is:

    (A) 11/12   (D) 23

    (B) 11   (E) 132

    (C) 12

72. The following chart depicts the ionization constants (K_a) for a number of weak acids. If you had a 1.0-molar solution of each acid, which would have the highest pH?

Acid	K_a
HSO_2^-	1.2×10^{-2}
HNO_2	4.0×10^{-4}
HF	7.2×10^{-4}
HOCl	3.5×10^{-8}
HCN	6.2×10^{-10}

(A) HSO_2^- (D) HOCl

(B) HNO_2 (E) HCN

(C) HF

73. What is the ratio of the rate of effusion of helium gas (molar mass = 4.0 g/mol) to the rate of effusion of oxygen gas (molar mass = 32.0 g/mol) at the same temperature and pressure?

(A) 2   (D) 8.0

(B) 4   (E) 16.0

(C) 0.125

74. 44.8 liters of a gas are collected in a lab under standard conditions. The number of molecules in this volume is:

(A) 112,000   (D) 18.06×10^{23}

(B) 6.02×10^{23} (E) 1,112,000

(C) 12.04×10^{23}

75. The second law of Thermodynamics states that:

(A) Energy is neither created nor destroyed, but changed from one form to another.

(B) Gas pressures are determined independently in a mixture

(C) Heat flows to a more concentrated medium.

(D) Matter is neither created nor destroyed.

(E) Spontaneous process tend toward increasing disorder.

AP Chemistry

Practice Exam 2

Section II

TIME: 90 minutes
55% of the entire test

(Answer sheets appear in the back of this book.)

The percentages given for the parts represent the score weightings for this section of the examination. You will be given 40 minutes for Part A and 50 minutes for Part B.

You may use a calculator on Part A, but not on Part B.

Be sure to write your answers in the space provided following each question. Pay attention to significant figures.

Part A

TIME: 40 minutes
40 percent

YOU MAY USE A CALCULATOR ON THIS PART.

Show your work clearly for full credit. Pay attention to significant figures in your answers.

Solve the following problem.

1. The value for the ionization constant, K_a, for hypochlorous acid, HOCl, is 3.2×10^{-8}.

    (a) Calculate the pH of a 0.030-molar solution of HOCl.

    (b) Calculate the percent dissociation of the solution in (A).

(c) Calculate the hydrogen ion concentration of a solution prepared by mixing equal volumes of a 0.030-molar HOCl and a 0.020-molar solution of sodium hypochlorite, NaOCl.

(d) Calculate the pH at which 50 mL of the 0.030 M HOCl solution is at the equivalence point after adding 50 mL of a standard NaOH solution.

(e) What needs to be added to the solution in part (C) to create a solution of maximum buffering ability?

Solve EITHER problem 2 or problem 3 in this part. A second problem will not be scored. (The problem you choose will be worth 20% of the score on Part II.)

2. Iron reacts with oxygen gas to form rust according to the following equation,

$$2 \, Fe \, (s) + 3/2 \, O_2 \, (g) \rightarrow Fe_2O_3 \, (s) \qquad \Delta H°_f = -824 \text{ kJ/mol}$$

(a) 25.0 grams of Fe (s) is mixed with 20.0 L of oxygen gas at 3.00 atm and 25 °C. What mass of iron oxide is produced?

(b) Identify the limiting reactant in this reaction. Support your conclusion with calculations.

(c) What further amount of mass of the limiting reactant would be needed to use up the remainder of the other reactant?

(d) What is the $\Delta S°$ for the reaction when it is just barely spontaneous?

3. The following data was collected for the reaction, $A \rightarrow B + C$.

Time (sec):	0	900	1800
[A] @ 25 °C:	50.8	19.7	7.62
[A] @ 35 °C:	80.0	26.7	8.90

(a) What is the rate law for the reaction?

(b) Calculate the specific rate constant and determine its units.

(c) Describe how to calculate the half-life from this information.

(d) Determine the energy of activation for this reaction.

(e) What will be the approximate concentration of A after 40 minutes (at 25 °C)?

Part B

TIME: 50 minutes

YOU MAY NOT USE A CALCULATOR ON THIS PART.

4. This question is worth 15% of Section II. Write the formulas of the reactants and products for FIVE of the following eight reactions. Show net ionic reactions only, where appropriate. Assume the reaction takes place in aqueous solution unless otherwise specified. Do not balance the reaction.

(a) A piece of zinc is placed in an aqueous solution of nitric acid.

(b) Nitrogen gas is combined with hydrogen gas under pressure in the presence of a catalyst.

(c) Zinc reacts with hydrochloric acid.

(d) Sulfur dioxide is mixed with hydrogen sulfide gas.

(e) Hydrogen is passed over heated solid iron (III) oxide.

(f) Hydrogen chloride is heated with oxygen in the presence of a catalyst.

(g) Iron oxide and aluminum are heated at a high temperature.

(h) Magnesium is burned in pure oxygen.

ANSWER BOTH OF THE FOLLOWING ESSAY QUESTIONS (15% each).

5. A student uses a bomb calorimeter to calculate the molar heat of combustion of a hydrocarbon.

(a) What are the units of the heat capacity of the calorimeter?

(b)   What information would you need to calculate the heat capacity of the calorimeter?

(c)   Describe how to calculate the heat of combustion per kg for the hydrocarbon using the calorimeter.

(d)   What is the most typical type of error that this student will get in her measurement, and in which direction will this error push the results?

ANSWER THE FOLLOWING LABORTATORY-BASED ESSAY QUESTION.

6.   You are given three unlabeled bottles, each containing small samples of one of the following metals: magnesium, aluminum, and silver. You are also given samples of the following reagents: pure water, a 1.0-molar solution of HCl, and a solution of concentrated nitric acid.

(a)   Which metal can be easily identified because it is much softer than the others? What chemical test using the available reagents would you use to confirm your conclusion?

(b)   Determine a chemical test using an available reagent that would distinguish between the two remaining metals.

(c)   Write a balanced equation for the one metal that reacts with concentrated nitric acid.

(d)   Which of the reagent solutions could be used to identify the existence of Pb^{2+} ions in solution? Write a balanced chemical reaction that would identify the lead ions.

ANSWER QUESTION 7 OR QUESTION 8 BELOW. ONLY ONE OF THESE TWO QUESTIONS WILL BE GRADED.

7.   Use your understanding of chemistry to give an explanation for each of the following.

(a)   He and Xe are both Nobel gases. Explain why compounds can be formed with Xe, but not with He.

(b)   Both fluorine and iodine are group VIIA elements. However, at 25 °C, F_2 is a gas, but I_2 is a solid.

(c) BH_3 is an acid, but NH_3 is a base.

(d)   The second ionization energy of potassium is much higher than the second ionization energy of magnesium, even though they are next to each other on the periodic table.

8.   A student is given two vials of two isomers of 2,3-dichloro,2-butene, $C_4H_6Cl_2$, and is asked to distinguish between the two molecules.

(a)   Draw the two possible isomers of this molecule.

(b)   Compare the hybridization of each of the four carbon atoms in the molecule.

(c)   How many pi bonds occur in this molecule, and where is (are) it (they) located?

(d)   Pi bonds are broken upon heating before sigma bonds. The student heats a mixture of the two isomers, the pi bond is broken, and at high temperatures the molecule freely rotates around each sigma bond. Which of the two isomers will natural re-form in greatest abundance, and why?

(e)   How can the student use melting points to distinguish between the two isomers?

AP Chemistry

Practice Exam 2

ANSWER KEY

Section I

1.	(D)	26.	(D)	51.	(D)
2.	(D)	27.	(B)	52.	(A)
3.	(B)	28.	(E)	53.	(C)
4.	(D)	29.	(B)	54.	(C)
5.	(A)	30.	(B)	55.	(D)
6.	(B)	31.	(E)	56.	(B)
7.	(D)	32.	(C)	57.	(B)
8.	(C)	33.	(C)	58.	(D)
9.	(A)	34.	(A)	59.	(C)
10.	(A)	35.	(E)	60.	(B)
11.	(B)	36.	(C)	61.	(B)
12.	(D)	37.	(A)	62.	(E)
13.	(C)	38.	(D)	63.	(A)
14.	(C)	39.	(C)	64.	(C)
15.	(C)	40.	(B)	65.	(D)
16.	(D)	41.	(A)	66.	(C)
17.	(C)	42.	(B)	67.	(D)
18.	(B)	43.	(B)	68.	(D)
19.	(C)	44.	(D)	69.	(B)
20.	(D)	45.	(C)	70.	(C)
21.	(E)	46.	(D)	71.	(D)
22.	(E)	47.	(B)	72.	(E)
23.	(D)	48.	(D)	73.	(B)
24.	(C)	49.	(D)	74.	(C)
25.	(A)	50.	(E)	75.	(E)

DETAILED EXPLANATIONS OF ANSWERS

Practice Exam 2

Section I

1.   **(D)**   Nonmetals tend to accept electrons to obey the octet rule. They have five or more electrons in their valence shell. Atom Y has seven, being very active and close to fulfillment.

2.   **(D)**   Z has four electrons. Four hydrogens, each with one electron, can share and fulfill Z with its remaining four. Hydrogen is also satisfied, gaining a second electron for fulfillment of its only energy shell. Four covalent bonds are formed.

3.   **(B)**   With 5 valence electrons, D is in need of 3 more for octet fulfillment.

4.   **(D)**   5.   **(A)**   6.   **(B)**   The two choices are general principles comparing solids and liquids for rapidity of particle movement and intermolecular distance. Liquid water does not freeze and become a solid until $0°$ C. Mercury, unlike most metals, is a liquid at room temperature.

7.   **(D)**   8.   **(C)**   9.   **(A)**   The most common oxygen-containing salt ends in the suffix "ate": $NaClO_3$ = sodium chlorate. Chlorine's oxidation state is +5, as sodium's is +1, and oxygen's total is -6 (3×-2). +5 and +1 balance the -6 oxidation state. The next lowest chlorine oxidation state ends in "ite": sodium chlorite, $NaClO_2$. Chlorine's oxidation state here is +3, along with sodium's +1 and oxygen's total -4. The next lowest chlorine oxidation state uses the "hypo. . .ite" prefix-suffix: $NaClO \rightarrow$ Na is +1, Cl is +1 and O is -2. The next lowest state uses the "ide" suffix: NaCl, sodium chloride. Chlorine's oxidation state is -1 to sodium's +1.

10.   **(A)**   11.   **(B)**   12.   **(D)**   13.   **(C)**   Alkanes have the general molecular formula C_nH_{2n+2}, such as butane, C_2H_6. Alkenes conform to C_nH_{2n}, for example butene, C_2H_4. Alkynes, CnH_{2n-2}, include butyne,

C_2H_2. Alcohols, such as butyl alcohol, include an OH in the carbon chain. Amines are nitrogen derivatives, and are not represented.

14. **(C)** $HC_2H_3O_2$ / $C_2H_3O_2^-$ is the only conjugate acid/base pair, each of which is different from the other by only a proton. Cu / Cu^{++} are different from each other by two electrons. N_2 / NH_3 are different from each by hydrogen atoms—protons and electrons. $Al(OH)_3$ / $[Al(OH)_4]^-$ are different by a hydroxide ion. PbI_2 / Pb^{2+} are different by two iodine atoms.

15. **(C)** Since nitrogen is in the second row, its highest energy electron is at n = 2, which is the first number. The second number signifies that its outer electron is in a p-orbital. The third number indicates the third p-orbital to receive an electron, since nitrogen is the third element in the p-block in the periodic table. The last number is the magnetic spin quantum number and signifies that the highest energy electron is the only electron in the orbital.

16. **(D)** The enthalpy of combustion for hydrogen, upon close inspection, is actually the same as the heat of formation for water.

$$\Delta H°_{reaction} = \Sigma H°_f \text{(products)} - \Sigma H°_f \text{(reactants)}$$

$$\Delta H°_{reaction} = -285.85 \text{ kJ/mol}$$

17. **(C)** Reaction rates of inorganic substances usually double with every 10°C increase in temperature. Therefore, if 35°C represents the new, doubled rate, then the original temperature must be 10° less: 35°C – 10°C = 25°C.

18. **(B)** The order is not derived from the stoichiometric coefficients unless it is understood to be a single step mechanism. The order is found from adding two exponents from the rate equation Rate = k $[A]^x[B]^y$ where order = x + y.

19. **(C)** Other color indicator changes are: congo red 4, malachite green 12, phenophthalein 9, thymol blue 3.

20. **(D)** Both pressures represent standard pressure while 25°C is considered the thermodynamic standard state; standard temperature for gases is 0°C, or 273K.

21. **(E)** By temperature conversion, C = 5/9 (F –32). C = 5/9 (122 – 32) = 50. A Centigrade value is converted to Kelvin by adding the constant 273: 50 + 273 = 323.

22. **(E)**   Two moles (4 grams) of hydrogen gas react with one mole (32 grams) of oxygen gas in this balanced reaction. Six grams of H_2 are 3 moles. By simple proportion, 1.5 moles of O_2 must react. One mole occupies 22.4 L at STP. 1.5 moles occupy 33.6 liters by simple proportion.

23. **(D)**   With atomic number 19 (19 electrons), the electrons will fill up n = 1 (2 electrons), n = 2 (8 electrons), and the s and p orbitals of n = 3. This array places potassium in group one of the periodic table.

24. **(C)**   Isotopes of an element have the same atomic number but their atomic mass varies due to a varying number of neutrons. This question compares two isotopes of oxygen.

25. **(A)**   Two electrons from calcium satisfy oxygen's requirement for eight valence electrons to obey the octet rule. They thus combine in a one-to-one ratio, CaO.

26. **(D)**   Beta rays consist of negatively charged particles moving close to the speed of light. Alpha rays are positive, and penetrating gamma rays are high frequency, near X-rays. All affect a photographic plate, a trait that led to their initial detection.

27. **(B)**   Cobalt is in group two of the periodic table and hence has two valence electrons. All elements of a given numbered family have that common valence electron number.

28. **(E)**   Iodine is at the bottom of the halogens in family seven of the periodic table. Elements that appear at the bottom of any family have more energy levels and are larger in size.

29. **(B)**   All of the choices are formed throughout the various steps of radioactive $^{238}_{92}U$ decay. $^{206}_{82}Pb$ is thus associated with $^{238}_{92}U$ in nature. The relative amounts of the two, along with knowledge of half-life periods, can be used to calculate the age of a geological structure harboring these two atoms.

30. **(B)**   The alkali metals are in family one of the period table. They are progressively more active as metals, losing their one valence electron as they descend through the vertical array.

31. **(E)** Xe, xenon, is found in family eight of the periodic table, the noble gases. All other choices are active metals or nonmetals of other families.

32. **(C)** Dalton's laws of partial pressures state that gases in a mixture exert their individual pressures independently.

33. **(C)** By the balanced equation, two moles (244 grams) of $KClO_3$ yield 3 moles of O_2 (96 grams). By simple proportion:

$$\frac{(2KClO_3-)}{3O_3} = \frac{244}{96} = \frac{x}{72} \text{ so } x = 183$$

34. **(A)** The equilibrium constant for the listed reaction is $1/K_b$, which, since $K_w = K_a \times K_b$, then equals K_a/K_w.

35. **(E)** With an atomic number of 21, the electron and proton numbers are each 21. For a mass of 45, 24 neutrons must exist with the 21 protons.

36. **(C)** An alpha particle consists of two protons and two neutrons as in a helium nucleus, $_2^4He$. In the bombardment, boron incorporates the two protons for an atomic number increase from 5 to 7. These two protons plus one captured neutron yield an atomic mass increase from 11 to 14, thus $_7^{14}N$ as in nitrogen. The second neutron remains free.

37. **(A)** Carbon is neither a strong metal nor a strong nonmetal and has less electron-attracting power than the strong nonmetals bromine, chlorine, fluorine, and oxygen, in their covalent bond formation.

38. **(D)** Methane, CH_4, is a symmetrical molecule in terms of the direction of its four covalent bonds. Each C–H bond is at an approximate 109 degree bond angle, oriented toward the corner of an imaginary tetrahedron, (a four-sided figure).

39. **(C)** Metals in family one and two of the periodic table have these characteristics. Note lithium's location in the periodic table.

40. **(B)** The respective cations, H+ and Na+, and anions, Cl⁻ and OH⁻, swap places in the change from reactants to products.

41. **(A)**   One mole of FeS, 88 grams (56 + 32) forms one mole of H_2S gas in the balanced equation. By simple proportion, one-quarter mole of the given 22 grams, thus yields one-quarter mole of H_2S. One mole of a gas fills 22.4 liters; thus .25 mole × 22.4 liters = 5.6 liters.

42. **(B)**   One mole of sucrose is 342 grams:

C 12 × 12 (atomic weight of carbon)   = 144 g
H 22 × 1 (atomic weight of hydrogen) =   22 g
O 11 × 16 (atomic weight of oxygen)   = 176 g

These total 342 grams; 342 grams in one liter makes a 1M-strength solution. In one-half liter, 500 ml, this measured amount is also halved.

43. **(B)**   Among reactants, uncombined potassium is 0. Hydrogen is +1 metallic behavior and chlorine is −1 (nonmetal) while combined in a compound. Among products, potassium is now combined, +1 (metal). Chlorine remains −1 as combined. Liberated hydrogen is uncombined as a liberated gas, 0.

44. **(D)**   Enzymes are proteins which act as catalysts for biochemical reactions.

45. **(C)**   Electronegativity is electron-attracting power. Fluorine, in the upper right-hand corner of the periodic table, is the most active nonmetal and has the highest electronegativity. Oxygen follows as very active. Aluminum is a metal, which means less electronegativity: it actually donates electrons. Sodium and cesium are metals, too, and cesium has the least electronegativity.

46. **(D)**   For each gas, a temperature is reached where the kinetic energy of the molecules is so great that no pressure, however large, can liquefy the gas. Any pressure is insufficient to compress gas molecules back to the liquid state where molecules are closer together. This temperature is the critical temperature. The accompanying pressure is the critical pressure.

47. **(B)**   For the general reaction

$$A \rightarrow B + C$$

The rate is written as

$$\text{rate} = [A]^n$$

where n is the experimentally determined order of the reaction. The only answer which conforms with the rate as written above is (B), i.e. rate [PCl_5]. In this case, n = 1.

48. **(D)**   The molar mass is found by adding the atomic masses of each atom in the formula. $(2 \times 12.011) + (4 \times 1.008) + (16) = 44$ g/mol.

49. **(D)**   The left-to-right reaction is exothermic, therefore, adding heat drives the reaction equilibrium to the left. From the equilibrium constant

$$K_{eq} = \frac{[H_2S]}{[H_2]\,[S]}$$

it is clear that an increase in the concentration of H_2S increases the value of this ratio, *i.e.*, the equilibrium is disturbed. To return to the equilibrium constant value, H_2S decomposes, so that the reaction is shifted to the left. Blocking H_2 removes reactant, inhibiting formation to the right side. Removing S has the same effect. Removing H_2S, however, lowers the value of the equilibrium constant. To restore it, more H_2S is produced, *i.e.*, the reaction shifts to the right. The above analysis is the application of Le Chatelier's principle.

50. **(E)**

$$32\ g = 2.0\ L\ solution \times \frac{04.0\ mol\ NaOH}{L\ NaOH\ solution} \times \frac{40\ g\ NaOH}{1\ mol\ NaOH}$$

51. **(D)**   Hydrochloric acid, HCl, almost completely ionizes in solution, therefore allows passage of electricity; *i.e.*, it acts as a conductor. The other four choices do not ionize.

52. **(A)**   For a reaction HA $\leftrightarrow$ H^+ + A^-, given initial concentrations:

[x] $\leftrightarrow$ 0 + 0 and equilibrium concentrations: [x–y] $\leftrightarrow$ [y]+[y], then the ionization constant K_a is

$$K_a = \frac{[y]\,[y]}{[x - y]}$$

$$K_a = \frac{[y]^z}{[x - y]}$$

If x >> y (x is much greater than y), then

$$K_a \sim \frac{[y]^2}{x}$$

In our example, $x = 0.5$ moles/L and $y = 2.9 \times 10^{-3}$; therefore

$$K_a = \frac{(2.9 \times 10^{-3})^2}{0.5 - 0.0029} \approx \frac{8.41 \times 10^{-6}}{0.5}$$

$$K_a = 16.82 \times 10^{-6} \approx 1.7 \times 10^{-5}$$

53. **(C)**   pOH is negative the log of a solution's hydroxyl ion concentration. A .0001M KOH solution furnishes 10^{-4} hydroxyl ions in moles per liter. Molarity and normality are the same for KOH, as it yields one hydroxyl ion per KOH unit. pOH = $-\log$ [OH–]; therefore pOH = $-\log 10^{-4}$ = 4.

54. **(C)**   Carbon has four valence electrons. Two occupy the smaller s orbital and the two remaining fill the larger p orbital.

55. **(D)**   Percent composition is found by dividing the mass contributed by one element by the total molar mass of the compound, then multiplying by 100%.

$$\frac{16 \text{ g O}}{40.31 \text{ g Mg O}} \times 100\% = 39.69\% = 40\%$$

56. **(B)**   The rate-determining step depends on the intermediate, I, which can be expressed in terms of A and B using the prior fast equilibrium step. Thus, in this mechanism, the rate is not proportional to just I and C, but A, B, and C.

57. **(B)**   Three molecules of O_2 (6 atoms) supply 2 water molecules (2 oxygen atoms) and 2 sulfur dioxide molecules (4 atoms). Four hydrogen atoms from H_2S (2×2) also supply the four hydrogens in the water produced (2×2).

58. **(D)**   The acid and base react by the equation:

$$HCl + NaOH \rightarrow HCl + H_2O.$$

Each compound donates single ions to form an NaCl unit. By this assumption: molarity of an acid x volume of an acid = (normality of a base) x (volume of a base).

By substitution:

$$0.01 \times 3 = 0.3 \times V_2$$

$$V_2 = \frac{0.01 \times 3 \text{ liters}}{0.3} = 0.1 \text{ liter}$$

0.1 liter = 100 mL

59. **(C)** Illustration A shows the molecular formula of glucose. (D) shows an amino acid's formula. (E) is cyclopropane. Both (B) and (C) are outlines of fatty acids. (B), however, is not saturated with hydrogen atoms, covalently bonded to its carbon chain. This is because of the double C–to–C bonds, limiting availability for hydrogen covalent bonding. Carbon's valence is four. The carbon atoms in illustration (C) are single bonded, leaving more bonding sites for hydrogen atoms. It is relatively saturated with these atoms. Fatty acids are the molecular sub-units of fat molecules.

60. **(B)** The ice cube will melt by gaining heat from the water. The temperature of the water drops below room temperature; therefore heat flows from the surroundings into the water until room temperature is attained. The resultant effect is an increase in energy for the ice and the water system. When the ice melts, it changes from an ordered to a disordered system. Entropy is a measure of disorder (randomness). The higher the disorder, the higher the entropy. In this case, energy and entropy both increase.

61. **(B)** The molar solubility can be found by equating the solubility product constant to the product of the molar concentrations of the dissolved ions. Therefore, in this case, the molar solubility is simply the square root of the solubility product constant of $PbCrO_4$.

$$x^2 = 1.0 \times 10^{-16}$$

$$x = 1.0 \times 10^{-8}$$

62. **(E)** Zinc oxide's formula weight is 81 (65 + 16). Therefore, 162 grams is twice this weight or two moles. If one mole liberates 84 calories, two liberates twice that amount of energy. The minus sign indicates energy liberation.

63. **(A)** The alcohol's molecular weight is 46: 24 (C_2) + 6 (6H) + 16 (O). Twenty-three grams is one-half mole. It, therefore, changes boiling and freezing points by one-half the stated increments.

64. **(C)** The other statements are the opposite of what is correct due to substances' ability to ionize (soluble) or not ionize (insoluble) among the molecules of the solvent water. Silver salts form insoluble precipitates except for the ionizing silver nitrate, $AgNO_3$.

65. **(D)** HCl is an acid. NaCl is formed from a strong acid and strong base. Na_2CO_3 is a product of a weak acid and strong base. NH_4CN is produced from two weak compounds. A strong acid, HCl, and weak base NH_4OH, react to produce NH_4Cl.

66. **(C)** This is a law applied every time an equation is balanced.

67. **(D)** Hematite is Fe_2O_3. Magnetite or lodestone is Fe_3O_4. Siderite is $FeCO_3$. All choices given are the most common iron ores in the earth's crust.

68. **(D)** The number of energy shells stays constant with the valence electrons tending to increase from left to right. Atomic numbers and mass change for each element.

69. **(B)** Hydrogen's most common atomic form has one proton and one electron.

70. **(C)** Boyle's law ($P_1V_1 = P_2V_2$) predicts an inverse pressure-volume relationship. A pressure increase means a volume decrease. The multiplied fraction is thus less than one:

$$500 \times \frac{760}{800} = 475$$

71. **(D)** Atomic mass is the sum of protons and neutrons. In a neutral atom, the number of positive protons equals the number of electrons. Hence, 11 is added to 12.

72. **(E)** The weakest acid, with the lowest K_a, would have the highest pH at any given concentration. HCN is by far the weakest acid on the list with the smallest ionization constant.

73. **(B)** Graham's law of effusion can be used to calculate how much faster hydrogen gas moves than oxygen gas.

$$\frac{M_{oxygen}}{M_{hydrogen}} = \frac{r_{hydrogen}^{2}}{r_{oxygen}^{2}} = \frac{32}{2} = 16$$

$(16)^{\frac{1}{2}} = 4$; hydrogen is 4 times faster than oxygen.

74. **(C)**   22.4 liters of a gas is occupied by one mole. This mole contains 6.02×10^{23} molecules, Avogadro's number. The given volume in this problem is twice that.

75. **(E)**   This is a strict statement of the law, predicting that the universe is gradually approaching randomness. Chemical reactions are a part of this.

Section II

1.

(a) $$HOCl\ (aq) \leftrightarrow H^+\ (aq) + OCl^-\ (aq)$$

Before equilibrium: 0.030 M   0   0

After equilibrium: 0.030 − x   x   x

$$K_a = \frac{(x^2)}{(0.030 - x)} = 3.2 \times 10^{-8}$$

$$x^2 = 3.2 \times 10^{-8} \times 0.030$$

$$x = [H^+] = 3.1 \times 10^{-5}; pH = -log\ [H^+]$$

$$pH = 4.50$$

(b)   Percent dissociation = 3.1×10^{-5} / $0.030 \times 100\% = 0.1\ \%$ dissociated

(c) $$[H^+] = \frac{K_a}{[OCl^-]} = \frac{(3.2 \times 10^{-8})\,(.03\ M)}{(.02\ M)} = 4.8 \times 10^{-8}\ M$$

(d) $HOCl\ (aq)$ + $OH- \leftrightarrow H_2O(aq) + OCl^-\ (aq)$

Before reaction: $.03 \times .05 = .0015$ mol   0   0

After reaction (mol):   0   0   0.0015 mol

After equilibrium (M):   x   x   0.0015 mol/.1L − x

$$K_b = \frac{(x^2)}{(0.015 - x)} = 3.1 \times 10^{-7}$$

$$x^2 = 3.1 \times 10^{-7} \times 0.015$$

$$x = [OH^-] = 6.8 \times 10^{-5}$$

$$[H^+] = 1.5 \times 10^{-10}$$

$$pH = 9.8$$

(e)   Additional sodium hypochlorite needs to be added so that the concentration of the weak acid equals the concentration of the weak base.

2.   (a)

$$25.0 \text{ g Fe} \times \frac{1 \text{ mol Fe}}{55.85 \text{ g Fe}} \times \frac{1 \text{ mol Fe}_2\text{O}_3}{2 \text{ mol Fe}} \times$$

$$\frac{159.7 \text{ g Fe}_2\text{O}_3}{1 \text{ mol Fe}_2\text{O}_3} = 35.74 \text{ g Fe}_2\text{O}_3$$

$$\frac{20.0 \text{ L} \times 3.0 \text{ atm K mol oxygen}}{.082 \text{ L atm } 298\text{K}} \times \frac{1 \text{ mol Fe}_2\text{O}_3}{1.5 \text{ mol oxygen}} \times$$

$$\frac{159.7 \text{ g Fe}_2\text{O}_3}{1 \text{ mol Fe}_2\text{O}_3} = 261 \text{ g Fe}_2\text{O}_3$$

Therefore, 35.74 g Fe_2O_3 is produced.

(b)   The calculations above demonstrate that iron (Fe) is the limiting reactant.

(c)

$$\text{total moles oxygen} = \frac{20.0 \text{ L} \times 3.0 \text{ atm K mol O}_2}{.082 \text{ L atm } 298\text{K}}$$

$$= 2.46 \text{ mol oxygen}$$

$$35.74 \text{ g Fe}_2\text{O}_3 \times \frac{1 \text{ mol Fe}_2\text{O}_3}{159.9 \text{ g Fe}_2\text{O}_3} \times \frac{1.5 \text{ mol O}_2}{1 \text{ mol Fe}_2\text{O}_3}$$

$$= 0.34 \text{ moles oxygen used}$$

moles oxygen to further react = total moles oxygen – moles used
= 2.46 – .34 = 2.12 moles

$$2.12 \text{ mol oxygen} \times \frac{2 \text{ mol Fe}}{1.5 \text{ mol O}_2} \times \frac{55.85 \text{ g Fe}}{1 \text{ mol Fe}} =$$

158 g Fe needs to be added

(d) $\Delta G° = \Delta H° - T\Delta S°$
$0 = \Delta H° - T\Delta S°$
$\Delta H° = T\Delta S°$
$\Delta S° = \Delta H°/T = -824 \text{ kJ}/ 298 \text{ K} = -2.7 \text{ kJ/K}$

3.   (a)   If the reaction is zero order, then the ratio of the change in concentration over time will be the same at any concentration. This can be tested by comparing any two concentration and time data points.

$$\frac{50.8 - 19.7}{900 - 0} = \frac{31.1}{900} = 0.0346$$

$$\frac{19.7 - 7.62}{1800 - 900} = \frac{12.08}{900} = 0.013$$

The two ratios do not match, so it is not a zero order.

If the reaction is first order, then the ratio of the change in the natural log of the concentration over time will be the same at any concentration.

$$\frac{\ln 50.8 / 19.7}{900} = \ln 2.58 / 900 = 0.001$$

$$\frac{\ln 19.7 / 7.62}{900} = \ln 2.58 / 900 = 0.001$$

The two ratios are identical, so the reaction is first order with respect to A.

(b)   The slope of the ratio calculated in the previous problem is the specific rate constant for the reaction.

$$k = \ln 2.58/900 = 0.001$$

The rate constant would be used in the rate law, where rate $= k$ [A]. The units of rate are M/sec; the units of [A] are M. Therefore, the units of the rate constant are 1/sec.

(c)   Half-life for first order reactions $= 0.693/k = 693$ sec

(d)   First find the specific rate constant at 35°C.

$$\frac{\ln 80 / 26.7}{900} = 0.0012 = k$$

Then use the following equation to find the activation energy.

$\ln (k_2/k_1) = E_a/R \ (1/T_1 - 1/T_2)$

$E_a = 8.31$ J/mol $(0.18)/0.00011 = 13600$ J/mol $= 13.6$ kJ/mol

(e)   The integrated rate law may be used to find the concentration at some time in the future.

$\ln[A] = -kt + \ln[A_{initial}] = -.001(2400) + \ln(50.8) = 1.53$

$[A] = e^{1.53} = 4.62 \text{ M}$

4. (a) $Zn \ (s) + 2HNO_3 \ (aq) \rightarrow Zn \ (NO_3)_2 \ (aq) + H_2$

   $Zn^0 + H^{+1} \ (aq) \rightarrow Zn^{+2} \ (aq) + H_2^0 \ (g)$

   (b) $N_2 \ (g) + 3H_2 \ (g) \rightarrow 2NH_3$

   $N^0 + H_2^0 \rightarrow N^{-3} \ H^{+1}$

   (c) $Zn \ (s) + 2HCl \rightarrow ZnCl_2 + H_2 \ (g)$

   $Zn^0 + H^{+1} \rightarrow Zn^{+2} + H^0$

   (d) $8SO_2 + 16H_2S \rightarrow 3S_8 + 16H_2O$

   $S^{+4} + S^{-2} \rightarrow S^0$

   (e) $Fe_2O_3 \ (s) + 3H_2 \ (g) \rightarrow 2Fe \ (s) + 3H_2O$

   $Fe^{+3} + H_2^0 \rightarrow Fe^0 + H^{+1}$

   (f) $4HCl \ (g) + O_2 \ (g) \rightarrow 2H_2O + 2Cl \ (g)$

   $Cl^{-1} + O_2^0 \rightarrow O^{-2} + Cl^0$

   (g) $Fe_2O_3 + 2Al \rightarrow Al_2O_3 + 2Fe$

   $Fe^{+3} + Al^0 \rightarrow Al^{+3} + Fe^0$

   (h) $2Mg + O_2 \rightarrow 2MgO$

   $Mg^0 + O_2^0 \rightarrow Mg^{+2}O^{-2}$

5. (a) The units for the calorimeter's heat capacity are J/°C or J/K, and represent the amount of heat that must be absorbed by the calorimeter in order to raise the temperature of the calorimeter by one degree or one Kelvin.

   (b) One would need to measure the temperature of the calorimeter when a specific amount of heat was added.

   (c) One would need to allow the reaction to proceed inside the calorimeter and measure the change in temperature of the calorimeter. Be sure to measure the amount of reactant that reacted, so that the amount of heat can be attributed to a specific amount of kg.

(d)   The typical error for calorimeters is that some of the heat of the reaction will be absorbed by the surroundings, and not all of the heat will go into raising the temperature of the calorimeter.

6.   (a)   Magnesium is much softer than the other metals. Also, the magnesium will readily produce hydrogen gas in a 1.0 molar HCl solution. Aluminum will eventually react slowly, but drastically so; and silver will not react at all.

(b)   Silver will react with nitric acid, but aluminum will not because of the protective oxide coating around it.

(c) $Ag + HNO_3 + H^+ \rightarrow Ag^+ + NO_2 + H_2O$

The oxidation state of nitrogen decreases by one, and the oxidation state of silver increases by one.

(d)   The hydrochloric acid will react with the soluble lead ions to produce a cloudy precipitate of lead (II) chloride. $Hcl + Pb \rightarrow PbCl_2$

7.   (a)   Xe will form compounds with highly electronegative elements. Expanded octets exist when a large molecule (such as Xe) is combined with a highly electronegative element (such as F). The electronegativity of one element draws into hybridization some of the electrons in the d-orbitals in the larger element, which allows for more than four bonds around the central atom. The He atom is very small; the electrons are held closely to the nucleus, and are not accessible for bonding.

(b)   Iodine is a solid and fluorine is a gas because iodine has much greater intermolecular attraction as a result of Van der Waals forces, or London forces. These forces are proportional to the number of electrons in a compound. Iodine has over six times more electrons than fluorine.

(c)   The largest difference in these properties has its source in the different number of valence electrons in boron and nitrogen. Boron has only three valence electrons; when it is fully bonded to hydrogen, it can act as an electron acceptor (Lewis acid) to get a full octet around it. Nitrogen has two unbonded electrons around it in addition to those electrons involved with bonds to hydrogen. The two unbonded electrons can be donated as an electron pair (Lewis base) or accept a proton (Brønsted base) in a reaction. The difference of an electron pair makes the difference between making the molecule an acid or a base.

(d)   Potassium has only one electron in its outer s-orbital, and magnesium has two. Once the outer s-orbital electrons are removed (one for potassium, two for magnesium) then it takes significantly more energy to ionize an electron out of the inner p-orbital. Therefore, potassium sees a large jump in ionization energies after the first electron is removed. Magnesium sees a large jump in ionization energies after the second electron is removed.

8.   (a)

$$\begin{array}{ccc} CH_3 & & CH_3 \\ \backslash & & / \\ C & = & C \\ / & & \backslash \\ Cl & & Cl \end{array} \qquad \text{cis isomer}$$

$$\begin{array}{ccc} CH_3 & & Cl \\ \backslash & & / \\ C & = & C \\ / & & \backslash \\ Cl & & CH_3 \end{array} \qquad \text{trans isomer}$$

(b)   The methyl group carbons are sp^3 hybridized, while the carbons attached to double bonds are sp^2 hybridized.

(c)   There is only one pi bond in this molecule; it is between the second and third carbons.

(d)   The trans isomer will tend to re-form upon heating, because the larger methyl groups will take up space and hinder the formation of the cis isomer.

(e)   In the compound, 2,3-dichloro, 2-butene, we have two isomers, the cis- and trans-isomers. The cis- and trans-isomers are diastereisomers (i.e, stereoisomers that are not mirror images of each other) or in this case more specifically geometric isomers. This means that they have the same molecular formula, but the substituents (in this case the methyl groups and chlorine) are respectively positioned in the cis and trans positions.

Diastereoisomers have different physical properties such as melting point. The cis-isomer will have the lower melting point temperature, and the trans-isomer the higher melting point temperature, and therefore can be separated on the basis on the differences in melting point.

▼
Practice
Exam 3

AP Chemistry

Practice Exam 3

Section I

TIME: 90 minutes
45% of the entire test

(Answer sheets appear in the back of this book.)

DIRECTIONS: Each set of lettered choices below refers to the numbered questions or statements immediately following it. Select the one lettered choice that best answers each question. A choice may be used once, more than once, or not at all in each set.

Part A

Questions 1 - 4

    (A) grayish solid

    (B) greenish-yellow gas

    (C) pale-yellow gas

    (D) reddish-brown gas

    (E) reddish-brown liquid

1. Br_2

2. Cl_2

3. F_2

4. I_2

Questions 5 - 7

        (A) barium   (D) magnesium

        (B) beryllium   (E) strontium

        (C) calcium

5.   Major component of limestone

6.   Least active by oxidation

7.   Least dense

Questions 8 - 11 refer to energy levels and the maximum number of electrons they can hold.

        (A) eight   (D) twelve

        (B) eighteen   (E) two

        (C) thirty-two

8. $n = 1$

9. $n = 2$

10. $n = 3$

11. $n = 4$

Directions: Each of the following questions or incomplete sentences is followed by five possible answers. Choose the best one in each case.

---

12.   Which of the following aqueous solutions demonstrates the highest boiling point?

     (A) 1.0 M $MgCl_2$

     (B) 1.0 M NaCl

     (C) 1.0 M HCl

     (D) 1.0 M glucose

     (E) 2.0 M KNO_3

13. A Fahrenheit temperature is converted to a corresponding Centigrade (Celsius) value by the equation: $C = \frac{5}{9} (F - 32)$. A recorded Fahrenheit value is 82 degrees. Its value on the Kelvin temperature scale is approximately:

    (A) 355.0 K   (D) 246 K

    (B) 27.7 K   (E) 300.7 K

    (C) 83.7 K

14. Consider the balanced equation:

    Fe+S $\rightarrow$ FeS

    Approximately what amount of sulfur in grams must be available for 28 grams of iron to react to form the compound?

    (A) 1   (D) 32

    (B) 8   (E) 64

    (C) 16

15. An element's atom most commonly has the following listing of sub-atomic particles:

    6 protons, 6 neutrons, 6 electrons.

    Select the following listing of particles that reveal an isotope to this given atom.

    (A) 6 protons, 6 neutrons, 4 electrons

    (B) 6 protons, 6 neutrons, 8 electrons

    (C) 6 protons, 8 neutrons, 6 electrons

    (D) 8 protons, 6 neutrons, 6 electrons

    (E) 8 protons, 8 neutrons, 6 electrons

16. Select the element with an atomic number of 15 and 5 electrons in its valence shell.

    (A) chlorine   (D) phosphorus

    (B) nitrogen   (E) sulfur

    (C) oxygen

17. Aluminum has three valence electrons; sulfur has six. Which of the following represents the formula of the most likely compound to turn when aluminum and sulfur combine?

    (A) AlS   (D) Al_2S_3

    (B) AlS_2 (E) Al_3S_2

    (C) AlS_3

18. The correct ranking of halogens, from most reactive to least reactive, is:

    (A) Cl-F-Br-I   (D) I-Br-Cl-F

    (B) F-Cl-Br-I   (E) Ne-Cl-Br-I

    (C) He-I-Br-Cl

19. In the periodic table, metals with low melting points appear just to the left and below the nonmetals. A metal with a probable low melting point is:

    (A) cadmium   (D) selenium

    (B) iron   (E) rubidium

    (C) lithium

20. Select the incorrect statement about the kinetic theory of gases.

    (A) Average energy of each particle is the same regardless of mass.

    (B) Distances between their molecules are large.

(C)   Their molecules are imperfectly inelastic.

(D)   Their motion is constant.

(E)   Velocity of molecules increases with increasing temperature.

21.   96 grams of oxygen are produced by chemical reaction from ozone. The number of moles of ozone required to produce this amount of oxygen is:

(A)   1   (D)   5

(B)   2   (E)   10

(C)   3

22.   Consider the reaction under standard lab conditions:

$N_2 + 3H_2 \rightarrow 2NH_3$

If 6 grams of hydrogen gas reacts, the volume it occupies in liters is:

(A)   2   (D)   67.2

(B)   3   (E)   100

(C)   22.4

23.   Consider a mixture of oxygen and hydrogen. The velocity of oxygen's molecules is less than hydrogen's by a factor of:

(A)   1/2   (D)   1/16

(B)   1/4   (E)   1/32

(C)   1/8

24.   Consider the following balanced equation:

$Zn + H_2SO_4 \rightarrow ZnSO_4 + H_2$

Zinc's oxidation number changes in this reaction from:

(A) 0 to +2   (D) +2 to –2

(B) 0 to +4   (E) +2 to –4

(C) +2 to +4

25. An example that shows dipole-dipole inermolecular attraction is:

(A) CH_4 (D) NaCl

(B) H_2 (E) O_2

(C) H_2O

26. Which of the acids below has the formula $HBrO_2$?

(A) bromic   (D) hypobromous

(B) bromous   (E) perbromic

(C) hydrobromic

27. A correct ranking of elements in order of decreasing electronegativity is:

(A) Ca-Li-Ba-K-Ca   (D) F-Br-H-Al-Rb

(B) H-I-Na-K-Ca   (E) Na-O-C-Ca-Li

(C) Ca-Al-P-S-F

28. The formula for tin (II) hydroxide is:

(A) CuO   (D) $Sn(OH)_2$

(B) $Ni(OH)_2$ (E) $Sn(OH)_4$

(C) $Ni(OH)_3$

29. Determine the <u>incorrect</u> statement:

    (A) In a first order gaseous reaction, if we decrease the volume of the container where the reaction is taking place, the velocity of the reaction will decrease.

    (B) A catalyst creates a new path for the reaction which requires a smaller activation energy.

    (C) Activation energy is constant for a certain reaction.

    (D) By increasing the temperature of a reaction, we increase the amount of molecules with sufficient energy to react.

    (E) All intermolecular collisions result in chemical reactions.

30. $N_2 + 3H_2 \leftrightarrow 2NH_3$ (g) + heat

    In this reversible reaction, the equilibrium shifts to the right because of all the following factors <u>except</u>:

    (A) adding heat

    (B) adding reactant amounts

    (C) formation of ammonia gas

    (D) increasing pressure on reactants

    (E) yielding an escaping gas

31. Consider the following reversible reaction:

    $H_2 + 3N_2 \leftrightarrow 2NH_3$

    Its equilibrium constant "K" is expressed as:

    (A) $\dfrac{[NH_3]}{[N_2][H_2]^3}$

    (D) $[NH^3]$

    (B) $\dfrac{[NH_3]^2}{[N_2]^3[H_2]}$

    (E) $[N_2]^2[H_2]^3$

    (C) $\dfrac{[NH_3]}{[N_2][H_2]}$

32. Select the compound that is <u>not</u> a conductor in aqueous solution:

   (A) CH_3OH (D) NaCl

   (B) $CuSO_4$ (E) NaOH

   (C) HCl

33. $H_2CO_3 \leftrightarrow H^+ + HCO_3$

   0.5 moles/liter of carbonic acid dissociates hydrogen and carbonic ions at 0.1 mole per liter, each in a lab aqueous setting. Its ionization constant is:

   (A) 1×10^{-2} (D) 2×10^1

   (B) 2×10^{-2} (E) 2×10^2

   (C) 1×10^2

34. Consider the reaction:

   $2Al + 3S \rightarrow Al_2S_3$

   The oxidation numbers of aluminum and sulfur in the product are, respectively:

   (A) 1,1   (D) 3,2

   (B) −2,3   (E) 3,−2

   (C) 2,−3

35. Complete ionization of a calcium hydroxide molecule yields:

   (A) Ca^{++}, OH^- (D) $2Ca^{++}$, $2OH^-$

   (B) Ca^{++}, $2OH^-$ (E) $3Ca^{++}$, OH^-

   (C) $2Ca^{++}$, OH^-

36. The molar solubility of strontium fluoride, MgF_2, is 1×10^{-3} in pure water. What is the K_{sp} for MgF_2?

    (A) 4×10^{-3} (D) 2×10^{-3}

    (B) 4×10^{-6} (E) 1×10^{-3}

    (C) 4×10^{-9}

37. Which of the following is the least polar molecule?

    (A) H_2 (D) C_2H_2

    (B) H_2O (E) NaH

    (C) H_2S

38. A set of kinetic experiments for the decomposition of a molecule, A, were recorded in the data table below. What is the order of the reaction with respect to A?

Trial	[A]	Initial rate of formation of C (M/sec)
1	0.01	0.002
2	0.03	0.006

    (A) zero order

    (B) first order

    (C) second order

    (D) third order

    (E) sixth order

39. Oxygen's valence shell electron configuration can be symbolized as:

    (A) $2s^2\,2p^2$ (D) $2s^4\,2p^4$

    (B) $2s^2\,2p^4$ (E) $2s^4\,2p^6$

    (C) $2s^4\,2p^2$

40. Calcium has an atomic number of 20. Its electron configuration can be summarized as:

   (A) $1s^2\,2s^2\,2p^6\,3s^2\,3p^6\,4s^2$

   (B) $1s^2\,2s^2\,2p^6\,3s^2\,3p^4\,4s^4$

   (C) $1s^2\,2s^4\,2p^4\,3s^2\,3p^6\,4s^2$

   (D) $1s^1\,2s^4\,2p^4\,3s^2\,3p^6\,4s^4$

   (E) $1s^1\,2s^3\,2p^5\,3s^1\,3p^6\,4s^2$

41. Consider the following unbalanced equation. Coefficients are missing:

   $$\underline{}NH_3 + \underline{}O_2 \rightarrow \underline{}NO + \underline{}H_2O$$

   To balance the equation, the four consecutive coefficients from left to right are:

   (A) 4, 5, 4, 6   (D) 5, 5, 4, 6

   (B) 4, 4, 5, 6   (E) 6, 5, 4, 4

   (C) 5, 4, 5, 6

42. Consider the following balanced equation. How many moles of hydrogen sulfide react with one mole of oxygen?

   $$2H_2S + 3O_2 \rightarrow 2SO_2 + 2H_2O$$

   (A) 2/3   (D) 2

   (B) 3/2   (E) 3

   (C) 1

43. Hydrogen, nitrogen, and oxygen combine in the following amounts to form a compound:

   H = 3.18g   O = 152.64g   N = 44.52g

   The probable formula for the compound is:

(A) HNO_2 (D) H_2N_2O

(B) HNO_3 (E) H_3NO_2

(C) H_2NO_3

44. Select the <u>incorrect</u> statement about radiation.

(A) Alpha rays exhibit low penetrating power.

(B) Alpha ray particles consist of 2 neutrons and 2 protons.

(C) Beta ray particles can move close to the speed of light.

(D) Beta ray particles possess a positive charge.

(E) Gamma rays lack a possession of charge.

$$^{238}_{92}U \rightarrow {}^{234}_{90}Th \rightarrow {}^{234}_{91}Pa \rightarrow$$

45. The next disintegration occurs as a result of an emission of a beta particle and results in:

(A) $^{226}_{88}Ra$ (D) $^{234}_{92}U$

(B) $^{226}_{86}Pa$ (E) $^{232}_{90}U$

(C) $^{230}_{90}Th$

46. A positive subatomic particle which is about equal in mass to the electron is the:

(A) proton   (D) neutron

(B) hyperon   (E) positron

(C) muon

47. In 1919, Rutherford bombarded nitrogen gas with high speed alpha particles. Complete the following equation summarizing the results.

$$^{14}_{7}N + {}^{4}_{2}He \rightarrow {}^{17}_{8}O + \underline{\hspace{2cm}}$$

(A) $_1^1H$ (D) $_2^4He$

(B) $_1^2H$ (E) $_{10}^{18}Ne$

(C) $_2^2He$

48. Identify the element which is converted to the phosphorous isotope and neutron when it collides with alpha particles.

$$\underline{\hspace{3cm}} + \, _2^4He \rightarrow \, _{15}^{30}P + \, _0^1H$$

(A) $_{13}^{27}Al$ (D) $_{25}^{55}Mn$

(B) $_7^{14}N$ (E) $_{15}^{31}P$

(C) $_{11}^{23}Na$

49. Light nuclei combine to yield somewhat heavier, stable nuclei with energy release. This is a definition of:

(A) atomic fission   (D) chain reaction

(B) atomic fusion   (E) radioactivity

(C) binding energy

50. Select the <u>incorrect</u> statement about the chemical activity at electrodes during electrolysis.

(A) Anions give up electrons.

(B) Cations take up electrons.

(C) Oxidation occurs at the anode.

(D) Proton transfer occurs in the reactions.

(E) Reduction occurs at the cathode.

Question 51 refers to the figure below.

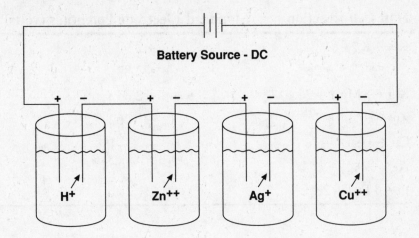

51. One faraday of electricity is passed through the series of solutions with different electrolytes. Select the correct statement about substances liberated at the electrodes.

    (A) 4.002 grams of hydrogen

    (B) 65.54 grams of zinc

    (C) 65.37 grams of copper

    (D) 107.86 grams of silver

    (E) 196.96 grams of gold

52. The approximate quantity of grams of aluminum needed to furnish 6.02×10^{23} electrons in an electrolytic cell is:

    (A) 3   (D) 27

    (B) 9   (E) 81

    (C) 18

Question 53 refers to the chart below.

Half Cell Reaction	Standard Electrode Potentials (volts)
$K \leftrightarrow K^+ + e^-$	+ 2.92
$Ca \leftrightarrow Ca^{++} + 2e^-$	+ 2.87
$Mg \leftrightarrow Mg^{++} + 2e^-$	+ 2.34
$Zn \leftrightarrow Zn^{++} + 2e^-$	+ .762
$Cu \leftrightarrow Cu^{++} + 2e^-$	- .344
$Ag \leftrightarrow Ag^+ + e^-$	- .7995
$Pt \leftrightarrow Pt^{++} + 2e^-$	- 1.2

53. A potential difference of 1.1068 is produced in an electrolysis set-up with the two half cell elements of:

    (A) calcium and silver

    (B) copper and zinc

    (C) magnesium and platinum

    (D) potassium and silver

    (E) zinc and silver

54. Select the metal with the highest ionization energy.

    (A) cesium   (D) rubidium

    (B) lithium   (E) sodium

    (C) potassium

55. Consider this reaction:

    $$C_8H_{18} + O_2 \rightarrow CO_2 + H_2O$$

    Under standard conditions, the volume of air in liters required for com-plete combustion of 228 grams of octane is about

(A) 22.4   (D) 1560

(B) 2.50   (E) 2800

(C) 560

56. A buffer solution was prepared by mixing 100 mL of a 1.2M NH_3 solution and 400 mL of a 0.5M NH_4Cl solution. What is the pH of this buffer solution, assuming a final volume of 500 mL and $K_b = 1.8 \times 10^{-5}$?

(A) $pH = 14 + pOH$

(B) $14 - \log\left[\dfrac{(1.8 \times 10^{-5}) \times (0.24)}{(0.4)}\right]$

(C) $\log\left[\dfrac{(1.8 \times 10^{-5}) \times (0.24)}{(0.4)}\right]$

(D) $14 + \log\left[\dfrac{(1.8 \times 10^{-5}) \times (0.24)}{(0.4)}\right]$

(E) None of the above

57. Determine ΔG° (free energy at standard conditions) for the reaction below, considering $K_p = 8$ at 25°C.

$2A(g) \leftrightarrow B(g)$

(A) $-2.303 \times (0.287) \times (25) \times \log 8$ [J]

(B) $-2.303 \times (8.314) \times (25) \times \log 8$ [J]

(C) $-2.303 \times (8.314) \times (298) \times \log \dfrac{1}{8}$ [J]

(D) $-2.303\ R\ T\ \log \dfrac{[B]^2}{[A]^2}$

(E) $-2.303 \times (8.314) \times (298) \times \log 8$ [J]

58. Which of the expressions below represents the correct rate law of the reaction?

    $2A + B \rightarrow C$

Experiment	[A]	[B]	initial rate (mole/l sec)
1	0.01	0.01	1.2
2	0.02	0.01	4.8
3	0.01	2	2.4
4	0.03	0.01	10.8
5	0.01	0.03	3.6

    (A) rate = K[A] [B]
    (B) rate = K[A]^2 [B]
    (C) rate = K[A]

    (D) rate = K[B]
    (E) rate = K[A] [B]^2

59. A sample of calcium carbonate (molar mass = 100 g) is analyzed. Assuming that all the calcium is combined with carbonate, what is the approximate percent of calcium in the sample?

    (A) 20%
    (B) 40%
    (C) 60%

    (D) 75%
    (E) 80%

60. $Cd + Cu^{2+} \rightarrow Cd^{2+} + Cu$

    The reaction above takes place in a voltaic cell in which all concentrations are equal to 1.0-molar. What will happen to the reaction quotient, Q, and the cell voltage potential, E, if the concentration of Cd^{2+} is increased?

    (A) Q and E both increase

    (B) Q increases, E decreases

    (C) Q and E both decreases

    (D) Q decreases, E increases

    (E) Q decreases, E remains the same

61. In a 0.1M aqueous solution of a monoprotic acid, 1% of the acid is dissociated. What is the appropriate pH of the solution?

(A) 11

(D) 7

(B) 3

(E) 8

(C) 5

62. The table below gives solubility product constants for a few salts of solver. From the table, we can conclude that the saturated solution with greatest value for $[Ag^+]$ is:

Salt	Solubility Product Constants
AgI	8.3×10^{-17}
AgBr	5.3×10^{-13}
AgCl	1.8×10^{-10}
$AgIO_3$	3.0×10^{-8}
$AgBrO_3$	5.3×10^{-5}

(A) AgI

(D) AgCl

(B) AgBr

(E) $AgBrO_3$

(C) $AgIO_3$

63. If 200 mL of N_2 at 25°C and pressure 400 mm Hg, and 200 mL of O_2 at 25°C and pressure 300 mm Hg are placed in a vessel with volume 700 mL, what is the total pressure of the mixture?

(A) 100 mm Hg

(D) 700 mm Hg

(B) 200 mm Hg

(E) 800 mm Hg

(C) 500 mm Hg

64. In which of the compounds below may CIS-TRANS isomerism occur?

(A) CH_4

(D) $C_2H_2(CH_3)_2$

(B) C_6H_6

(E) C_2H_6

(C) C_2H_4

65. What is the $[H^+]$ of a 1.0 M solution of phenol, which has a K_a of 1.6 x 10^{-10}?

(A) 1.6×10^{-10}

(D) 2.0×10^{-6}

(B) 2.0×10^{-5}

(E) 4.0×10^{-6}

(C) 4.0×10^{-5}

66. Methane, CH_4, has a heat of formation of –18 in kilocalories per mole. Select the correct statement for a reaction producing 48 grams of methane:

(A) $\Delta H = 9$ kcal

(B) $\Delta H = 18$ kcal

(C) $\Delta H = -18$ kcal

(D) $\Delta H = -36$ kcal

(E) $\Delta H = -54$ kcal

67. A certain substance with molecular weight 62 g × mole^{-1} will cause an aqueous solution to have a change of freezing point of 1.86°/m, where m stands for molal. What would be the change in the freezing point of an aqueous solution containing 200 g of H_2O, if we added 8g of this substance?

(A) 2.4 °C

(D) 0.6 °C

(B) 1.2 °C

(E) 0 °C

(C) 3.6 °C

68. A given atom has an atomic mass of 23 and an atomic number of 11. Select the <u>incorrect</u> statement about its atomic structure.

    (A) Eight electrons are in its outermost energy shell.

    (B) Its number of electrons is 11.

    (C) Its number of protons is 11.

    (D) Most of its mass is in the nucleus.

    (E) The number of neutrons is 12.

69. The most common element in the earth's crust, by weight, is:

    (A) aluminum   (D) oxygen

    (B) calcium   (E) silicon

    (C) iron

70. The Russian chemist Mendeleev first arranged 63 known elements in order of their increasing:

    (A) atomic number   (D) electron number

    (B) atomic weight   (E) silicon

    (C) boiling point

71. The greatest bond energy in kcal per mole is found with:

    (A) C–C   (D) H–F

    (B) H–Br   (E) H–I

    (C) H–Cl

72. An example of a metal which is ductile and malleable is:

    (A) Au   (D) K

    (B) Cd   (E) Na

    (C) Hg

73. A 300 mL volume of gas experiences a pressure change from 1000 mm of mercury to 760 mm of mercury, with other laboratory factors held constant. Its new volume in mL is:

(A) 131.6

(D) 500.8

(B) 228.0

(E) 1000.0

(C) 394.8

Questions 74 and 75 refer to the list of elements in the activity series below.

Activity Series

K
Ba
Ca
Na
Mg
Al
Mn
Zn
Cr
Fe
Co
Ni
Sn
Pb
H
Sb
Bi
Cu
Hg
Ag
Pt
Au

74. Among manganese, lead, iron, chromium, and copper, the least easily oxidized metal is:

    (A) chromium

    (D) lead

    (B) copper

    (E) manganese

    (C) iron

75. What mass of acetic acid will be consumed by 10.0 grams of NaOH in the reaction below?

    $$HC_2H_3O_2 + OH^- \leftrightarrow H_2O + C_2H_3O_2^-$$

    (A) 1.5 grams

    (D) 6.6 grams

    (B) 15 grams

    (E) 66 grams

    (C) 0.66 grams

AP Chemistry

Practice Exam 3

Section II

TIME: 90 minutes
55% of the entire test

(Answer sheets appear in the back of this book.)

The percentages given for the parts represent the score weightings for this section of the examination. You will be given 40 minutes for Part A and 50 minutes for Part B.

You may use a calculator on Part A, but not on Part B.

Be sure to write your answers in the space provided following each question. Pay attention to significant figures.

Part A

TIME: 40 minutes
40 percent

YOU MAY USE A CALCULATOR ON THIS PART.

Show your work clearly for full credit. Pay attention to significant figures in your answers.

Solve the following problem.

1. An unknown monoprotic organic acid is 0.8% dissociated when put into an aqueous solution. A 0.682-gram sample was dissolved in sufficient water to make 50 mL of a solution that was titrated with

0.135-molar NaOH solution. The equivalence point was reached after the addition of 28.4 mL of the NaOH solution.

(a) Calculate the number of moles of acid in the original sample.

(b) Calculate the molecular weight of the acid, HA.

(c) Calculate the ionization constant, K_a, of the acid, HA.

(d) Calculate Gibbs free energy, $\Delta G°$, for the dissociation of this monoprotic acid.

(e) Calculate the pH at the equivalence point.

Solve EITHER problem 2 or problem 3 below. Only one of these two questions will be graded. (The problem you choose will be worth 20% of the score on Part II.)

2. (a) Determine the empirical formula of the hydrocarbon that contains 75% carbon by mass.

(b) The molar mass of the molecule in part a is 16.0 g/mol. What is the density of the gas at 25 °C and 2.00 atm?

(c) The combustion of 4.0 grams of the hydrocarbon takes place in an insulated container that has a heat capacity of 12.50 J/g °C.

   (i) Write the balanced combustion reaction.

   (ii) What is the approximate ΔH for the reaction, in J/mol, if the calorimeter increases in temperature by 62.2 °C?

(d) 10.0 grams of the hydrocarbon is combined with 10.0 grams of oxygen gas in a rigid 2.0 L container at 25 °C. How many moles of carbon dioxide are produced?

3. A solution of H_2SO_4 was electrolyzed using inert platinum electrodes.

(a) Write the balanced half-reactions for the anode and cathode in this cell.

(b) How many coulombs passed through the cell in 90 minutes at 8.0 amperes?

(c) How many moles of electrons pass through the cell while the current flows?

(d) What number of moles of gas was produced at the cathode after the cell operated for 90 minutes at 8.0 amperes?

(e) What total volume of gas, at STP, could be produced by this cell if it operated for 100 minutes at 20.0 amperes?

Part B

TIME: 50 minutes

YOU MAY NOT USE A CALCULATOR ON THIS PART.

4. This question is worth 15% of Section II. Write the formulas of the reactants and products for FIVE of the following eight reactions. Show net ionic reactions only, where appropriate. Assume the reaction takes place in aqueous solution unless otherwise specified. Do not balance the reaction.

(a) Iron filings are dropped into a blue solution of copper (II) sulfate

(b) Solid iodine reacts with concentrated nitric acid

(c) Copper is exposed to excess oxygen

(d) Hydrogen sulfide is added to an aqueous solution of hydrogen peroxide

(e) Lead II sulfide is added to an aqueous solution of hydrogen peroxide.

(f) Liquid hydrogen is combined with gaseous oxygen

(g) Xenon II floride is placed into a water bath

(h) Manganese oxide solid is added to hydrochloric acid

ANSWER BOTH OF THE FOLLOWING ESSAY QUESTIONS (15% each).

5. Use principles of bonding and structure to explain each of the following.

    (a) The bond length between carbons is shorter in C_2H_2 than it is in C_2H_6.

    (b) The hydrogen-oxygen bond angle in water is 105°.

    (c) The bond lengths in SO_3 are all identical and shorter than the sulfur-oxygen single bond.

    (d) The HCN bond angle is linear, while the CO_3^{2-} bond angle is not.

ANSWER THE FOLLOWING LABORTATORY-BASED ESSAY QUESTION.

6. Describe a separate laboratory procedure to accomplish each of the following procedures. Where appropriate, write the balanced reaction for any chemical change that takes place during your procedure.

    (a) Isolate pure barium sulfate from barium chloride.

    (b) Create a solution of copper (II) nitrate from a sample of solid copper chloride.

    (c) Remove the lead from a heterogeneous mixture of solid lead nitrate and solid lead sulfate.

    (d) Distinguish between two liquid samples: pure water and an aqueous solution that contains dissolved ions.

ANSWER QUESTION 7 OR QUESTION 8 BELOW. ONLY ONE OF THESE TWO QUESTIONS WILL BE GRADED.

7. The acid ionization constants for three different weak acids are given below.

$$HSO_4^- \qquad 1.3 \times 10^{-2}$$

$$HCO_3^- \qquad 4.2 \times 10^{-7}$$

$$H_2PO_4^- \qquad 6.2 \times 10^{-8}$$

(a) Which of the above weak acids would be best to use to prepare a buffer with a pH of 7.2?

(b) How would you prepare the buffer solution mentioned in the previous question?

(c) If the concentrations of all dissolves species in the previous question were doubled, how would the pH of the buffer solution be affected? Explain your answer.

(d) In titrating all of the above weak acids with a strong base, which would be fully neutralized at the lowest pH? Explain your answer.

8. $NH_4HS\ (s) \leftrightarrow NH_3\ (g) + H_2S\ (g) \qquad \Delta H\ =\ +93\ kJ$

The equilibrium above is established by placing solid ammonium hydrogen sulfide in an empty container at 298 K. Once equilibrium is established, some of the solid remains in the container, and each of the following events takes place. Answer the following questions and give reasons for your answers.

(a) What happens to the amounts of all the reactants and products if the container is heated to a temperature higher than 298 K?

(b) What happens to the equilibrium amounts of the reactants and products if the container is put under greater pressure?

(c) What happens to the partial pressure of ammonium gas when hydrogen sulfide gas is introduced into the container?

(d) What happens to the amount of mass of the solid ammonium hydrogen sulfide when hydrogen sulfide gas is introduced into the container?

AP Chemistry

Practice Exam 3

ANSWER KEY

Section I

1.	(E)	26.	(B)	51.	(D)
2.	(B)	27.	(D)	52.	(B)
3.	(C)	28.	(D)	53.	(B)
4.	(A)	29.	(E)	54.	(B)
5.	(C)	30.	(A)	55.	(E)
6.	(B)	31.	(B)	56.	(D)
7.	(D)	32.	(A)	57.	(E)
8.	(E)	33.	(B)	58.	(B)
9.	(A)	34.	(E)	59.	(B)
10.	(B)	35.	(B)	60.	(B)
11.	(C)	36.	(C)	61.	(B)
12.	(A)	37.	(A)	62.	(E)
13.	(E)	38.	(B)	63.	(B)
14.	(C)	39.	(B)	64.	(D)
15.	(C)	40.	(A)	65.	(B)
16.	(D)	41.	(A)	66.	(E)
17.	(D)	42.	(A)	67.	(B)
18.	(B)	43.	(B)	68.	(A)
19.	(A)	44.	(D)	69.	(D)
20.	(C)	45.	(D)	70.	(B)
21.	(B)	46.	(E)	71.	(D)
22.	(D)	47.	(A)	72.	(A)
23.	(B)	48.	(A)	73.	(C)
24.	(A)	49.	(B)	74.	(B)
25.	(C)	50.	(D)	75.	(B)

DETAILED EXPLANATIONS OF ANSWERS

Practice Exam 3

Section I

1. **(E)** 2. **(B)** 3. **(C)** 4. **(A)** Each is a straight-forward fact from common lab observation.

5. **(C)** 6. **(B)** 7. **(D)** Limestone is mainly calcium carbonate, $CaCO_3$, with some iron and magnesium carbonates plus other impurities. For any periodic family of metals, metals are more easily oxidized when moving down the family. Beryllium is at the top of the alkali earth family, II A, in the periodic table. Although magnesium's atomic mass (24) is greater than beryllium's (9), it is within the sphere of an atom with one more energy shell. Thus this metal is slightly less dense than beryllium while also being tough, malleable, and ductile.

8. **(E)** 9. **(A)** 10. **(B)** 11. **(C)** K, L, M, and N rank the energy levels from the inside out with a 2–8–18–32 capacity for electrons.

12. **(A)** The solution that yields the greatest number of dissolved particles will increase the boiling point of water (a colligative property) the most. One should look for the highest concentration that produces the greatest number of dissolved particles. 1.0 M of magnesium chloride solution will put one mole of magnesium ions and two moles of chloride ions into solution—that's three moles for every mole dissolved.

13. **(E)** By computation with the formula, 82 degrees F becomes 27.7 degrees C. Centigrade to Kelvin conversion requires adding the constant 273: K=C+273.

14. **(C)** By consulting the periodic table, iron atoms have an atomic weight of about 56 while sulfur is 32. They combine in an atom-to-atom ratio, or a unitary gram equivalent to a unitary gram equivalent ratio. Thus 56 grams of iron combine with 32 grams of sulfur. By proportion, if iron is halved from 56 to 28, sulfur is halved from 32 to 16.

15. **(C)** Isotopes of an atom have the same atomic number but a different atomic mass, due to a varying number of neutrons. Choice (C) fits this requirement.

16. **(D)** The electron array is 2–8–5 among three energy levels. Checking phosphorus in the periodic table shows phosphorus in family five with the atomic number 15.

17. **(D)** Aluminum, as a metal, has three electrons to offer in its outer shell. As a nonmetal, sulfur needs two electrons to fill its outer capacity of eight by the octet rule. Two aluminum atoms with three electrons each can satisfy 3 sulfur atoms each in need of 2 electrons. The subscripts stand for the number of atoms of each element.

18. **(B)** Halogens are family seven of the periodic table. In a nonmetal family, the higher the element's position in the family, the greater its activity. Note the ranking of halogens from top to bottom in family seven.

19. **(A)** Using this principle, notice only cadmium (Cd) fits this table location. It is below and to the left of the metal (left side) and nonmetal (right side) stepline.

20. **(C)** In the kinetic theory, all collisions are perfectly elastic. Upon collision, they rebound with perfect bounce and without energy loss.

21. **(B)** 96 grams of O_2 total 3 moles by division: 96 grams divided by 32 grams (the molecular weight of oxygen). Two moles of ozone are equivalent to 96 grams. Its molecular weight is 48, or 3×16. Thus a mole is 48 grams. Two moles are therefore 96 grams. The balanced equation is: $2\,O_3 \rightarrow 3\,O_2$

22. **(D)** A gram molecular weight or mole of any gas occupies 22.4 liters. One mole of hydrogen gas weighs two grams. Six grams constitute three moles. 3×22.4 equals 67.2.

23. **(B)**   Since the kinetic energy is given by:

$$K_e = \frac{1}{2}\,mv^2 \text{ we can conclude:}$$

$$\frac{1}{2}m_{H_2}v_{H_2} = \frac{1}{2}m_{o_2}v^2{}_{o_2}$$

$$\Rightarrow 2v^2{}_{H_2} = 32v^2{}_{o_2}$$

$$v_{o_2}{}^2 = \frac{2}{32}v_{H_2}{}^2$$

$$v_o = \frac{1}{16}v_H$$

24. **(A)**   Zinc lacks an oxidation number initially in an uncombined state. It then loses two electrons and becomes +2 to couple with the –2 sulfate ion in $ZnSO_4$.

25. **(C)**   A dipole is an electrically asymmetrical molecule due to the unequal sharing of electron pairs between the spheres of bonding atoms. The two shared electron pairs of water spend more time in the command of oxygen's sphere than hydrogen's with its lower attracting power. Sodium chloride is not molecular but ionic. Methane (CH_4), hydrogen gas and oxygen gas share electron pairs equally and are thus nonpolar molecules.

26. **(B)**   By rules of nomenclature, a suffix, a prefix, or both are added to the word bromine to indicate its oxidation state, as shown in the table below:

compound	oxidation state of Br	name
$HBrO_3$	+5	bromic acid
$HBrO_2$	+3	bromous acid
$HBrO$	+1	hypobromous acid
HBr	–1	hydrobromic acid
$HBrO_4$	+7	perbromic acid

Note: All bromine oxidation states are computed algebraically, considering that each O atom is –2 and H atom is +1.

27. **(D)**   Electronegativity is the relative attracting force of the elements for electrons in a covalent bond. Nonmetals attract electrons, and fluorine is the most active nonmetal. Bromine is beneath it in the halogen family and is less active than fluorine, but it is still a very reactive nonmetal. Hydrogen is somewhat like a metal, but with less electron-attracting power. Aluminum and other metals in the middle of the periodic table have lower electronegativities than either F, Br, or H. Therefore, choice (D) gives a series of elements in order of decreasing electronegativity.

28. **(D)**   Sn, from the Latin word "stannous," is the symbol for tin. The radical "OH" has a valence of –1 and since Sn has a +2 valence the formula for tin (II) hydroxide becomes $Sn(OH)_2$.

29. **(E)**   Not all collisions result in chemical reactions: only the collisions between molecules with an amount of energy greater than or equal to the activation energy result in such chemical reactions.

30. **(A)**   Adding reactant amounts increases frequency of collision for more product formation. Removing ammonia, an escaping product gas, creates a void filled by an equilibrium shift to the right to form more NH_3. In the equation, four gas volumes form two. By Le Chatelier's principle, an altered equilibrium reacts to a stress to relieve the stress. Pressurizing the high-volume reactants forces the reaction to the right to relieve this stress. The reaction, however, is exothermic, producing heat, and therefore the right-to-left direction absorbs heat. Adding heat pushes it in this direction.

31. **(B)**   "K," the proportionality for reaction rate, is derived by the multiplication of product molar amounts divided by the multiplication of reactant's molar amounts. Coefficients in the balanced equation translate into exponents outside the bracketed molar amounts of the molecules.

32. **(A)** CH_3OH is nonpolar methyl alcohol or wood alcohol. Strong acids (HC1), strong bases (NaOH), or salts ($CuSO_4$, NaCl) have ionizing properties that make them electrolytes, capable of conducting an electric current in water.

33. **(B)**   The ionization constant is computed by the multiplication of product mole amounts over the mole amount of ionizing reactant. By division:

$$\frac{.1 \times .1}{.5} = \frac{.01}{.5} = 0.02 = 2 \times 10^{-2}$$

34. **(E)** Aluminum, a metal, is electropositive, +3. Three electrons from each of its two atoms fulfill the nonmetal sulfur's need for two electrons. So sulfur is –2.

35. **(B)** Calcium hydroxide's formula is $Ca(OH)_2$. One molecule thus dissociates into one calcium ion (Ca^{+2}) and two hydroxyl (OH^-) ions.

36. **(C)** The relationship between the solubility product constant and molar solubility for a compound that produces three moles of ions for every mole of solid dissolved is,

$$K_{sp} = 4x^3 = 4(1 \times 10^{-3})^3 = 4 \times 10^{-9}$$

37. **(A)** Hydrogen gas is the least polar because it is bonded to itself as a diatomic molecule. Therefore, there is no difference in electronegative between the two atoms in the bond, and it is entirely non-polar.

38. **(B)** Since the rate of decomposition increases by a factor of three when the concentration of A is increased by a factor of three, then it is a linear relationship between A and the rate, and it is first order with respect to A.

39. **(B)** Oxygen, in family six of the periodic table, has six valence electrons. Two of them saturate the smaller s orbital with 4 remaining for the larger p orbital.

40. **(A)** Since oxygen has atomic number 20, the first shell can hold a maximum of 2 electrons. Eight plus eight fill out the next two shells with two left over for a fourth outer shell. s and p refer to the two different shaped orbital spheres within the three energy levels beyond the first.

41. **(A)** Four ammonia molecules offer the 12 hydrogens needed for 6 water molecules. Six water molecules require 6 oxygens. Five O_2 molecules offer these 6 as a reactant, plus the four additional oxygens (5×2 total) for the four NO molecules among the products.

42. **(A)** If 2 moles of H_2S react with 3 moles of oxygen, $^2/_3$ moles react with 1 mole:

$$\frac{2}{3} = \frac{X}{1}; X = \frac{2}{3}$$

43. **(B)** Solution:

First calculate the number of moles of each element present.

$$1 \text{ mole H} = 1.0\text{g}$$
$$1 \text{ mole O} = 16.0\text{g}$$
$$1 \text{ mole N} = 14.0\text{g}$$

Therefore, number of moles of H is

$$\frac{3.18 \text{ g}}{1 \text{ g/mole}} = 3.18 \text{ moles H}$$

number of moles of O is

$$\frac{152.64 \text{ g}}{16 \text{ g/mole}} = 9.54 \text{ moles O}$$

number of moles of N is

$$\frac{44.52 \text{ g}}{14 \text{ g/mole}} = 3.18 \text{ moles N}$$

The smallest number is used to find the simplest ratio in which the elements combine as

$$\text{H: } \frac{3.18}{3.18} = 1 \qquad \text{O: } \frac{9.54}{3.18} = 3 \qquad \text{N: } \frac{3.18}{3.18} = 1$$

Therefore, the simplest molecular formula is HNO_3.

44. **(D)** All statements are true except this one. Beta ray particles, known as high-speed electrons, have a negative charge.

45. **(D)** The first step results from emission of an alpha particle, loss of 2 protons, and 2 neutrons. Thus atomic number decreases by 2 (2 protons) and atomic mass drops by 4. The second step involves emission of a beta particle (electron), which increases atomic number by one, but does not affect atomic mass. Note that the same alteration occurs from protactinium, Pa, to $^{234}_{92}U$ in this well-known sequence from uranium's isotope of 238.

46. **(E)** Each of the three basic subatomic particles has an antiparticle with equal mass, but opposite electric charge and magnetic moment. The positron (positive electron) has approximately the same mass as the electron but with positive charge.

47. **(A)**   An alpha particle has two protons and two electrons. In-corporation of one of its protons and two neutrons increases the original nitrogen's atomic number and mass to 8 (7+1) and 17 (14+3), respectively. A free proton, or hydrogen ion, $_1^1H$, is left over.

48. **(A)**   The helium nucleus, actually an alpha particle with two protons and two neutrons, adds two protons to aluminum to increase atomic number from 13 to 15. Adding one of its neutrons as well, mass is increased from 27 to 30. One free neutron remains. Working backwards from $_{15}^{30}P$ yields $_{13}^{27}Al$ by subtraction.

49. **(B)**   This is a straight-forward definition of atomic fusion as op-posed to a splitting or fission.

50. **(D)**   During electrolysis, anions, or negative ions, move to an an-ode and release electrons (oxidation). The electrons move through a metal-lic conductor to the cathode where the electrons are accepted (reduction). Thus the electrons move from one electrode to another.

51. **(D)**   For every faraday of electricity that is passed through a series of electrolytes, one gram equivalent weight of an element is released at an electrode. The corresponding numbers for atomic weights are found from the periodic table. Silver, Ag, is the only correctly stated gram weight.

52. **(B)**   A monovalent element such as hydrogen, H+, requires its entire gram equivalent weight to furnish 6.02×10^{23} electrons. In this case, each atom furnishes one electron. Aluminum is trivalent, furnishing three electrons per atom. Therefore, only one-third of its gram equivalent weight is needed. $^1/_3 \times 27$ (Al) = 9 grams.

53. **(B)**   The potential difference is calculated by determining the more easily oxidized metal's potential, and subtracting the standard elec-trode potential from it. Only a subtraction of .762 (Zn)–(–.344) (Cu) yields a difference of 1.1068. Zinc loses electrons more easily than copper.

54. **(B)**   Ionization energy is the energy needed to move one or more electrons from the neutral atoms. All choices are alkali metals from Group 1A of the periodic table. Although all these metals tend to lose their single valence electron and ionize, lithium has only two energy shells, with its electron close to the nucleus attracting sphere. Therefore, more energy is needed to attract its valence electron from the atom.

55. **(E)**   After balancing the reaction we obtain:

$$2\,C_8H_{18} + 25\,O_2 \rightarrow 16\,CO_2 + 18\,H_2O$$

Octane's molecular weight is 114: $C(8 \times 12) + H(18 \times 1)$. Thus one mole weighs 114 grams. From the balanced equation, two moles (228 grams) react with twenty-five moles of oxygen gas. At STP, one mole of a gas occupies 22.4 liters. By proportion, the 25 reacting moles occupy 560 liters (22.4×25). Since oxygen is about one-fifth of the atmosphere, 560 is multiplied by five for the air volume required.

56. **(D)**   The total amount of NH_3 added is:

$$1.2\,\frac{\text{mole}}{L} \times 0.1\,L = 0.12\,\text{mole}$$

The total amount of NH_4^+ added is:

$$0.5\,\frac{\text{mole}}{L} \times 0.4\,L = 0.2\,\text{mole}$$

Therefore the "new" concentrations for a total volume of $(0.1 + 0.4)$ L are:

$$[NH_3] = \frac{0.12}{0.5} = 0.24\,M$$

$$[NH_4^+] = \frac{0.2}{0.5} = 0.4\,M$$

From the reaction below:

$$NH_3 + H_2O \leftrightarrow NH_4^+ + OH^-$$

We obtain the expression for K_b:

$$K_b = \frac{[NH_4^+]\,[OH^-]}{[NH_3]}$$

$$[OH^-] = \frac{(1.8 \times 10^{-5}) \times (0.24\,M)}{0.4\,M}$$

$$pOH = -\log [OH^-] = -\log \left[\frac{(1.8 \times 10^{-5}) \times (0.24)}{(0.4)} \right]$$

$$pH = 14 - pOH$$

$$ph = 14 + \log \left[\frac{(1.8 \times 10^{-5}) \times (0.24)}{(0.4)} \right]$$

$pOH = 4.966$ and $pH = 14 - pOH = 9.0334$

$pH \approx 9.03$

57. **(E)** ΔG° is given by the expression below:

$\Delta G^{\circ} = -2.303RT \log K_p$

$\Delta G^{\circ} = -2.303 \times (8.314) \times (298) \times \log 8 \ [J]$

58. **(B)** Solution:

Let the rate be expressed as follows:

$\text{rate} = k[A]^n[B]^m$

To find n, examine the data and find the ratios of rates for reactions where [B] was kept constant as:

$$\frac{\text{rate}_2}{\text{rate}_1} = \frac{k[2A]^n[B]^m}{k[A]^n[B]^m} = \frac{4.8}{1.2} = 4$$

Simplifying we have

$2^n = 4 = 2^2$

$\rightarrow \quad n = 2$

or $\quad \dfrac{\text{rate}_4}{\text{rate}_1} = \dfrac{k[3A]^n}{k[A]} \dfrac{[B]^m}{[B]^m} = \dfrac{10.8}{1.2} = 9$

$\rightarrow \quad 3^n = 9 = 3^2$

$n = 2.$

Similarly for m consider reactions where [A] = constant.

$$\frac{\text{rate}_3}{\text{rate}_1} = \frac{k[A]^n[2B]^m}{k[A]^n[B]} = \frac{2.4}{1.2} = 2$$

or $2m = 2$

$\rightarrow$ $m = 1$

or $\dfrac{\text{rate}_5}{\text{rate}_1} = \dfrac{k[A]^n[3B]^m}{k[A]^n[B]^m} = \dfrac{3.6}{1.2} = 3$

$3m = 3$

$m = 1$; therefore rate $= k[A]^2[B]$.

59. **(B)**   Percent composition is found by dividing the mass contributed by one element by the total mass of the compound, then multiplying by 100%.

$$40\% \text{ Ca} = \frac{40 \text{ g Ca}}{100 \text{ g CaCO}_3} \times 100\%$$

60. **(B)**   As the concentration of a product increases, the Q ratio also increases. Le Chatelier's principle suggests that with increasing products, the tendency for the reaction to continue to proceed forward is diminished. The Nernst equation would support this idea quantitatively and would show a lower cell voltage as the reactant is used up and the product accumulates.

61. **(B)**   The dissociation equation is given below:

$CH_3COOH \leftrightarrow H^+ + CH_3COO^-$

If the dissociation is 1%, it means that 0.1×0.01 molecules dissociated and generated 0.1×0.01 molecules of H+ or $[H^+] = 1 \times 10^{-3}$, so pH = 3.

62. **(E)**   The solution with greatest $[Ag^+]$ is the solution with the greatest solubility product, which is $AgBrO_3$.

63. **(B)**   According to Dalton's law, "the total pressure of a mixture of gases is the summation of the pressures of the individual gases if they occupied alone the volume of the mixture."

$$\frac{P_1V_1}{T_1} = \frac{PV}{T} \qquad \text{where}$$

$T = T_1$

$V = 700$

$P = ?$

$$P = \frac{(400)(200)}{700} = \frac{80000}{700} \quad \text{where}$$

$$\frac{P_2 V_2}{T_2} = \frac{P^1 V^1}{T^1}$$

$T^1 = T_2$

$V = 700$

$P = ?$

$$\frac{300 \times 200}{700} = P^1 = \frac{600}{7} \quad \text{P total} = P + P^1 = \frac{800 + 600}{7} =$$

$$\frac{1400}{7} = 200 \text{ mm}$$

64. **(D)** CIS-TRANS isomerism occurs only in compounds which divide the molecule into two parts, so that two different configurations are possible. Two possibilities are shown below:

```
  H     CH₃      CH₃    CH₃
   \    /         \     /
    C = C          C = C
   /    \         /     \
  H     CH₃      H       H
```

65. **(B)** The proton concentration in moles per liter is simply the square root of the ionization constant for a one molar solution of the acid.

$$K_a = \frac{(x^2)}{(1.0)} = 4.0 \times 10^{-10}$$

$$x^2 = 4.0 \times 10^{-10}$$

$$x = [H^+] = 2.0 \times 10^{-5}$$

66. **(E)** The negative sign to the heat per mole in kilocalories means that the heat is liberated. One mole of methane is 16 grams: 12 g C + 4 (1 g O). Therefore three moles liberates 54 kilocalories or 3×18.

67. **(B)** The first step consists of determining the molarity of the solution, which is obtained by dividing the mass of the solute by its molecular weight:

$$\text{Molarity} = \frac{8}{62} = 0.13 \text{ mole}$$

To obtain the molality, it is necessary to divide the molarity by the mass of solvent as below:

$$\text{Molality} = \frac{\text{molarity}}{K_g \text{ of solvent}} = \frac{0.13}{0.2} = 0.65 \text{ m}$$

The change in freezing point Δt_f is:

$$\frac{1.86 \, ^\circ C}{M} \times 0.65 \text{ m} = 1.2 \, ^\circ C$$

68. **(A)** By definition, atomic number is the number of protons or electrons. With 11 electrons, its electron arrangement is 2-8-1 over three energy levels. If the atomic number is 23, however, 12 neutrons must add to 11 protons for this total mass by simple subtraction. Note its outer level has one electron.

69. **(D)** Oxygen constitutes about 49%, followed by silicon (25%), aluminum (7%), iron (5%), and calcium (3.5%) in the earth's crust.

70. **(B)** This is a historical fact. The modern periodic table ranks a larger array of elements by atomic number.

71. **(D)** Fluorine's high electronegativity (electron-attracting power) yields a strong force with the metallic-acting hydrogen. Fluorine is the most active nonmetal, topping chlorine, bromine, and iodine, which possess decreasing electronegativity moving down the halogen family, (Group 7A in the periodic table). Carbon, with a valence of four, is neither strongly metallic nor nonmetallic. Its electronegativity is less than most strong nonmetals.

72. **(A)** "Au" is the symbol for gold, which is malleable (capable of being hammered into a desired shape) and ductile (capable of being drawn into a wire). Metals such as Fe, Cu, Ni, and Pt in the middle of the periodic table have these properties. Cadmium (Cd), mercury (Hg), potassium (K), and sodium (Na) lack this table location and these properties.

73. **(C)** Boyle's law ($P_1V_1 = P_2V_2$) states that gas volume varies by inverse proportion with a pressure change. Pressure is reduced here so the gas will expand:

$$300 \times \frac{1000}{760} = 394.8 \text{ ml}$$

74. **(B)** Oxidation is the loss of electrons. Copper, Cu, is lowest on the series among the list of choices with a tendency to do this.

75. **(B)**

$$15 \text{ g acetic acid} = 10.0 \text{ g NaOH} \times \frac{1 \text{ mol NaOH}}{40 \text{ g NaOH}} \times$$

$$\frac{1 \text{ mol acetic acid}}{1 \text{ mol NaOH}} \times \frac{60 \text{ g acetic acid}}{1 \text{ mol acetic acid}}$$

Section II

1. (a) At the equivalence point, the moles of acid equal the moles of base added. Moles acid = moles base = 0.0284 L $\times$ 0.135 mol/L = 0.003834 mol acid

(b) 0.682 g/ 0.003834 mol = 177.8 g/mol

(c) $K_a = \dfrac{[H^+]\,[A^-]}{[HA]} = (0.008)(0.008) = 6.4 \times 10^{-5}$

(d) $\Delta G = -\,RT \ln K = -\,(8.31\ J)\,(298)\ \ln\,(6.4 \times 10^{-5}) = 23900\ J = 23.9\ kJ$

(e) $K_b = \dfrac{[OH^-]\,[HA]}{[A]} = \dfrac{x^2}{.003834\ mol/.0784\ L} = 1.6 \times 10^{-10}$

$x = [OH^-] = 2.8 \times 10^{-6}$

$[H^+] = 3.6 \times 10^{-9}$

$pH = 8.4$

2. (a)

$75\ g\ C \times \dfrac{1.0\ mol\ C}{12.011\ g\ C} = 6.244\ mol\ C$

$25\ g\ H \times \dfrac{1.0\ mol\ H}{1.008\ g\ H} = 24.801\ mol\ H$

The empirical formula is CH_4

(b) d = P (molar mass)/ RT = (2.0 atm) (16 g/mol)/(0.082 L atm/ mol K)(298 K)= 1.3 g/L

(c) (i) $CH_4 + 2\,O_2 \rightarrow CO_2 + 2\,H_2O$

(ii) $62.2\ ^\circ C \times 12.5\ J/^\circ C\ /\ 0.25\ mol = 3110\ J/mol$

(d)

$$10 \text{ g methane} \times \frac{1 \text{ mol methane}}{16 \text{ g methane}} \times \frac{1 \text{ mol carbon dioxide}}{1 \text{ mole methane}} =$$

0.625 mol carbon dioxide

$$10 \text{ g oxygen} \times \frac{1 \text{ mol oxygen}}{32 \text{ g oxygen}} \times \frac{1 \text{ mol carbon dioxide}}{2 \text{ mole oxygen}} =$$

0.156 mol carbon dioxide

Therefore, 0.156 mol of carbon dioxide is formed; oxygen is the limiting reactant.

3.   (a)

Cathode: $2H_2O \ (l) \rightarrow 2OH^- \ (aq) + H_2 \ (g)$

Anode: $H_2O \ (l) \rightarrow 2H^+ \ (aq) + O_2 \ (g)$

(b)

$$43,200 \text{ C} = 8.0 \text{ A} \times 5400 \text{ sec} \times \frac{\text{C}}{\text{A sec}}$$

(c)

$$0.45 \text{ mol electrons} = 8.0 \text{ A} \times 5400 \text{ sec} \times \frac{\text{C}}{\text{A sec}} \times \frac{1.0 \text{ mol e}^-}{96,485 \text{ C}}$$

(d)

$$0.22 \text{ mol} = 8.0 \text{ A} \times 5400 \text{ sec} \times \frac{\text{C}}{\text{A sec}} \times$$

$$\frac{1.0 \text{ mol e}^-}{96,485 \text{ C}} \times \frac{1.0 \text{ mol gas}}{2 \text{ mol e}^-}$$

(e)   Remember that gas is being produced at both the cathode and the anode. For every four moles of electrons, two moles of hydrogen gas and one mole of oxygen gas are produced.

$$0.93 \text{ mol} = 20.0 \text{ A} \times 6000 \text{ sec} \times \frac{C}{A \text{ sec}} \times$$

$$\frac{1.0 \text{ mol e}^-}{96,485 \text{ C}} \times \frac{3 \text{ mol gas}}{4 \text{ mol e}^-}$$

4.   (a)   Fe (s) + $CuSO_4$ (aq) → $FeSO_4$ (aq) + Cu (s)

          Fe^0 (s) + Cu^{+2} (aq) → Fe^{+2} (aq) + Cu^0 (s)

   (b) $3I_2$ + $10HNO_3$ (aq) → 6 HIO_3 + 10NO + $2H_2O$

          $I2^0$ + N^{+5} (aq) → I^{+5} + N^{+4}

   (c)   2Cu (s) + O_2 (g) → 2CuO (s)

          Cu^0 + $O2^0$ → $Cu^{+2}O^{-2}$

   (d) $8H_2S$ + $8H_2O_2$ → S_8 (s) + $16H_2O$

          S^{-2} + O^{-1} → S^0 + O^{-2}

   (e)   PbS + $4H_2O_2$ → PSO_4 + $4H_2O$ (l)

          S^{-2} + O^{-1} → S^{-6} + O^{-2}

   (f) $2H_2$ (l) + O^2 (g) → $2H_2O$ (g)

          H^0 + O^0 → $H^{+1}O^{-2}$

   (g) $2XeF_2$ (s) + $4H_2O$ (l) → 2Xe (s) + $2O_2$ (g) + $4H_2F$ (g)

          Xe^{+2} + O^{-2} → Xe^0 + $O2^0$

   (h) MnO_2 + 4HCl (aq) → $MnCl_2$ (aq) + Cl_2 (g) + $2H_2O$ (l)

          Mn^{+4} + Cl^{-1} → Mn^{+2} + Cl^0

5.   (a)   The bond length between the carbons in C_2H_2 is much shorter than the carbon bond in ethane. C_2H_2 has a triple bond between the two carbons. The pi bonding pulls the carbons closer together, and since bond length is proportional to bond strength, the stronger triple bond is shorter.

   (b)   Even though water has four electron pairs around it, like methane, the actual bond angle between the oxygen-hydrogen bonds is slightly less than the tetrahedral 109°. The unbonded electrons around the oxygen take up more space because they are not confined between two nuclei in a sigma bond.

(c)   The sulfur trioxide molecule requires a resonance structure to properly model the bond between the sulfur and each oxygen atom. An extra electron pair from the sulfur atom is delocalized and create some pi-bonding with all three oxygen atoms. This creates a bond that is slightly stronger, and shorter, than a sulfur-oxygen single sigma bond.

(d)   The carbon in the hydrogen cyanide molecule demonstrates *sp* hybridization, so its two hybridized electrons separate as far from each other as possible. This puts the hybridized electrons 180° apart and creates a linear molecule. On the other hand, the central carbon in the carbonate molecule shows a planar geometry to maximize the distance between the slightly-stronger-than-single bonds to each of three oxygen atoms.

6.   (a)   Adding concentrated sulfuric acid would precipitate solid barium sulfate from a solution of barium chloride.

$$Ba^{2+} (aq) + SO_4^- (aq) \rightarrow BaSO_4 (s)$$

(b)   Adding excess concentrated nitric acid will create a solution of copper (II) nitrate by oxidizing the copper and, since nitric acid is a strong acid, the unreacted nitrate ions will be free in solution. (However, some of the nitrate ions will be reduced to nitrogen dioxide and leave the reaction as a brown gas.) Remember, the number of electrons lost with the copper must be equal to the number of electrons gained by the nitrogen.

$$Cu (s) + 4 H+ + 2 NO_3^- (aq) \rightarrow Cu^{2+} (aq) + 2 NO_2 (g) + 2 H_2 0$$

(c)   Stirring the solid mixture into a solution of sulfuric acid will put virtually all of the lead together with sulfate ions. The lead will leave the lead nitrate, which is soluble, and combine with the sulfate in the sulfuric acid to form a white precipitate. The solid can then be filtered off, thereby removing the lead entirely from the mixture.

$$Pb^{2+} (aq) + SO_4^- (aq) \rightarrow PbSO_4 (s)$$

(d)   Checking the conductivity will distinguish between a sample of pure water and an aqueous solution with dissolved ions. The pure water is not a conductor and will not allow electricity to flow through it. However, a solution with dissolved ions in it contains mobile charges that will carry an electric current very easily.

7.   (a)   The best buffer system to buffer at pH 7.2 would be the dihydrogen phosphate in combination with its conjugate base, hydrogen phos-

phate. The pK$_a$ of this acid equals 7.2, which signifies that this is the pH where the moles of the weak acid in solution equal the moles of its conjugate base in solution.

(b)   To prepare this buffer, put equimolar amounts of sodium dihydrogen phosphate and disodium hydrogen phosphate into solution together.

(c)   The pH of the buffer would not change because the ratio of the weak acid to its conjugate base would not change. Only when this ratio changes, does it change the value for pH calculated in the Henderson-Hasselbach equation.

(d)   The acid that would be fully neutralized at the lowest pH would be the strongest acid, or the acid with the highest K$_a$, which would be the hydrogen sulfate ion.

8.   (a)   Since the reaction is endothermic, heating the reaction further will result in a shift toward the left, toward reforming the ammonium hydrogen sulfide and using up ammonia and hydrogen sulfide gas.

(b)   When the system is put under pressure, the equilibrium will shift to minimize the change, and reduce the number of gas moles. This will cause the equilibrium to shift to the left toward reforming ammonium hydrogen sulfide and using up ammonia and hydrogen sulfide gas.

(c)   If hydrogen sulfide gas is added to the system, it will cause the equilibrium to shift to the left and react with the ammonia gas to form ammonium hydrogen sulfide. The amount of ammonia gas will decrease.

(d)   The amount of solid ammonium hydrogen sulfide will increase when hydrogen sulfide gas is introduced into the container. Like the above questions, this is another example of Le Chatelier's principle, where the equilibrium will shift to minimize change. This is also considered the law of mass action, where adding a compound on one side of an equilibrium will cause the reaction to go in the other direction, using up what was added.

Practice
Exam 4

AP Chemistry

Practice Exam 4

Section I

TIME: 90 minutes
45% of the entire test

(Answer sheets appear in the back of this book.)

DIRECTIONS: Each set of lettered choices below refers to the numbered questions or statements immediately following it. Select the one lettered choice that best answers each question. A choice may be used once, more than once, or not at all in each set.

Part A

Questions 1 – 3

(A) I   (D) Ga

(B) Kr   (E) At

(C) Sr

1.   Which element has the characteristics of a metalloid?

2.   Which element is an inert gas?

3.   Which of the elements is the most metallic?

Questions 4 – 6

    (A) Calcium carbonate

    (B) Stannous fluoride

    (C) Acetic acid

    (D) Formaldehyde

    (E) Acetylsalicylic acid

4.   Used as a preservative in embalming procedures

5.   Used daily as a dental cleanser

6.   Commonly found in aspirin

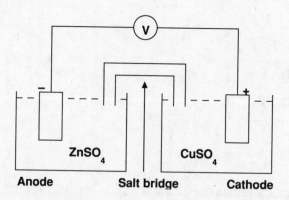

Given two solutions, $ZnSO_4$(1M) and $CuSO_4$(1M), answer **questions 7 – 9** based on this diagram.

7. What reaction, if any, takes place at the cathode?

   (A) $Cu^{2+} + 2e^- \rightarrow Cu$ (D) $Zn \rightarrow Zn^{2+} + 2e^-$

   (B) $Zn^{2+} + 2e^- \rightarrow Zn$ (E) none of the above

   (C) $Cu \rightarrow Cu^{2+} + 2e^-$

8. What is the purpose of the salt bridge?

   (A) to allow the two solutions to mix

   (B) to allow copper to migrate to the other cell and vice-versa

   (C) to allow the positive and negative ions to migrate

   (D) to allow counterclockwise flow of current

   (E) the purpose of the bridge is unimportant in this diagram

9. Which of the following equations can be used to calculate the emf of this voltaic cell at various concentrations?

   (A) $E = E° - \dfrac{0.05915}{n} \log Q$

   (B) $E = q - w$

   (C) $E = E°$ products $- E°$ reactants

   (D) $E = E° - \dfrac{0.05915}{n} \ln Q$

   (E) none of the above

Part B

Directions: Each of the following questions or incomplete sentences is followed by five possible answers. Choose the best one in each case.

10. Allotropes are best described as

    (A) having the same composition but occurring in different molecular structures.

(B) being without definite shape.

(C) having both acid and base properties.

(D) elements with more than one molecular or crystalline form and with different physical and chemical properties.

(E) having the same number of protons and electrons, but a different number of neutrons

11. Hydrolysis of sodium carbonate yields

(A) a strong acid and a strong base

(B) a weak acid and a strong base

(C) a weak acid and a weak base

(D) a strong acid and a weak base

(E) none of the above

12. What volume does 34 grams of ammonia gas occupy at standard temperature and pressure? (assume ideal behavior)

(A) 22.4 L

(B) 44.8 L

(C) 11.2 L

(D) 0.1 L

(E) 0 L

13. Which of the following is <u>not</u> a homogeneous mixture?

(A) sugar in water

(B) salt in water

(C) sand in water

(D) gasoline

(E) soft drinks

14. Rutherford's most significant discovery in nuclear chemistry is that

(A) the volume occupied by an atom is largely empty space

(B) the gold atom has a dense nucleus

(C) alpha particles radiate through gold foil

(D) the negative electron region is unaffected by the positive $\propto$ –particle

(E) the $\propto$ –particle passes mostly undeflected because of the extremely small size of the atom

15. Which of the following represents the structure of a noble gas?

(A) $^{19}_{9}X$

(B) $^{21}_{10}X$

(C) $^{17}_{8}X$

(D) $^{15}_{7}X$

(E) $^{13}_{6}X$

16. What is the functional group $R - \overset{\overset{\displaystyle O}{\|}}{C} - OH$ representative of?

(A) Ethers

(B) Alcohols

(C) Acids

(D) Aldehydes

(E) Esters

17. What mass of chlorine gas, Cl_2, could be contained in a 3.0-liter flask at 2.0 atm and 400 K?

(A) 0.077 g

(B) 1.0 g

(C) 6.5 g

(D) 13.0 g

(E) 8.5 g

18. Which of the following contains the largest <u>number</u> of atoms or molecules?

(A) 49 g of Fe

(B) 5 liters of H_2 at STP

(C) 150 g of ethanol

(D) 10 liters of ozone at STP

(E) 80 g of calcium carbide

19. What mass of chlorine gas, Cl_2, should be contained in a 3.0-liter flask at 2.0 atm and 400 K?

   (A) 0.077 g

   (B) 1.0 g

   (C) 6.5 g

   (D) 13.0 g

   (E) 8.5 g

20. The abbreviated electronic configuration of an element of atomic number 42 can be:

   (A) $[Kr]5s^14d^5$

   (B) $[Kr]5s^24d^4$

   (C) $[Kr]4d^6$

   (D) $[Kr]5s^25p^4$

   (E) $[Kr]5s5p^5$

21. Which of the following is/are paramagnetic?

   I. Fe^{2+}
   II. Fe^{3+}
   III. CO^{3+}
   IV. Ni^{2+}

   (A) I and IV

   (B) I only

   (C) II only

   (D) I and II

   (E) All the ions listed.

22. For the following reaction, calculate an approximate value for the change in free energy and determine whether or not the reaction is spontaneous under standard conditions.

$$2\ HCN\ (g) + 4.5\ O_2\ (g) \rightarrow H_2O\ (l) + 2\ CO_2\ (g) + 2\ NO_2\ (g)$$

Compound	$\Delta G_f°$ (kJ/mol)
NO_2	52
HCN	125
CO_2	-394
H_2O	-237

(A) -230 kJ/mol, yes   (D) +230 kJ/mol, no

(B) +2300 kJ/mol, yes   (E) +2300 kJ/mol, no

(C) -2300 kJ/mol, yes

23. What will be the shape of a molecule when the central atom is surrounded by five atoms and the molecule does <u>not</u> contain lone pairs of electrons?

(A) tetrahedral   (D) planar

(B) triangular   (E) octahedral

(C) triangular bipyramid

24. Which of the following is most likely to be found on the striking surface of a matchbox?

(A) lead oxide   (D) calcium carbide

(B) white phosphorus   (E) sodium peroxide

(C) red phosphorus

25. Calculate the specific rate constant for the reaction, $A + B \rightarrow C$, that is represented by the kinetic data in the chart below.

Trial	[A]	[B]	Initial rate of formation of C (M/sec)
1	0.10	0.40	0.02
2	0.10	0.80	0.04
3	0.20	0.80	0.16

(A) $2.0 \text{ mol}^2/L^2 \text{ sec}$

(B) $0.1 \text{ L}^2/\text{mol}^2 \text{ sec}$

(C) $4.0 \text{ mol}/L \text{ sec}$

(D) $2.5 \text{ mol}^2/L^2 \text{ sec}$

(E) $0.5 \text{ L}^2/\text{mol}^2 \text{ sec}$

26. In which of the following is iodine not used?

    (A) preparation of antiseptics

    (B) preparation of some medicines

    (C) photographic film

    (D) audio-recording tapes

    (E) dye compounds

27. VSEPR method is used to

    (A) predict the geometries of an atom.

    (B) estimate the energy levels of orbitals in an atom.

    (C) estimate electronegativities of elements.

    (D) predict the geometries of molecules and ions.

    (E) There is no such thing as a VSEPR method.

28. At 25 °C, the K_{sp} for $CaSO_4$ and Ag_2SO_4 are 2.4×10^{-5} and 1.2×10^{-5}, respectively. Which of the following is true?

    (A) The solubility of $CaSO_4$ is twice that of Ag_2SO_4.

    (B) The solubility of Ag_2SO_4 is twice that of $CaSO_4$.

(C)   The solubility of Ag_2SO_4 is sensitive to the square of the sulphate ion concentration.

(D)   The solubilities of $CaSO_4$ and Ag_2SO_4 are equal.

(E)   The solubilities of Ag_2SO_4 and $CaSO_4$ in mol liter^{-1} differ by a factor of 2.9.

29.   For the molecules listed below, the resultant dipole moments are oriented as (from left to right)

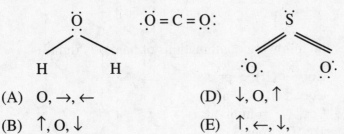

(A) $O, \rightarrow, \leftarrow$ (D) $\downarrow, O, \uparrow$

(B) $\uparrow, O, \downarrow$ (E) $\uparrow, \leftarrow, \downarrow,$

(C) $\uparrow, O, \uparrow$

30.   The balanced equation of the reaction of MnO_4 in an acidic medium to produce MnO_4 and MnO_2 is

(A) $3MnO_4 + 4H^+ \rightarrow 2MnO_4 + MnO_2 + 2H_2O$

(B) $3MnO_4 \rightarrow 2MnO_4 + MnO_2 + O_2$

(C) $2MnO_4 + 2H_2O \rightarrow MnO_4 + MnO_2 + 2O_2 + 2H_2$

(D) $2MnO_4 + 2OH^- \rightarrow MnO_4 + MnO_2 + O_2 + H_2$

(E) $MnO_4 \rightarrow H_2O$

31.   Metathesis reactions usually involve

(A)   a transfer of protons

(B)   an exchange of ions with the formation of one or more insoluble salts

(C)   an electron and neutron transfer

(D)   acid-base reactions

(E)   chromatography

32. Which of the following salts are soluble?

    I. $(NH_4)_2CO_3$
    II. $CaSO_4$
    III. $PbCl_2$
    IV. $AgClO_4$

    (A) I and III only   (D) II, III and IV

    (B) I and IV only   (E) II and IV only

    (C) I, II and IV

33. Which of the following combinations of names is right?

    I.   Copper (II): cupric
    II. Cobalt (II): cobaltic
    III. Lead (II): plumbous
    IV. Tin (II): stannic

    (A) I and III   (D) II only

    (B) I, II and IV   (E) none of the above

    (C) III only

34. In which of the following solutions will iron sulfide, FeS, be most soluble?

    (A) pure water

    (B) 2.0 M NaOH

    (C) 1.0 M NaOH

    (D) 2.0 M H_2SO_4

    (E) 2.0 M HCl

35. An important application of colligative properties of solutions is

    (A) the determination of boiling points

    (B) the determination of heat of fusion

    (C) the determination of molecular weight

(D)   the determination of atomic weight

(E)   the evaluation of electronegativities

36.   The diagram below is used to describe a reaction path. What are y, x and z respectively?

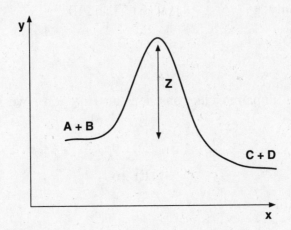

(A) temperature, volume, pressure

(B)   activation energy, potential energy and temperature

(C)   potential energy, reaction coordinate and activation energy

(D)   distance, time, concentration

(E)   time, distance, concentration.

37.   The specific rate constant of the natural radioactive potassium iso-tope $^{40}_{19}K$ is 5.33 x 10^{-10} year $^{-1}$, so the half-life of $^{40}_{19}K$ is:

(A) 1.3×10^9 years   (D) 5.33×10^5 years

(B) 1.3×10^{-9} years   (E) 2.665×10^{-10} years

(C) $9 \times 10^{1.3}$ years

38. Which of the following is/are both a Brønsted-Lowry base and a Lewis base?

    I. NH_3
    II. BBr_3
    III. H_2O
    IV. NaOH

(A) I and IV   (D) II and III

(B) IV only   (E) I and III

(C) I only

39. How many unpaired electrons does an Ho^{3+} ion have in its ground state?

(A) 3   (D) 0

(B) 5   (E) 6

(C) 4

40. What is the electron configuration of Ir^{+3} ion in its ground state?

(A) $[Xe]4f^{14}5d^{4}6s^{2}$ (D) $[Xe]4f^{11}5d^{7}6s^{2}$

(B) $[Xe]4f^{14}5d^{6}$ (E) $[Xe]4f^{13}5d^{6}6s^{1}$

(C) $[Xe]4f^{14}5d^{5}6s^{1}$

41. Predict the most common oxidation states of europium and scandium

(A) −1 and −3, respectively.

(B) +1 and +1, respectively.

(C) +1 and +2, respectively.

(D) +4 and +3, respectively.

(E) +2 and +3, respectively.

42. Solutions of alums are

    (A) basic   (D) saturated with Ca^{2+} ions

    (B) neutral   (E) isomorphous

    (C) acidic

Questions 43 – 45 refer to the statement below: A voltaic cell consists of a combination of a standard silver electrode and another silver electrode in which the concentration of silver ions is $10^{-3}M$, $E^0_{Ag+/Ag} = 0.80V$.

43. Which of the following is true?

    (A) The standard electrode is the cathode.

    (B) The standard electrode is the anode.

    (C) There will be no electron transfer.

    (D) This cell will work like a perpetual source of energy.

    (E) A reaction will not occur.

44. The cell standard potential, $E^°_{cell}$, is

    (A) 0.00 V   (D) +1.6V

    (B) + 0.80V   (E) –1.6V

    (C) – 0.80V

45. Which of the following is false?

    (A) The overall cell potential depends on the difference in concentration between the two solutions.

    (B) The overall cell potential is negative so no reaction takes place.

    (C) The overall cell potential is positive so the cell works.

    (D) Copper will be deposited at the standard electrode.

    (E) The electrode immersed in the 10^{-3} M solution will lose weight.

46. 25.0 mL of 0.100 M HCl is titrated with 0.15 M NaOH. The pH of the acid solution after 10 mL of base added is

    (A) $-\log\left(\dfrac{1 \text{ m mol}}{25 \text{ mL}}\right)$

    (D) $-\log\left(\dfrac{1 \text{ m mol}}{35 \text{ mL}}\right)$

    (B) $\log\left(\dfrac{1 \text{ m mol}}{35 \text{ mL}}\right)$

    (E) $-\log\left(\dfrac{1.5 \text{ m mol}}{35 \text{ mL}}\right)$

    (C) $-\log\left(\dfrac{1 \text{ m mol}}{1 \text{ L}}\right)$

47. Which of the following is most soluble in water?

    (A) hexanol

    (D) acetylene

    (B) benzene

    (E) hexanoic acid

    (C) acetic acid

48. Which of the following has the highest boiling point?

    (A) $CH_3CH_2CH_2CO_2H$

    (B) $CH_3CH_2CH_2CH_2CHO$

    (C) $CH_3CH_2CH_2CH_2CH_2OH$

    (D) $CH_3(CH_2)_4CH_3$

    (E) $CH_3CH_2 - \overset{\displaystyle ||}{\underset{\displaystyle O}{C}} - CH_2CH_3$

49. Which of the following pairs of elements have almost the same atomic size?

    (A) Sc and Y

    (D) Mg and Ca

    (B) B and Al

    (E) Be and Mg

    (C) Al and Ga

50. Which of the following molecules or ions can act as either an acid or a base?

    (A) OH^- (D) $H_2PO_4^-$

    (B) H_3O^+ (E) NH_4^+

    (C) $C_2H_3O_2^-$

51. What is the pressure at Point A on the following phase diagram?

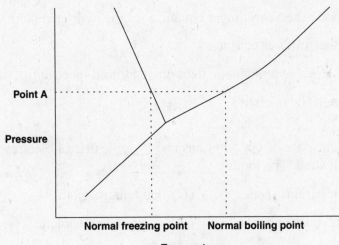

    (A) 1.0 atm   (D) 5.0 atm

    (B) 1.8 atm   (E) 10.0 atm

    (C) 2.0 atm

52. Which of the following is used to refine silicon semiconductors?

    (A) electrolysis   (D) precipitation

    (B) zone refining   (E) chromatography

    (C) distillation

53. Which gas has a rate of diffusion 0.25 times that of hydrogen at the same temperature and pressure?

    (A) CH_4 (D) N_2

    (B) PH_3 (E) O_2

    (C) Argon

54. Which of the following molecules shows a hydrogen bonding?

    (A) water   (D) carbon dioxide

    (B) hydrochloric acid   (E) sodium chloride

    (C) silver nitrate

55. The spin quantum number, or m_s is obtained as a result of

    (A) the Heisenberg Uncertainty Principle

    (B) solving the Schrödinger equation for the hydrogen atom

    (C) Rutherford's experiment

    (D) the effect of a magnetic field on an atomic spectrum

    (E) spin of the nucleus

56. The ground state of Ga^{3+} ion has an _____pair of electrons in its outermost shell. The ion is _____

    (A) odd, paramagnetic   (D) odd, diamagnetic

    (B) even, paramagnetic   (E) even, ferromagnetic

    (C) even, diamagnetic

57. An alloy of iron and gallium has 63.8% iron composition. If 351.25 g of the alloy is completely dissolved in H_2SO_4 to produce Fe^{2+} and Ga^{3+} ions, what is the volume of H_2 collected at STP (neglecting the vapor pressure of air)?

    (A) 156.8 L   (D) 78.4 L

    (B) 123.2 L   (E) 145.6 L

    (C) 246.2 L

58. The reaction $A(g) + B(g) \leftrightarrow 2C(g) + D(s)$ has K_p of 0.65 at T = 298 K. If at the beginning P_A = 2 atm, P_B = 5 atm, and P_C = 4 atm, then initially

    (A) the free energy of the reaction is zero.

    (B) the reaction will proceed from left to right.

    (C) the reaction will proceed from right to left.

(D) the system will be at equilibrium.

(E) the free energy of the reaction is negative.

59. Use the information from the following table to calculate the approximate standard change of enthalpy in kJ/mol for the combustion of coal.

Substance	ΔH_f° (kJ/mol)
C (s)	0.0
CO_2 (g)	−393.5
H_2O (l)	−285.85
O_2 (g)	0.0

(A) 0

(B) +286

(C) −698

(D) −286

(E) −394

60. Which of the following aqueous solutions has the lowest melting point?

(A) pure water

(B) 1.0 M NaCl

(C) 1.0 M sucrose

(D) 1.0 M $MgCl_2$

(E) 1.0 M HCl

61. What is the volume of H_2O which can be condensed after the complete combustion of 2240 L of ethane (volume of gas measured at STP?

(A) 10.8 mL

(B) 10.8 L

(C) 5.4 L

(D) 5.4 mL

(E) 3.0 L

62. Given the mechanism below for the oxidation of nitrogen (II) oxide; determine which expression gives the rate of formation of NO_2?

$$NO + NO \overset{k_1}{\underset{k_1}{\leftrightarrow}} N_2O_2 \quad \text{Fast equilibrium}$$

$$N_2O_2 + O_2 \overset{k_3}{\rightarrow} 2NO_2$$

(A) $k_3[N_2O_2][O_2]$

(B) $\frac{k_1}{k_2} k_3[NO]^2[O_2]$

(C) $\frac{k_2}{k_1} k_3[NO]^2[O_2]$

(D) $2\frac{k_2}{k_1} k_3[NO][O_2]$

(E) $2\frac{k_1}{k_2} k_3[NO][O_2]$

63. The pOH of a 1.0 M solution of HCl is:

(A) 1   (D) 0

(B) 13   (E) 15

(C) 14

64. If the pOH of solution A is 2.5 and the pOH of B is 10.1, then which of the following is true?

(A) Solution A has a higher concentration of protons than B.

(B) Solution B is more basic than solution A.

(C) Solution A is more basic than solution B.

(D) Solution A is more acidic than solution B.

(E) Solution B has a higher concentration of hydroxyl ions than A.

65. K_c for a reaction $A(g) + 3B(g) \leftrightarrow 2C(g) + 2D(s)$ has units

(A) $mole^{-2}liter^{2}$

(D) $mole^{-1}liter$

(B) $mole^{2}liter^{-2}$

(E) $mole^{-1}liter^{-1}$

(C) $mole\,liter^{-2}$

66. The density of gaseous SO_3 at 15 °C, 50 mmHg and R = 0.0821 liter-atm/(mole • K) is:

(A) 0.223 g/liter

(D) 0.357 liter/g

(B) 0.223 liter g^{-1}

(E) 0.357 g/liter

(C) 169.17 g/liter

67. Cryolite (Na_3AlF_6) is added to Al_2O_3 during electrolysis of Al_2O_2 to

(A) obtain higher purity Al

(B) permit the electrolysis at a lower temperature

(C) increase the solubility of Al_2O_3 for electrolysis

(D) increase the conductivity of Al_2O_3

(E) react with the oxygen in Al_2O_2 and hence free the Al metal

68. Which of the following is acetone?

(A) $CH_3CH_2CH_2{-}OH$

(B)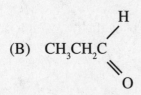

(C) $CH_3{-}O{-}CH_2CH_3$

(D) CH_3COCH_3

(E) $CH_3CH_2CH_3$
    |
    OH

69. Carbon dioxide sublimes. Which physical transformation occurs in sublimation?

    (A) gas to liquid   (D) solid to gas

    (B) gas to solid   (E) solid to liquid

    (C) solid to liquid to gas

70. What is the type of hybridization used by chlorine in the ClF_4 ion?

    (A) sp^3d^2 (D) sp^2d^3

    (B) p^3d^3 (E) sp^3sd

    (C) p^3d^3

71. 15 g of ethane reacts with chlorine to yield 15 g of 1-chloropropane. The percent yield of ethyl chloride is:

    (A) 46.5%   (D) 93.0%

    (B) 50.0%   (E) 23.3%

    (C) 100.0%

72. The K_a for acetic acid is 1.8×10^{-5}. Calculate the approximate equilibrium constant for the reaction below.

    $$HC_2H_3O_2 + OH^- \leftrightarrow H_2O + C_2H_3O_2^-$$

    (A) 1.8×10^{-5} (D) 5.5×10^4

    (B) 1.8×10^9 (E) 1.0×10^{-14}

    (C) 1.0×10^{14}

73. Based on the standard reduction potentials listed below, which of the following is the strongest reducing agent?

    Fe^{2+} / Fe   −0.44 V

    Pb^{2+} / Pb   −0.13 V

    Ag^+ / Ag   +0.80 V

    (A) Fe   (D) Ag

    (B) Fe^{2+} (E) Ag^+

    (C) Pb

74. Refer to the diagram below.

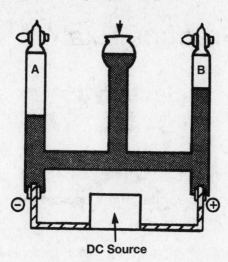

H$_2$O + dilute H$_2$SO$_4$

DC Source

Which of the following is the anode reaction?

(A) $2H_2O \leftrightarrow H_3O^+ + OH^-$

(B) $H_2O \leftrightarrow \dfrac{1}{2}O_2 + H_2$

(C) $H_2O \leftrightarrow H^+ + OH^-$

(D) $H_2O \leftrightarrow \dfrac{1}{2}O_2 + 2H^+ + 2e^-$

(E) $2H_2O \overset{+2e-}{\leftrightarrow} H_2 + 2OH^-$

75. A hydrocarbon that contains only carbon and hydrogen is composed of 75% carbon. What is the empirical formula for the compound?

(A) CH_2 (D) C_2H_5

(B) CH_3 (E) C_2H_7

(C) CH_4

AP Chemistry

Practice Exam 4

Section II

TIME: 90 minutes
55% of the entire test

(Answer sheets appear in the back of this book.)

The percentages given for the parts represent the score weightings for this section of the examination. You will be given 40 minutes for Part A and 50 minutes for Part B.

You may use a calculator on Part A, but not on Part B.

Be sure to write your answers in the space provided following each question. Pay attention to significant figures.

Part A

TIME: 40 minutes
40 percent

YOU MAY USE A CALCULATOR ON THIS PART.

Show your work clearly for full credit. Pay attention to significant figures in your answers.

Solve the following problem.

1.   The solubility of iron (II) hydroxide, $Fe(OH)_2$, is 1.43×10^{-3} g/L at 25 °C.

   (a) Write the balanced equation for the solubility equilibrium.

   (b) Write the expression for the solubility product constant, K_{sp}, and calculate its value.

   (c) Calculate the pH of a saturated solution of $Fe(OH)_2$ at 25 °C.

   (d) A 50.0-milliliter sample of 0.002-molar $FeSO_4$ solution is added to 50.0-milliliters of 0.003-molar NaOH solution. Will a precipitate form? Show calculations to support your answer.

   (e) How is the solubility of iron (II) hydroxide affected if the pH of the solution is lowered? Use calculations to support your answer.

Solve EITHER problem 2 or problem 3 below. Only one of these two questions will be graded. (The problem you choose will be worth 20% of the score on Part II.)

2.   A student dissolves 2.00 grams of an unknown solute into 125 grams of benzene to find the molar mass of an unknown compound. The normal melting point for benzene is 5.5 °C, while its molal freezing point constant is 5.12 °C kg / mol.

   (a) The student compares the cooling curve of the solution of benzene and the unknown with the cooling curve for pure benzene. The difference in the melting points on the two cooling curves is 0.55 °C. At what temperature did the solution freeze?

   (b) Calculate the molality of the unknown solute.

   (c) Calculate the molar mass of the unknown solute.

   (d) The percent composition of the unknown solute is 78.9 % carbon, 10.6 % hydrogen, and 10.5 % oxygen. Calculate the molecular formula of the unknown.

   (e) Suggest a structure for the formula that is consistent with the results. Explain briefly why the structure that you propose is appropriate given these experimental results.

3.   To standardize a solution of potassium permanganate, 0.157 g of sodium oxalate was dissolved in water, acidified, and titrated with the permanganate solution.

   (a)   Write a balanced equation for the reaction.

   (b)   If 15.3 mL of the potassium permanganate solution were needed, what is its molarity?

   (c)   What is the mass of potassium permanganate in the 15.3 mL solution?

   (d)   Find the volume of the above potassium permanganate solution required to titrate 0.105 mole solution of ferrous sulfate.

Part B

TIME: 50 minutes

YOU MAY NOT USE A CALCULATOR ON THIS PART.

4.   This question is worth 15% of Section II. Write the formulas of the reactants and products for FIVE of the following eight reactions. Show net ionic reactions only, where appropriate. Assume the reaction takes place in aqueous solution unless otherwise specified. Do not balance the reaction.

   (a)   An aqueous solution of nitric acid poured over solid copper (I) oxide

   (b)   Hydrogen gas passed over Tungsten (VI) oxide

   (c)   Zinc added to copper sulfate

   (d)   Ammonia gas passed over copper oxide

   (e)   Carbon dioxide gas mixed with methane gas

   (f)   Zinc oxide added to hot coke

   (g)   Manganese dropped into an aqueous hydrochloric acid bath

   (h)   Solid cobalt in an atmosphere of chlorine gas

ANSWER BOTH OF THE FOLLOWING ESSAY QUESTIONS (15% each).

5. Explain each of the following based on principles of atomic structure or position on the periodic table.

    (a) Within a family, the ionic radius increases as the atomic number increases.

    (b) The first ionization energy of aluminum is lower than the first ionization energy of magnesium.

    (c) The second ionization energy of sodium is about three times greater than the second ionization energy of magnesium.

    (d) For magnesium, the difference between the second and third ionization energies is much larger than the difference between the first and second ionization energies.

ANSWER THE FOLLOWING LABORTATORY-BASED ESSAY QUESTION.

6. Use principles of bonding and/or intermolecular forces to explain each of the following laboratory observations:

    (a) Argon has a higher boiling point that does neon.

    (b) Solid silver is an excellent conductor of electricity, but solid silver iodide is not.

    (c) NH_3 is soluble in water, but BF_3 is not.

    (d) Silicon and carbon are both in the same group on the periodic table. However the oxide of silicone is a solid, but the oxide of carbon is not.

ANSWER QUESTION 7 OR QUESTION 8 BELOW. ONLY ONE OF THESE TWO QUESTIONS WILL BE GRADED

7.   Explain the following:

(a)   Hydrogen peroxide is kep in dark brown bottles. Explain the antiseptic action of hydrogen peroxide.

(b)   Ethyl chloride acts as a fast acting local anesthetic.

(c)   A lake freezes on the surface but not at the bottom.

(d)   Aerosol cans carry a warning: "Do Not Incinerate."

8.   What are the differences between:

(a)   Amorphous and crystalline solids?

(b)   Molecular and ionic crystals?

(c)   Polar molecular and non-polar molecular crystals?

(d)   Ionic and network covalent crystals?

AP Chemistry

Practice Exam 4

ANSWER KEY

Section I

1.	(E)	26.	(D)	51.	(A)
2.	(B)	27.	(D)	52.	(B)
3.	(D)	28.	(E)	53.	(E)
4.	(D)	29.	(B)	54.	(A)
5.	(B)	30.	(A)	55.	(D)
6.	(E)	31.	(B)	56.	(D)
7.	(A)	32.	(B)	57.	(B)
8.	(C)	33.	(A)	58.	(C)
9.	(A)	34.	(D)	59.	(E)
10.	(D)	35.	(C)	60.	(D)
11.	(B)	36.	(C)	61.	(C)
12.	(B)	37.	(A)	62.	(B)
13.	(C)	38.	(E)	63.	(C)
14.	(A)	39.	(C)	64.	(C)
15.	(B)	40.	(B)	65.	(A)
16.	(C)	41.	(E)	66.	(A)
17.	(D)	42.	(C)	67.	(B)
18.	(C)	43.	(A)	68.	(D)
19.	(D)	44.	(A)	69.	(D)
20.	(A)	45.	(B)	70.	(A)
21.	(E)	46.	(D)	71.	(A)
22.	(C)	47.	(C)	72.	(B)
23.	(C)	48.	(A)	73.	(A)
24.	(C)	49.	(C)	74.	(D)
25.	(E)	50.	(D)	75.	(C)

DETAILED EXPLANATIONS OF ANSWERS

Practice Exam 4

Section I

1.   **(E)**   Metalloids cannot be satisfactorily identified as being either metals or non-metals for they possess some properties of each. They are usually identified as the staircase elements.

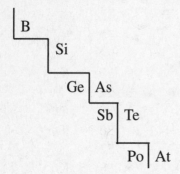

Note that At has mostly metallic properties; therefore it is not included in the staircase.

2.   **(B)**   Krypton is a member of the noble gas family otherwise known as inert gases. These gases, due to their filled valence shells, are quite unreactive, hence the term "inert gas."

3.   **(D)**   Metals are located on the left of the periodic table, while the non-metals are listed on the right side. Of all the elements listed, Sr is the element furthest to the left of the periodic table and, therefore, the most metallic. Sr is also located in the group IIA generally known as the alkaline-earth metals.

4.   **(D)**   Actually the liquid form of formaldehyde, called formalin, is used to preserve tissue specimen.

5.   **(B)**   Stannous fluoride is the active ingredient in certain brand name toothpastes which capitalize on the oxidizing effectiveness of fluoride ions.

6.   **(E)** $CH_3COOC_6H_4COOH$, acetylsalicylic acid, is the white crystalline compound commonly used to reduce pain and fever in the form of aspirin.

7.   **(A)**   Oxidation takes place at the anode while reduction takes place at the cathode. Alternatives (C) and (D) are wrong since they both describe oxidative processes. Upon reviewing the cell solution, choice (A) is the correct answer.

8.   **(C)**   The purpose of a salt bridge is to allow the positive and negative ions to migrate from cell to cell and thus allows a current to flow while preventing the two solutions from mixing. The current flows clockwise in this cell.

9.   **(A)**   In order to calculate the emf value of a voltaic cell at various concentrations we use the Nernst equation

$$E = E° - \frac{0.05915}{n} \log Q$$

where E = the emf for the reaction at the new concentration
       E° = the standard electrode potential
       n = the number of moles of electrons involved in the half reactions
       Q = the reaction quotient

10. **(D)**   Allotropes are elements with more than one form due to molecular structure differences, as in O_2 and O_3 (see figure below), or as a result of differences in the arrangement of atoms or molecules, as with diamond and graphite, which are allotropic forms of carbon.

ozone   oxygen

11. **(B)**   The reaction of a salt with water yields acid and base products.

$$Na_2CO_3 + 2H_2O \leftrightarrow 2NaOH + H_2CO_3$$

strong base weak acid

12. **(B)**   Since one mole of ideal gas occupies a volume of 22.4 liters at STP we have:

$$\frac{34 \text{ grams of } NH_3}{17 \text{ grams (M.W. of } NH_3)} = 2 \text{ moles of } NH_3 \times \frac{22.4 \text{ liters}}{1 \text{ mole of } NH_3}$$

$$= 44.8 \text{ liters of } NH_3$$

M.W. = molecular weight.

13. **(C)**   A homogeneous mixture is one of uniform composition. All of the choices are homogeneous except for the heterogeneous mixture of sand in water, in which case you can see the separate bits of sand dispersed in the water medium.

14. **(A)**   Rutherford projected a beam of $\propto$-particles from a radioactive source onto very thin gold foil. Most passed through without deflection, a few were diverted from their paths and very few were deflected back towards the source. Rutherford therefore concluded that: 1) the atom consists largely of empty space and 2) each atom must contain a heavy positively charged body (the nucleus) due to the repulsions.

15. **(B)**   X represents an element.

$$_{\text{atom number}}^{\text{atomic mass}} X$$

Based solely on the atomic number we can conclude

that $_{10}^{21}X$ must represent the noble gas neon.

16. **(C)** The functional group is representative of an acid (e.g. acetic acid CH_3-COOH).

Other functional groups such as:

$$R-O-R, \qquad R-COH, \quad R-\underset{\underset{O}{||}}{C}-H, \qquad R-\overset{\overset{O}{||}}{C}-OR$$

represent ethers, alcohols, aldehydes, and esters respectively.

17. **(D)**

$$\text{mass} = \frac{PV \text{ (molar mass)}}{RT} = \frac{2.0 \text{ atm} \times K \text{ mol} \times 3.0 \text{ L} \times 70.90 \text{ g}}{0.082 \text{ L atm} \quad 400 \text{ K}}$$

$$= 13 \text{ grams}$$

18. **(C)**

(A) Atomic weight of Fe = 55.8g $mole^{-1}$

; therefore there are $\dfrac{49}{55.8} \approx 0.88$ moles of Fe

1 mole element will contain Avogadro's number of atoms which is 6.026×10^{23}

; therefore no. of atoms in 55.8g of Fe = $0.88 \times 6.026 \times 10^{23}$
$$= 5.3 \times 10^{23} \text{ atoms.}$$

(B) at STP 1 mole of gas occupies 22.4 L

No. of moles of 5 L of gas is $\dfrac{5}{22.4} \times 1 = 0.22$ moles

No. of molecules present is no. of moles × Avogadro's number =

$$0.22 \times 6.026 \times 10^{23} = 1.3 \times 10^{23} \text{ molecules}$$

(C) Ethanol has the molecular formula C_2H_5OH

Molecular weight of ethanol = $(2 \times 12) + 6 + 16 = 24 + 22 = 46$ g/mol

; therefore no. of moles in 150 g of $C_2H_5OH = \dfrac{1 \text{ mol}}{46 \text{ g}} = 3.26$

No. of molecules $= 3.26 \times 6.026 \times 10^{23} = 19.65 \times 10^{23}$ molecules

(D) 10 L of O_3 at STP contains 10/22.4 moles of O_3.

; therefore no. of moles of $O_3 = \dfrac{10}{22.4} \times 6.026 \times 10^{23} = 2.69 \times 10^{23}$ molecules

(E) The no. of molecules in 80 g of calcium carbide is

$$\frac{80}{\text{Mol. Wt. of } Ca_2C} \times 6.026 \times 10^{23} =$$

$$\frac{80}{92.16} \times 6.026 \times 10^{23} = 5.23 \times 10^{23} \text{ molecules}$$

; therefore the answer is (C) 150 g of ethanol contains the largest number of molecules (19.65×10^{23} molecules).

19. **(D)**

$$\text{Mass} = \text{PV (molar mass)} = \frac{(2.0 \ \text{atm}) (K \text{ mol}) (3.0 \text{ L}) (70.90 \text{ g})}{(0.0821 \text{ L atm}) (400 \text{ K})}$$

$$= 13 \text{ grams}$$

20. **(A)** The abbreviated electronic configuration of an element of atomic number 42 is [Kr] $5s^1 4d^5$, where [Kr] stands for the electronic arrangement of Krypton, element 36, indicating the filling of all sublevels through $4p^6$. The remaining 6 electrons go into 5s and 4d orbitals. The $5s^1 4d^5$ configuration is preferred over the $5s^2 4d^4$ configuration because of the stability of the half-filled 4d sublevel.

21. **(E)** An atom, ion or a molecule with one or more unpaired electrons exhibits paramagnetism (they are slightly attracted into a magnetic field). Those with all electrons paired are diamagnetic (slightly repelled by a magnetic field). All the ions listed have unpaired electrons in their valence shell. The ions have the following electron configurations:

Fe^{2+}: [Ar]$3d^6$ with 4 unpaired electrons in the 3d orbitals

Fe^{3+}: $[Ar]3d^5$ with 5 unpaired electrons

CO^{3+}: $[Ar]3d^6$ with 4 unpaired electrons

Ni^{2+}: $[Ar]3d^{10}$ with two unpaired electrons in the 3d orbitals.

$$(\uparrow\downarrow) \quad (\uparrow\downarrow) \quad (\uparrow\downarrow) \quad (\uparrow) \quad (\uparrow)$$

22. **(C)** The reaction is spontaneous because the change in free energy is less than zero.

$$\Delta G°_{reaction} = \Sigma\Delta G°_f(\text{products}) - \Sigma\Delta G°_f(\text{reactants})$$

$$\Delta G°_{reaction} = [(2 \times -237) + (4 \times -394) + (4 \times 52)] - (4 \times 125)$$

$$\Delta G°_{reaction} = -2342 \text{ kJ}$$

23. **(C)** This problem in molecular geometry can be solved by considering an electrostatic model. This is done by arranging all electrical charges of the same sign on the surface of a given sphere so that they have maximum stability. The possible stable positions on the sphere depend on the number of charges: two charges will be arranged in diametrically opposite positions; three charges will be arranged on the circumference of a circle bounding the sphere at 120° to each other; four will occupy the vertices of a regular tetrahedron. The most stable arrangements for five and six charges will be a triangular (triagonal) bipyramid and an octahedral respectively. Therefore, for a central atom surrounded by five atoms, the geometrical shape of the molecule will be a triangular bipyramid. PCl_5 is an example of such a molecule.

24. **(C)** While phosphorous and red phosphorous are two allotropic forms of phosphorous, red phosphorous ignites by friction. Mixed with fine sand, it is used on striking surfaces of matchboxes. Although its structure is unknown, red phosphorous is less reactive than white phosphorous, which burns spontaneously in air.

25. **(E)** Since the rate equation is third order (rate $= k \, [A]^2 \, [B]$), then solving for the specific rate constant would yield the following.

$$k = \frac{\text{rate}}{[A]^2 \, [B]} = \frac{.02 \text{ M/sec}}{.04 \text{ M}^3} = 0.5 \frac{L^2 \text{ sec}}{\text{mol}^2}$$

26. **(D)**   Iodine is not used in the making of audio-recording tapes. These employ a coating of metallic oxides with magnetic properties like iron oxides.

27. **(D)**   VSEPR is an acronym for valence-shell electron-pair repulsion. It states that bonding electron pairs and lone electron pairs of an atom will arrange themselves in space so as to minimize electron-pair repulsion around that atom. It is used to predict the geometries of various molecules and ions.

28. **(E)** K_{sp} is the solubility product of a slightly soluble salt.

For $CaSO_4$ $K_{sp} = [Ca^{2+}] [SO_4^{2-}]$

If we let X represent the concentration of SO_4^{2-} anions in mole liter^{-1},

$CaSO_4$ dissociates in equimolar proportions so

$$K_{sp} = [Ca^{2+}] [SO_4^{2-}] = [X] [X] = X_1^2 = 2.4 \times 10^{-5}$$

; therefore $X_1 \approx 5. \times 10^{-3}$ moleliter^{-1}

For Ag_2SO_4 the K_{sp} expression is different because $Ag_2SO_4 \leftrightarrow 2\ Ag^+ + SO_4^{2-}$ *i.e.*, each mole of Ag_2SO_4 produces 2 moles of Ag^+ and one mole of SO_4^{2-} ions

$$[Ag^+] = 2X_2 \text{ and } [SO_4^{2-}] = X_2$$
$$K_{sp} = [Ag+]2 [SO_4^{2-}] = (2X_2)^2 (X_2)$$
$$K_{sp} = 4X^3 = 1.2 \times 10^{-5}$$
$$X_2 = 0.0144$$
$$X_2 = 14.4 \times 10^{-3}$$
$$\frac{X_2}{X_1} = \frac{14.4 \times 10^{-3}}{5 \times 10^{-3}} = 2.9$$

29. **(B)**   The dipole moment of a bond is directed from the partial positive charge to the partial negative charge or from the less electronegative to the more electronegative atom in the bond.

Example: H – Cl

$\xrightarrow{\quad \propto +\qquad \propto -\quad}$ direction of dipole moment.

If the molecule contains more than one bond moment, then the resultant dipole moment is the vector sum of all the bond moments.

Thus for H_2O we have:

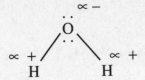

bond moments: ☐☐

 resultant dipole moment is oriented according to the resultant
i.e.: ↑

For CO_2 we have:

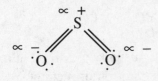

bond moments   ←——⊣   ⊢——→

The vector sum is zero, therefore the resultant dipole moment is 0.

For SO_2

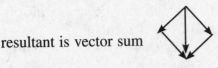

bond moments

resultant is vector sum ◇ is oriented as ↓ so the combination of

resultant dipole moments is ↑, O, ↓

30. **(A)** The reaction is

$$MnO_4^= \rightarrow MnO_4^- + MnO$$

This is a type of disproportionation reaction, MnO_4^- reacting with itself to produce MnO_4^{-2} and MnO_2 in acidic medium. "Acidic medium" informs us that the balanced equation may involve H^+ and/or H_2O on either side of the equation. We will use the ion-electron method to balance the equation. We write two half-reactions as follows:

1st half-reaction

$$MnO_4^{-2} \rightarrow MnO_4^-$$

The oxidation state of Mn changes from +6 to +7 in MnO_4^-, so the preceding is an oxidation reaction.

$$MnO_4^{2-} \rightarrow MnO_4^- + e^- \qquad \text{(oxidation)}$$

2nd half reaction

$$MnO_4^{2-} \rightarrow MnO_2 \qquad \text{(reduction)}$$

Here Mn is changed from +6 to +4. To account for the deficiency of oxygen on the right-hand side of the equation, we add H_2O, remembering that the reaction is occuring in acidic solution, which corresponds to adding H^+ to the left-hand side of the equation and balance it as

$$MnO_4^{2-} + 4H^+ + 2e^- \rightarrow MnO_2 + 2H_2O$$

For the electron gain and loss to balance, multiply the oxidation half-reaction by 2 and add the half-reactions.

$$
\begin{array}{lll}
2MnO_4^{2-} & \rightarrow 2MnO_4^- + 2e^- & \text{(oxidation)} \\
+\ MnO_4^{-2} + 4H^+ + 2e^- & \rightarrow MnO_2 + 2H_2O & \text{(reduction)} \\
\hline
3MnO_4^{2-} + 4H^+ & \rightarrow 2MnO_4^- + MnO_2 + 2H_2O &
\end{array}
$$

31. **(B)** Reactions that occur in solution are usually classified into, (i) proton transfer or acid-base reactions, (ii) precipitation or metathesis, (iii) electron transfer or oxidation-reduction reactions.

Metathesis involves the exchange of ions with the formation of one or more salts. (Note: Another type of reaction which may occur not in solution is synthesis or formation of compounds from elements.)

32. **(B)** From the solubility rules we know that

(1) all $(IA)^+$ and NH_4^+ salts are soluble, therefore I is soluble.

(2) all sulfates are soluble except sulfates of Pb^{+2}, Ca^{2+}, Sr^{2+} and Ba^{2+}, therefore, II is not soluble.

(3) also all halides are soluble except halides of Pb^{+2}, Ag^+, Hg^{2+} and Tl^+, therefore, $PbCl_2$ is insoluble.

(4) all salts of NO_3^-, ClO_4^-, ClO_3^- and $C_2H_3O_2^-$ ions are soluble, therefore IV is soluble.

33. **(A)**   Cations in the common higher oxidation state are named by adding the suffix –ic to a stem.

Cations in the common lower oxidation state are named by adding the suffix –ous to a stem.

The common cations for copper, cobalt, lead and tin are

      Cu: Cu^+ (cuprous)
            Cu^{2+} (cupric)

      Co: Co^{2+} (cobaltous)

      Pb: Pb^{2+} (plumbous)

      Sn: Sn^{+2} (stannous)
           Sn^{4+} (stannic)

34. **(D)**   The sulfide ion is used up and removed from the reaction by the acid, because hydrogen sulfide gas is produced. With the removal of the sulfide ion, mass action draws more and more iron sulfide into solution. In this way, the solubility of iron sulfide is maximized in an acidic solution. Option D is the answer that involves the highest concentration of acidic solution, and will therefore allow the most iron sulfide to dissolve.

35. **(C)**   Properties of a solution that depend only on the concentration of the solute and not on its nature, are called colligative properties. Examples are the freezing-point depression, boiling point elevation, osmotic pressure and vapor pressure depression. Each of these can be used to find the molecular weight of an unknown solute.

36. **(C)**

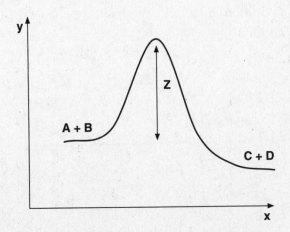

The above diagram is a plot of the potential energy (E) possessed by molecules as a function of the reaction coordinate. As A and B approach each other, the potential energy of the system increases to a maximum, which corresponds to an activated complex. The difference in energy between A + B and the activated complex is called the activation energy. In the diagram above, y = E = potential energy, x = reaction coordinate, and z = activation energy.

37. **(A)**   Radioactive decay is governed by a first-order rate law
R → P

Rate = k[R]   The minus sign indicates a rate of decrease.

[R] - amount present at time t

k – specific rate constant

$$T_{1/2} = \frac{.693}{k}$$

$$T_{1/2} = \frac{.693 \text{ yr}}{5.33 \times 10^{-10}}$$

$$T_{1/2} = 1.3 \times 10^{9} \text{ yr}$$

38. **(E)**   By the Brønsted-Lowry definition, an acid is any substance that can donate protons and a base is a substance that accepts protons. By this definition, NH_3 and H_2O are Brønsted bases because:

$$NH_3 + H^+ \rightarrow NH_4^+$$

$$H_2O + H^+ \rightarrow H_3O^+$$

By the Lewis definition an acid is an electron-pair acceptor and a base is an electron-pair donor in a chemical reaction.

By this definition we again see that NH_3 and H_2O are Lewis bases because

$$H - \overset{..}{N} - H + H+ \qquad \longrightarrow \qquad \left[H - \overset{\overset{\displaystyle H}{|}}{N} - H \right]^{+}$$
with H below the nitrogen on the left.

and

$$H - \overset{\cdot\cdot}{\underset{\underset{H}{|}}{O}} + H^+ \longrightarrow \left[H - \overset{\cdot\cdot}{\underset{\underset{H}{|}}{O}} - H \right]^+$$

hydronium ion

BBr_3 is a Lewis acid because boron in BBr_3 has a vacant 2p orbital which can accept a pair of electrons, *e.g.*,

$$\overset{\cdot\cdot}{N} H_3 + B Br_3 \rightarrow H_3N \rightarrow B Br_3$$

NaOH is neither a Brønsted base nor a Lewis base. It is an Arrhenius base. An Arrhenius acid is a substance that produces hydrogen ions or protons in aqueous solution. An Arrhenius base produces hydroxide ions.

39. **(C)**   The electron configuration of holmium (Ho) with atomic number 67 is [Xe] $4f^{11}6s^2$.

Hence that of Ho^{+3} is $[Xe]4f^{10}$ in the ground state. 4f has seven degenerate (i.e. equal energy) orbitals with the 10 electrons distributed by Hund's rule as:

$$\underline{\uparrow\downarrow} \quad \underline{\uparrow\downarrow} \quad \underline{\uparrow\downarrow} \quad \underline{\uparrow} \quad \underline{\uparrow} \quad \underline{\uparrow} \quad \underline{\uparrow}$$

Thus we have 4 unpaired electrons.

40. **(B)**   One may assume that when removing electrons to form stable cations, the electrons would leave the orbitals in the reverse order in which they were filled. This is true to some extent; but there are many exceptions especially in the transition elements. A good rule to follow is that the electrons that are removed from an atom or ion are those with the maximum value of the principal quantum number n; and of this set of electrons the easiest to remove are those with the maximum L.

Ir^{+3} is formed by removal of 3 electrons from Ir which has an electron configuration $[Xe]4f^{14}5d^76s^2$. So by the rule given, the first 2 electrons would leave the $6s^2$ and the third from $5d^7$ orbitals to give a ground state configuration of $[Xe]4f^{14}5d^6$.

41. **(E)**   The tendency to achieve completely filled and, to a lesser extent, half-filled shells, controls the chemistry of most elements of the periodic table. Therefore, Eu, with configuration $[Xe]4f^76s^2$, will lose the $6s^2$ electron to attain a half-filled $4f^7$ configuration, with oxidation state equal

to +2. For Sc, with configuration $[Ar]3d^14s^2$, the most stable ion will be obtained with the loss of 3 electrons from $4s^2$ and $3d^1$ to achieve the configuration of Argon:$[Ne]3s^23p^6$, oxidation state equals +3.

42. **(C)**   Alums are double salts of the general formula M^+M^{3+} $(SO_4)_2$ $12H_2O$ where M^+ can be Na^+, K^+, Ag^+, NH_4^+ and other +1 ions.

M^{3+} can be Al^{3+}, Fe^{+3}, Cr^{+3}, Mn^{+3}.

The most common alums are aluminum salts (therefore the name alum). Solutions of alum are acidic because of the hydrolysis of the aluminum ion.

$$Al^{3+} + H_2O \rightarrow \downarrow Al(OH)_3 + 3H^+$$

(E) is not a correct answer because although crystals of alum are isomorphous, i.e. of the same crystalline form, we cannot speak of solutions being isomorphous. Isomorphism refers to crystalline forms and not to solutions.

43. **(A)**   44.   **(A)**   45.   **(B)**

The cell in these problems is called the concentration cell.

Let the half-cell equations be:

anode:	$Ag \rightarrow Ag^+_{dilute} + e^-$	$\Sigma^\circ = -0.8V$
cathode:	$Ag^+_{std} + e^- \rightarrow Ag$	$\Sigma^\circ = +0.8V$

overall: $Ag^+_{std} + Ag \rightarrow Ag^+_{dilute} + Ag,$ $\Sigma^\circ = 0.00V$

= 0.00V which answers (44). To find out if the reaction will take place as written we use a Nernst equation to evaluate the cell potential.

$$E_{cell} = E^\circ_{cell} - \frac{0.059}{n} \log \left\{ \frac{[Ag^+_{dilute}]}{[Ag^+_{std.}]} \right\}$$

n = 1 in this example

$$\therefore E_{cell} = -0.059 \log \frac{10^{-3}}{1.0} = -0.059 \times (-3)$$

$$E_{cell} = 0.177$$

Since E_{cell} is positive, the reaction will proceed as written; if E_{cell}, however, had been negative then it would imply that we had written the equation in the wrong direction. From the half-cell reactions we conclude that the standard electrode is the cathode so the only correct statement in 43 is (A).

43 (D) is false since the cell will stop functioning after the concentration of Ag^+ ions around the electrodes evens out. The only false statement in 45 is (B) since we found from the Nernst equation that $E_{cell} = +0.117$.

46. **(D)** The number of moles of base added is

$$10 \text{ mL} \times 0.15 = 1.5 \text{ m mol}$$

The reaction of the base and acid is:

$$HCl + NaOH \rightarrow NaCl + H_2O$$

so 1.5 m mole of HCl reacts.

The amount of acid remaining is

$$(25.0 \text{ mL} \times 0.1) - 1.5 \text{ m mol} = 2.5 - 1.5 = 1 \text{ m mol}$$

The new volume in which this acid exists is

$$V_T = 25 + 10 = 35 \text{ mL}$$

$$\text{concentration of protons } [H^+] = \frac{1 \text{ m mol}}{35 \text{ mL}}$$

$$pH = -\log\left(\frac{1 \text{ m mol}}{35 \text{ mL}}\right)$$

47. **(C)** The most polar of the organic substances listed is acetic acid CH_3COOH therefore it is the most soluble.

48. **(A)** The compounds listed are approximately the same molecular weight, but the boiling point of the acid is relatively higher as a result of intermolecular hydrogen bonding between two molecules.

$$CH_3CH_2CH_2 - C \overset{\displaystyle \ddot{O} : \ldots \ldots H - O}{\underset{\displaystyle \ddot{O} - H \ldots \ldots : \ddot{O}}{\Big\langle}} \; C - CH_2CH_2CH_3$$

49. **(C)** In the periodic table as one moves down a group, the atomic size increases as a result of an increase in the principal quantum number n, corresponding to a decrease in the attraction force to the nucleus. But as one moves from left to right across a period, the atomic size decreases

as a result of an increase in nuclear charge while n remains constant. The decrease in atomic size as one moves across the first transition elements (*n* and *l* constant) results in gallium having the same size as aluminum, and germanium having the same size as silicon.

50. **(D)** Only the dihydrogen phosphate ion is able to either donate a proton (in the presence of a base) or accept a proton (in the presence of a very strong acid). The hydroxide ion (option A) can't donate a proton. The hydronium ion (option B) can't accept a further proton. The acetate ion (option C) can't donate another proton. The ammonium ion (option E) can't accept a further proton.

51. **(A)** The pressure at point A corresponds to the normal freezing and boiling points, so it must be 1.0 atm.

52. **(B)** Of the listed answers, only zone refining is used to purify silicon. Zone refining involves melting a rod of an element near one end and moving the heat source slowly to the opposite end of the rod. The impurities being more soluble in the melt than in the solid will move along the rod and concentrate at one end of the rod. This end is discarded leaving a pure rod.

53. **(E)** Graham's law of diffusion relates the diffusion rate and molecular weight of gases as

$$\frac{\text{rate (A)}}{\text{rate (B)}} = \sqrt{\frac{MW_B}{MW_A}}$$

$$\frac{\text{rate (A)}}{\text{rate (H}_2)} = 0.25$$

$$0.25 = \sqrt{\frac{2}{MW_A}}$$

$$0.0625 = \frac{2}{MW_A}$$

$$MW_A = \frac{2}{0.0625} = 2 \times 16 = 32$$

54. **(A)** Hydrogen bonding, the intramolecular force that occurs between a hydrogen covalently bonded to N, O, or F in one molecule and a nonbonding pair of electrons on N, O, or F in another molecule. Water is the most commonly encountered molecule that shows hydrogen bonding. The electron pair in the covalent bond between O and H is shifted toward the more electronegative oxygen, leaving the hydrogen partially positive in charge. This leads to a strong intramolecular attraction with a nonbonding pair of electrons on the oxygen of a nearby water molecule. That attraction is the hydrogen bond.

55. **(D)** There are four quantum numbers which describe an electron in an atom. Three of the quantum numbers, the principal (n), the azimuthal (l) and the magnetic quantum number m_l are obtained from the solution of the Schrödinger equation. The fourth, the spin quantum number m_s, is needed to explain the behavior of atomic spectra in a magnetic field. The electron has spin and therefore a magnetic moment which can be directed up or down.

56. **(D)** The electronic configuration of Ga is $[Ar]3d^{10}4s^24p^1$ so Ga^+ has configuration $[Ar]3d^{10}$. So there are 5 pairs of electrons in the outermost shell which now is 3d. 5 is an odd number.

The magnetic nature of the atom depends on the presence of an unpaired electron in the atom or ion. If the atom or ion contains one or more unpaired electrons it is paramagnetic. If it contains no unpaired electrons, it is diamagnetic.

57. **(B)** 351.25g of alloy contain:

Fe: $0.638 \times 351.25 = 224$ g of Fe

or $\dfrac{224}{56}$

$56 \approx$ atomic weight of Fe

Ga: $351.25 - 224 = 127.25$ g of Ga

or 1 mole of Ga since atomic wt. of Ga = 127.25

H_2SO_4 supplies $2H^+$ ions in solution per H_2SO_4

; therefore $Fe + 2H^+ \rightarrow Fe^{2+} + H_2\uparrow$

$2\,Ga + 6H^+ \rightarrow 2Ga^{3+} + 3H_2$

1 mole of Fe gives 1 mole of H_2 hence 4 moles of Fe will yield 4 moles of H_2.

2 moles of Ga gives 3 moles of H_2, hence 1 mole of Ga will yield 1.5 moles of H_2.

; therefore 351.25g of alloy gives 5.5 moles of H_2

At STP one mole of a gas occupies 22.4 L

; therefore the volume occupied by 5.5 moles of H_2 = 22.4 L × 5.5 gives V = 123.2 L

58. **(C)** The direction of a reaction is determined by ΔG. If $\Delta G < 0$, then the reaction proceeds spontaneously as written. If $\Delta G > 0$ then it will proceed in the reverse direction of the written equation.

For the reaction $A(g) + B(g) \rightarrow 2C(g) + Ds$

$$\Delta G = \Delta G^\circ + RT \ln \frac{[C]^2}{[A][B]}$$

$$\Delta G = \Delta G^\circ + RT \ln \frac{(P_c)^2}{(P_A)(P_B)}$$

If at any moment $Q > K$ then $\Delta G > 0$ and the reaction from left to right is not spontaneous but spontaneous from right to left. Since $\Delta G < 0$ for this direction, the reaction will take place in this direction, *i.e.*, right to left until equilibrium is established.

If $Q = K$, the reaction is at equilibrium.

If $Q < K$, $Q < 0$ the reaction proceeds from left to right until equilibrium is reached.

In the example $Q = \dfrac{(P_c)^2}{(P_A)(P_B)} = \dfrac{4^2}{2 \times 5} = \dfrac{16}{10} = 1.6$

$Q = 1.6 > 0.65 = K_p$

$\Delta G > O$ and reaction will proceed from right to left.

59. **(E)** The combustion of coal is simply the heat of formation of carbon dioxide.

60. **(D)**   The solution with the lowest melting point will have the greatest number of particles dissolved in it. The 1.0 M magnesium chloride has three moles dissolved in it for each liter of solution. The next greatest number of dissolved particles would come from the sodium chloride and the hydrochloric acid, each of which would donate two moles of dissolved ions for each mole of compound.

61. **(C)**   At STP 2240 L of ethane contains

$$\frac{2240}{22.4} = 100 \text{ moles of ethane using that 1 mole of a gas occupies 22.4 L}$$

at STP.

The equation for the complete combustion of ethane is

$$2C_2H_6 + 14O_2 \rightarrow 4CO_2 + 6H_2O$$

1 mole of C_2H_6 yields 3 moles of H_2O
; therefore 100 moles of C_2H_6 yields 300 moles of H_2O
1 mole of H_2O is 18 g
; therefore 300 moles weighs $300 \times 18 = 5400$ g $= 5.4$ kg
1 kg of H_2O occupies a volume of 1 L
; therefore volume of water condensed $= 5.4$ L

62. **(B)**   Given the mechanism as:

$$NO + NO \overset{k_1}{\underset{k_2}{\leftrightarrow}} N_2O_2$$

$$N_2O_2 + O_2 \overset{k_3}{\rightarrow} 2NO_2$$

Then the rate of formation of NO_2 is

$$\text{Rate} = k_3[N_2O_2] [O_2\}$$

The concentration of N_2O_2 is found from the equilibrium relation

$$k_1[NO] [NO] = k_2[N_2O_2]$$

$$[N_2O_2] = \frac{k_1}{k_2} [NO]^2$$

$$\text{the rate} = \frac{k_1}{k_2} [NO]^2[O_2]$$

63. **(C)**   HCl dissociates completely

; therefore $[H^+] = 1.0$

$pOH = 14 - pH$

$pH = -log[H^+] = -log 1 = 0.0$

; therefore $pOH = 14 - 0 = 14$

64. **(C)**   Given that pOH of A is 2.5

$pH = 14 - 2.5 = 11.5$ (basic solution)

$[H+] = 10^{-11.5} = 10^{-12} \times 10 + {}^{0.5} = 3.16 \times 10^{-12}M$

pOH of $B = 10.1$

$pH = 14 - 10.1 = 3.9$ (acidic solution)

$log[H^+] = -3.9$

$[H^+] = 10^{-3.9} = 10^{-4} \times 10^{+0.1} = 1.3 \times 10^{-4}M$

(A) and (B) state the same fact and are both wrong.

65. **(A)**   At equilibrium $A(g) + 3B(g)$ $2C(g) + 2D(s)$ has equilibrium constant as shown below:

$$K_c = \frac{[C]^2}{[A][B]^3} \frac{[mole/L]^2}{[mole/L][mole/L]^3}$$

$[Kc] = mole^{-2}\ liter^2$

66. **(A)**   For n moles of gas

$PV = nRT$

$PV = \frac{m}{M}RT,$ M = molecular weight

m = mass of gas

$density\ d = \frac{mass}{volume}$

$d = \frac{m}{v} = \frac{PM}{RT}$

Molecular weight of SO_3 is

$M_{SO_3} = 32+3\ (16) = 80$ g/mole

$P = 50$ mmHg $= 50/760$ atm $= 0.066$ atm

$T = 15 + 273 = 288$ K

$R = 0.0821$ liter • atm/(mole • K)

$$d = \frac{0.066 \times 80}{0.0821 \times 288} = 0.223 \text{ g/liter}$$

67. **(B)** Electrolysis of Al_2O_3 takes place in a molten state. Al_2O_3 has a melting point of about 2000 °C. Charles Hall found that a mixture of cryolite (Na_3AlF_6) and Al_2O_3 melts at about 1000 °C. At present other materials are used to produce even lower melting temperatures.

68. **(D)** Acetone is a ketone. Ketones are distinguished by the presence of C = O, the carbonyl group. Acetone has the structural formula

$$\begin{array}{c} O \\ \parallel \\ CH_3 - C - CH_3 \end{array}$$

69. **(D)** Sublimation describes the transformation from a solid to a gas without becoming a liquid.

70. **(A)** Chlorine is the central atom in ClF_4^-. The ground state electronic configuration of chlorine is

Cl: [Ne] $3s^2 3p^5$

3s   3p

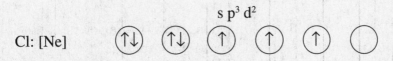

To accommodate 3F atoms and the lone pair of F– chlorine uses 2 of the 3d orbitals.

                    3s   3p   3d

Cl: [Ne]

These six orbitals are hybridized to give 6 equivalent $3sp^3d^2$ orbitals.

                                s p^3 d^2

Cl: [Ne]

Then the bonding of ClF_4^- is

$$s\,p^3\,d^2$$

Cl: [Ne]   ⟨↑↓⟩   ⟨↑↓⟩   ⟨↑↓⟩   ⟨↑↓⟩   ⟨↑↓⟩   ⟨↑↓⟩

                   F   F   F   F⁻

71. **(A)**   The reaction is

$$Cl_2 + CH_3CH_3 \rightarrow CH_3CH_2Cl + HCl$$

1 mole of ethane is $(2 \times 12\text{ g}) + 6 = 30$ g.

From the equation 1 mole C_2H_6 yields 1 mole of C_5H_5Cl

1 mole of C_2H_5 Cl weighs $(2 \times 12\text{ g}) + 5\text{ g} + 35.5\text{ g} = 64.5$ g

30 g of ethane theoretically should give 64.5 g of ethyl chloride. The amount of ethyl chloride obtained from 15 g of ethane is:

$$\text{amount of } C_2H_5Cl = \frac{15}{30} \times 64.5\text{ g} = 32.25\text{ g}$$

Therefore the theoretical yield is 32.25 g.

But the actual yield is 15 g.

$$\text{Therefore percent yield} = \frac{15}{32.25} \times 100 = 46.5\%$$

72. **(B)**   The reaction as shown is the reverse of the K_b reaction. The equilibrium constant for this reaction is simply the K_a divided by K_w, or simply add 14 to the exponent of the acid dissociation constant.

73. **(A)**   The iron reduction potential is the lowest, so it is most easily oxidized—not reduced. Since it is the most easily oxidized, then it acts as the reducing agent most easily.

74. **(D)**   The oxidation reaction is

$$H_2O \rightarrow \frac{1}{2}O_2 + 2H^+ + 2e^-$$

Reaction E is a reduction while reactions A and C are not electrochemical in nature. Reaction B is the overall reaction for the cell.

75. **(C)** The quick way to look at this is that the carbon is three-fourths of the molecule by mass, so 12 grams (1 mole) of carbon must go with 4 grams (4 moles) of hydrogen. Or, to check with the complete calculation,

$$75 \text{ g C} \times \frac{1.0 \text{ mol C}}{12.011 \text{ g C}} = 6.2 \text{ mol C}$$

$$25 \text{ g H} \times \frac{1.0 \text{ mol H}}{1.008 \text{ g H}} = 24.8 \text{ mol H}$$

Empirical formula: CH_4

Section II

1.   (a) $Fe(OH)_2$ (s) $\leftrightarrow$ Fe^{2+} (aq) $+$ 2 OH^- (aq)

     (b) $K_{sp} = [Fe^{2+}][OH^-]^2 = (1.6 \times 10^{-5})(3.2 \times 10^{-5})^2 = 1.6 \times 10^{-14}$

     (c)   First convert the solubility in g/L into molar solubility to find $[OH^-]$ at saturation.

     1.43×10^{-3} g/L $\times$ 1 mol/89.9 g $= 1.6 \times 10^{-5}$ mol/L

     $[OH^-] = 2 \times$ molar solubility $= 3.2 \times 10^{-5}$ mol/L

     $[H^+] = 3.1 \times 10^{-10}$ mol/L

     pH = 9.5

     (d)   First find the new molar concentrations of each ion that could potentially precipitate, then calculate Q using the solubility product constant expression. Finally, compare Q with the solubility product constant. If Q is larger, then a precipitate will form.

$$[Fe^{2+}] = \frac{0.0500 \text{ L Fe solution}}{.1 \text{ L combine soln.}} \times \frac{0.002 \text{ mol } Fe^{2+}}{\text{L Fe solution}} =$$

     0.001 M Fe^{2+}

$$[OH^-] = \frac{0.0500 \text{ L OH solution}}{.1 \text{ L combine soln.}} \times \frac{0.003 \text{ mol } OH^-}{\text{L OH solution}} =$$

     0.0015 M OH^-

     $Q = (.001)(.0015)^2 = 2.2 \times 10^{-9}$

     $K_{sp} = (1.6 \times 10^{-5})(3.2 \times 10^{-5})^2 = 1.6 \times 10^{-14}$

     Q is less than K_{sp} so a precipitate does not form.

     (e)   The solubility increases with a decreased pH because the hydroxide ions are used up, and more iron hydroxide can dissolve. For example, at pH 6, the molar solubility is 1.6×10^{15}.

2. (a) $5.5\,°C - 0.55\,°C = 4.95\,°C$

    (b) $m = \dfrac{\Delta T}{k_f\, i} = \dfrac{0.55\,°C\,mol}{5.12\,°C\,kg} = 0.107\ molal$

    (c)   First find the number of moles of the unknown in the solution.

    0.0134 moles unknown $=$

    $\dfrac{0.107\ \text{moles unknown}}{\text{kg solvent}} \times 0.125\ \text{kg solvent}$

    $\text{molar mass} = \dfrac{\text{grams of unknown}}{\text{moles of unknown}} = \dfrac{2.00\ \text{g unknown}}{0.0134\ \text{mol unknown}}$

    $= 149.3\ g/mol$

    (d)

    $78.9\ g\ C \times \dfrac{1\ mol\ C}{12.011\ g} = 6.569\ mol$

    $10.6\ g\ H \times \dfrac{1\ mol\ H}{1.008\ g} = 10.516\ mol$

    $10.5\ g\ O \times \dfrac{1\ mol\ O}{16.0\ g} = 0.656\ mol$

This gives a simplest ratio of $C_{10}H_{16}O$, which has a molar mass of 152.2 g/mol. Therefore, the empirical formula is most likely the same as the molecular formula.

    (e)   There are several possible structures, but the proposed structure should be non-polar, since it had to dissolve in a non-polar solvent in this experiment.

3. (a)   The reaction occurring between the permanganate and oxalate ions is an oxidation-reduction reaction, as shown below:

The ionic equation is

$$MnO_4^- + C_2O_4^{2-} \rightarrow Mn^{2+} + CO_2\ \text{(acid solution)}$$

The half-reactions are

reduction: $MnO_4^- + 8H^+ + 5e^- \rightarrow Mn^{2+} + 4H_2O$

oxidation: $C_2O_4^- \rightarrow 2CO_2 + 2e^-$

To balance the overall reaction we need $10e^-$ in each half reaction. So we multiply the oxidation half-reaction by 5 and the reduction half-reaction by 2 and add the two half-reactions

$2MnO_4^- + 5C_2O_4^- + 16H^+ \rightarrow 2Mn^{2+} + 10CO_2 + 8H_2O$

(b)   The number of moles of $Na_2C_2O_4$ dissolved is:

$$n \text{ of } Na_2C_2O_4 = \frac{0.157}{\text{molecular weight (m.w.) of } Na_2C_2O_4} =$$

m.w. of $Na_2C_2O_4 = (2 \times 23 \text{ g}) + (2 \times 12 \text{ g}) + (4 \times 16 \text{ g}) = 134 \text{ g/mol}$

$$n \text{ of } Na_2C_2O_4 = \frac{0.157 \text{ mol}}{134 \text{ g/mol}} = 1.17 \times 10^{-3} \text{ mole}$$

From the balanced equation we know that 5 moles of oxalate react with 2 moles of MnO_4^-. One mole oxalate reacts with $\frac{2}{5}$ mole MnO_4^- 1.17 $\times 10^{-3}$ oxalate reacts with $1.17 \times 10^{-3} \times \frac{2}{5}$ mole of MnO_4^-

; therefore number of moles MnO_4^- is

$1.17 \times 10^{-3} \times = 0.465 \times 10^{-3}$ moles

0.465×10^{-3} moles of MnO_4^- are contained in 15.3 mL

; therefore the molarity of $KMnO_4$ solution is

$$M \text{ of } KMnO_4 = \frac{0.465 \times 10^{-3} \text{ mole}}{15.3 \times 10^{-3} \text{ L}}$$

M of $KMnO_4 = 3.039 \times 10^{-2}$ mole/L

Molarity of $KMnO_4 = 0.03$ M.

(c)   The mass of $KMnO_4$ in 15.3 mL solution is:

M of $KMnO_4$ = M.W. of $KMnO_4 \times n$ $KMnO_4$

M.W. of $KMnO_4 = 39 \text{ g} + 55 \text{ g} + (16 \text{ g} \times 4) = 94 \text{ g} + 64 \text{ g} = 158 \text{ g/mol}$

M of $KMnO_4 = 158 \text{ g/mol} \times 0.465 \times 10^{-3} \text{ mol} = 0.073 \text{ g}$.

(d)   We need a balanced equation to solve the problem.

Reduction half-reaction

$$MnO_4^- + 8H^+ + 5e^- \rightarrow Mn^{2+} + 4H_2O$$

Oxidation half-reaction

$$Fe^{2+} \rightarrow Fe^{3+} + e^-$$

Multiply oxidation half-reaction by 5 and add to reduction half-reaction to get the overall balanced equation.

$$MnO_4^- + 8H^+ + 5Fe^{2+} \rightarrow Mn^{2+} + 5Fe^{3+} + 4H_2O$$

25 mL of $FeSO_4$ contains:

25×10^{-3} L $\times 0.105 = 2.625 \ 10^{-3}$ mole of Fe^{2+} ions

From the balanced equation:

5 moles Fe^{2+} react with 1 mole MnO_4^-

1 mole Fe^{2+} reacts with $\frac{1}{5}$ mole MnO_4^-

2.625 $\times 10^{-3}$ mole Fe^{2+} reacts with 2.625 $\times 10^{-3} \times 5$ moles MnO_4
$= 0.523 \times 10^{-3}$ mole MnO_4^-

Number of moles = Molarity $\times$ Volume

$$Volume = \frac{Number \ of \ Moles}{Molarity}$$

$$Volume \ of \ KMnO_4 = \frac{0.523 \times 10^{-3} \ moles}{0.03} = 17.43 \times 10^{-3} \ L$$

Volume of $KMnO_4 = 17.43$ ml

4.   (a) $HNO_3 \ (aq) + Cu_2O(s) \rightarrow Cu(NO_3)_2 \ (aq) + NO(g) + H_2O(l)$

             $N^{+5} + Cu^{+1} \rightarrow Cu^{+2} + N^{+2}$

       (b) $WO_3(s) + 3H_2(g) \rightarrow W(s) + 3H_2O(g)$

             $W^{+6} + H^0 \rightarrow W^0 + H^{+1}$

       (c) $Zn + CuSO_4 \rightarrow ZnSO_4 + Cu$

             $Zn^0 + Cu^{+2} \rightarrow Zn^{+2} \ Cu^0$

(d) $2NH_3(g) + 3CuO(s) \rightarrow N_2(g) + 3Cu(s) + 3H_2O(g)$

$N^{-3} + Cu^{+2} \rightarrow N^0 + Cu^0$

(e) $3CO_2(g) + CH_4(g) \rightarrow 4CO(g) + 2H_2O(g)$

$C^{+4} + C^{-4} \rightarrow C^{+2}$

(f) $ZnO(s) + C(s) \rightarrow Zn(g) + CO(g)$

$Zn^{+2} + C^0 \rightarrow Zn^0 + C^{+2}$

(g) $Mn(s) + 2HCl(aq) \rightarrow MnCl_2 + H_2(g)$

$Mn^0 + H^{+1} \rightarrow Mn^{+2} + H^0$

(h) $Co(s) + Cl_2(g) \rightarrow CoCl_2(g)$

$Co^0 + Cl^0 \rightarrow Co^{+2}Cl^{-1}$

5.   (a)   The ionic radius increases as the atomic number increases within each family simply because the outer electrons are further away from the nucleus for larger and larger elements. Positive ions are smaller than the complete atoms, while negative ions are larger. Whatever type of ion, the similarly charged ion underneath the element on the periodic chart will simply carry one more shell of electrons, which increases its radius.

(b)   The first ionization energy of aluminum is smaller than the first ionization of magnesium because its highest energy electron is a singular electron in a p-orbital. Magnesium's highest energy electron (and hence the first removed) is one of two electrons in a s-orbital. S-orbital electrons are relatively easy to remove, but with two electrons in an orbital, there is some attraction to each other as a result of the opposite magnetic fields induced from the "spin" of the electron. The first electron to be removed from aluminum has no other electron to keep it in the orbital.

(c)   The second ionization energy of sodium is about three times that of the second of magnesium for two primary reasons. First, the second ionization for sodium requires the removal of a much more tightly held p-orbital electron. Second, the electron to be removed from sodium is significantly closer to the nucleus and experiences a greater effective nuclear charge, and therefore attraction.

(d)   Similarly, the difference between the second and third ionization energies in magnesium represent the need to remove a p-orbital electron. The smaller difference between the first and second ionization energies represents only the difference between one outer s-orbital electron and the second, slightly more closely held, s-orbital electron.

6.　(a)　Argon has a higher boiling point than neon because of the increased number of electrons in it, which contribute to greater London forces and higher intermolecular attraction.

　　(b)　Silver metal is an excellent conductor of electricity because it is held together with a metallic "electron sea" attraction. That is, the energy levels of its d-electrons are so close to that of nearby atoms that those electrons move easily from atom to atom (delocalized). This electron mobility promotes thermal and electrical conductivity. Silver iodide is an ionic compound, with its valence electrons donated to the iodine atom to form the iodide ion. This electron is localized around the iodine atom, and is not mobile enough to allow the compound to conduct electricity.

　　(c)　Ammonia is a polar molecule, and therefore soluble in water. Boron trifluoride is not a polar molecule, and therefore not soluble in water. Even though the formulas of the two fluorides are similar, nitrogen has two more electrons in its valence shell, which results in a pyramidal shape when the nitrogen atom is bonded to three fluorine atoms. The high electronegativity of the fluorine atoms pulls on the electrons from nitrogen is an unbalanced manner, creating a separation of charge—or polarity—within the ammonia molecule. Boron tirfluoride is polar because the fluorine atoms pull evenly at 120 degree angles on each of the three boron valence electrons.

　　(d)　While silicon and carbon both have the same number of valence electrons, silicon oxide is bound together and to other silicon and oxygen atoms in a continuous covalent crystal lattice. Whereas carbon dioxide has two covalent bonds between the carbon and each of the oxygen atoms, but very weak intermolecular attraction between one molecule of carbon dioxide and another.

7.　(a)　In the presence of light, hydrogen peroxide decomposes to form water and oxygen:

$$2H_2O_2 \xrightarrow{\text{light}} 2H_2O + O_2 \uparrow$$

To prevent H_2O_2 from decomposing, it is stored in dark-brown bottles which prevent light from reaching the liquid.

Hydrogen peroxide acts as an antiseptic because as the hydrogen peroxides decomposes, it produces a very reactive atomic oxygen. Bacteria, which are organic in composition, are easily oxidized (and therefore killed) by the atomic oxygen.

$$2H_2O_2 \rightarrow 2H_2O + 2[O] \rightarrow O_2$$

oxidation   organic
material

(b)   Ethyl chloride, CH_3CH_2Cl has a very low boiling point (about 13 °C). It exists as a gas under normal conditions. It liquefies under pressure. When it is sprayed on the skin, it evaporates very quickly and in doing so, it absorbs energy from the skin. The skin and the nerve endings in the skin are cooled. The skin, therefore, feels numb under the action of ethyl chloride.

(c)   The volume of water increases as it changes from the liquid state to the solid. This is because of hydrogen bonding. In the liquid state, the water molecules can be forced together because the hydrogen bonding is randomly oriented. In the solid state, however, the molecules are arranged in a regular crystal lattice and the molecules cannot be squashed together as in the liquid state. The density of ice is, therefore, lower than water (at 4° C density of H_2O = 1.000 g/cm³, at 0 °C density of ice = 0.998 g/cm³). So, when the lake freezes, the ice which is less dense rises to the surface of the lake. The layer of ice at the surface also acts as an insulator and so lakes rarely freeze all the way to the bottom. Fish and other aquatic life can therefore survive in the lake during the winter.

(d)   Aerosol cans always contain vapors although it may seem to us to be empty. They become "empty" when the pressure inside is equal to the pressure outside. If an empty can is incinerated, i.e., if the temperature is raised to very high temperatures, the volume and pressure of the vapor increases according to the gas laws. Since the volume of the can is fixed, the volume of the gas will be constant; as a result, the pressure of the vapor is dramatically increased. A stage is reached where the can cannot contain the pressure built in it. It will rupture with an explosion of the expanding gases. The explosion can cause material damage or human injury.

8.   (a)   There are two types of solids: amorphous and crystalline.

Crystals are solids bounded by planar surfaces. Amorphous substances have no definite form.

Particles in a crystal are well ordered whereas those in an amorphous substance are chaotic, i.e., arranged in a random manner.

Crystals have sharp and definite melting points, while amorphous solids soften as they are heated and melt over a range of temperatures. Examples of crystals are NaCl and quartz; amorphous are tar and glass solids.

The differences between molecular, ionic, and covalent crystals lie in the types of particles present at the lattice points and the nature of the attractive forces between them.

The lattice of molecular crystals are occupied by molecules or atoms, in ionic crystals by ions, and in covalent crystals by atoms.

The binding forces in molecular crystals consist only of atoms and nonpolar molecules for example: Ar, O_2, and naphthalene (the binding forces are London forces). In crystals of polar molecules, like SO_2, the binding forces are dipole-dipole attractions. In some molecular crystals where the polar molecules contain hydrogen, *e.g.*, H_2O, NH_3, and HF, the molecules are attracted in the crystal by hydrogen bonding.

In ionic crystals such as NaCl (salt), the binding forces are electrostatic.

In covalent crystals, a network of covalent bonds links the atoms throughout the solid. Examples of covalent crystals are carborundum (SiC), quartz (SiO_2), and diamond (C).

Molecular crystals are soft and have low melting points since their lattice energies are small.

Ionic crystals have large lattice energies; therefore, such crystals are hard and have high melting points. They are also brittle because external forces can cause planes of ions to slip by one another. These planes pass from a condition of mutual attraction to one of mutual repulsion.

All the crystals are poor conductors of electricity because the electrons are bound to individual molecules in molecular crystals and are localized in covalent bonds in covalent crystals; ions in ionic crystals are fixed rigidly in place. (When ionic crystals melt, they conduct electricity, but then they are no longer crystals.)

(b)   Ionic crystals are more brittle and have higher melting and boiling points than molecular crystals. Some molecular crystals will be waxy and more volatile; all will be softer than ionic crystals.

(c)   Polar molecular crystals will have a higher melting and boiling point than non-polar molecular crystals. The latter will tend to be more waxy, and be more volatile—and possibly smelly.

(d)   Ionic crystals are brittle and have much lower melting and boiling points than network covalent crystals. The latter are exceptionally hard and durable.

Practice
Exam 5

AP Chemistry

Practice Exam 5

Section I

TIME: 90 minutes
45% of the entire test

(Answer sheets appear in the back of this book.)

DIRECTIONS: Each set of lettered choices below refers to the numbered questions or statements immediately following it. Select the one lettered choice that best answers each question. A choice may be used once, more than once, or not at all in each set.

Part A

Questions 1 – 5

(A) carbon, oxygen

(B) chlorine, bromine

(C) aluminum, galium

(D) zinc, mercury

(E) silver, gold

1.   Are members of the halogen family

2.   Exist in well-known allotropic forms

3. In their standard states at 25°C one element is a gas and the other is a liquid

4. These elements, when combined, form an amalgam

Questions 5 – 9

       (A) $K(s) + H_2O(aq)$

       (B) $O_2(g) + 2H_2(g)$

       (C) $AgNO_3(aq) + NaCl(aq)$

       (D) $He(g) + Ar(g)$

       (E) $NaOH(aq) + HC(aq)$

5. An oxidation-reduction process that yields water as a product

6. The product of this reaction is an insoluble precipitate

7. A very exothermic process that is kinetically slow at room temperature

8. No product is expected from this reaction

9. This reaction produces a solution pH»8

Questions 10 – 14

       (A) tetrahedral

       (B) square-planar

       (C) trigonal-bipyramidal

       (D) trigonal-pyramidal

       (E) octahedral

10. the geometry of CCl_4

11. the geometry of XeF_4

12. the geometry of NH_3

13. the geometry of PCl_5

14. the geometry of CCl_3

Directions: Each of the questions or incomplete statements below is followed by five suggested answers or completions. Select the one that is best in each case.

Questions 15 – 19 are based on the following information: A student is given a soluble sodium salt containing one of 8 possible anions: acetate, chloride, bromide, iodide, sulfide, sulfate, and phosphate.

15. What cations other than sodium will likely form soluble salts with all the anions?

    (A) Zn^{2+}, Pb^{2+}, K^+ (D) K^+, NH_4^+

    (B) Pb^{2+}, Hg^{2+}, Fe^{2+} (E) Fe^{2+}

    (C) Ca^{2+}, Mg^{2+}

16. Three to four drops of $AgNO_3$ are added to a solution of the salt. No precipitate results. Which anions are absent?

    (A) Cl^-, Br^-, I^-

    (B) Cl^-, Br^-, CH_3COO^-, I^-

    (C) Cl^-, Br^-, I^-, S^{2-}, PO_4^{3-}

(D) Cl⁻ only

(E) Br⁻ only

17. Suppose that a precipitate did form in the reaction in Question 16 and it is then treated with a few drops of nitric acid. No change is observed. Which anions can be present?

(A) $Cl^-, Br^-, I^-, SO_4^{2-}$ (D) Cl^-, Br^-, I^- only

(B) CH_3COO^-, NO_3^- (E) no ionization will occur

(C) $Cl^-, Br^-, I^-, SO_4^{2-}$

18. The student treats some fresh solution of the salt with $BaCl_2$. A precipitate forms. Which anions could have been present?

(A) SO_4^{2-}, PO_4^{3-} (D) Br^- only

(B) Br^-, Cl^-, I^- (E) NO_3^- only

(C) CH_3COO^- only

19. After various tests, the student has identified the anion and 4 drops of ethyl alcohol are added to a small amount of the salt. The student completes a specific test as follows: 2 drops of 18M H_2SO_4 and then 4 drops of ethyl alcohol. After the solution is heated, a fruity odor is produced. What is the anion?

(A) Cl^- (D) SO_4^{2-}

(B) S^{2-} (E) PO_4^{3-}

(C) CH_3COO^-

20. Which one of the following species has not been correctly matched with its number of neutrons and electrons?

(A) $_7^{14}N$ 7 neutrons, 7 electrons

(B) $_8^{16}O^{2-}$ 8 neutrons, 10 electrons

(C) $_{24}^{53}Cr^{2+}$ 29 neutrons, 26 electrons

(D)   He 2 neutrons, 2 electrons

(E)   C 7 neutrons, 6 electrons

21.   Determine the oxidation state of Mn in $KMnO_4$

(A)   +1   (D)   +7

(B)   +3   (E)   −1

(C)   +5

22.   Which of the following graphs is a valid representation of Boyle's Law?

(A)   (B)

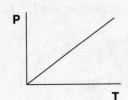   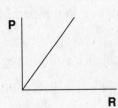

(C)   (D)

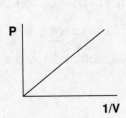   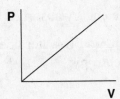

(E)

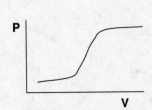

23.

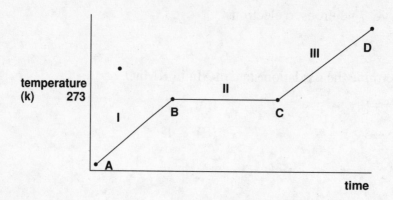

The above sketch represents a warming curve for water at 1 atm pressure. Select the one <u>incorrect</u> statement. (Note: C_I = heat capacity of water in region I, ΔT = change in temperature between points specified, ΔH_f = heat of fusion.)

(A) Water is a solid in region I of the curve.

(B) Water exists in a solid/liquid equilibrium in region II.

(C) The energy absorbed by a sample of mass N in the temperature range A to C is $(C_I) (\Delta T_{A'B}) (N) + (\Delta H_f) (\Delta T_{B'C}) (N)$.

(D) The energy absorbed by a sample in the range B to C is $\Delta H_f N$.

(E) In region II water doesn't gain any kinetic energy but does gain in entropy.

24. According to Hund's rule, how many unpaired electrons does the ground state of iron have?

(A) 6   (D) 3

(B) 5   (E) 2

(C) 4

25. Arrange the following neutral gaseous atoms in order of decreasing atomic radius.

S, Mg, F, Cl

(A) Mg>S>Cl>F

(D) S>Mg>Cl>F

(B) F>Cl>S>Mg

(E) Cl>S>F>Mg

(C) Cl>F>S>Mg

26. What volume of .5 M H_2SO_4 will neutralize 100 mL of .2 M NaOH?

(A) 400 mL

(D) 20 mL

(B) 200 mL

(E) 2 mL

(C) 100 mL

27. Copper metal will replace silver ions in solution, resulting in the production of silver metal and copper ions. This indicates the following:

(A) Silver has a higher oxidation potential than copper.

(B) A combustion reaction is occurring.

(C) Copper has a higher oxidation potential than silver.

(D) Silver is much less soluble than copper.

(E) Copper metal is readily reduced.

28. How many moles of chlorine gas are produced when one mole of $Cr_2O_7^{2-}$ reacts in the following unbalanced raction?

$Cr_2O_7^{2-}(aq) + Cl^-(aq) \rightarrow Cr^{3+}(aq) + Cl_2(g)$ (acidic solution)

(A) 1

(D) 4

(B) 2

(E) 8

(C) 3

29. Which of the following compounds have only nonpolar bonds?

    (A) KO_2

    (B) NaF

    (C) HF

    (D) KBr

    (E) I_2

30. Determine the formal charge of N in acetonitrile (CH_3CN).

    (A) –2

    (B) –1

    (C) 0

    (D) +1

    (E) +2

31. Arrange the following ion pairs in order of increasing lattice energy

    $LiCl, BaCl_2, LiBr, LiI$

    (A) $LiI, LiBr, LiCl, BaCl_2$

    (B) $BaCl_2, LiI, LiBr, LiCl$

    (C) $BaCl_2, LiCI, LiBr, LiI$

    (D) $LiCl, LiBr, LiI, BaCl_2$

    (E) $LiCl, BaCl_2, LiI, LiBr$

32. Lithium (AW=6.941 g/mole) exists as two naturally occurring iso-topes, $_3^6Li$ and $_3^7Li$ with relative atomic masses of 6.015 and 7.016. Find the percent abundances of the two isotopes.

    (A) 23.1, 46.2

    (B) 74.30, 25.70

    (C) 90, 10

    (D) 92.51, 7.49

    (E) 94.63, 5.37

33.

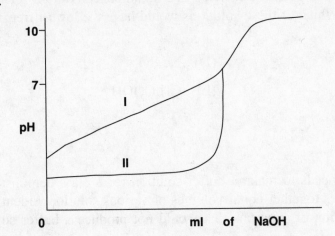

Above is a sketch of two acid-base titration curves. The curves represent the different monoprotic acids of identical concentration titrated with .100 M NaOH. Identify the correct association of acid with its titration curve.

(A) curve I HCl, curve II HBr

(B) curve I CH_3COOH, curve II HCl

(C) curve I HBr, curve II CH_3COOH

(D) curve I HNO_3, curve II HNO_2

(E) curve I CH_3COOH, curve II H_2SO_4

34. What is the oxidation state of iron in the coordination complex Na_2K_2 $[Fe(CN)_6]$?

(A) –2   (D) +2

(B) –1   (E) +3

(C) +1

35. Suppose that solutions are made up in 1 molal concentrations for five substances. Which of these solutions would have the lowest freezing point?

(A) NaBr

(D) Na_2SO_4

(B) $C_6H_{12}O_6$

(E) CH_3COOH

(C) NaCl

36. A professor needs to make a buffer solution for a class demonstration. He mixes together equal volumes of various solutions. Identify the combination of solutions that would <u>not</u> produce a buffer solution.

(A) 1 M CH_3COOH, 1 M HCl, .2 M $NaCH_3COO$

(B) 1 M CH_3COOH, 1 M $NaCH_3COO$

(C) 1 M CH_3COOH, .5 M NaOH

(D) 1 M CH_3COOH, 1 M HCl, 1 M NaOH, 1 M $NaCH_3COO$

(E) 2 M NH_3, 1 M HCl

37. What is the molar mass of the molecule, NH_3?

(A) 4.0 g/mol

(D) 17.0 g/mol

(B) 7.0 g/mol

(E) 20.0 g/mol

(C) 10.0 g/mol

38. Which of the following has a Van't Hoff factor approximately equal to 1.2?

(A) NaCl

(D) H_2SO_4

(B) $MgCl_2$

(E) glucose

(C) $HC_2H_3O_2$

39. What mass of HCl is needed to dilute to 1.0-liter to create a solution with pH 1.0?

   (A) 0.10 g   (D) 3.5 g

   (B) 35 g   (E) 7.0 g

   (C) 0.35 g

40. The species O_2^-

   (A) has 2 unpaired electrons

   (B) has 1 unpaired electron

   (C) has 0 unpaired electrons

   (D) has a bond order of $2\frac{1}{2}$

   (E) has a bond order of 2

41. Choose the correct statement pertaining to the following energy diagram.

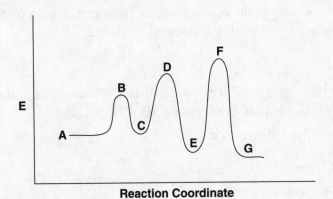

Reaction Coordinate

   (A) The reaction A → G is endothermic.

   (B) k_3 is larger than k_1.

   (C) Species B is called an intermediate product.

   (D) Species E is kinetically and thermodynamically more stable than species C.

   (E) The rate determining step involves reaction C → E.

42. The compound

```
     H    H
     |    |
  H–C–O–C–H
     |    |
     H    H
```

is best described as being a(n)

(A) alcohol

(D) ester

(B) alkene

(E) carboxylic acid

(C) ether

43. Which of the following is true of the reaction $2A(g) + B(g)\ C(g)$?

(A) In a reaction starting with equal moles of A and B, reagent B is the limiting reagent.

(B) The rate equation can be expressed as Rate = $k[A]^2 [B]$.

(C) There is an increase in the entropy of the system.

(D) If the reaction is endothermic, a decrease in temperature will favor formation of reactant.

(E) The percent yield of the reaction is determined as (moles of C produced/moles of A consumed) x 100%.

44. The reaction $2A(g) + 2B(g) \rightarrow 2C(l)$ is a spontaneous and exothermic reaction. What are the signs of ΔG, ΔH, ΔS, and ΔE?

	ΔG	ΔH	ΔS	ΔE
(A)	+	+	+	–
(B)	+	+	–	+
(C)	–	–	+	–
(D)	–	–	–	+
(E)	–	–	–	–

45. An oxide of phosphorus contains 56.36% oxygen by mass. What is the empirical formula of the oxide?

(MW P = 30.97 g/mol, MW O = 16.00 g/mol)

(A) PO_2

(B) PO_3

(C) P_2O_4

(D) P_2O_5

(E) P_3O_7

46. Determine the density of methane gas (MW = 16.0 g/mole) at 25 °C and 6.00 atm

(A) 3.77 g/L

(B) 10.4 g/L

(C) 46.8 g/L

(D) 3.92 g/L

(E) 1.21 g/L

47. Calculate the number of moles of carbon dioxide produced during the combustion of 2 moles of ethane (C_2H_6)

(A) 2

(B) 4

(C) 6

(D) 8

(E) 10

48. A gas at 25°C occupies a 10 liter volume at P atm pressure. The gas is allowed to expand to a volume of 15 liters at 377 °C. What is the new pressure?

(A) 1.45

(B) 1.45P

(C) 1.45/P

(D) 1.07

(E) 1.07/P

Question 49 refers to the diagram below.

$$\begin{array}{ccccccc} H & H & & H & H & & \\ | & | & & | & | & & \\ H-C_1-C_2 & = & C_3 & = & C_4-N-H & & \\ | & & & & & & \\ H & & & & & & \end{array}$$

49. In the above compound what is the hybridization state for C_3?

    (A) sp   (D) sp^4

    (B) sp^2 (E) sp^3d

    (C) sp^3

50. Use this table to answer the following question.

Substance	$S°$ (J/ K mol)
C_2H_2 (g)	249.0
CO_2 (g)	213.6
H_2O (l)	69.96
O_2 (g)	205.0

    The numeric value for the standard change in entropy for the combustion of C_2H_2 (g) is closest to

    (A) -267 J/mol K   (D) +497 J/mol K

    (B) +267 J/mol K   (E) -763 J/mol K

    (C) -497 J/mol K

51. Which of the following statements is false?

    (A) The energy of the universe is constant.

    (B) $\Delta S > 0$ for a spontaneous process.

    (C) The entropy of the universe tends toward a maximum.

(D) Entropy is a measure of increasing disorder.

(E) The entropy of a perfect crystal of a pure substance at 0°C is zero.

52. Which of the following gases would be expected to show the greatest deviation from ideal behavior?

(A) H_2

(B) H_2S

(C) H_2O

(D) O_2

(E) CH_4

53. Determine ΔH in kcal for the reaction $2C(s) + O_2(g) \; 2CO(g)$. Additional information:

(i) $CO_2(g) \rightarrow O_2(g) + C(s)$ ΔH = 94.1 kcal

(ii) $CO_2(g) \rightarrow O_2(g) + CO(g)$ ΔH = 67.7 kcal

(A) −52.8

(B) −26.4

(C) +26.4

(D) −161.8

(E) 100

54. The Ksp for BaF_2 is 1.7×10^{-6}. What is the solubility of fluoride in moles per liter?

(A) $\left(\dfrac{1.7 \times 10^{-6}}{4} \right)^{\frac{1}{3}}$

(B) $2(1.7 \times 10^{-6})^{\frac{1}{3}}$

(C) $2\left(\dfrac{1.7 \times 10^{-6}}{4} \right)^{\frac{1}{3}}$

(D) $(1.7 \times 10^{-6})^{\frac{1}{3}}$

(E) $(1.7 \times 10^{-6})^{3}$

55. A galvanic cell can be represented as Pt(s)|Sn^{2+} (aq,1M), Sn^{4+} (aq, 1M) || Fe^{2+} (aq, 1M), Fe^{3+} (aq, 1M) | Pt(s). What reaction is occurring at the anode?

(A) $Pt \rightarrow Pt^{2+} + 2e^-$

(B) $Sn^{2+} \rightarrow Sn^{4+} + 2e^-$

(C) $Pt \rightarrow Sn^{2+} + 2e^-$

(D) $Fe^{2+} \rightarrow Fe^{3+} + 1e^-$

(E) $Fe^{3+} + 1e^- \rightarrow Fe^{2+}$

56. Identify the incorrect Lewis structure(s).

(A) CH_4

$$\begin{array}{c} H \\ | \\ H - C - H \\ | \\ H \end{array}$$

(B) NH_3O

$$\begin{array}{c} H \\ | \\ H - N - \overset{..}{\underset{..}{O}} \\ | \\ H \end{array} \leftrightarrow \begin{array}{c} H \\ | \\ H - N = \overset{..}{\underset{..}{O}} \\ | \\ H \end{array}$$

(C) C_2H_3N

$$\begin{array}{c} H \\ | \\ H - C - C \equiv N: \\ | \\ H \end{array}$$

(D) NH_4^+

$$\begin{array}{c} H \\ | \\ H - N - H \\ | \\ H \end{array}$$

(E) NO_2^- $[O = N - O]^- \leftrightarrow [O - N = O]^-$

57. The reaction $2H_2 + NO \rightarrow H_2O + \frac{1}{2} N_2$ has a rate law of the form: rate = $k[H_2]^x [NO]^y$

Find the sum of x and y from the given data.

experiment	[H$_2$]	[NO]	rate (M s^{-1})
a	1.0 x 10^{-3}	4.6 x 10^{-2}	3.1 x 10^{-4}
b	2.0 x 10^{-3}	4.6 x 10^{-2}	6.2 x 10^{-4}
c	1.0 x 10^{-3}	1.84 x 10^{-1}	5.0 x 10^{-3}

(A) 1/2

(B) 2

(C) 3

(D) 4

(E) 5

58. $COCl_2(g) \rightarrow CO(g) + Cl_2(g)$ Kp = 6.7 x 10^{-9} atm (100°C)

For the above reaction, equal pressures of the reagent and products (Pressure of CO = Pressure of COCl$_2$ = Pressure of Cl$_2$ = 1 atm) are placed in a flask.

At equilibrium (100 °C) it is true that

(A) the total pressure of the system must remain at 3 atm.

(B) P of CO and P of Cl must decrease from their initial values.

(C) P of CO and P of Cl must increase from their initial values.

(D) P of COCl$_2$ remains constant.

(E) final pressures cannot be determined because a volume is not specified.

59. At 298 K, $\Delta G° = 90.3$ kJ for the reaction $HgO(s) \leftrightarrow Hg(g) + \frac{1}{2}O_2(g)$. Calculate Kp at 298 K

(A) $e\left(-\dfrac{90,300}{8.314 \times 298}\right)$

(B) $e\left(-\dfrac{90.30}{8.314 \times 298}\right)$

(C) $e\left(\dfrac{90,300}{8.314 \times 298}\right)$

(D) $e\left(\dfrac{90.30}{8.314 \times 298}\right)$

(E) $\ln k = \dfrac{[Hg][O_2]^{\frac{1}{2}}}{[HgO]}$

60. Calculate the molecular weight of an unknown gas X if the ratio of its effusion rate to that of He is .378 (AW of He = 4.00 g/mol)

    (A) 9.47   (D) 28.0

    (B) 42.3   (E) 32.0

    (C) 10.6

61. What is the value of "x" in the nuclear reaction

    $^{31}_{14}\text{Si} \rightarrow \, ^{x}_{15}\text{P} + \, ^{0}_{-1}\beta?$

    (A) 28   (D) 32

    (B) 30   (E) 33

    (C) 31

62. Aqua regia is a strong acid that can dissolve even gold and platinum. It consists of a mixture of two strong monoprotic acids. These acids are

    (A) nitric and sulfuric

    (B) hydrochloric and hydrofluoric

    (C) hydrochloric and nitric

    (D) nitric and acetic

    (E) perchloric and ammonia

63. A solution is made by combining 1 mole of ethanol and 2 moles of water. What is the total vapor pressure above the solution? (At the same temperature, the vapor pressure of pure ethanol is .53 atm and the vapor pressure of water is .24 atm.)

    (A) .34 atm   (D) .56 atm

    (B) .41 atm   (E) .77 atm

    (C) .43 atm

64. The K_a of HCN is 1.0×10^{-10}. What is the approximate pH of a 1.0-molar solution of HCN?

    (A) 1   (D) 7

    (B) 3   (E) 10

    (C) 5

65. An amphoteric substance

    (A) is both easily oxidized and reduced

    (B) is inert and unreactive

    (C) can act as both an acid and a base

    (D) can dissolve many solids

    (E) is hydrophobic

66. Compounds that can form hydrogen bonds with water include

    (A) CH_4 (D) NH_3, HF, CH_3OH

    (B) CH_4, HF   (E) NaCl

    (C) CH_3OH, HF, CCl_4

67. The net ionic equation that represents the reaction of aqueous hydrochloric acid with aqueous ammonia is

    (A) $HCl(aq) + NH_3(aq) \rightarrow NH_4^+(aq)$

    (B) $HCl(aq) + NH_3(aq) \rightarrow NH_4^+(aq) + Cl^-(aq)$

    (C) $H^+(aq) + NH_3(aq) \rightarrow NH_4^+(aq)$

    (D) $H^+(aq) + Cl^-(aq) + NH_4^+(aq) + OH^-(aq) \rightarrow H_2O(aq) + NH_4^+(aq) + Cl^-(aq)$

    (E) $H^+(aq) + NH_4^+(aq) + OH^-(aq) \rightarrow H_2O(aq) + NH_4^+(aq)$

68. All of the following are colligative properties except

    (A) osmotic pressure

    (B) pH of buffer solutions

    (C) vapor pressure

    (D) boiling point elevation

    (E) freezing point depression

69. What is the molar concentration of a 0.50-liter sample of a mono-protic acid if it was completely neutralized by 20 mL of 0.1-molar NaOH solution?

    (A) 0.001 M   (D) 0.10 M

    (B) 0.004 M   (E) 1.0 M

    (C) 0.05 M

70. The kinetics of a reaction in which two reactants, A and B, react to-gether to form a product, C is studied and the results are recorded in the chart below. What is the order of the reaction with respect to A and B, respectively?

Trial	[A]	[B]	Initial rate of formation of C (M/sec)
1	0.20	0.40	0.001
2	0.20	0.80	0.001
3	0.40	0.80	0.004

    (A) first order with respect to A; first order with respect to B

    (B) first order with respect to A; zero order with respect to B

    (C) zero order with respect to A; first order with respect to B

    (D) zero order with respect to A; second order with respect to B

    (E) second order with respect to A; zero order with respect to B

71. $H_2O + (CH_3)_3N \rightarrow (CH_3)_3NH^+ + OH^-$

    For the above reaction, which conjugate acid-base pair is correctly listed?

    (A) H_2O, $(CH_3)_3N$ (D) H_2O, H^+

    (B) $(CH_3)_3NH^+$, OH^- (E) H_2O, OH^-

    (C) H_2O, $(CH_3)_3NH^+$

72. Arrange the acids in order of increasing strength

    (A) HCl_1O_4, H_2SO_4, H_3PO_4, $HClO$

    (B) $HClO$, $HClO_4$, H_2SO_4, H_3PO_4

    (C) H_3PO_4, H_2SO_4, $HClO_4$, $HClO$

    (D) $HClO$, H_3PO_4, H_2SO_4, $HClO_4$

    (E) H_3PO_4, H_2SO_4, $HClO$, $HClO_4$

73. Calculate the solubility (in moles/liter) of $Zn(OH)_2$ in a solution buffered at pH 8. (Ksp of $Zn(OH)_2 = 1.8 \times 10^{-14}$)

    (A) 1.0×10^{-8} (D) $1.7 \times 10^{+5}$

    (B) 1.7×10^{-5} (E) 1.8×10^{-2}

    (C) $1.8 \times 10^{+2}$

74. Molten NaCl was electrolyzed with a constant current of 2.0 amperes for 120 seconds. What number of coulombs passed through the cell during this time?

    (A) 2 C

    (B) 24 C

    (C) 60 C

    (D) 120 C

    (E) 240 C

75. Which of the following demonstrates pi bonding?

   (A) OH^-

   (B) H^+

   (C) C_2H_2

   (D) H_2S

   (E) KCl

AP Chemistry

Practice Exam 5

Section II

TIME: 90 minutes
55% of the entire test

(Answer sheets appear in the back of this book.)

The percentages given for the parts represent the score weightings for this section of the examination. You will be given 40 minutes for Part A and 50 minutes for Part B.

You may use a calculator on Part A, but not on Part B.

Be sure to write your answers in the space provided following each question. Pay attention to significant figures.

Part A

TIME: 40 minutes
40 percent

YOU MAY USE A CALCULATOR ON THIS PART.

Show your work clearly for full credit. Pay attention to significant figures in your answers.

Solve the following problem.

1. Sodium hydrogen carbonate, NaHCO$_3$, decomposes according to the following reaction.

    $$2 \, NaHCO_3 \, (s) \rightarrow Na_2CO_3 \, (s) + H_2O \, (g) + CO_2 \, (g)$$

    A sample of 100.0-grams of sodium hydrogen carbonate is placed in an evacuated rigid 5.00-liter container and the temperature is raised to 433 K.

    (a) The total pressure in the container at 433 K is 7.76 atm once equilibrium is reached. Calculate the number of moles of water vapor present at equilibrium.

    (b) Write the equilibrium expression for the equilibrium constant, K$_p$, and calculate its value at 433 K.

    (c) How many grams of the original solid remain in the container under the conditions described in (a)?

    (d) Use Le Chatelier's principle to predict what would happen to the partial pressure of carbon dioxide in the container if the container's volume were decreased.

    (e) Calculate K$_c$ for this reaction.

Solve EITHER problem 2 or problem 3 below. Only one of these two questions will be graded. (The problem you choose will be worth 20% of the score on Part II.)

2. 30.2 grams of nitrogen gas and 14.0 grams of oxygen gas exist in a rigid 2.0 L container at 400 K.

    (a) Calculate the total pressure in the container.

    (b) What is the mole fraction of oxygen gas?

    (c) What is the partial pressure exerted by the oxygen?

    (d) A combustion reaction takes place to form nitrogen dioxide.

        (i) Write the balanced equation for this reaction.

        (ii) What is the mass of the product that is formed?

        (iii) What is the limiting reactant?

    (e)   After the combustion reaction has proceeded, the container develops a microscopic leak. Which gas will leak out fastest, and why?

3.   An electrochemical cell at 298 K is made to generate the aqueous reaction $Cr^{2+} + Mn \rightarrow Cr + Mn^{2+}$.

    (a)   Calculate $E°_{cell}$.

    (b)   Calculate E_{cell} when $[Cr^{2+}] = .0021$ M and $[Mn^{2+}] = .31$ M. Is the reaction spontaneous as written?

    (c)   Determine the value of ΔG for the reaction in (b).

    (d)   Suppose the concentrations in (b) were reversed. Determine the new E_{cell}. Is the reaction spontaneous as written?

Part B

TIME: 50 minutes

YOU MAY NOT USE A CALCULATOR ON THIS PART.

4.   This question is worth 15% of Section II. Write the formulas of the reactants and products for FIVE of the following eight reactions. Show net ionic reactions only, where appropriate. Assume the reaction takes place in aqueous solution unless otherwise specified. Do not balance the reaction.

    (a)   Aqueous chlorine mixed with aqueous potassium bromide solution

    (b)   Passing of hydrogen over heated copper oxide

    (c)   Zinc added to mercurial (II) oxide

    (d)   Aluminum exposed to oxygen

    (e)   Manganese mixed with chromium III chloride

    (f)   Mixture of aqueous solution of iron III chloride and tin (II) chloride

(g) Hot zinc sulfide exposed to excess oxygen

(h) Gaseous methane mixed with oxygen

ANSWER BOTH OF THE FOLLOWING ESSAY QUESTIONS (15% each).

5. Limestone (calcium carbonate) can be converted to calcium bicarbonate when it comes in contact with water containing some dissolved carbon dioxide:

$$CaCO_3(s) + CO_2 (g) + H_2O(l) \leftrightarrow Ca^{2+}(aq) + 2HCO_3^- (aq)$$

Briefly explain Le Chatelier's principle, and then use it to predict how each of the following affects the amount of bicarbonate ion produced.

(a) The pressure of CO_2 is increased.

(b) $CaCl_2$, a source of Ca^{2+} ion, is added.

(c) Half of the calcium carbonate is removed.

(d) An inert gas, Ar, is added, which increases the total pressure.

(e) A catalyst is added to the system.

ANSWER THE FOLLOWING LABORTATORY-BASED ESSAY QUESTION.

6. You are given four bottles, each containing a few grams of a solid crystalline substance. You are told that the substances are glucose, sodium iodide, aluminum oxide, and zinc sulfate.

(a) What single test could you use to identify glucose from the rest of the samples?

(b) What ion could you add to solutions of these samples that would yield a yellow precipitate from one of the samples?

(c)   Write the reaction that each of these substances undergoes when put into pure water.

(d)   Describe how you could use freezing point determination to determine between each of these substances.

ANSWER QUESTION 7 OR QUESTION 8 BELOW. ONLY ONE OF THESE TWO QUESTIONS WILL BE GRADED.

7.   a)   Use the kinetic-molecular model to briefly describe why most gases are best described by the ideal gas equation, and not the van der Waals equation.

     b)   Discuss briefly the properties of gas molecules that cause deviations from ideal behavior.

     c)   At 25 °C and 1.0 atm pressure, which of the following gases shows the greatest deviation from ideal behavior? Give two reasons for your choice.

$$H_2S \quad H_2 \quad O_2$$

     d)   Identify the two constants in the van der Waals equation that are different from the variables in the ideal gas equation, and briefly describe the properties that each constant represents.

8.   Give explanations of the following, on the basis of your knowledge of coordination chemistry.

     (a)   A sample of the compound K_3 $[Fe(CN)_6]$ is weighed in the presence and absence of a magnetic field. The weight of the sample was greater in the former case.

     (b)   Many transition metal complexes are colored.

     (c)   The complex $[Pt(NH_3)_2Cl_2]$, which has a square-planar geometry, has two isomers.

     (d)   An octahedral complex of composition $CO(NH_3)_5 BrCl$ is dissolved in water and found to consist of two ions, one of which is a bromide ion.

AP Chemistry

Practice Exam 5

ANSWER KEY

Section I

1.	(B)	26.	(D)	51.	(E)
2.	(A)	27.	(C)	52.	(B)
3.	(B)	28.	(C)	53.	(A)
4.	(D)	29.	(E)	54.	(C)
5.	(B)	30.	(C)	55.	(B)
6.	(C)	31.	(A)	56.	(B)
7.	(B)	32.	(D)	57.	(C)
8.	(D)	33.	(B)	58.	(B)
9.	(A)	34.	(D)	59.	(A)
10.	(A)	35.	(D)	60.	(D)
11.	(B)	36.	(A)	61.	(C)
12.	(D)	37.	(D)	62.	(C)
13.	(C)	38.	(C)	63.	(A)
14.	(D)	39.	(D)	64.	(C)
15.	(D)	40.	(B)	65.	(C)
16.	(C)	41.	(D)	66.	(D)
17.	(E)	42.	(C)	67.	(C)
18.	(A)	43.	(D)	68.	(B)
19.	(C)	44.	(D)	69.	(B)
20.	(C)	45.	(D)	70.	(E)
21.	(D)	46.	(D)	71.	(E)
22.	(C)	47.	(B)	72.	(D)
23.	(C)	48.	(B)	73.	(E)
24.	(C)	49.	(A)	74.	(E)
25.	(A)	50.	(A)	75.	(C)

DETAILED EXPLANATIONS OF ANSWERS

Practice Exam 5

Section I

1.   **(B)**   Members of the group containing F, Cl, Br, I, and At are called halogens.

2.   **(A)**   Allotropes are different forms of the same element. Diamond and graphite are allotropes of carbon; dioxygen (O_2) and ozone (O_3) are allotropes of oxygen.

3.   **(B)**   At 25° C, chlorine is a gas and bromine is a liquid. Though mercury (choice D) is a liquid; zinc is a solid.

4.   **(D)**   An amalgam is a solution of any metal in mercury.

5.   **(B)** O_2 is reduced and H_2 is oxidized to form H_2O.

6.   **(C)**   When Ag^+ and Cl^- combine, a precipitate of AgCl forms immediately. This is a useful reaction for qualitative analysis.

7.   **(B)**   This reaction is very violent and exothermic, but at room temperature there is not enough activation energy to initiate the reaction.

8.   **(D)**   The noble gases are generally inert and unreactive, especially with each other, under ordinary conditions. However, the heavier elements (Xe, Kr, Rn) will react, especially with oxygen and fluorine.

9.   **(A)** $K(s) + H_2O (aq) \rightarrow KOH (aq) + \frac{1}{2}H_2(g)$. The potassium hydroxide generates a very basic solution.

10.   **(A)** CCl_4 has 4 bonding atoms; hence, from the Valence Shell Electron Pair Repulsion theory (VSEPR), CCl_4 has a tetrahedral geometry.

11. **(B)** XeF_4 has 4 bonding atoms and 2 orbitals with lone pairs of electrons; hence, it has a square-planar geometry.

12. **(D)** NH_3 has 3 bonding atoms and 1 orbital with a lone pair of electrons; hence, it has a trigonal-pyramidal geometry.

13. **(C)** PCl_5 has 5 bonding atoms; hence, it has a trigonal-bipyramidal geometry.

14. **(D)** CCl_3^- has 3 bonding atoms and 1 orbital with a lone pair of electrons; hence, it has a trigonal-pyramidal geometry.

15. **(D)** Salts with the cations Na^+, K^+, or NH_4^+ are usually very soluble.

16. **(C)** These ions form insoluble precipitates with silver.

17. **(E)** The silver salts of Cl^-, Br^-, I^-, and S^{2-} remain insoluble in strongly acidic solution.

18. **(A)** Ba^{2+} will form insoluble salts with sulfate and phosphate.

19. **(C)** In acidic solution, the acetate ion reacts with ethyl alcohol to form ethyl acetate, an ester. Esters often have fruity odors.

20. **(C)** $^{53}_{24}Cr^{2+}$ has 29 neutrons and only 22 electrons. Neutral chromium possesses as many electrons as protons (AN=24), but the dipositive species loses 2 electrons.

21. **(D)** The charge on the permanganate ion is –1. Thus, with oxygen possessing the normal –2 state, manganese has a +7 oxidation state.

22. **(C)** Boyle's law states that at constant temperature, the volume of a gas is inversely proportional to its pressure. Mathematically, this is represented as $PV = k$, where k is a constant. Rearranging, $P = k/V$. Thus, a plot of P versus 1/V should yield a straight line.

23. **(C)** The second part of the equation is incorrect. The energy gained in region II equals $\Delta H_f N$. There is no temperature change during the melting process. All the energy gained is involved in the change from solid to liquid structure – an entropy gain.

24. **(C)**   The ground state configuration of iron is $[Ar]\ 4s^2 3d^6$. There are five d orbitals and with minimum pairing Fe has <u>4</u> unpaired electrons.

25. **(A)**   Atomic radius increases as the principal quantum number, n, increases, thus $Cl > F$. Within a row (or same principal quantum number) size decreases as the atomic number increases, thus $Mg > S > Cl$.

26. **(D)**   Use $V_A \times M_A = V_B \times M_B$ and solve for V_A: $V_A = (V_B \times M_B)/M_A$ where $V_B = 100$ mL, $M_B = .2$ M and $M_A = 1$ M. Note that $M_A = 1$ M because H_2SO_4 is diprotic.

27. **(C)**   The unbalanced reaction occurring is $Cu + Ag^+ \rightarrow Cu^{2+} + Ag$. For the reaction to proceed, copper must be easier to oxidize than silver. Thus, copper must have a higher oxidation potential than silver. Choice (B) is a redox reaction. (D) is incorrect because both silver and copper metal are insoluble. (E) is incorrect because metals are not readily reduced.

28. **(C)**   This is a redox reaction and must be balanced accordingly:

$$Cr_2O_7^{2-} + 6e^- \rightarrow 2Cr^{3+}$$

$$\underline{6Cl^- \rightarrow 3Cl_2 + 6e^-}$$

$$1Cr_2O_7{}^{2-} + 6Cl^- \rightarrow 2Cr^{3+} + 3Cl_2$$

29. **(E)**   The polarity of a bond can be estimated by the difference in electronegativity (ΔEN) between the 2 atoms in the bond. The compounds in A to D are ionic (large ΔEN). ΔEN for I_2 is, of course, zero.

30. **(C)**   Formal charge = (valence electrons) – (nonbonding electrons) $- \frac{1}{2}$ (bonding electrons). For N in CH_3CN, formal charge $= 5 - 2 - \frac{1}{2}(6) = 0$.

31. **(A)**   Lattice energy depends on (i) ionic charge (a greater charge results in a greater lattice energy), (ii) ionic radius (a smaller sum of the ionic radii results in a greater lattice energy), and (iii) lattice geometry. Here, ionic charge (Ba^{2+} versus Li^+) and ionic radius ($Cl^- < Br^- < I^-$) are the important factors.

32. **(D)** Let x = fraction of $_3^6Li$ and $1 - x$ = fraction of $_3^7Li$ 6.015x + 7.016 (1 – x) = 6.941. x = .0749 or 7.49%; 1 – x = .9251 or 92.51%.

33. **(B)** Curve II breaks sharply to an equivalence point at pH = 7. This behavior is consistent with that of a strong acid (monoprotic HCl). Curve I breaks less sharply to an equivalence point pH > 7. This behavior is consistent with that of a weak acid such as acetic acid. At the equivalence point, the pH is basic due to water hydrolysis by acetate.

34. **(D)** The oxidation states are known for the other atoms in the compound Na^+, K^+, and CN^{-1}. Thus, by difference, the oxidation state of iron is +2 as the compound has an overall zero charge.

35. **(D)** Freezing point depression is a colligative property – it depends on the number of moles of particles (ions, molecules, etc.) in solution. The 1 molal Na_2SO_4 ionizes into a 3 molal concentration of ions (1 $Na_2SO_4 \rightarrow 2\,Na^+ + SO_4^{2-}$). This is greater than any of the other choices and will result in the solution with the lowest freezing point.

36. **(A)** A buffer solution contains a weak acid (or base) and the salt of its conjugate base (or acid). Solutions B-D, when mixed, yield CH_3COOH and $NaCH_3COO$. Solution E, when mixed, yields NH_3 and NH_4Cl. These are buffer solutions. Solution A yields CH_3COOH, HCl, and NaCl. There is no $NaCH_3COO$ remaining, hence we do not have a buffer.

37. **(D)** The molar mass can be found by adding together the atomic weights of each atom in the formula. 14 g/mol (for nitrogen) + 3×1 g/mol (for the hydrogens) = 17 g/mol.

38. **(C)** To get a fractional Van't Hoff factor, you should look for the molecule that is partially, but not completely ionized in water. The only molecule that fits that description is the weak acid, acetic acid.

39. **(D)**

$$3.5 \text{ g acid} = 1.0 \text{ liter solution} \times \frac{0.10 \text{ mol acid}}{\text{L solution}} \times \frac{35 \text{ g acid}}{\text{mol acid}}$$

40. **(B)** The MO (molecular orbital) bonding schemes for simple diatomic species must be used to answer this question. For O_2^- the MO scheme is $(\sigma1s)^2(\sigma*1s)^2(\sigma2s)^2(\sigma*2s)^2(\sigma2p)(\pi2p)^4(\pi*2p)^3$.

O_2^- has 3 net bonding electrons and a BO (bond order) of $1^1/_2$. It also has 1 unpaired electron (2 electrons in one of the π^* orbitals and the 1 unpaired electron in the other π^* orbital).

41. **(D)**   Species E is lower in energy than species C and is thermo-dynamically more stable. It is also kinetically more stable because of the larger activation energies (proportional to the height of the "hills") for the forward and reverse reactions.

42. **(C)**   The –C–O–C– linkage is characteristic of an ether.

43. **(D)**   The application of Le Chatelier's principle provides a solution: heat + 2A + B $\rightarrow$ C. The removal of heat (decrease in temperature) shifts the reaction equation toward the formation of reactants. Note that (B) would only be a true statement if this reaction were identified as the rate-limiting (or slowest) step.

44. **(D)**   A spontaneous, exothermic reaction must have, by definition, a negative ΔH and negative ΔG. If ΔG is negative then, also by definition, ΔE is positive. Since 3 mol of gas forms 2 mol of liquid, the entropy has decreased, thus, ΔS is negative.

45. **(D)**

    Per 100 g, the mass of P is 43.64 g and that of O is 56.36 g.

    43.64 g P = 1.409 mol; 56.36 g O = 3.521 mol

    P:O (mol) is 1:2.5 or 2:5 Thus, the formula is P_2O_5.

46. **(D)**   Density = mass/volume = (MW) (P/RT) = 3.92 g/L.

47. **(B)**   The answer is determined from the correctly balanced equation $2C_2H_6 + 7O_2 \rightarrow 4CO_2 + 6H_2O$.

48. **(B)** $P_1V_1/T_1 = P_2V_2/T_2$ where $P_1 = P$, $V_1 = 10$ L, $T_1 = 298$, $T_2 = 650$ K, $V_2 = 15$ L, $P_2 = ?$ $P_2 = 1.45$ P

49. **(A)** C_3 has two bonds and two π bonds. We need two hybrid orbitals for the two bonds; hence, C_3 is sp hybridized.

50. **(A)** The balanced chemical equation for this reaction is:

$$C_2H_2 + \tfrac{5}{2}O_2 \rightarrow 2CO_2 + H_2O$$

$$\Delta S^\circ_{reaction} = \Sigma S^\circ \text{ (products)} - \Sigma S^\circ \text{ (reactants)}$$

$$\Delta S^\circ_{reaction} = [(2 \times 213.6) + (70)] - [(249) + (2.5 \times 205)]$$

$$\Delta S^\circ_{reaction} = -264.2 \text{ J/K}$$

51. **(E)** Choice E would correctly state the third law of thermodynamics if the temperature was listed as 0 K.

52. **(B)** The ideal gas law assumes that there is no intermolecular attraction and that the volume of the gas molecules are insignificant relative to the space between the molecules. Therefore, gases that are large molecules and/or demonstrate strong intermolecular attraction are likely to be non-ideal gases. Hydrogen sulfide is both the largest gas molecule of the options, and it shows very strong intermolecular attraction because of the difference in electronegativity between hydrogen and sulfur. Water vapor also shows strong intermolecular attraction, but it is a much smaller molecule.

53. **(A)** The reaction equation is obtained as $-2(i) + 2\,(ii)$:

$$2C + 2O_2 \rightarrow 2CO_2 - 188.2 \text{ kcal}$$

$$\underline{2CO_2 \rightarrow O_2 + 2CO + 135.4 \text{ kcal}}$$

$$2C + O_2 \rightarrow 2CO - 52.8 \text{ kcal}$$

54. **(C)**

$$BaF_2 \rightarrow Ba^{2+} + 2F^-;\ Ksp = 1.7 \times 10^{-6} = [Ba^{2+}]\,[F^-]^2$$

Let $x = [Ba^{2+}]$ and $2x = [F^-]$; $(x)\,(2x)^2 = 4x^3 = 1.7 \times 10^{-6}$;

$$x = \left(\frac{1.7 \times 10^{-6}}{4} \right)^{\frac{1}{3}}$$

$$[F^-] = 2x = 2\left(\frac{1.7 \times 10^{-6}}{4} \right)^{\frac{1}{3}}$$

55. **(B)** In cell notation, the anodic (oxidation) reaction is indicated to the left of the double vertical bars. Sn^{2+} is oxidized to Sn^{4+}. Note that the Pt is inert, and it serves as the electrode. Choice E represents the cathodic (reduction) reaction.

56. **(B)**   One of the resonance forms of (B) places 10 electrons around the N– a violation of the octet rule for a second row element. A far better structure is

$$H - \overset{\overset{\displaystyle H}{\displaystyle |}}{\underset{\displaystyle \cdot\cdot}{N}} - \overset{\cdot\cdot}{\underset{\cdot\cdot}{O}} - H$$

57. **(C)**   To determine x, use the data from exp a and b, where the H_2 concentration varies but the NO concentration is the same. Thus, rate (b)/rate (a) = 2 = $k[H_2]\,^x/_b\,[NO]\,^y/_b\,/\,k[H_2]\,^x/_a\,[NO]\,^y/_a = (2.0 \times 10^{-3}\,/\,1.0 \times 10^{-3})^x = 2^x$; x = 1. In a similar way, use exp a and c to determine y; y = 2.

58. **(B)**   The use of a reaction quotient (Q) will help determine the direction of the reaction as it achieves equilibrium.

Q = $[CO]\,[Cl_2]\,/\,[COCl_2]$ = (1) (1) / (1) = 1 Comparing Q with Kp, we see that to achieve equilibrium, there must be a decrease in product concentration and an increase in reactant concentration.

59. **(A)**   Use $\Delta G = -RT \ln K$ where ΔG = 90,300 J mol^{-1}, T = 298 K, and R = 8.314 J mol^{-1} K^{-1}.

$$\ln K = \frac{-90,300}{8.314 \times 298} \quad K = e\left(\frac{-90,300}{8.314 \times 298}\right)$$

60. **(D)**   Effusion rates of gases are related as $r_A\,/\,r_B = (MW_B/\,MW_A)^{1/2}$ Thus, $r_x\,/\,r_{He}$ = .378 = $(4/x)^{1/2}$ x = 28.0.

61. **(C)**   An understanding of the several radioactive decay processes is important. Here, the process is beta decay. The mass number on the left must be balanced by an equal mass on the right. Since the beta particle has a zero mass, the mass of P must be 31.

62. **(C)**   Hydrochloric and nitric acids are the only listed pair of strong, monoprotic acids.

63. **(A)**   Applying Raoult's law, we can solve the problem:

$P_A = P_A°X_A$ (P_A = vapor pressure of compound A above the solution, P_Ao = vapor pressure of pure compound A, X_A = mole fraction of compound A). Let A = ethanol, B = water. $P_{total} = P_A + P_B = P_A°X_A + P_B°X_B$ = (.53) (.33) + (.24) (.67) = .34 atm.

64. **(C)** The square root of the ionization constant will give the molar proton concentration (10^{-5}). The negative of the exponent of the proton concentration gives the pH, or 5.

65. **(C)** Amphoteric or amphiprotic substances can function as either bases or acids, depending on conditions. Water, pure acetic acid, and liquid ammonia are examples of amphoteric substances.

66. **(D)** A hydrogen bond is a bond formed by the coulombic attraction between a hydrogen atom that is bonded to a strongly electronegative element (usually O, F, N) and another strongly electronegative element (O, F, N). The presence of hydrogen does not by itself ensure hydrogen bonding capability (*e.g.*, CH_4).

67. **(C)** Since HCl is a strong acid, it dissociates completely. Thus, a chloride ion is not chemically involved in the reaction and is not in the net ionic equation.

68. **(B)** pH is not a colligative property as it depends on specific properties of acids and bases (Ka, K_b) and not just their concentration.

69. **(B)** At neutralization, the moles of acid equal the moles of base. There are $0.02 \times 0.1 = 0.002$ moles of base, so there must also be 0.002 moles of acid in the 0.5 liter sample; that would require a acid solution concentration of 0.004 moles per liter.

70. **(E)** The reaction rate is proportional to the square of the concentration of A, which means the reaction is second order with respect to A. The reaction rate does not change at all when the concentration of B changes, so it is zero order with respect to B. Combined, the reaction is second order overall.

71. **(E)** Conjugate acid-base pairs consist of an acid and base related by the exchange of a proton. These are H_2O, OH^- and $(CH_3)_3 N$, $(CH3)_3NH^+$.

72. **(D)** The strength of oxyacids depends on the electronegativity and oxidation state of the central atom of the acid. The greater that both of these are, the greater the strength of the acid. If H_aXO_b represents a general oxyacid, then $b - a$ is proportionate to acid strength. Thus, $HClO_4$ is a strong acid and HClO is weak.

73. **(E)** $Zn(OH)_2$ $Zn^{2+} + 2OH^-$ $Ksp = 1.8 \times 10^{-14} = [Zn^{2+}] [OH^-]^2$
A pH 8 solution means that OH^- concentration is 10^{-6}. Let x = $[Zn^{2+}]$;
$10^{-6} = [OH^-]$ $1.8 \times 10^{-14} = (x) (10^{-6})^2$; x = 1.8×10^{-2}

74. **(E)**

$$240 \ C = 2.0 \ A \times 120 \ sec \ x \ \frac{C}{A \ sec}$$

75. **(C)** Acetylene shows a triple bond between the two carbons, which contains two pi bonds. In multiple bonds, the first bond is a sigma bond, where electrons are shared along the internuclear axis. Any additional bonding is created by the sideways overlap of unhybridized p-orbitals above and below the internuclear axis. None of the other options for answers contain multiple covalent bonds between any two atoms.

Section II

1. (a)

$$PV/RT = \frac{7.76 \text{ atm K mol} \times 5.00 \text{ L}}{0.082 \text{ L atm } 433 \text{ k}} = 1.09 \text{ moles total}$$

Half of those moles are due to water (0.545 mol) since carbon dioxide and water are produced in equimolar amounts.

(b) Pressure of water vapor = pressure carbon dioxide = 3.88 atm (half of total pressure for each.)

$$K_p = (H_2O)(CO_2) = (3.88 \text{ atm})(3.88 \text{ atm}) = 15.0$$

(c) First, find the amount that reacted to produce 0.545 mol each of water and carbon dioxide. Since the balanced equation states that two moles of sodium hydrogen carbonate react to produce one mole each of water and carbon dioxide, then 1.09 moles of reactant must have decomposed.

Mass reacted =

$$1.09 \text{ mol NaHCO}_3 \times \frac{85 \text{ g NaHCO}_3}{1 \text{ mol NaHCO}_3}$$

$$= 92.6 \text{ g NaHCO}_3$$

Therefore, $100 - 92.6 = 7.4$ g remain.

(d) Decreasing the volume would decreased the amount of space for the gas molecules, and equilibrium would have been established with less reacting. The partial pressure would be the same, but less carbon dioxide would be in the container.

(e)

$$\frac{K_p}{(RT)^{\Delta n}} = K_c = 15.0 / (0.082 \times 433)^2 = 0.0118$$

2.   (a)

total mol $=$ mol N_2 $+$ mol O_2 $=$

$$\frac{(30.2 \text{ g} \times 1 \text{ mol } N_2)}{28 \text{ g}} + \frac{(14.0 \text{ g} \times 1 \text{ mol } O_2)}{32 \text{ g}}$$

$= 1.52$ mol

$$P = nRT/V = \frac{1.52 \text{ mol} \times 0.082 \text{ L atm} \times 400 \text{ K}}{2.0 \text{ L} \qquad \text{K mol}}$$

$= 25.0$ atm

(b)   moles nitrogen $= 1.08$ mol

moles oxygen $= 0.438$ mol

mole fraction of oxygen $= 0.438 / (1.08 + 0.438) = 0.289$

(c)   Partial pressure $=$ total pressure $\times$ mole fraction

$= 25.0$ atm $\times 0.289 = 7.23$ atm

(d)   (i) $N_2 + 2 O_2 \rightarrow 2 NO_2$

(ii) 20.15 g nitrogen dioxide are produced from 0.438 moles oxygen.

(iii) The reaction begins with 1.08 mol of nitrogen and 0.428 mol oxygen. Since twice as many moles of oxygen than nitrogen are needed, and there is less than half the number of moles of nitrogen, then the oxygen runs out first, and oxygen is the limiting reactant.

(e)   The nitrogen leaks out slightly faster because it is the smaller molecule and has a greater molecular speed at any given temperature.

3.   (a)   From the useful information we may determine $E°$:

$Cr^{2+} + 2e^-$ $\qquad$ $Cr -0.91$ V

$\underline{Mn \qquad\qquad\quad Mn^{2+} + 2e^- + 1.03 \text{ V}}$

$Cr^2 + Mn$ $\qquad$ $Cr^2 + Mn^2 \ E° = +0.12V$

(b)   We use the Nernst equation:

$E_{cell} = E° - .059/n \ln ([Mn^{2+}] / [Cr^{2+}])$ where n (no. of electrons transferred) $= 2$

$$E_{cell} = .12 - .059/2 \ \ln\left(\frac{.31}{.0021}\right) = \underline{-0.027 \ V}$$

The reaction is not spontaneous as written (a negative E_{cell}).

(c) $\Delta G = -nFE$

$\Delta G = -(2) \ (96,500 \ \text{coulomb}) \ (-0.027 \ V) = 5.2 \times 10^3 \ J$

(d) $E_{cell} = .12 - .059/2 \ \ln\left(\frac{.0021}{.31}\right) = \underline{0.27 \ V}$

The reaction is spontaneous (a positive E_{cell}).

4. (a) $Cl_2(aq) + 2KBr(aq) \rightarrow Br_2(aq) + 2KCl(aq)$

$Cl_2^0(aq) + 2Br^{-1}(aq) \rightarrow Br_2(aq) + 2Cl^{-1}(aq)$

(b) $CuO(s) + H_2(g) \rightarrow Cu(s) + H_2O(g)$

$Cu^{+2} + H_2^0 \rightarrow Cu^0 + H^{+1}$

(c) $Zn(s) + HgO(s) \rightarrow ZnO(s) + Hg(l)$

$Zn^0 + Hg^{+2} \rightarrow Zn^{+2} + Hg^0$

(d) $4Al(s) + 3O_2(g) \rightarrow 2Al_2O_3(s)$

$Al^0 + O_2^0 \rightarrow Al^{+3}O^{-2}$

(e) $3Mn(s) + 2CrCl_3 \rightarrow 2Cr(s) + 3MnCl_2$

$Mn^0 + Cr^{+3} \rightarrow Cr^0 + Mn^{+2}$

(f) $2FeCl_3(aq) + SnCl_2(aq) \rightarrow 2FeCl_2(aq) + SnCl_4(aq)$

$Fe^{+3} + Sn^{+2} \rightarrow Fe^{+2} + Sn^{+4}$

(g) $2ZnS(s) + 3O_2(g) \rightarrow 2ZnO(s) + 2SO_2(g)$

$S^{-2} + O_2^0 \rightarrow S^{+4}O^{-2}$

(h) $CH_4(g) + 2O_2(g) \rightarrow CO_2(s) + 2H_2O(l)$

$C^{-4} + O_2^0 \rightarrow C^{+4} + O^{-2}$

5.   Le Chatelier's Principle states that if a stress is applied to a chemical system, the system will react in such a way that it relieves the applied stress. For the reaction:

$K = [HCO_3^-] [Ca^{2+}] / P$ of CO

(a)   The stress of added CO_2 pressure is relieved by an increase in the amount of bicarbonate.

(b)   The stress of added Ca^{2+} is relieved by its reaction with bicarbonate to form the reactants; hence, there is a decrease in the amount of the bicarbonate.

(c)   Note that $CaCO_3$ (s), as a solid, is not part of the equilibrium expression. Thus, there is no change to the amount of bicarbonate formed.

(d)   Since Ar is not part of the equilibrium, there should be no change in the amount of bicarbonate formed.

(e)   A catalyst speeds up a reaction but does not change the final equilibrium point. There is no change in the bicarbonate formed.

6.   (a)   When solutions are created from each sample, the glucose solution is the only one that will dissolve but not conduct electricity because it doesn't dissociate into ions.

(b)   Adding chloride ions (such as with HCl) would precipitate lead iodide ion in the following reaction,

Pb^{2+} *(aq)* $+ 2\, I^-$ *(aq)* $\rightarrow PbI_2$ *(s)*

(c)   glucose *(s)* $\rightarrow$ glucose *(aq)*

NaI *(s)* $\leftrightarrow Na^+$ *(aq)* $+ I^-$ *(aq)*

Al_2O_3 *(s)* $\leftrightarrow$ no reaction

$ZnSO_4$ *(s)* $\leftrightarrow Zn^{2+}$ *(aq)* $+ SO_4^{2-}$ *(aq)*

(d)   Aluminum oxide is determined because of its lack of solubility with water. Glucose has a Van't Hoff factor of 1.0 because it doesn't dissociate. Whereas both sodium iodide and zinc sulfate have a Van't Hoff factor of 2.0, since one mole dissolved creates two moles of ions in solution for both compounds. The latter two would show the same freezing point.

7. (a) At common temperatures and pressures, most gases do not demonstrate significant intermolecular attraction to be able to neglect that variable in the Van der Waals equation. Additionally, gases have enough kinetic energy to be able to create significant space between them, so their molecular volume is negligible compared to the space between the molecules. Therefore, that variable in the Van der Waals equation can be neglected. The resulting equation upon neglecting those two variables is the ideal gas law equation.

(b) To extend from the answer in part (a) above, at high pressures and low temperatures, gas molecules get close enough together so that for some gases intermolecular attraction and the molecular volume are significant enough to allow the gas behavior to deviate from the ideal gas law.

(c) Both oxygen and hydrogen gases, as diatomic molecules, are not polar, and are not likely to demonstrate strong intermolecular attraction. However, hydrogen sulfide is a more polar molecule and will be the first to show non-ideal behavior because of intermolecular attraction. Additionally, hydrogen sulfide is the largest of the molecules, so it would be the first to deviate from the ideal gas law due to molecular volume.

(d) "a" is a constant that is unique for each gas which represents the strength of intermolecular attraction for that gas. "b" is the molecular volume of one mole of the gas.

8. (a) The compound contains unpaired d electrons and is paramagnetic. As a result, it weighs more in a magnetic field.

(b) The color of a compound is caused by the compound absorbing selected wavelengths of visible light. In transition metal complexes, absorption can occur by exciting electrons from one d orbital to another d orbital that is higher in energy.

(c) The complex has two geometric isomers—cis (the same type of ligands on the same side) and trans (the same type of ligands on the opposite side:

trans   cis

(d)   The complex must be of the structure $[CO(NH_3)_5Cl]Br$. The chloride must be covalently bonded to the metal, while the bromide is ionic. Thus, the two ions produced in solution are of the form $[CO(NH_3)_5Cl]^{-1}$ and Br^{-1}.

Practice
Exam 6

AP Chemistry

Practice Exam 6

Section I

TIME: 90 minutes
           45% of the entire test

(Answer sheets appear in the back of this book.)

> **DIRECTIONS:** Each set of lettered choices below refers to the numbered questions or statements immediately following it. Select the one lettered choice that best answers each question. A choice may be used once, more than once, or not at all in each set.

Part A

1. How many grams of oxygen are needed for the complete combustion of 39.0 g of C_6H_6? The molecular weight of C_6H_6 is 78.0.

   $2\,C_6H_6 + 15\,O_2 \rightarrow 12\,CO_2 + 6H_2O$

   (A) 3.75 g   (D) 60.0 g

   (B) 120.0 g   (E) 292.5 g

   (C) 32.0 g

2. How many molecules are there in 22 g of CO_2? The molecular weight of CO_2 is 44 g mol.

   (A) 3   (D) 9.03×10^{23}

   (B) 6.02×10^{23} (E) 3.01×10^{23}

   (C) 44

3. What is the percent carbon in sucrose, $C_{12}H_{22}O_{11}$?

(A) 42.1   (D) 6.0

(B) 3.5   (E) 26.6

(C) 12.0

4. An atom containing which of the following number of protons, neutrons and electrons would be an isotope of hydrogen?

	protons	neutrons	electrons
(A)	0	1	1
(B)	1	2	1
(C)	0	0	1
(D)	2	1	2
(E)	2	0	2

5. A compound was found to contain only carbon, hydrogen and oxygen. The percent composition was determined as 40.0% C, 6.7% H and 53.3% O. The emperical formula of this compound is:

(A) C_2H_4O (D) CH_2O

(B) C_6HO_8 (E) C_3H_6O

(C) CHO

6. Which one of the following species has a noble gas configuration?

(A) Be^+ (D) H^+

(B) N^- (E) O^{2+}

(C) Mg^{2+}

7. Which one of the following compounds is an Iron (III) oxide?

    (A) FeO

    (B) Fe_3O_4

    (C) FeO_2

    (D) Fe_2O_3

    (E) Fe_2O

8. A sample of a pure gas occupied a volume of 500 mL at a temperature of 27 °C and a pressure of .4 atm. The number of moles present in this sample is:

    (A) .045

    (B) .008

    (C) .091

    (D) 8.13

    (E) .182

9. The molecular weight of 0.25 g of a gas that occupies a volume of 100 mL at a pressure of 2.5 atm and a temperature of 25 °C is:

    (A) 28.0

    (B) 12.2

    (C) 2.05

    (D) 20.5

    (E) 24.4

10. The pair of atoms that are most likely to form a covalent compound are:

    (A) H and He

    (B) Na and F

    (C) H and Cl

    (D) Li and F

    (E) Na and Cl

11. What is the hydronium ion concentration, H_3O^+ of a solution that has a hydroxide concentration of 1.4 x 10^{-4} M?

    (A) 7.2×10^{-11}

    (B) 1.4×10^{-10}

    (C) 1.0×10^{-14}

    (D) 1.8×10^{-5}

    (E) 7.0×10^{-7}

12. What is the pH of a solution that has a hydronium ion concentration, H_3O^+ of 1.2×10^{-4}?

(A) 3.92   (D) 5.20

(B) 4.00   (E) 7.90

(C) 3.80

13. The H^+ concentration of a .01 molar solution of HCN is:

(The K_i for HCN is 4×10^{-10})

(A) 2.5×10^{-11} M   (D) 2×10^{-6} M

(B) .01 M   (E) 2×10^{-5} M

(C) 4×10^{-10} M

14. What is the frequency of electromagnetic radiation that has a wavelength of 600 nm? (The velocity of light is 3.0×10^8 m/s)

(A) 2.0×10^{-15} s^{-1} (D) 5.0×10^{14} s^{-1}

(B) 2.0×10^{14} s^{-1} (E) 3.0×10^8 s^{-1}

(C) 6.64×10^{18} s^{-1}

15. The energy of electromagnetic radiation whose frequency is 8.00×10^{11} s^{-1} is: (Planck's constant is 6.63×10^{-34} j/s)

(A) 1.2×10^{45} j   (D) 8×10^{-46} j

(B) 6.02×10^{23} j   (E) 3.0×10^8 j

(C) 5.30×10^{-22} j

Questions 16 and 17

Choose the letter answer which best describes the gas law that follows the graphs shown.

(A) Graham's Law

(D) Gay – Lussac's Law

(B) Boyle's Law

(E) Avogadro's Law

(C) Charles' Law

16.

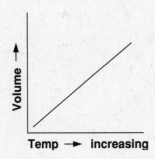

17.

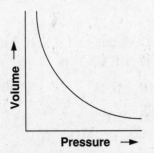

18. What is the molarity of a solution that is prepared by dissolving 32.0 g of KCl in enough water to make 425 mL of solution?

    (A) 1.0

    (B) 2.3

    (C) 1.0×10^{-3}

    (D) .425

    (E) .0075

19. What would the freezing point of a solution containing 8.0 g of ethylene glycol $(C_2H_6O_2)$ in 100 g of H_2O? (The K^f for H_2O is 1.86° C/M and the freezing point of pure water is 0 ° C.)

    (A) 0.0 °C

    (B) −1.8 °C

    (C) +2.4 °C

    (D) + 0.2 °C

    (E) −2.4 °C

20. Which of the following pairs are allotropes?

    (A) H_2O D_2O

    (B) O_2 O_3

    (C) HCl   HBr

    (D) Cl_2 F_2

    (E) Fe_2O_3 Fe_3O_4

21. A saturated solution of AgCl was found to contain 1.3×10^{-5} mol/L of Ag^+. The solubility product constant, K_{sp} of AgCl is:

    (A) 1.30×10^{-5}

    (B) 1.14×10^{-5}

    (C) 2.60×10^{-5}

    (D) 1.80×10^{-10}

    (E) 2.60×10^{-10}

22. Which of the following salts will have the greatest freezing point depression for a .1 M solution of the salt?

    (A) Na_2SO_4 (D) KNO_3

    (B) NaCl   (E) NH_4Cl

    (C) KCl

23. The molecular orbital diagram shown below:

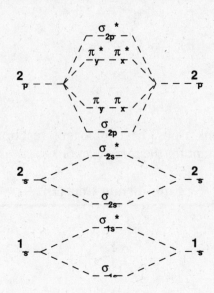

    is correct for which species listed:

    (A) NO   (D) CO

    (B) CO+   (E) F_2

    (C) NO+

24. If the specific heat of aluminum is .89 j / °C g, how many joules are required to heat 23.2 g of aluminum from 30 °C to 80 °C?

    (A) 45   (D) 1,032

    (B) 1,160   (E) 50

    (C) 20

25. Which one of the following compounds contains chlorine in a positive oxidation state?

   (A) HCl

   (B) KCl

   (C) $HClO_3$

   (D) PCl_3

   (E) NH_4Cl

26. Which of the following is a superoxide?

   (A) $KClO_3$

   (B) RbO_2

   (C) FeO

   (D) H_2O_2

   (E) Na_2O_2

27. Use the equilibrium constants from the component reactions to calculate the equilibrium constant for the total reaction.

REACTION	Equilibrium Constant
Cl_2 $+$ $\leftrightarrow$ 2 Cl	K_1
Cl $+$ CO $\leftrightarrow$ COCl	K_2
COCl $+$ Cl $\leftrightarrow$ $COCl_2$	K_3
Cl_2 $+$ CO $\leftrightarrow$ $COCl_2$	K_{total}

   (A) $K_1 + K_2 + K_3$

   (B) $K_1 \times K_2 \times K_3$

   (C) $K_1 - K_2 - K_3$

   (D) $K_1 + K_2 - K_3$

   (E) none of the above

28. How many times faster will hydrogen effuse from the same effusion apparatus than nitrogen at the same temperature?

   (A) 14.0

   (B) .3

   (C) 5.3

   (D) 3.8

   (E) 2.7

29. What is the Normality of a solution that contains 23.2 g of H_2SO_4 and enough water to make 400 mL of solution?

    (A) 2.4   (D) 6.0

    (B) .60   (E) .50

    (C) 1.2

30. If a certain number of moles of a gas occupied a volume of 200 ml at 25°C, what volume would it occupy if it was heated to 40°C at a constant pressure?

    (A) 210 mL   (D) 500 mL

    (B) 320 mL   (E) 120 mL

    (C) 230 mL

31. Using molecular orbital theory predict the bond order of the He_2^+.

    (A) 1/2   (D) 3

    (B) 1   (E) 1/4

    (C) 0

32. Which one of the following accounts for the disappearance of the purple color of MnO_4^- ion when it reacts with Fe^{2+} in acid solution?

    (A) MnO_4^- forms a complex with Fe^{2+}.

    (B) The MnO_4^- is reduced to the colorless Mn^{2+} ion.

    (C) The MnO_4^- is oxidized.

    (D) MnO_4^- is colorless in acid solution.

    (E) The presence of water is in the system.

33. Which is the correct electron configuration for a Cr atom?

    (A) [Ar] $4s^23d^4$ (D) [Ar] $4s^13d^5$

    (B) [Ar] $4s^13d^4$ (E) [Ar] $4s^23d^5$

    (C) [Ar] $4s^23d^6$

34. For the reaction

    $2A + 1B \rightarrow 2C$

    The following rate data was obtained:

Experiment	initial conc. of A mol/l	initial conc. of B mol/l	initial rate mol/l sec
1	.5	.5	10
2	.5	1.0	20
3	.5	1.5	30
4	1.0	.5	40

    Which expression below states the rate law for the reaction above?

    (A) Rate = k $[A]^2$ [B]

    (B) Rate = k [A] [B]

    (C) Rate = k $[A]^2$ $[B]^2$

    (D) Rate = k $[A]^3$

    (E) Rate = k $[A]^2$ $[B]^3$

35. The high boiling point of H_2O relative to the boiling points of H_2S, H_2Se and H_2Te can be attributed to:

    (A) the molecular weight of H_2O

    (B) the covalent bonds between H and O

    (C) the atomic number of oxygen

    (D) the ability of water to absorb oxygen

    (E) the ability of water to form hydrogen bonds

36. For the reaction

    $N_2 (g) + O_2 (g) \rightarrow 2 NO (g)$

    $\Delta G°$ for the reaction is $+ 174$ kJ. This reaction would:

    (A) be at equilibrium

    (B) proceed spontaneously

    (C) have a negative $\Delta H°$

    (D) not proceed spontaneously

    (E) exothermic

37. From the heats of reaction, $\Delta H°$, for

    $C(graphite) + O_2(g) \rightarrow CO_2(g)$ $\Delta H° = -394$ kj

    $CO(g) + \frac{1}{2}O_2 \rightarrow CO_2(g)$ $\Delta H_o = -284$ kj

    The calculated $\Delta H°$ for the reaction:

    $C(graphite) + \frac{1}{2}O_2(g) \rightarrow CO(g)$

    is:

    (A) 0   (D) -678 kj

    (B) $+18$ kj   (E) -110 kj

    (C) -18 kj

38. In the reaction

    $HCN + H_2O \leftrightarrow H_3O^+ + CN^-$

    which species are functioning as Brønsted bases?

    (A) only H_2O (D) CN^- and HCN

    (B) HCN and H_3O^+ (E) H_3O^+ and CN^-

    (C) H_2O and CN^-

39. How many grams of copper would be produced by the reduction of Cu^{2+} if 3.0 amperes of current are passed through a copper (II) nitrate solution for 1 hour?

    (A) 18.20   (D) 7.12

    (B) 3.56   (E) 63.50

    (C) 31.80

40. The half life of $^{224}_{88}Rn$ is 3.64 days. How many μg of $^{224}_{88}Rn$ would be left after 18.2 days if the starting amount weighed 2.0 μg?

    (A) .06   (D) .69

    (B) .40   (E) none

    (C) .19

41. A saturated solution of Ag_2CrO_4 was found to have a CrO_4 concentration of 1.30×10^{-4} M. The K_{sp} for Ag_2CrO_4 is:

    (A) 1.70×10^{-8} (D) 1.7×10^{-12}

    (B) 4.4×10^{-8} (E) 8.8×10^{-12}

    (C) 3.4×10^{-8}

42. One atom of hydrogen weighs:

    (A) 1.00 g   (D) 2.00 g

    (B) 22.4 g   (E) 6.02×10^{23} g

    (C) 1.66×10^{-24} g

43. Which one of the following is paramagnetic?

    (A) He   (D) F⁻

    (B) Be   (E) Li

    (C) Cl⁻

44. What volume of a 1.3 M solution of NaCl contains 2.3 g of NaCl?

    (A) 130 mL   (D) 177 mL

    (B) 30.2 mL   (E) 1.3 mL

    (C) 3.9 mL

45. If oxygen is collected over water at 25 °C and at a pressure of 760 tor, the pressure due to just the oxygen is: (the vapor pressure of H_2O at 25 °C is 19.0 torr)

    (A) 779 torr   (D) 741 torr

    (B) 760 torr   (E) 1 torr

    (C) 19 torr

46. Which of the following is not a colligative property of a solution?

    (A) freezing point

    (B) vapor pressure over the solution

    (C) molecular weight of the solute

    (D) boiling point

    (E) none of the above

47. Which of the following solutions does not constitute a buffer pair?

    (A) .2M NH_4OH and .1M NH_4Cl

    (B) .2M NaCl and .1M HCl

    (C) .1M acetic acid and .05M sodium acetate

    (D) .1M NH_4OH and .1M $(NH_4)_2SO_4$

    (E) .1M formic acid and .1M sodium formate

48. What is the hydrogen ion concentration of a buffer solution that is .05M in acetic acid and .1M in sodium acetate. (The K_i for acetic acid is 1.8×10^{-5}.)

    (A) 9.0×10^{-6} (D) 1.8×10^{-6}

    (B) 1.8×10^{-5} (E) 1.0×10^{-7}

    (C) 1.0×10^{-14}

49. What is the mole fraction of CH_3OH in a solution that contains 53.0 g of water, 20.3 g of CH_3OH and 15.0 g of CH_3CH_2OH?

    (A) .33   (D) .96

    (B) .48   (E) .16

    (C) 1.22

50. For the reaction at 298 K:

    $A(g) + B(g) \rightarrow C(g)$

    the value of K_p is 1×10^{10} atm^{-1}. The value for $\Delta G°$ expressed in kJ is:

    (A) 0   (D) $+ 57.1$

    (B) $- 57.1$ (E) $+ 83.7$

    (C) $- 27.3$

51. For the following reaction at 500 K

    $C(s) + CO_2(g) \qquad 2CO(g)$

    the equilibrium mixture contained CO_2 and CO at partial pressures of 7.6 atm and 3.2 atm respectively. The value of the K_p is:

    (A) 2.4 atm   (D) 1.0 atm

    (B) 18.1 atm   (E) .4 atm

    (C) .6 atm

52. $Br_2 (l) \rightarrow Br_2 (g)$

    The equilibrium vapor pressure of bromine gas is 0.281 atm at 25 °C? What is the K_p for the above reaction at 25 °C?

    (A) 0 atm

    (B) 0.281 atm

    (C) $(0.281)^2$ atm

    (D) 1.0 atm

    (E) 760 mm Hg.

53. Which of the following is the weakest acid?

    (A) HCl   (D) HF

    (B) HBr   (E) H_2SO_4

    (C) HI

54. How many moles of $KClO_3$ must be decomposed to produce 3.20 g of O_2?

    (A) .10   (D) .14

    (B) .30   (E) .07

    (C) .24

55. Which of the following has the highest first ionization potential?

    (A) Na   (D) P

    (B) Ar   (E) Si

    (C) Mg

56. How many mL of 0.5 NaOH are required to just neutralize 50 mL of 0.2N HCl?

    (A) 25   (D) 50

    (B) 100   (E) 40

    (C) 20

57. In the Van der Waal's equation:

$$\left(P + \frac{n^2a}{V^2}\right)(V - nb) = nRT$$

The constant a is best described as a correction factor due to:

    (A) temperature

    (B) intermolecular attractions of real gases

    (C) the molecular weights of gases

    (D) the volume of the actual gas molecules

    (E) the specific heat of the gas molecules

58. Which of the following statements is correct concerning the reaction:

$Fe^{2+} + 2H^+ + NO_3^- \rightarrow Fe^{3+} + NO_2 + H_2O$

    (A) Fe^{3+} is oxidized and H^+ is reduced.

    (B) Fe^{2+} is oxidized and nitrogen is reduced.

    (C) Fe^{2+} and H^+ are oxidized.

    (D) Oxygen is oxidized.

    (E) H^+ and oxygen are reduced.

59. Thioacetamide is used as a reagent in quantitative analysis to form precipitates of Fe^{3+}, Ni^{2+}, CO^{2+}, Mn^{2+}, and Zn^{2+}. This reagent is used because it provides a convenient method of generating which of the following materials in aqueous solution?

(A) H_2SO_4

(B) H_2S

(C) SO_3

(D) SO_2

(E) both SO_3 and SO_2

60. The standard free energy, $\Delta G°$ expressed in kj for the reaction below at 25 °C is:

$$Cd + Pb^{2+} \rightarrow Cd^{2+} + Pb \quad E° = +.28V$$

(A) -27

(B) -54

(C) $+27$

(D) -108

(E) 0

61. Which of the following salts would hydrolize to form a solution whose pH is below 7?

(A) $CaCl_2$

(B) CH_3COONa

(C) $NaCl$

(D) NH_4Cl

(E) $BaCl_2$

62. For the reaction:

$$FeCl_2 \text{ (aq)} + KMnO_4 \text{ (aq)} + HCl \text{ (aq)} \rightarrow FeCl_3 \text{ (aq)} + MnCl_2 \text{ (aq)} + KCl \text{ (aq)} + H_2O \text{ (l)}$$

the net ionic equation is:

(A) $Fe^{2+} \rightarrow Fe^{3+}$

(B) $Fe^{2+} + Mn^{7+}O_4^- + H^+ \rightarrow Fe^{3+} + Mn^{2+} + H_2O$

(C) $MnO_4^- + H^+ \rightarrow Mn^{2+} + H_2O$

(D) $FeCl_2 + MnO_4^- \rightarrow FeCl_3 + Mn^{2+}$

(E) $MnO_4^- \rightarrow Mn^{+2}$

63. What do the following ions have in common?

Mg^{2+} O^{2-} F$^-$ Na$^+$

(A) they are isoelectronic

(B) the same number of protons

(C) they are metal ions

(D) they have the same atomic radius

(E) none of the above

64. VSEPR theory predicts that the geometry of the ICl_4^- ion is:

(A) tetrahedral   (D) linear

(B) square planar   (E) trigonal pyramidal

(C) octahedral

65. Which of the following can best be described as a polar covalent molecule?

(A) Cl_2 (D) H_2

(B) HCl   (E) NaCl

(C) KCl

66. Use the chart below to answer the following question.

Substance	ΔG_f° (kJ/mol)
C_2H_2 (g)	209.0
CO_2 (g)	-394.0
H_2O (l)	-237.0
O_2 (g)	0.0

Which of the following represents the approximate change in standard free energy per mole for the combustion of C_2H_2 (g)?

(A)   –20 kJ/mol

(B)   +20 kJ/mol

(C)   –100 kJ/mol

(D)   –1200 kJ/mol

(E)   +1200 kJ/mol

67. Which of the following is an example of a hydride?

(A) HCl   (D) HF

(B) H_2O (E) H_2S

(C) LiH

68. A catalyst will increase the rate of a chemical reaction by:

(A)   shifting the equilibrium to the right

(B)   lowering the activation energy

(C)   shifting the equilibrium to the left

(D)   increasing the activation energy

(E)   has no effect

69. In the correctly balanced equation for the reaction:

$MnO_4^- + Cl^- + H^+ \leftrightarrow Mn^{2+} + Cl_2 + H_2O$

The coefficients for Cl^- and H^+ are respectively:

(A)   10 and 8   (D) 5 and 5

(B)   10 and 16   (E) 5 and 10

(C)   5 and 8

70. Which one of the following hydroxides is amphoteric?

    (A) $Ba(OH)_2$ (D) $Al(OH)_3$

    (B) $Ca(OH)_2$ (E) NaOH

    (C) $Mg(OH)_2$

71. Which of the following would have the lowest entropy at 25 °C?

    (A) NaCl(s)   (D) He(g)

    (B) $H_2(g)$ (E) both H_2 and He

    (C) $H_2O(l)$

72. From the data below, calculate the $\Delta H°$, expressed in kj, for the reaction:

    $2Na(s) + 2H_2O(l) \rightarrow 2NaOH(s) + H_2(g)$

Substance	$\Delta H°$ kj/mol
$H_2O(l)$	−285.8
NaOH(s)	−426.7
$H_2(g)$	−241.8

    (A) − 281.8   (D) + 712.5

    (B) + 140.9   (E) zero

    (C) − 712.5

73. For which one of the following equilibrium equations will K_p equal K_c?

    (A) $PCl_5 \leftrightarrow PCl_3 + Cl_2$

    (B) $COCl_2 \leftrightarrow CO + Cl_2$

    (C) $H_2 + I_2 \leftrightarrow 2HI$

    (D) $3H_2 + N_2 \leftrightarrow 2NH_3$

    (E) $2SO_3 \leftrightarrow 2SO_2 + O_2$

74. The weak electrolyte is:

(A) HNO_3

(D) NaCl

(B) KI

(E) NH_4OH

(C) HCl

75. The following phase diagram was obtained for compound X:

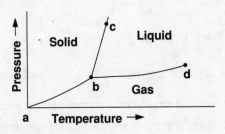

The melting point of X would:

(A)   be independent of pressure

(B)   increase as pressure increases

(C)   decrease as pressure increases

(D)   depends on the amount of X present

(E)   both (C) and (D)

AP Chemistry

Practice Exam 6

Section II

TIME: 90 minutes
55% of the entire test

(Answer sheets appear in the back of this book.)

The percentages given for the parts represent the score weightings for this section of the examination. You will be given 40 minutes for Part A and 50 minutes for Part B.

You may use a calculator on Part A, but not on Part B.

Be sure to write your answers in the space provided following each question. Pay attention to significant figures.

Part A

TIME: 40 minutes
40 percent

YOU MAY USE A CALCULATOR ON THIS PART.

Show your work clearly for full credit. Pay attention to significant figures in your answers.

Solve the following problem.

1. The value for the ionization constant, K_a, for hydrocyanic acid, HCN, is 6.2×10^{-10}.

    (a) Calculate the pH of a 0.040-molar solution of HCN.

    (b) Calculate the percent dissociation of the solution in (a).

    (c) Write the net ionic equation for the titration of HCN with a standardized solution of NaOH.

    (d) Calculate the equilibrium constant for the titration of HCN.

    (e) Calculation the hydrogen ion concentration of a solution prepared by mixing equal volumes of a 0.050-molar HCN and a 0.030-molar solution of sodium cyanide, NaCN.

    (f) The K_{sp} for $Mg(OH)_2$ is 1.5×10^{-11}. Calculate the molar solubility of magnesium hydroxide in the solution indicated in part (a).

Solve EITHER problem 2 or problem 3 below. Only one of these two questions will be graded. (The problem you choose will be worth 20% of the score on Part II.)

2. A student intends to carry out an oxidation-reduction titration for the reaction,

    $$Fe^{2+} + H^+ + MnO_4^- \rightarrow Fe^{3+} + Mn^{2+} + H_2O$$

    (a) Balance the above equation.

    (b) 10.0 grams of iron (II) nitrate and 10.0 gram of potassium permanganate are put into a 0.80 L solution of 2.0 M nitric acid. What are the resulting values for $[Fe^{2+}]$ and $[MnO_4^-]$?

    (c) As the reaction proceeds to completion, what is the mass of Fe^{3+} that is produced?

    (d) What is the limiting reactant?

    (e) What is the pH of the remaining solution after the reaction is complete?

3. A set of kinetic experiments were performed on the reaction
    $A + 2B \rightarrow C$, and the following data was obtained.

Trial	[A]	[B]	Initial rate of formation of C (M/sec)
1	0.10	0.40	0.02
2	0.10	0.80	0.02
3	0.20	0.80	0.16

(a) Determine the order of the reaction with respect to each
     reactant and write the overall rate law for the reaction.

(b) Calculate the value and units of the rate constant for the
     reaction.

(c) The temperature is increased by 10 K and trial number 3
     is repeated. What would you anticipate to be the initial
     rate of formation of C, and why?

(d) One person suggested the following rate mechanism for
     the reaction. Prove whether or not the proposed mecha-
     nism is consistent with the rate law of the reaction. If the
     mechanism is not consistent with the rate law, suggest a
     mechanism that would be.

Step one:	A	$\leftrightarrow$	2 I	slow
Step two:	B + I	$\leftrightarrow$	C	fast equilibrium
Step three	B + I	$\leftrightarrow$	C	fast equilibrium

Total reaction: $A + 2B \leftrightarrow C$

Part B

TIME: 50 minutes

YOU MAY NOT USE A CALCULATOR ON THIS PART.

4. This question is worth 15% of Section II. Write the formulas of the reactants and products for FIVE of the following eight reactions. Show net ionic reactions only, where appropriate. Assume the reaction takes place in aqueous solution unless otherwise specified. Do not balance the reaction.

   (a) Magnesium metal in an aqueous solution of sulfuric acid

   (b) Nitrogen oxide gas in the presence of hydrogen gas

   (c) Iodine mixed with hydrogen sulfide

   (d) Oxygen and ammonia gases react

   (e) Zinc (II) chloride in the presence of magnesium

   (f) Mercurial (II) oxide in aqueous hydrogen peroxide

   (g) Steam passed over hot coke

   (h) Copper exposed to fluorine gas

ANSWER BOTH OF THE FOLLOWING ESSAY QUESTIONS (15% each).

5. The location of an element on the periodic table will determine whether or not an element is a metal or a nonmetal.

   (a) Identify the major traits of metals.

   (b) Give an explanation for three of these traits based on atomic structure.

   (c) How do the traits of metals and nonmetals influence the attraction between like elements?

   (d) How do the different metallic traits of elements differ among different groups and families on the periodic table?

ANSWER THE FOLLOWING LABORTATORY-BASED ESSAY QUESTION.

6. Construct a flow chart that details the procedures for the separation and identification of the Group I metal ions: Hg_2^{2+}, Ag^+, Pb^{+2}. Your answer should include a discussion of why the separations are achieved, as well as a specific listing of the reagents that are utilized in the final identification of the metal ions.

ANSWER QUESTION 7 OR QUESTION 8 BELOW. ONLY ONE OF THESE TWO QUESTIONS WILL BE GRADED (15%), ANSWER ONE OF THE FOLLOWING ESSAY QUESTIONS.

7. Iodine-131 is an unstable nuclide with a half-life of 8.1 days.

   (a) If 80.0 grams of Iodine-131 is created from nuclear bombardment, how long will it take for there to only be 5.0 grams left?

   (b) Explain why the nucleus of the Iodine-131 atom weighs less than the sum of the individual neutrons, protons, and electrons of which it is made.

   (c) Describe the difference between alpha, beta, and gamma decay.

   (d) Which type of decay is Iodine-131 most likely undergoing, and why?

   (e) What are the units of the rate constant? Why are these units the same for all radioactive decay?

8. Give the scientific explanation for the following:

   (a) Real gases tend to behave non-ideally at low temperatures and high temperatures.

   (b) Fish kills are more prevalent in the summer than in the winter.

(c)   Ethylene glycol-based antifreeze offers protection both against freezing in the winter and boil over in the summer.

(d)   The endpoint determined by an indicator might or might not correspond to the equivalent point in an acid-base titration.

AP Chemistry

Practice Exam 6

ANSWER KEY

Section I

#		#		#	
1.	(B)	26.	(B)	51.	(B)
2.	(E)	27.	(B)	52.	(B)
3.	(A)	28.	(D)	53.	(D)
4.	(B)	29.	(C)	54.	(E)
5.	(D)	30.	(A)	55.	(B)
6.	(C)	31.	(A)	56.	(C)
7.	(D)	32.	(B)	57.	(B)
8.	(B)	33.	(D)	58.	(B)
9.	(E)	34.	(A)	59.	(B)
10.	(C)	35.	(E)	60.	(B)
11.	(A)	36.	(D)	61.	(D)
12.	(A)	37.	(E)	62.	(B)
13.	(D)	38.	(C)	63.	(A)
14.	(D)	39.	(B)	64.	(B)
15.	(C)	40.	(A)	65.	(B)
16.	(C)	41.	(E)	66.	(D)
17.	(B)	42.	(C)	67.	(C)
18.	(A)	43.	(E)	68.	(B)
19.	(E)	44.	(B)	69.	(B)
20.	(B)	45.	(D)	70.	(D)
21.	(D)	46.	(C)	71.	(A)
22.	(A)	47.	(B)	72.	(A)
23.	(B)	48.	(A)	73.	(C)
24.	(D)	49.	(E)	74.	(E)
25.	(C)	50.	(B)	75.	(B)

DETAILED EXPLANATIONS OF ANSWERS

Practice Exam 6

Section I

1. **(B)** According to the equation:

$$2C_6H_6 + 15O_2 \rightarrow 12CO_2 + 6H_2O$$

for every 2 moles of C_6H_6, 15 moles of oxygen are required for the complete combustion of the C_6H_6. Therefore it is necessary to find the number of moles of C_6H_6 in 39.0 g. Since the number of moles is always equal to:

$$\text{moles} = \frac{g}{MW} = \frac{39.0}{78.0} = 0.5 \text{ moles of } C_6H_6$$

According to the balanced equation for every 2 moles of C_6H_6, 15 moles of oxygen are required. Therefore

$$\frac{2 \text{ moles } C_6H_6}{.5 \text{ moles } C_6H_6} \qquad \frac{15 \text{ moles } O_2}{x \text{ moles } O_2}$$

$x = 3.75$ moles of oxygen are needed for .5 moles of C_6H_6. However the question asked for the answer expressed in grams, and so we must now convert 3.75 moles of O_2 to grams of O_2. Since moles = g/MW the number of grams can be calculated by

g = moles x MW

g = 3.75 moles $\times$ 32 g/mole

g = 120 g of oxygen.

2. **(E)** The number of molecules in one mole is given by Avogadro's number which is: 1 mole of molecules contains 6.02×10^{23} molecules. Since the amount of CO_2 given is 22 g it is first necessary to find the number of moles of CO_2 in 22 g. This is calculated from:

$$\text{moles} = \frac{\text{g}}{\text{MW}} = \frac{22\text{ g}}{44\text{ g/mol}} = 0.5\text{ moles of CO}_2$$

It is now necessary to calculate the number of molecules in .5 moles of CO_2. This is obtained using Avogadro's number.

$$\frac{1\text{ mole}}{0.5\text{ moles}} = \frac{6.02 \times 10^{23}\text{ molecules}}{x\text{ molecules}}$$

$$x = 3.01 \times 10^{23}\text{ molecules}$$

3.   **(A)**   The percent of an element in a compound is equal to the weight of that element divided by the total weight of the compound times 100. Therefore the percent carbon in sucrose is equal to

$$\%C = \frac{12 \times \text{atomic weight of C}}{\text{molecular weight of sucrose}} \times 100$$

$$= \frac{12 \times 12.0\text{ g}}{(12 \times 12)C + (22 \times 1)H + (16 \times 11)O} \times 100$$

$$= \frac{144}{342} \times 100 = 42.1\%\text{ carbon}$$

4.   **(B)**   Atoms that have the same number of protons but differ in the number of neutrons they contain are referred to as isotopes. For the element hydrogen there are three forms, Hydrogen or Protium, Deuterium, and Tritium which occur naturally. In each of the three forms the number of protons and electrons is identical but they contain a different number of neutrons. The only difference between isotopes is the number of neutrons. Thus isotopes of hydrogen will all contain 1 proton and 1 electron but will have additional neutrons. Of the choices listed the only one that could be an isotope of hydrogen would be (B), since it has the same atomic number as hydrogen, but has two additional neutrons.

Isotopes of Hydrogen

	Atomic number	protons	neutrons	electrons
Hydrogen	1	1	0	1
Deuterium	1	1	1	1
Tritium	1	1	2	1

In this case the isotope of hydrogen would be tritium.

5.   **(D)**   The empirical formula of a compound tells us the relative number of moles or atoms of each element it contains. From the data given above it is possible to calculate the mole ratio of each element. In a 100 g sample there would be 40 g of carbon, 6.7 g of hydrogen and 53.3 g of oxygen. Therefore the number of moles of each element would be:

$$\text{moles of C} = \frac{\text{g of C}}{\text{at. wt. C}} = \frac{40.0g}{12.0g} = 3.3$$

$$\text{moles of H} = \frac{\text{g of H}}{\text{at. wt. H}} = \frac{6.7g}{1.0g} = 6.7$$

$$\text{moles of O} = \frac{\text{g of O}}{\text{at. wt. O}} = \frac{53.3g}{16.0g} = 3.3$$

The molar ratio is then

$$C_{3.3}H_{6.7}O_{3.3}$$

The relative whole number ratio of each can be found by dividing each by the smallest number, which in this case is 3.3:

C	H	O
$\dfrac{3.3}{3.3} = 1$	$\dfrac{6.7}{3.3} = 2$	$\dfrac{3.3}{3.3} = 1$

Therefore the empirical formula would be CH_2O.

6.   **(C)**   A noble gas configuration is one in which all of the available energy levels contained in the atom are completely occupied by electrons. For example He has a configuration $1s^2$ and Ne has a configuration $1s^22s^22p^6$. In both cases these elements contain the maximum number of electrons that their available energy levels can contain. The configurations for the species given are:

Be^+	3 electrons	$1s^22s^1$
N^-	8 electrons	$1s^22s^22p^4$
Mg^{2+}	10 electrons	$1s^22s^22p^6$
H^+	0 electrons	
O^{2+}	6 electrons	$1s^22s^22p^2$

The only one that has a noble gas configuration is Mg^{2+} which has the same electron configuration as Ne which is also $1s^22s^22p^6$.

7.   **(D)**   All oxides contain oxygen in an oxidation state of –2. Thus in all of the above compounds the oxidation state of the oxygen is –2. Since all compounds are neutral we may assign the oxidation state of the Iron as follows:

FeO   Since oxygen is –2 the iron must be +2 for the compound to be neutral.

Fe_3O_4 Each oxygen is –2 for a total charge of $-2 \times 4 = -8$. Therefore the oxidation state of the iron must be

$$\frac{-8}{3} = -2\frac{1}{2}$$

Fe_2O_3 Each oxygen is –2 for a total charge of $-2 \times 3 = -6$, therefore the iron is $+6/2 = 3$.

Fe_2O The oxygen is –2, therefore total charge due to the two iron atoms is +2 hence the oxidation state of the iron would be +1.

8.   **(B)**   We can use the ideal gas law, $PV = nRT$ to solve for the number of moles. By rearranging we have:

$$n = \frac{PV}{RT}$$

To solve this equation we must use the correct units. Using $R = .082$ L • atm / K • mol we must express the pressure in atmospheres, the volume in liters and the temperature in K.

V = 500 mL = .5 L

P = .4 atm.

T = 27 ºC + 273 K = 300 K

Substituting

$$n = \frac{.4 \text{ atm} \times .5 \text{ L}}{.082 \dfrac{1 \text{ atm}}{\text{mole K}} \times 300 \text{ K}} = .008 \text{ moles}$$

9.   **(E)**   Using the ideal gas law $PV = nRT$ and rearranging:

$$n = \frac{PV}{RT}$$

and since $n = \dfrac{g}{MW}$

we now have $\dfrac{g}{MW} = \dfrac{PV}{RT}$

and solving for MW gives us MW =

$$MW = \dfrac{g\,RT}{PV}$$

Using the ideal gas law constant R = .082 L • atm / K • mol

we make the substitutions $\quad$ g = 0.25

$\qquad\qquad\qquad\qquad\qquad$ pressure = 2.5 atm

$\qquad\qquad\qquad\qquad\qquad$ volume (in liters) = .1

$\qquad\qquad\qquad\qquad\qquad$ temperature = 25 °C = 298 K

$$MW = \dfrac{0.25\ g\ \times\ .082\ \dfrac{1\ atm}{mole\ K}\ \times\ 298\ K}{2.5\ atm\ \times\ .1}$$

MW = 24.4 g / mole

10. **(C)** Covalent bonding occurs when an electron pair is shared between two atoms, whereas ionic bonding will occur when one atom has a tendency to lose one or more electrons and the other atom has a tendency to gain electrons. This process will result in the formation of a positive and a negative ion which will result in the formation of an ionic bond (i.e., Na^+Cl^-). In covalent bonding both atoms will have a tendency to gain electrons. In the simplest example of covalent bonding, the H_2 molecule is formed when one hydrogen atom H ($1s^1$) shares its electron with a second hydrogen atom,

$\qquad$ H : H

In this process of sharing electron pairs, both hydrogen atoms now have effectively obtained their next nearest noble gas configuration which is a very stable configuration.

In the answers listed the only pair of atoms that can form a covalent bond is H and Cl.

Both the H and $\cdot\ddot{\text{Cl}}$: would each like to gain 1 electron to achieve a pseudo noble gas configuration. This results in hydrogen achieving the pseudo helium configuration and Cl achieving the pseudo argon configuration:

$$H : \ddot{\text{Cl}} :$$

11. **(A)** The hydronium ion concentration can be calculated from the ion – product constant for water, K_w,

$$K_w = [H_3O^+][OH^-] = 1 \times 10^{-14}$$

Due to the auto ionization of water both the OH^- and the H_3O^+ ions exist in acid or basic solutions. However the product of the OH^- ion concentration and the H_3O^+ ion concentration will always be equal to 1×10^{-14}, therefore substituting the OH^- concentration into the K_w expression we can calculate the H_3O^+ ion concentration.

$$K_w = [H_3O^+][OH^-] = 1 \times 10^{-14}$$

$$H_3O_+ = \frac{1 \times 10^{-14}}{1.4 \times 10^{-4}} = 7.2 \times 10^{-11}$$

12. **(A)** The pH of a solution is defined as $pH = -\log[H^+]$

Therefore
$$pH = -\log(1.2 \times 10^{-4})$$
$$= -\log 1.2 + \log 10^{-4}$$

The log of 1.2 is obtained either from a log table or from a calculator that has a log function key. The log of 10^{-4} is –4. Therefore:

$$pH = -(.079 - 4.00)$$
$$= -(-3.92)$$
$$= 3.92$$

13. **(D)** Since a K_i is given, the acid is a weak acid and reaches a state of equilibrium. In this case $HCN \leftrightarrow H^+ + CN^-$ and the expression for the equilibrium constant is

$$K_i = \frac{[H^+][CN^-]}{HCN} = 4 \times 10^{-10}$$

The initial amount of HCN present is .01 Molar; however the amount at equilibrium is .01 minus the amount that has ionized (.01 – x). For x amount that ionizes there will be x amount of H^+ and CN^- ions:

$$0.01 - x \qquad\qquad x \qquad\quad x$$
$$\text{HCN} \qquad \leftrightarrow \qquad \text{H}^+ \qquad \text{CN}^-$$

To solve for the H^+ concentration we substitute

$$\frac{(x)\ (x)}{0.01 - x} = 4 \times 10^{-10}$$

Since x is very small compared to the total amount of acid present we may neglect it in the denominator without introducing a measurable error, thus

$$\frac{x^2}{0.01} = 4 \times 10^{-10}$$

$$x^2 = 4 \times 10^{-12}$$

$$x = [\text{H}^+] = 2 \times 10^{-6}$$

14. **(D)** Since the velocity of light is expressed in meters per second and the wavelength is expressed in nm it is necessary to convert nm to meters before calculating the frequency form:

$$v = \frac{c}{\lambda}$$

Since $\dfrac{1\ \text{nm}}{600\ \text{nm}} = \dfrac{1 \times 10^{-9}\ \text{m}}{x\text{m}}$

Solving for x we find $\qquad x = 6.0 \times 10^{-7}\ \text{m}$

Substituting this wavelength we have

$$v = \frac{3.0 \times 10^8\ \text{m/s}}{6.0\ x\ 10^{-7}\ \text{m}}$$

$$v = .5 \times 10^{15}\ \text{s}^{-1}$$
$$\text{or}$$
$$5.0 \times 10^{14}\ \text{s}^{-1}$$

15. **(C)** The energy of electromagnetic radiation is equal to the frequency times Planck's constant

$$\begin{aligned}
E &= hv \\
E &= (6.63 \times 10^{-34}\ \text{j/s})\ (8.00 \times 10^{11}\ \text{1/s}) \\
&= 53.0 \times 10^{-23}\ \text{j} \\
&= 5.3 \times 10^{-22}\ \text{j}
\end{aligned}$$

16. **(C)**   The graph in question 16 is a representation of Charles' Law which states that at constant pressure the volume of a given quantity of a gas varies directly with temperature. $V \propto T$

17. **(B)**   The graph in 17 is a representation of Boyle's Law which states that at constant temperature the volume of a fixed quantity of a gas is inversely proportional to the pressure:

$$V \propto \frac{1}{p}$$

It can be seen from the graph that as the pressure increases, the volume decreases, as stated in Boyle's Law.

18. **(A)**   The molarity of a solution is defined as the number of moles of solute in a liter of solution

$$\text{Molarity} = \frac{\text{moles of solute}}{\text{liters of solution}}$$

To solve this problem we must first determine the number of moles of KCl in 32.0 g of KCl, which is:

$$\text{Moles} = \frac{\text{g of KCl}}{\text{MW of KCl}} = \frac{32.0 \text{ g}}{74.6 \text{ g/mole}} = .428 \text{ moles}$$

Substituting into this expression for molarity and expressing the volume in liters,

$$M = \frac{.428 \text{ moles}}{.425 \text{ liters}} = 1.0$$

19. **(E)**   The presence of a non-volatile solute such as $C_2H_6O_2$ will depress the freezing point of the solution according to Raoult's Law. The freezing point depression is given by the expression:

$$\Delta T = K_f \bullet m$$

Where K_f is the freezing point depression constant, ΔT is the change in the freezing point, and m is the molality of the solution, or

$$m = \frac{\text{moles of solute}}{\text{kg of solvent}}$$

and since the number of moles $= \dfrac{\text{g of solute}}{\text{MW of solute}}$

we now have $m = \dfrac{\dfrac{\text{g of solute}}{\text{MW of solute}}}{\text{kg of solvent}}$

Substituting this expression for molality in the first equation we have,

$$\Delta T = Kf \, \dfrac{\dfrac{\text{g of solute}}{\text{MW of solute}}}{\text{kg solvent}}$$

$$\Delta T = 1.86 \left(\dfrac{\dfrac{8.0}{62.0}}{.1} \right)$$

$$\Delta T = 2.4$$

Since the normal freezing point of water is 0.0 °C the freezing point of this solution will be 2.4 °C lower than pure H_2O or – 2.4 °C.

20. **(B)**   Ozone, O_3 and oxygen, O_2 are allotropes. Allotropes are two forms of the same element that differ in their bonding or molecular structure. In the ozone form of oxygen the structure is

Whereas in the diatomic form of oxygen the structure is $O = O$.

Other examples of allotropes are carbon in the graphite and diamond form, and sulfur in its S_2, S_6, and S_8 forms.

21. **(D)**   In a saturated solution of AgCl the following equilibrium is established

$$AgCl_{(solid)} \leftrightarrow Ag^+_{(aq)} + Cl^-_{(aq)}$$

and the expression for the K_{sp} is:

$$K_{sp} = [Ag^+] \, [Cl^-]$$

To calculate the K_{sp} it is necessary to know both the Ag^+ and Cl^- ion concentration. The Ag^+ concentration is given as 1.34×10^{-5} M. Since for every mole of AgCl that ionizes there will be 1 mole of both Ag^+ and

Cl⁻. The Ag^+ concentration is 1.34×10^{-5} M and the Cl⁻ will also be 1.34×10^{-5} M. Substituting the concentration of both Ag^+ and Cl⁻

$$K_{sp} = [1.34 \times 10^{-5}][1.34 \times 10^{-5}]$$
$$K_{sp} = 1.80 \times 10^{-10}$$

22. **(A)**   The freezing point depression or boiling point elevation of a solution depends on the number of particles present in the solution. A solution that contains a strong electrolyte such as the salts listed above will depress the freezing point according to the number of particles that are produced when the salt dissolves and ionizes completely. When Na_2SO_4 ionizes it forms 2 Na^+ and 1 SO_4^{2-} ions:

$$Na_2SO_4 \rightarrow 2\,Na^+ + 1\,SO_4^{2-}$$

So the effective molality of the solution will be three times the molality of the undissociated Na_2SO_4. The other salts will only produce an effective molality 2 times the undissociated form of the salt.

$$NaCl \rightarrow Na^+ + Cl^-$$

Therefore the freezing point depression would be the greatest for Na_2SO_4.

23. **(B)**   In molecular orbital diagrams all of the electrons contained in the molecule or ion are placed in the energy levels according to both the auf bau principle and Hund's rule. In the diagram above there are thirteen electrons. The number of electrons for the species listed as possible answers are:

Species	Number of electrons
NO	N = 7, O = 8 total = 15
CO^+	C = 6, O = 8 However since it is a +1 ion, the species contains 1 less electron than the neutral molecule or a total of $6 + 8 - 1 = 13$
NO^+	N = 7, O = 8 − 1 (since the species is a + 1 ion). $7 + 8 - 1 = 14$
CO	C = 6, O = 8 total = 14
F_2	each F has 9 for a total of 18

Since the molecular orbital diagram shows a total of 13 electrons, it represents the CO^+ species.

24. **(D)**   The specific heat of a substance is the amount of heat required to produce a change of 1 °C in 1 g of the substance. For aluminum it requires .89 joules to raise 1 g of Al 1 °C, therefore the heat required to raise 23.2 g from 30 °C to 80°C, or a change of 50°, will be equal to

q = mass × specific heat × temperature change

q = 23.2 g × .89 j / °C g × 50 °C

q = 1,032 joules

25. **(C)**   Group VII A elements assume the – 1 oxidation state in all their binary compounds with metals and with the ammonium ion, NH_4^+. However, Cl, Br, and I can exist in positive oxidation states of +1, +3, +5, and +7 in covalently bonded species that contain more electronegative elements. An example of such species are:

	Oxidation state of Chlorine
ClO^-	+1
ClO_2^-	+3
ClO_3^-	+5
ClO_4^-	+7

The compound $HClO_3$ is the only compound listed that contains chlorine in a positive oxidation state.

26. **(B)**   Compounds that contain oxygen in the minus 2 oxidation state are called oxides. Oxygen can also react with active metals to form peroxides which contain the O_2^{2-} ion, and the superoxides which contain the O_2^- ion. RbO_2 is the only superoxide listed. Rb only forms the Rb^+ ion; therefore the compound RbO_2 must contain the superoxide ion O_2^-.

27. **(B)**   When reactions are added together to get a total reaction, the equilibrium constants of the component reactions are multiplied together to get the equilibrium constant for the total reaction.

28. **(D)**   Graham's law of effusion states that the rates of effusion of gases are inversely proportional to the square roots of their molecular weights or densities.

$$\text{rate of effusion} \propto \frac{1}{\sqrt{MW}}$$

$$\text{rate of effusion} \times \sqrt{MW} = t_0 \text{ a constant}$$

Hence when 2 gases effuse from the same apparatus at the same conditions:

$$\frac{\text{rate}_A}{\text{rate}_B} = \frac{\sqrt{MW_B}}{\sqrt{MW_A}}$$

Substituting the molecular weight for N_2 and H_2:

$$\frac{\text{rate } H_2}{\text{rate } N_2} = \frac{\sqrt{28}}{\sqrt{2}} = \frac{5.29}{1.41} = 3.8$$

29. **(C)**   Normality is defined as the number of equivalent weights of solute per liter of solution.

$$N = \frac{\text{Number of equivalent weights}}{1}$$

To solve this problem we must first determine the number of equivalent weights there are in 23.2 g of H_2SO_4. For acids the equivalent weight is defined as the mass of the acid that will furnish 1 mole of hydrogen ions. Since 1 mole of H_2SO_4 (98.0 g) produces 2 moles of H^+ ions,

$$H_2SO_4 \rightarrow 2H^+ + SO_4^-$$

its equivalent weight is 1/2 the molecular weight or 49.0 g. The number of equivalent weights in 23.2 g of H_2SO_4 will be:

$$\text{The number of equivalent weights} = \frac{\text{g present}}{\text{equivalent weight of } H_2SO_4}$$

$$= \frac{23.2 \text{ g}}{49.0 \text{ g/eq wt}}$$

$$= .47$$

and the Normality is then calculated by

$$N = \frac{\text{Number of eq wt}}{\text{liter}}$$

$$N = \frac{.47 \text{ eq wt}}{.40 \text{ l}} = 1.2 \text{ N}$$

30. **(A)**   Charles' Law states that the volume is directly proportional to temperature at constant pressure. Therefore

$$\frac{V}{T} = k$$

in this problem

$$
\begin{aligned}
V_1 &= 200 \text{ mL} \\
T_1 &= 25\ ^\circ\text{C} + 273\ ^\circ\text{C} = 298\ ^\circ\text{K} \\
V_2 &= \text{unknown} \\
T_2 &= 40\ ^\circ\text{C} + 273\ ^\circ\text{C} = 313\ ^\circ\text{K}
\end{aligned}
$$

Thus

$$\frac{200 \text{ mL}}{298 \text{ K}} = \frac{V_2}{313 \text{ K}}$$

and $V_2 = \dfrac{200 \text{ mL} \times 313 \text{ K}}{298 \text{ K}} = 210 \text{ mL}$

Note: In all problems involving the gas laws the temperature <u>must</u> be expressed in degrees Kelvin (K).

31. **(A)**   The electron configuration of He is $1s^2$. In He_2^+ the only orbitals available for molecular orbital formation are the $1s$. The $1s$ from each He will interact to form a $1s$ bonding orbital and a $1s$ antibonding orbital.

He He_2^+ He

1s   σ antibonding

                               1s

                               σ bonding

Placing the 3 electrons in the He_2^+ ion in the molecular orbital diagram we have

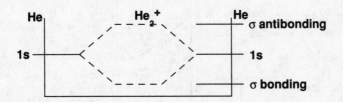

The bond order is then equal to

$$\text{Bond order} = \frac{\text{\# of e in bonding MO} - \text{\# or e in antibonding MO}}{2}$$

by substitution,

$$= \frac{2-1}{2} = 1/2$$

32. **(B)**   When MnO_4^- reacts with Fe^{2+} in acid solution, the following reaction occurs

$$MnO_4^- + Fe^{2+} + H^+ \rightarrow Fe^{3+} + Mn^{2+} + H_2O$$

The Mn in MnO_4^- which is in the +7 oxidation state, is reduced to Mn^{2+} which is almost colorless. The Fe^{2+} is oxidized by the MnO_4^- ion to Fe^{3+} and in turn the MnO_4^- is reduced to Mn^{2+}.

33. **(D)**   Electrons fill the energy levels according to the auf bau principle and Hund's rule. This means the electron will fill the lowest energy levels first and will tend to remain unpaired, unless there is an opportunity to achieve a 1/2 filled or completely filled d level by promotion of one s electron to the d level. The correct energy level diagram for the first transition series is

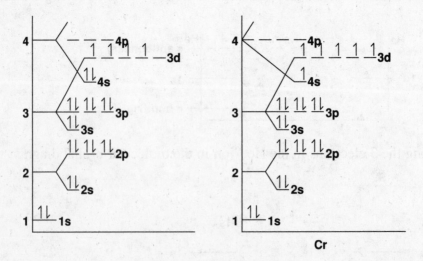

Cr

Since Cr has 24 electrons we would expect a configuration of $4s^2 3d^4$ as shown above; however in the case of Cr we could achieve a more stable 1/2 filled $3d$ level by promotion of one $4s$ electron to the $3d$ level. The more stable configuration of $4s^1 sd^5$ is achieved in this manner.

Note: Only 1 electron from an s level can be promoted to the d level to achieve the more stable 1/2 filled or completely filled d level.

34. **(A)** The generalized rate for this reaction can be expressed as

RATE = $k [A]^x [B]^y$

The values of x and y are determined from the experimental data. In experiment 1 and 2 the concentration of A is constant but the concentration of B has been doubled. The effect of doubling B increased the rate by a factor of 2. Also in experiment 1 and 3 a tripling of B triples the rate. Hence the concentration of B is to the first power and the exponent y must be equal to 1. In experiment 1 and 4 the concentration of B is constant but the concentration of A is doubled. We see that by doubling the concentration of A the rate increases by a factor of 4. Therefore the value of the exponent x must be to the second power, x = 2. The overall rate is then

RATE = $k [A]^2 [B]$

35. **(E)** The abnormally high boiling point of H_2O in comparison to H_2S, H_2Se and H_2Te is due to the ability of water to extensively hydrogen bond. Hydrogen bonding is and inter-molecular attraction that exists between water molecules. This attraction occurs when hydrogen is covalently bonded to a small electronegative atom such as oxygen. The result is that the hydrogen atom develops a partial positive charge $^+$ and the oxygen being highly electronegative develops a partial negative charge $^-$.

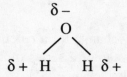

The water molecule will be attracted to other water molecules forming what is referred to as hydrogen bonds.

$$\delta- \qquad \delta+$$
$$O \qquad\quad H$$

$$\diagup \quad \diagdown \delta+ \qquad \diagdown \quad \delta-$$

$$\delta+ \ H \qquad H \ \delta+ \qquad O - H \ \delta+$$

$$\diagdown \qquad\qquad \diagup$$

$$O - H \ \delta+$$

$$\diagup$$

$$H$$

This dipole – dipole interaction is strong in water, and the molecules are highly attracted to one another. These forces are responsible for H_2O being a liquid at room temperature rather than a gas.

36. **(D)** $\Delta G°$ is the Gibb's free energy and may be calculated from the values of $\Delta H°$ (enthalpy) and $\Delta S°$ (entropy) by the relationship

$$\Delta G° = \Delta H° - T \ \Delta S°$$

The value of $\Delta G°$ will predict if the reaction is spontaneous, non-spontaneous or at equilibrium.

    IF $\Delta G°$ is positive the reaction is non-spontaneous

            $\Delta G° = 0$ system is at equilibrium

            $\Delta G°$ is negative the reaction is spontaneous

Since the values of $°G°$ for the reaction given is +174 kj the reaction will not proceed as written (non-spontaneous) but the reverse reaction,

$$2NO(g) \rightarrow N_2(g) + O_2(g)$$

$$\Delta G° = -174kj$$

could be spontaneous.

37. **(E)** According to Hess' Law the enthalpy change for a reaction is the same whether the reaction takes place in one step or a series of steps. We can utilize this law to determine the enthalpy change $\Delta H°$ for the reaction

$$C(\text{graphite}) + \frac{1}{2}O_2 \rightarrow CO(g)$$

first by reversing the reaction

$$CO_2(g) + \frac{1}{2}O_2 \rightarrow CO_2(g) \qquad \Delta H° = -284 \text{ kJ}$$

we have

$$CO_2(g) \rightarrow CO(g) + \frac{1}{2}O_2 \quad \Delta H° = +284 \text{ kj}$$

and adding it to the reaction

$$C(\text{graphite}) + \frac{1}{2}O_2(g) \rightarrow CO_2(g) \qquad \Delta H° = -394 \text{ kj}$$

$$\underline{CO_2(g) \rightarrow CO(g) + \frac{1}{2}O_2 \qquad\qquad\qquad \Delta H° = +284 \text{ kj}}$$

We get $C(\text{graphite}) + \frac{1}{2}O_2(g) \rightarrow CO(g) \qquad \Delta H° = -110 \text{ kj}$

Note: When reversing the reaction we must also change the sign of $\Delta H°$.

38. **(C)**   The Danish chemist J.N. Brønsted defined an acid as a species that can donate a hydrogen ion, and a base as a hydrogen ion acceptor. In the given reaction in the forward direction

$$HCN + H_2O \rightarrow H_3O^+ + CN^-$$

the HCN is donating a hydrogen ion to the water molecule. Hence the HCN is a Brønsted acid and the water is functioning as a Brønsted base. In the reverse reaction

$$H_3O^+ + CN^- \rightarrow HCN + H_2O$$

the hydronium ion, H_3O^+ is donating a hydrogen to the CN^- ion, hence it is functioning as a Brønsted acid and the CN^- ion is functioning as a Brønsted base.

39. **(B)**   The equation for the reaction is

$$Cu^{2+} + 2e^- \rightarrow Cu$$

From Faraday's Law it is known that 96,500 coulombs will reduce 1 equivalent weight of a substance at the cathode. Since

1 coulomb = 1 ampere × seconds,

the number of coulombs passing through the solution is calculated by converting 1 hour to seconds and multiplying by the number of amperes.

coulombs = 3.0 amp × 3600 sec

= 10,800 coulombs

In the reaction copper is undergoing a 2-electron reduction, so the equivalent weight of copper is:

$$eq \quad \text{wt of Cu} = \frac{MW}{\text{change in \# of } e^-}$$

$$= \frac{63.5}{2} = 31.8 \text{ g/eq wt}$$

Knowing 96,500 coulombs will deposit 1 eq wt. of copper or 31.8 g in this reduction we can calculate the weight of copper that results when 10,000 coulombs are passed through the solution:

$$\frac{96,500 \text{ coul}}{10,800} = \frac{31.8 \text{ g}}{xg}$$

$$x = 3.56$$

40. **(A)** For first order kinetics we can evaluate the rate constant from

$$T_{1/2} = \frac{.693}{k}$$

$$k = \frac{.693}{T_{1/2}} = \frac{.693}{3.64} = .190 \text{ day}^{-1}$$

The ratio of initial concentration of the Rn, A_o, to the concentration, A, after time T is given by

$$\log \frac{A_o}{A} = \frac{kT}{2.303}$$

Substituting the values of k and T

$$\log \frac{A_o}{A} = \frac{.190 \text{ days}^{-1} \ 18.2 \text{ days}}{2.303} = \frac{.345}{2.303}$$

$$\log \frac{A_o}{A} = 1.50$$

Taking the anti log of both sides

$$\frac{A_o}{A} = 31.7$$

and since the initial concentration, A_o was 2.0 µg we can calculate the final concentration:

$$A = \frac{A_o}{31.7} = \frac{2.0\ \mu g}{31.7} = .06\ \mu g$$

41. **(E)** In a saturated solution solid Ag_2CrO_4 is in equilibrium with its ions as shown by

$$Ag_2CrO_4 \leftrightarrow 2Ag^+ + CrO_4^{2-}$$

The CrO_4^{-2} concentration is given as 1.30×10^{-4}. To calculate the K_{sp} for Ag_2CrO_4 it is necessary to find the Ag^+ concentration. From the equation above it can be seen that in the dissolution of Ag_2CrO_4 will produce two moles of Ag^+ for each mole of CrO_4^{2-}. Hence if the CrO_4^{2-} ion concentration is 1.3×10^{-4}, the Ag^+ must be twice that amount or 2.60×10^{-4} M.

The expression for the K_{sp} of Ag_2CrO_4 is:

$$K_{sp} = [Ag^+]^2\ [CrO_4^{2-}]$$

Substituting the concentration of both Ag^+ and CrO_4^{2-}

$$
\begin{aligned}
K_{sp} &= [2.60 \times 10^{-4}]^2\ [1.3 \times 10^{-4}] \\
&= [6.76 \times 10^{-8}]\ [1.3 \times 10^{-4}] \\
&= 8.8 \times 10^{-12}
\end{aligned}
$$

42. **(C)** 1 mole of atoms contains Avogadro's number of particles, $6.02 \times 10^{23.}$ Since the atomic weight (the weight of one mole of hydrogen atoms) is 1.00 g, the weight of one atom of hydrogen can be calculated by:

$$\frac{1\ \text{atom of H}}{6.02 \times 10^{23}\ \text{atoms/mol}} = \frac{X\ g}{1.00\ \text{g/mol}}$$

Solving for X,

$$X = \frac{1\ \text{atom of H}}{6.02 \times 10^{23}\ \text{atoms/mol}}$$

$$X = 1.66 \times 10^{-24}\ g$$

43. **(E)** Atoms or molecules that contain one or more unpaired electrons are said to be paramagnetic. Paramagnetic material will be weakly attracted into a magnetic field. Atoms in which all the electrons are paired are referred to as diamagnetic and will be weakly repelled from a magnetic field.

To solve this problem it is necessary to examine the electron configuration of each species and determine if it contains unpaired electrons. The configurations are:

He	$1s^2$
Be	$1s^2\,2s^2$
Cl^-	$1s^2\,2s^2\,2p^6\,3s^2\,3p^6$
F^-	$1s^2\,2s^2\,2p^6$
Li	$1s^2\,2s^1$

From the above configurations it can be seen that only Li has an unpaired electron and is therefore paramagnetic.

The others all contain outer levels that are completely filled, and all electrons are therefore paired.

44. **(B)** The molarity, M, is defined as the number of moles of solute per liter of solution.

$$M = \frac{\text{moles}}{V_1}$$

Rearranging and solving for volume, we have

$$V = \frac{\text{moles}}{M}$$

Since the problem is asking for the number of grams it is necessary to substitute g/MW for the number of moles.

$$V = \frac{\dfrac{G}{MW}}{M} = \frac{\dfrac{2.3\text{ g}}{58.5\text{ g/mol}}}{1.3\text{ mol/L}}$$

$$V = 0.0302\text{ L or }30.2\text{ mL}$$

45. **(D)** According to Dalton's Law of partial pressures the total pressure is equal to the sum of the partial pressures …

$$P_T = P_a + P_b + P_c + \ldots$$

In this case there are two gases present in the container, the oxygen and the water vapor. Since the vapor pressure of water is 19 torr at 25 °C, the partial pressure of the water vapor is 19 torr and the total pressure in the container is 760 torr. From Dalton's Law we can calculate the pressure due to just the oxygen.

$$P_{total} = P_{O_2} + P_{H_2O\ vapor}$$
$$760\ torr = P_{O_2} + 19\ torr$$
$$P_{O_2} = 760\ torr - 19\ torr$$
$$= 741\ torr$$

46. **(C)**   Physical properties of solutions that only depend on the **number** of particles that are present, and not the **kind** of particles that are present are referred to as colligative properties.

It has been shown that a non-volatile solute in a solution will retard the rate of excape of solvent molecules in the solution. The total number of solvent molecules per unit area on the surface is reduced because of the presence of the solute. This results in a lowering of the vapor pressure of the solution. The lowering of the vapor pressure depresses the freezing point of the solution from that of only the pure solvent. The vapor pressure lowering is Raoult's Law, which states that the vapor pressure of a solvent in a solution decreases as the mole fraction of the solution decreases. The molecular weight of a solute does not effect the total number of particles in a solution. For example, 1 mole of NaCl and 1 mole of KCl will both produce the same number of particles when dissolved in a solvent, but NaCl and KCl have different molecular weights.

47. **(B)**   Buffer solutions contain conjugate acid – base pairs. They are usually prepared by mixing either a weak acid and a salt of the weak acid or a weak base and a salt of the weak base. In the answers given, only (B), .2M NaCl and .1M HCl, does not meet the requirement of a buffer. HCl is a strong acid. The others given are either a weak acid and a salt of the weak acid, or a weak base and a salt of the weak base.

48. **(A)**   Acetic acid ionizes,

$$HC_2H_3O_2 \leftrightarrow H^+ + C_2H_3O_2^-$$

and sodium acetate completely dissociates,

$$NaC_2H_3O_2 \rightarrow Na^+ + C_2H_3O_2^-$$

The solution is a buffer solution since it is composed of a weak acid and a salt of the weak acid. The hydrogen ion concentration of such a buffer can be calculated from the expression:

$$H^+ = \frac{[acid]}{[salt]} \times K_i$$

$$[H^+] = \frac{.05}{.1} \times 1.8 \times 10^{-5}$$

$$= .90 \times 10^{-5} \text{ or } 9.0 \times 10^{-6}$$

49. **(E)**   The mole fraction of a component in a solution is the number of moles of that component divided by the total number of moles,

$$X_{CH_3OH} = \frac{\text{moles of } CH_3OH}{\text{total number of moles present in solution}}$$

The number of moles of each component:

$$\text{moles } H_2O \; \frac{53.0}{18.0} = 2.90 \quad \text{moles } CH_3OH = \frac{20.3}{32.0} = .63$$

$$\text{moles } CH_3CH_2OH = \frac{15.0}{46.0} = .32$$

Therefore the mole fraction of CH_3OH is:

$$X_{CH_3OH} = \frac{.63}{2.90 + .63 + .32}$$

$$= \frac{.63}{3.85} = .16$$

50. **(B)**   The relationship between K_p and Gibb's free energy, $\Delta G°$, is given by the expression

$$\Delta G = -2.303 \; RT \log K_p$$

Where R is the ideal gas law constant, 8.314 expressed in joules/mole and T is the temperature expressed in degrees Kelvin.

$$\Delta G = -(2.303)(8.314)(298) \log 1 \times 10^{10}$$

$$\Delta G = -5706 \, [\log 1 + \log 10^{10}]$$

$$= -5706 \, [0 + 10]$$

$$= -57060 \text{ J} \sim 57.1 \text{ kJ}$$

51. **(B)** K_p is the notation for the equilibrium constant when the concentrations of both the reactants and products are expressed in terms of their partial pressures. The K_p is defined for this reaction as

$$K_p = \frac{P^2CO2}{PCO}$$

By convention concentrations and partial pressures for pure liquids and solids are omitted from the equilibrium constant expression. Therefore,

$$K_p = \frac{7.6^2}{3.2} = 18.1 \text{ atm}$$

52. **(B)**   The gaseous equilibrium constant is composed of only those compounds that are in the gas phase. For a process that only involves a single gas in the reaction—a phase change from liquid to gas, for example—the equilibrium expression consists only of the pressure of the gas at equilibrium, which is the definition of the equilibrium vapor pressure of the gas.

53. **(D)**   All of the hydrogen halides are colorless gases that dissolve in water to give acid solutions. HCl, HBr, and HI ionize extensively and are strong acids. However HF only ionizes slightly in water. In order for ionization to occur the hydrogen – halogen bond must be broken:

$HX \leftrightarrow H^+ + X^-$

The H – F bond is considerably stronger than either the bonds in H – Cl, H – Br or H – I, and ionization is more difficult. In addition, when HF ionizes,

$HF \leftrightarrow H^+ + F^-$

a second ionization reaction also takes place due to hydrogen bonding. This results in the formation of the hydrogen difluoride ion:

$F^- + HF \leftrightarrow HF_2^-$

This hydrogen bonding effectively ties up some of the HF molecules and inhibits their dissociation.

54. **(E)** $KClO_3$ readily decomposes to liberate O_2 by the reaction

$KClO_3 \xrightarrow{\Delta} KCl + O_2$

Before this problem can be solved, the equation must be balanced:

$$2KClO_3 \rightarrow 2KCl + 3O_2$$

Form the balanced equation it can be seen that for every 3 moles of oxygen that are produced, 2 moles of $KClO_3$ are required. It is necessary to determine the number of moles of O_2 in 3.20 g:

$$moles = \frac{3.20 \text{ g}}{32.0 \text{ g/mol}} = .10 \text{ mol}$$

If 2 moles of $KClO_3$ will produce 3 moles of oxygen, then the amount of $KClO_3$ required can be determined:

$$\frac{2KClO_3}{3O_2} = \frac{X \ KClO_3}{.10 \ O_2}$$

$$X = .07 \text{ mol of } KClO_3$$

55. **(B)**   Ionization energies, I, of an atom is the amount of energy required to remove an electron from the gaseous atom. Electrons that are loosely held by the nucleus will have low ionization energies, consequently the ionization energies decrease as the size of the atoms increase. The size of atoms decrease moving from right to left on the periodic chart due to the increase in the effective nuclear charge. In the series given, Ar would have the highest first ionization potential. It has the stable noble gas configuration and is the smallest element in the series.

56. **(C)**   At the point of neutralization the number of equivalent weights of the acid is exactly equal to the number of equivalent weights of the base present.

Since

$$Normality = \frac{\# \text{ of eq wt}}{V_L}$$

then, # of eq wt $= N \times V_L$

and at the neutralization point,

$$\# \text{ eq wt}_{Acid} = \# \text{ eq wt}_{Base}$$

Therefore,

$$V_B \times N_B \quad = V_A \times N_A$$

$$V_B = \frac{V_A \times N_A}{N_B} = \frac{50 \text{ mL} \times 2N}{0.5}$$

$$V_B = 20 \text{ mL}$$

57. **(B)**   The Ideal gas law equation, PV = nRT derived from kinetic and molecular theory neglects two important factors in regard to real gases. First it neglects the actual volume of gas molecules, and secondly, it does not take into account the intermolecular forces that real gases exhibit.

The factor *b* in the Van der Waal equation is a correction for the actual volume of the gas molecules and the factor *a* is a correction of the pressure due to the intermolecular attractions that occur in real gases.

58. **(B)**   To determine what is being oxidized and reduced the oxidation states of each species must be determined.

     Fe^{2+} is being oxidized to Fe^{3+}.

There is no change in either the oxygen or hydrogen, being –2 and +1 respectively on both sides of the equation.

Examining the nitrogen, we see it changes from +5 in NO_3^- to + 4 in NO_2.

Therefore the Fe^{2+} is being oxidized and nitrogen in NO_3^- is being reduced.

59. **(B)**   Thioacetamide CH_3CSNH_2 will hydrolize in aqueous solutions according to the following equation:

$$H_3CSNH_2 + H_2O \rightarrow CH_3COO^- + NH_4^+ + H_2S$$

to produce hydrogen sulfide, H_2S, which is used as a reagent to form characteristic metal sulfides that are used in identifying the metal ion listed.

60. **(B)**   The standard free energy for an electrochemical cell is related to the standard electrode potential E° by:

$$\Delta G° = -nFE°$$

–   where n is the number of electrons involved in the oxidation - reduction reaction.

–   E° is the standard electrode potential

–   F is Faraday's constant, 96.487 kJ/V

The value of $\Delta G°$ is then equal to

$$\Delta G° = -2 \times 96.487 \text{kJ/V} \times .28\text{V}$$
$$\Delta G° = -54 \text{ kJ}$$

61. **(D)** Salts of weak acids and strong bases will hydrolize to produce basic solutions whereas salts of weak bases and strong acids will hydrolize to form acid solutions. Both $CaCl_2$ and $NaCl$ are salts formed from the reaction of strong acids with strong bases and will not hydrolize, *i.e.*,

$$HCl + NaOH \rightarrow NaCl + H_2O$$

Sodium acetate CH_3COONa is a salt of a weak acid and a strong base:

$$CH_3COOH + NaOH \rightarrow CH_3COO^-Na^+ + H_2O$$

The acetate ion, CH_3COO^- will hydrolize;

$$CH_3COO^- + HOH \leftrightarrow CH_3COOH + OH^-$$

forming OH^- ions which are basic. The salt of a weak base and a strong acid, will hydrolize to form an acid solution. NH_4Cl is such a salt and the NH_4^+ ion will hydrolize:

$$NH_4^+ + HOH \qquad H_3O^+ + NH_3$$

forming the Hydronium ion resulting in an acid solution whose pH is below 7.

62. **(B)** In the net ionic equation only ions in solution that appear unchanged on both sides of the equation are omitted. If an ion changes in any way during the reaction it must be shown in the net ionic equation. In the reaction the chloride ions are not oxidized or reduced, and do not undergo any changes and are therefore omitted. On the other hand, the Fe in $FeCl_2$ is oxidized to Fe^{3+} in $FeCl_3$ and must be shown in the net ionic equation as Fe^{2+} going to Fe^{3+}. Also, the Mn in MnO_4^- changes from Mn^{7+} to Mn^{2+} and must also be shown in the net ionic equation. Since the reaction is taking place in aqueous acid solution, the H^+ ion in HCl is shown on the reactant side of the equation, and the water is shown on the product side. Both the reactants and products are soluble in water and they are written in their ionic form in the net ionic equation, *e.g.*, $KMnO_4$ is written as MnO_4^-. In view of these changes in oxidation states, the only correct net ionic equation is choice (B).

63. **(A)** The only commonality among the ions listed is they all contain 10 electrons and have the same election configuration

$1s^2 2s^2 2p^6$

Ions or atoms that have the same electron configurations are said to be iso-electronic.

64. **(B)** Valence Shell Electron Pair Repulsion (VSEPR) is a convenient method of predicting molecular geometries based on the fact that electron pairs, either bonded pairs or lone pairs tend to orient themselves as far from one another as possible to reduce electron pair - electron pair repulsion. Iodine has seven valence electrons and since the charge on the ion, ICl_4^- is negative, it is viewed as having eight electrons associated with it. Of the eight electrons, four are involved in bonding (four shared electron pairs) leaving four electrons or two pairs that are nonbonding):

total electron pairs = 2 (lone pairs) + 4 (bonding pairs) = 6

The possible structure for the arrangement of the six pairs of electrons (4 bonding pairs and 2 lone pairs) is then either (A) or (B).

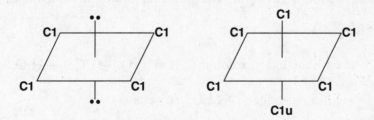

To chose the correct structure we evaluate the lone pair – lone pair interaction, and then the lone pair – bonding pair interaction.

Structure (A)   Structure (B)
0 LP – LP @ 90°   1 LP – LP @ 90°
8 LP – BP @ 90°   6 LP – BP @ 90°

Evaluating these interactions we see that structure (B) has a lone pair – lone pair interaction at 90°. This is a highly unfavorable situation and is not expected to occur. Hence structure (A) is favored. The atoms in ICl_4^- are all in a plane and the geometry of the molecule is best described as square planar.

Note: Although structure (B) has two less lone pairs – bonding pair interactions it is not sufficient to overcome the repulsion of the lone pair – lone pair interactions at 90°.

65. **(B)**   A polar covalent molecule must contain atoms of different electronegativities. Immediately it is recognized that H_2 and Cl_2 are not polar molecules. For a covalent bond to form, there must be a sharing of electron pairs. Both hydrogen and chlorine will form covalent bonds by the sharing of an electron pair.

H: C̈l:

In doing so, each element has achieved a stable inert gas configuration. Since chlorine is more electronegative than hydrogen it will develop a partial negative charge with respect to hydrogen. HCl is a polar covalent molecule.

$\delta +$ $\delta -$

H   Cl

Both NaCl and KCl are ionically bonded. The electropositive metal donates an electron to the non metal forming a M^+ ion and the non-metal X^- ion. This interaction between the two ions constitutes an ionic bond,

$K^+ Cl^-$ or $Na^+ Cl^-$

66. **(D)**   The combustion reaction is $C_2H_2 + \dfrac{3}{2} O_2 \rightarrow 2CO_2 + H_2O$

$\Delta G°_{reaction} = \Sigma \Delta G_{°f} (\text{products}) - \Sigma \Delta G°_f (\text{reactants})$

$\Delta G°_{reaction} = [(2 \times -394) + (-237)] - (209)$

$\Delta G°_{reaction} = -1234 \text{ kJ}$

67. **(C)**   Hydrides are compounds which contain hydrogen in the minus one oxidation state, H^-. They are formed when hydrogen reacts with group IA elements or the more active elements of Group IIA, Ca, Sr and Ba.

$2 \text{ Li} + H_2 \rightarrow 2 \text{ LiH}$

The other compounds listed all contain hydrogen in the plus one oxidation state and are not hydrides. In the case of LiH the hydrogen is in the minus one oxidation state since Li can only be in the plus one oxidation state. LiH is the only hydride of the possible choices, hence the correct answer is (C).

68. **(B)**   A catalyst increases the rate of a chemical reaction by lowering the activation energy. The activation energy of a reaction is the amount

of energy the molecules or atoms must have, so that when they collide the collision will result in product formation. A lower activation energy means there will be a greater number of molecules possessing sufficient kinetic energy to form products. This will result in a greater reaction rate.

69. **(B)** The first step in balancing this equation is to assign the oxidation numbers of each reactant and product:

$$\overset{+7}{MnO_4^-} + \overset{-1}{Cl^-}\ H^+ \rightarrow \overset{+2}{Mn} + \overset{0}{Cl_2} + H_2O$$

Therefore: $Mn^{7+} \rightarrow Mn^{2+}$ 5 electron change
  $2Cl^- \rightarrow Cl_2^{\,°}$ 2 electron change

To balance the number of electrons in the oxidation with the number in the reduction we multiply the manganese by 2 and the chloride by 5 and place these coefficients in the equation as shown below:

$$2MnO_4^- + 10Cl^- + ?H^+ \rightarrow 2Mn^{2+} + 5Cl_2 + ?H_2O$$

Next the charges on both sides of the equation are balanced by adding H+ ions to the left side. The charges are:

Left	Right
$(2x)\,(-1) + (10x)\,(-1)$	$(2x)\,(+2)$
or	
-12	$+4$

Therefore to balance the charges on each side we add 16 H^+ to the left.

$$2MnO_4^- + 10Cl^- + 16H^+ \rightarrow 2\ Mn^{2+} + 5Cl_2 + ?H_2O$$

Now 8 moles of H_2O must be added to the right side, to balance the hydrogens on the left side. The oxygens should now also be balanced and the correct balanced equation is then:

$$2MnO_4^- + 10Cl^- + 16H^+ \rightarrow 2\ Mn^{2+} + 5Cl_2 + 8H_2O$$

70. **(D)** Amphoteric compounds can function as either acids or bases. Hydroxides of Group I metals form solutions that are strongly basic when dissolved in water. Hydroxides of Group II metals although less soluble than Group I hydroxides also form basic solutions when dissolved in water. Hydroxides of metals that are of intermediate electronegativity and in relatively high oxidation states are usually amphoteric. $Al(OH)_3$ can function either as an acid or a base:

$$Al(OH)_3 + 3OH^- \rightarrow AlO_3^{3-} + 3 H_2O \qquad \text{(as an acid)}$$

$$\text{or}$$

$$Al(OH)_3 + 3H^+ \rightarrow Al^{3+} + 3H_2O \qquad \text{(as a base)}$$

The metal hydroxides that exhibit amphoteric behavior are generally found along the diagonal of the periodic table that separates the metals from the non-metals.

71. **(A)** The third law of thermodynamics states that the entropy of a perfect crystal at 0 K is zero. Entropy is the randomness or disorder in a system. The greater the disorder, the higher is its entropy. In the choices given, both H_2 and He are gases. The molecules are highly disordered and the entropy would be high. In liquid water, the entropy would be lower than the gases but the molecules are essentially random. In the solid, NaCl, the molecules are held rigid in the crystal structure. Therefore it would be a more structured environment or less random, hence the entropy is low.

72. **(A)** The standard heat of reaction, $\Delta H°$ is equal to the sum of the heats of the products minus the sum of the heats of the reactants:

$$\Delta H° = \Sigma \Delta H \text{ products } - \Sigma \Delta H \text{ reactants}$$

$$\Delta H° = \left(2 (\Delta H° \text{ NaOH}) + (\Delta H°H_2)\right) - \left(2 (\Delta H° \text{ H}_2O) + 2(\Delta H° \text{ Na})\right)$$

By convention the standard heats of formation of an element in its most stable form is zero. Thus both $H_2(g)$ and $Na(s)$ equal zero, then:

$$\begin{aligned}\Delta H° &= 2 (-426.7) - 2 (-285.8) \text{ *}\\ &= -853.4 - (-571.6)\\ &= -853.4 + 571.6\\ &= -281.8 \text{ kJ}\end{aligned}$$

*Note: the enthalpies given in the table above are in units of kJ/mol, therefore it is necessary to multiply by the number of moles of each substance as represented in the balanced equation to calculate the $\Delta H°$ for the overall reaction.

73. **(C)** K_c is the equilibrium constant when the concentrations are expressed in moles per liter. Kp is the equilibrium constant where the partial pressures of the gases is used in place of the molar concentrations. The relationship between K_p and K_c is:

$$K_p = K_c(RT)^{\Delta n}$$

where Δn is the change in the number of moles of the gas upon going from reactants to products. The correct answer is (C), since there is no change in the number of moles in going from reactants to products. Thus $\Delta n = 0$ and K_p will then be equal to K_c.

74. **(E)**   A weak electrolyte is one that when dissolved in water produces a low percentage of ions. Most of the material will remain in its undissociated form. NaCl, HCl, KI, and HNO_3 all dissociate completely when dissolved in water and are strong electrolytes. NH_4OH on the other hand only ionizes to a very small extent according to the equation:

$$NH_4OH \leftrightarrow NH_4^+ + OH^-$$

where most of the NH_4OH will remain in the undissociated form.

75. **(B)**   A phase diagram relates the pressure and the temperatures at which the gaseous, liquid and solid states of a material can exist. In this question, we are interested in the relationship between the temperature at which the material changes from a solid to a liquid, which is the melting point, and the pressure. This corresponds to the line indicated by b – c. It is apparent that this line slants to the right which shows that an increase in the pressure will cause an increase in the temperature at which this material melts.

Section II

1. (a)

$$HCN \ (aq) \leftrightarrow H^+ \ (aq) + CN^- \ (aq)$$

Before equilibrium: 0.040 M   0   0

After equilibrium: 0.040 – x   x   x

$$K_a = \frac{(x^2)}{(0.040 - x)} = 6.2 \times 10^{-10}$$

$x^2 = 6.2 \times 10^{-10} \times 0.040$

$x = [H^+] = 5.0 \times 10^{-6}$; pH = –log $[H^+]$

pH =   5.30

(b)   Percent dissociation = 5.0×10^{-6} / $0.040 \times 100\%$ = .013% dissociated

(c) $HCN + OH^- \leftrightarrow H_2O + CN^-$

(d)

$$K = \frac{1}{K_b} = \frac{K_a}{K_w} = \frac{[CN^-]}{[OH^-][HCN]} =$$

$6.2 \times 10^{-10} / 10^{-14} = 6.2 \times 10^4$

(e)

$$[H^+] = \frac{K_a \, [HCN]}{[CN^-]} = \frac{(6.2 \times 10^{-10})(.05 \text{ M})}{(.03 \text{ M})} = 1.0 \times 10^{-9} \text{ M}$$

(f)

$[H^+] = 1.0 \times 10^{-9} M$

$[OH^-] = 1.0 \times 10^{-5} M$

molar solubility = $x = K_{sp}$ / $[OH^-]^2 = 1.5 \times 10^{-11} / (2.0 \times 10^{-9})^2 = 3.8 \times 10^6$

2. (a)

Oxidation: $5[Fe^{+2} \rightarrow Fe^{+3} + 1e^-]$
                    $_{+2}$ $_{+3}$

Reduction: $5e^- + Mn^{7+} \rightarrow Mn^{2+}$
                          $_{+7}$ $_{+2}$

$5Fe^{2+} + 8H+ + MnO_4^- \rightarrow 5Fe^{3+} + Mn^{2+} + 4H_2O$

(b)

$$10.00 \text{ g Fe(NO}_3)_2 \times \frac{1 \text{ mol Fe(NO}_3)_2}{179.85 \text{ g Fe(NO}_3)_2} \times$$

$$\frac{1}{.8 \text{ L solution}} = 0.07 \text{ M Fe(NO}_3)_2$$

$$10.00 \text{ g KMnO}_4 \times \frac{1 \text{ mol KMnO}_4}{157.9 \text{ g KMnO}_4} \times$$

$$\frac{1}{.8 \text{ L solution}} = 0.08 \text{ M KMnO}_4$$

(c)   (d)

From the prior calculations, we know the following are present:

$$0.0556 \text{ mol Fe} \times \frac{55.85 \text{ g Fe}}{1 \text{ mol Fe}} = 3.10 \text{ g Fe}$$

$$0.0633 \text{ mol KMnO}_4 \times \frac{5 \text{ mol Fe}}{1 \text{ mol KMnO}_4} \times$$

$$\frac{55.85 \text{ g Fe}}{1 \text{ mol Fe}} = 17.7 \text{ g Fe}$$

Therefore, iron nitrate is the limiting reactant, and 3.10 of Fe is formed.

(e)   To find the pH, consider how many moles per liter of protons you started with, subtract those used during the reaction, then find the protons that exist in the solution once the reaction is complete.

Initial moles H^+: 0.8 L solution $\times \dfrac{2.0 \text{ mol } H^+}{\text{L solution}}$

$= 1.6 \text{ mol } H^+$

Moles H^+ used: 0.0556 mol Fe $\times \dfrac{8 \text{ mol } H^+}{5 \text{ mol Fe}}$

$= 0.089 \text{ mol } H^+$ used

moles H^+ remaining: 1.6 mol $- 0.089$ mol $= 1.511$ mol H^+

$[H^+] = 1.511$ mol$/0.8$ L $= 1.89$ M; pH $= -\log [H^+]$

pH $= -0.28$

3. (a) By inspection, the order of the reaction is second order with respect to A and zero order with respect to B. The overall rate equation is: rate $= k[A]^2$.

(b) rate $= k[A]^2$ gives the relationship used to find the value and units of the specific rate constant; solve for the constant using the values from any one of the experiments.

$k = $ rate$/[A]^2 = 0.02$ M/sec $/ (0.1$ M$)^2 = 2.0$ L/mol sec

(c) We would anticipate that the initial rate of formation would approximately double for every increase in 10 K. The increased heat increases both the frequency of collisions, and increases the proportion of those collisions that effectively lead to a reaction (overcome the activation energy).

(d) The suggested mechanism would imply kinetics that are first order with respect to A, which does not fit the experimental data. Students will have to be creative on suggesting mechanisms, one possible mechanism that is second order with respect to A during the slow step might be the following.

2 A	$\rightarrow$	I	slow step
I + B	$\rightarrow$	J	fast equilibrium
I + B	$\rightarrow$	J	fast equilibrium
2 J	$\rightarrow$	A + C	

| A + 2B | $\rightarrow$ | C | |

4.   (a) $Mg(s) + H_2SO_4(aq) \rightarrow MgSO_4(aq) + H_2(g)$

            $Mg^0 + H^+(aq) \rightarrow Mg^{+2}(aq) + H_2{}^0(g)$

   (b) $2NO(g) + 2H_2(g) \rightarrow N_2(g) + 2H_2O(g)$

            $N^{+2} + H^0 \rightarrow N^0 + H^{+1}$

   (c) $I_2(s) + H_2S(aq) \rightarrow S(s) + 2HI(aq)$

            $I^0 + S^{-2} \rightarrow S^0 + I^{-1}$

   (d) $4NH_3(g) + 5O_2 \rightarrow 4NO(g) + 6H_2O(l)$

            $N^{-3} + O^0 \rightarrow N^{+2} + O^{-2}$

   (e) $ZnCl_2 + Mg \rightarrow MgCl_2 + Zn$

            $Zn^{+2} + Mg^0 \rightarrow Mg^{+2} + Zn^0$

   (f) $HgO(s) + H_2O_2(aq) \rightarrow Hg + H_2O + O_2$

            $Hg^{+2} + O^{-1} \rightarrow Hg^0 + O^{-2}$

   (g) $H_2O(g) + C(s) \rightarrow CO(g) + H_2(g)$

            $H^{+1} + C^0 \rightarrow C^{+2} + H^0$

   (h) $Cu(s) + F_2(g) \rightarrow CuF_2(s)$

            $Cu^0 + F^0 \rightarrow Cu^{+2} + F^{-1}$

5.   (a)   Metals tend to become +2 ions, and certainly positive ions. They have luster, are malleable, and ductile. Metals easily conduct heat and electricity. Their oxides tend to be basic, but transition metals create an acid solution when put into water.

      (b)   Most metals have two electrons in an outer *s*-orbital, so tend to loose those two electrons to become +2 ions when combined with other elements (although many metals are able to achieve other oxidation states). Luster, malleability, and ductility are all a result of the "electron sea" bonding that hold metals together. The electrons are more mobile and allow the movement of one nucleus relative to another in a way that is not possible with covalent and ionic bonds. The mobility of the electrons also explains the thermal and electrical conductivity.

(c)   The "electron sea" aspect of metallic bonding was described in the prior question. Added to that, the shared electrons of covalent bonding in non-metals is consistent with their higher electronegativity.

(d)   Different groups of metals have unique characteristics. For example, IA metals all tend to become +1 ions because they only have one electron in their outer s-orbital. Also, copper, silver, and mercury are able to easily become +1 ions because the promotion of one s-orbital electron to fill the d-orbitals leaves only one s-orbital electron, which is easily pulled away. Likewise, those metals under iron (Ru, Os) easily take the +3 oxidation state because they have 6 electrons in their d-orbitals, and easily loose one of the d-orbital electrons (along with the s-orbital electrons) to achieve a set of half-filled d-orbitals.

6.   In order to construct a flow chart detailing the separations of Hg^{+2}_2, Ag^+, and Pb^{+2}, it must be realized that each of these metal ions form insoluble chloride salts.

$$Ag^+ + Cl^- \rightarrow AgCl(s)$$

$$Pb^{+2} + 2Cl^- \rightarrow PbCl_2(s)$$

$$Hg^{2+}_2 + 2Cl^- \rightarrow Hg_2Cl_2(s)$$

This is the basis of the separation of these Group I metals from other metal ions that might be in solution. When the unknown solution is treated with 3M HCl, the precipitate that forms will be be a mixture of Hg_2Cl_2, AgCl, and $PbCl_2$.

In order to separate and identify these metal chlorides, we must take advantage of the different chemical and physical properties of these precipitated metal chlorides.

Of the three metal chlorides, lead chloride is particularly soluble in boiling water. The $PbCl_2$ may then be separated by treating the precipitate with boiling water, and decanting off the water from the remaining solid. The decanted solution will contain only the Pb^{+2} ions. The Pb^{+2} ion can be confirmed by the presence of a yellow precipitate upon treatment with CrO_4^{-2}.

$$Pb^{+2} + CrO_4^{-2} \rightarrow PbCrO_4$$

yellow precipitate

Next, the solid precipitate left behind after the treatment with boiling water will contain both the AgCl and Hg_2Cl_2, which must now be separated and identified. The separation is achieved by adding concentrated ammonium hydroxide, NH_4OH, to the precipitate containing both the AgCl(s) and the $Hg_2Cl_2(s)$. If Hg_2^{2+} ion is present, a black precipitate, containing Hg + $HgNH_2Cl$, will result. The AgCl(s) will form the soluble salt $Ag(NH_3)_2^+$ Cl^- and will go back into solution. The filtrate is then separated from the Hg^-HgNH_2Cl precipitate. This soluble silver salt can then be reprecipitated from the filtrate with concentrated nitric acid, HNO_3, and a white precipitate of AgCl(s) will result, confirming the presence of the Ag+ ion.

The following flow chart summarized the procedure for the separation and identification of the group I metals:

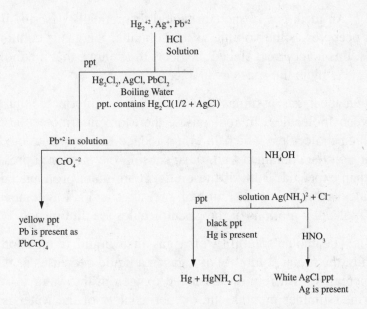

7.   (a)   It takes four half-lives to get from 80 grams of the isotope to 5 grams. $4 \times 8.1 = 32.4$ days.

(b)   The difference in mass described in this question is called the mass defect, and represents an amount of energy (through $E = mc^2$) called the binding energy of the atom.

(c)   Alpha decay releases an alpha particle from an unstable nucleus. An alpha particle is composed of two neutrons and two protons; losing it decreases the atom's mass number by four and atomic number by two. Beta decay involves the loss of a neutrino from the nucleus (AP students don't have to know that) which further decomposes into an electron as it leaves the atom, carrying with it a -1 nuclear charge and converting a neutron into a proton. As a result, beta decay does not change the mass number, but it increases the atomic number by one. Gamma particles are just high energy photons that carry energy, and often accompany both alpha and beta decay.

(d)   Since Iodine-131 is a relatively light element (compared to the heavy unstable elements on the periodic table) and the mass number is higher than the mass number of the stable isotope, it is most likely undergoing beta decay.

(e)   All radioactive decay is directly proportional to the amount of material that remains, and is therefore always demonstrates first order kinetics. Therefore, the rate constant for radioactive decay is a first order constant (see the Kinetics chapter), so its units are 1/sec.

8.   (a)   An ideal gas is one that would theoretically describe the volume a gas occupies as the volume of the container the gas is contained in. In actuality, this is incorrect since it neglects the volume that the molecules themselves occupy in the space available.

Secondly, an ideal gas assumes that there are no intermolecular attractions between molecules. In real gases, there are intermolecular attractions between molecules, which in effect reduce the frequency and force of collisions on the container wall, thus, causing the measured pressure to be lower than expected. Both of these effects are more pronounced when the molecules are close together, at high pressures and at low temperatures where the molecular motions of the gas molecules are diminished.

(b)   The molar solubility of a gas in a liquid is an exothermic process, thus, the molar solubility of a gas in a liquid decreases as the temperature increases. Fish rely on dissolved oxygen in the water to survive. In the warmer summer months, the oxygen content of the water is lower than in the colder months. When the oxygen level is reduced significantly, massive fish kills occur.

(c)   The addition of a non-volatile solute (ethylene glycol) to a solvent will reduce the vapor pressure above the solution, since the solute molecules will retard the rate of escape of the solvent molecules. The net effect is that the boiling point of the solution will be higher than that of the pure solvent. This will also cause a depression in freezing point. The freezing point depression or boiling point elevation is dependent on the concentration of the solute in the solution and can be expressed by the equations

$$\Delta T_{f.p.} = K_f m$$
$$\Delta T_{B.p.} = K_B m$$

where ΔT is the change in the boiling point from that of the pure solvent to that of the solution, K_f and K_B are the freezing point depression or boiling point elevation constants for the specific solvent, and m is the molality of the solution. For example, the K_f for water is 1.86 °C/m, and the boiling point elevation constant for water is

K_b = .512 °C/m.

For a 1.0 molal solution of ethylene glycol, the freezing point depression and the boiling point elevation will be respectively:

$$\Delta T_{f.p.} = 1.86 \text{ °C/m} \times 1.0m$$

$$\Delta T_{f.p.} = 1.86 \text{ °C}$$

$$\Delta T_{B.P.} = .512 \text{ °C/m} \times 1.0m$$

$$\Delta T_{B.P.} = .512 \text{ °C}$$

Thus, the 1 molal solution will boil at 100.000 °C + .512 = 100.512 °C and freeze at 0.00 °C + –1.86 °C = –1.86 °C.

(d)   The choice of indicators is important when attempting to determine the equivalence point in an acid base titration. For example, when a 1 molar HCl solution is titrated with a 1 molar NaOH solution the pH at the equivalence point will be 7.0

$$HCl + NaOH \rightarrow NaCl + H_2O$$

since the salt NaCl does not hydrolyze.

In selecting an indicator for this titration, it is necessary to choose one that has a color change as close to 7.0 as possible, which corresponds to the pH at the equivalence point. Examine the table below:

indicator	color in acid range	color in base range	pH range
thymol blue	pink	yellow	1.2 – 2.8
phenolphthalein	colorless	red	8.3 – 10.0
alizarian yellow	colorless	yellow	10.2 – 12.1

It is obvious that the best choice for the titration described above would be phenolphthalein, since a pronounced color change would occur at a pH of 8.3, which is close to the equivalence point of the titration. If either of the other two indicators listed were used, the equivalence point would not correspond to the color change range of the indicators.

In summary, it is always necessary to choose an indicator that has a color change as close to the pH at the equivalence point as possible.

Advanced Placement Examination in
CHEMISTRY
Exam 1

1. Ⓐ Ⓑ Ⓒ Ⓓ Ⓔ   26. Ⓐ Ⓑ Ⓒ Ⓓ Ⓔ   51. Ⓐ Ⓑ Ⓒ Ⓓ Ⓔ
2. Ⓐ Ⓑ Ⓒ Ⓓ Ⓔ   27. Ⓐ Ⓑ Ⓒ Ⓓ Ⓔ   52. Ⓐ Ⓑ Ⓒ Ⓓ Ⓔ
3. Ⓐ Ⓑ Ⓒ Ⓓ Ⓔ   28. Ⓐ Ⓑ Ⓒ Ⓓ Ⓔ   53. Ⓐ Ⓑ Ⓒ Ⓓ Ⓔ
4. Ⓐ Ⓑ Ⓒ Ⓓ Ⓔ   29. Ⓐ Ⓑ Ⓒ Ⓓ Ⓔ   54. Ⓐ Ⓑ Ⓒ Ⓓ Ⓔ
5. Ⓐ Ⓑ Ⓒ Ⓓ Ⓔ   30. Ⓐ Ⓑ Ⓒ Ⓓ Ⓔ   55. Ⓐ Ⓑ Ⓒ Ⓓ Ⓔ
6. Ⓐ Ⓑ Ⓒ Ⓓ Ⓔ   31. Ⓐ Ⓑ Ⓒ Ⓓ Ⓔ   56. Ⓐ Ⓑ Ⓒ Ⓓ Ⓔ
7. Ⓐ Ⓑ Ⓒ Ⓓ Ⓔ   32. Ⓐ Ⓑ Ⓒ Ⓓ Ⓔ   57. Ⓐ Ⓑ Ⓒ Ⓓ Ⓔ
8. Ⓐ Ⓑ Ⓒ Ⓓ Ⓔ   33. Ⓐ Ⓑ Ⓒ Ⓓ Ⓔ   58. Ⓐ Ⓑ Ⓒ Ⓓ Ⓔ
9. Ⓐ Ⓑ Ⓒ Ⓓ Ⓔ   34. Ⓐ Ⓑ Ⓒ Ⓓ Ⓔ   59. Ⓐ Ⓑ Ⓒ Ⓓ Ⓔ
10. Ⓐ Ⓑ Ⓒ Ⓓ Ⓔ   35. Ⓐ Ⓑ Ⓒ Ⓓ Ⓔ   60. Ⓐ Ⓑ Ⓒ Ⓓ Ⓔ
11. Ⓐ Ⓑ Ⓒ Ⓓ Ⓔ   36. Ⓐ Ⓑ Ⓒ Ⓓ Ⓔ   61. Ⓐ Ⓑ Ⓒ Ⓓ Ⓔ
12. Ⓐ Ⓑ Ⓒ Ⓓ Ⓔ   37. Ⓐ Ⓑ Ⓒ Ⓓ Ⓔ   62. Ⓐ Ⓑ Ⓒ Ⓓ Ⓔ
13. Ⓐ Ⓑ Ⓒ Ⓓ Ⓔ   38. Ⓐ Ⓑ Ⓒ Ⓓ Ⓔ   63. Ⓐ Ⓑ Ⓒ Ⓓ Ⓔ
14. Ⓐ Ⓑ Ⓒ Ⓓ Ⓔ   39. Ⓐ Ⓑ Ⓒ Ⓓ Ⓔ   64. Ⓐ Ⓑ Ⓒ Ⓓ Ⓔ
15. Ⓐ Ⓑ Ⓒ Ⓓ Ⓔ   40. Ⓐ Ⓑ Ⓒ Ⓓ Ⓔ   65. Ⓐ Ⓑ Ⓒ Ⓓ Ⓔ
16. Ⓐ Ⓑ Ⓒ Ⓓ Ⓔ   41. Ⓐ Ⓑ Ⓒ Ⓓ Ⓔ   66. Ⓐ Ⓑ Ⓒ Ⓓ Ⓔ
17. Ⓐ Ⓑ Ⓒ Ⓓ Ⓔ   42. Ⓐ Ⓑ Ⓒ Ⓓ Ⓔ   67. Ⓐ Ⓑ Ⓒ Ⓓ Ⓔ
18. Ⓐ Ⓑ Ⓒ Ⓓ Ⓔ   43. Ⓐ Ⓑ Ⓒ Ⓓ Ⓔ   68. Ⓐ Ⓑ Ⓒ Ⓓ Ⓔ
19. Ⓐ Ⓑ Ⓒ Ⓓ Ⓔ   44. Ⓐ Ⓑ Ⓒ Ⓓ Ⓔ   69. Ⓐ Ⓑ Ⓒ Ⓓ Ⓔ
20. Ⓐ Ⓑ Ⓒ Ⓓ Ⓔ   45. Ⓐ Ⓑ Ⓒ Ⓓ Ⓔ   70. Ⓐ Ⓑ Ⓒ Ⓓ Ⓔ
21. Ⓐ Ⓑ Ⓒ Ⓓ Ⓔ   46. Ⓐ Ⓑ Ⓒ Ⓓ Ⓔ   71. Ⓐ Ⓑ Ⓒ Ⓓ Ⓔ
22. Ⓐ Ⓑ Ⓒ Ⓓ Ⓔ   47. Ⓐ Ⓑ Ⓒ Ⓓ Ⓔ   72. Ⓐ Ⓑ Ⓒ Ⓓ Ⓔ
23. Ⓐ Ⓑ Ⓒ Ⓓ Ⓔ   48. Ⓐ Ⓑ Ⓒ Ⓓ Ⓔ   73. Ⓐ Ⓑ Ⓒ Ⓓ Ⓔ
24. Ⓐ Ⓑ Ⓒ Ⓓ Ⓔ   49. Ⓐ Ⓑ Ⓒ Ⓓ Ⓔ   74. Ⓐ Ⓑ Ⓒ Ⓓ Ⓔ
25. Ⓐ Ⓑ Ⓒ Ⓓ Ⓔ   50. Ⓐ Ⓑ Ⓒ Ⓓ Ⓔ   75. Ⓐ Ⓑ Ⓒ Ⓓ Ⓔ

AP CHEMISTRY
EXAM 1 – PART II

AP CHEMISTRY
EXAM 1 – PART II

Advanced Placement Examination in
CHEMISTRY
Exam 2

1. Ⓐ Ⓑ Ⓒ Ⓓ Ⓔ
2. Ⓐ Ⓑ Ⓒ Ⓓ Ⓔ
3. Ⓐ Ⓑ Ⓒ Ⓓ Ⓔ
4. Ⓐ Ⓑ Ⓒ Ⓓ Ⓔ
5. Ⓐ Ⓑ Ⓒ Ⓓ Ⓔ
6. Ⓐ Ⓑ Ⓒ Ⓓ Ⓔ
7. Ⓐ Ⓑ Ⓒ Ⓓ Ⓔ
8. Ⓐ Ⓑ Ⓒ Ⓓ Ⓔ
9. Ⓐ Ⓑ Ⓒ Ⓓ Ⓔ
10. Ⓐ Ⓑ Ⓒ Ⓓ Ⓔ
11. Ⓐ Ⓑ Ⓒ Ⓓ Ⓔ
12. Ⓐ Ⓑ Ⓒ Ⓓ Ⓔ
13. Ⓐ Ⓑ Ⓒ Ⓓ Ⓔ
14. Ⓐ Ⓑ Ⓒ Ⓓ Ⓔ
15. Ⓐ Ⓑ Ⓒ Ⓓ Ⓔ
16. Ⓐ Ⓑ Ⓒ Ⓓ Ⓔ
17. Ⓐ Ⓑ Ⓒ Ⓓ Ⓔ
18. Ⓐ Ⓑ Ⓒ Ⓓ Ⓔ
19. Ⓐ Ⓑ Ⓒ Ⓓ Ⓔ
20. Ⓐ Ⓑ Ⓒ Ⓓ Ⓔ
21. Ⓐ Ⓑ Ⓒ Ⓓ Ⓔ
22. Ⓐ Ⓑ Ⓒ Ⓓ Ⓔ
23. Ⓐ Ⓑ Ⓒ Ⓓ Ⓔ
24. Ⓐ Ⓑ Ⓒ Ⓓ Ⓔ
25. Ⓐ Ⓑ Ⓒ Ⓓ Ⓔ

26. Ⓐ Ⓑ Ⓒ Ⓓ Ⓔ
27. Ⓐ Ⓑ Ⓒ Ⓓ Ⓔ
28. Ⓐ Ⓑ Ⓒ Ⓓ Ⓔ
29. Ⓐ Ⓑ Ⓒ Ⓓ Ⓔ
30. Ⓐ Ⓑ Ⓒ Ⓓ Ⓔ
31. Ⓐ Ⓑ Ⓒ Ⓓ Ⓔ
32. Ⓐ Ⓑ Ⓒ Ⓓ Ⓔ
33. Ⓐ Ⓑ Ⓒ Ⓓ Ⓔ
34. Ⓐ Ⓑ Ⓒ Ⓓ Ⓔ
35. Ⓐ Ⓑ Ⓒ Ⓓ Ⓔ
36. Ⓐ Ⓑ Ⓒ Ⓓ Ⓔ
37. Ⓐ Ⓑ Ⓒ Ⓓ Ⓔ
38. Ⓐ Ⓑ Ⓒ Ⓓ Ⓔ
39. Ⓐ Ⓑ Ⓒ Ⓓ Ⓔ
40. Ⓐ Ⓑ Ⓒ Ⓓ Ⓔ
41. Ⓐ Ⓑ Ⓒ Ⓓ Ⓔ
42. Ⓐ Ⓑ Ⓒ Ⓓ Ⓔ
43. Ⓐ Ⓑ Ⓒ Ⓓ Ⓔ
44. Ⓐ Ⓑ Ⓒ Ⓓ Ⓔ
45. Ⓐ Ⓑ Ⓒ Ⓓ Ⓔ
46. Ⓐ Ⓑ Ⓒ Ⓓ Ⓔ
47. Ⓐ Ⓑ Ⓒ Ⓓ Ⓔ
48. Ⓐ Ⓑ Ⓒ Ⓓ Ⓔ
49. Ⓐ Ⓑ Ⓒ Ⓓ Ⓔ
50. Ⓐ Ⓑ Ⓒ Ⓓ Ⓔ

51. Ⓐ Ⓑ Ⓒ Ⓓ Ⓔ
52. Ⓐ Ⓑ Ⓒ Ⓓ Ⓔ
53. Ⓐ Ⓑ Ⓒ Ⓓ Ⓔ
54. Ⓐ Ⓑ Ⓒ Ⓓ Ⓔ
55. Ⓐ Ⓑ Ⓒ Ⓓ Ⓔ
56. Ⓐ Ⓑ Ⓒ Ⓓ Ⓔ
57. Ⓐ Ⓑ Ⓒ Ⓓ Ⓔ
58. Ⓐ Ⓑ Ⓒ Ⓓ Ⓔ
59. Ⓐ Ⓑ Ⓒ Ⓓ Ⓔ
60. Ⓐ Ⓑ Ⓒ Ⓓ Ⓔ
61. Ⓐ Ⓑ Ⓒ Ⓓ Ⓔ
62. Ⓐ Ⓑ Ⓒ Ⓓ Ⓔ
63. Ⓐ Ⓑ Ⓒ Ⓓ Ⓔ
64. Ⓐ Ⓑ Ⓒ Ⓓ Ⓔ
65. Ⓐ Ⓑ Ⓒ Ⓓ Ⓔ
66. Ⓐ Ⓑ Ⓒ Ⓓ Ⓔ
67. Ⓐ Ⓑ Ⓒ Ⓓ Ⓔ
68. Ⓐ Ⓑ Ⓒ Ⓓ Ⓔ
69. Ⓐ Ⓑ Ⓒ Ⓓ Ⓔ
70. Ⓐ Ⓑ Ⓒ Ⓓ Ⓔ
71. Ⓐ Ⓑ Ⓒ Ⓓ Ⓔ
72. Ⓐ Ⓑ Ⓒ Ⓓ Ⓔ
73. Ⓐ Ⓑ Ⓒ Ⓓ Ⓔ
74. Ⓐ Ⓑ Ⓒ Ⓓ Ⓔ
75. Ⓐ Ⓑ Ⓒ Ⓓ Ⓔ

AP CHEMISTRY
EXAM 2 – PART II

AP CHEMISTRY
EXAM 2 – PART II

Advanced Placement Examination in
CHEMISTRY
Exam 3

1. Ⓐ Ⓑ Ⓒ Ⓓ Ⓔ
2. Ⓐ Ⓑ Ⓒ Ⓓ Ⓔ
3. Ⓐ Ⓑ Ⓒ Ⓓ Ⓔ
4. Ⓐ Ⓑ Ⓒ Ⓓ Ⓔ
5. Ⓐ Ⓑ Ⓒ Ⓓ Ⓔ
6. Ⓐ Ⓑ Ⓒ Ⓓ Ⓔ
7. Ⓐ Ⓑ Ⓒ Ⓓ Ⓔ
8. Ⓐ Ⓑ Ⓒ Ⓓ Ⓔ
9. Ⓐ Ⓑ Ⓒ Ⓓ Ⓔ
10. Ⓐ Ⓑ Ⓒ Ⓓ Ⓔ
11. Ⓐ Ⓑ Ⓒ Ⓓ Ⓔ
12. Ⓐ Ⓑ Ⓒ Ⓓ Ⓔ
13. Ⓐ Ⓑ Ⓒ Ⓓ Ⓔ
14. Ⓐ Ⓑ Ⓒ Ⓓ Ⓔ
15. Ⓐ Ⓑ Ⓒ Ⓓ Ⓔ
16. Ⓐ Ⓑ Ⓒ Ⓓ Ⓔ
17. Ⓐ Ⓑ Ⓒ Ⓓ Ⓔ
18. Ⓐ Ⓑ Ⓒ Ⓓ Ⓔ
19. Ⓐ Ⓑ Ⓒ Ⓓ Ⓔ
20. Ⓐ Ⓑ Ⓒ Ⓓ Ⓔ
21. Ⓐ Ⓑ Ⓒ Ⓓ Ⓔ
22. Ⓐ Ⓑ Ⓒ Ⓓ Ⓔ
23. Ⓐ Ⓑ Ⓒ Ⓓ Ⓔ
24. Ⓐ Ⓑ Ⓒ Ⓓ Ⓔ
25. Ⓐ Ⓑ Ⓒ Ⓓ Ⓔ

26. Ⓐ Ⓑ Ⓒ Ⓓ Ⓔ
27. Ⓐ Ⓑ Ⓒ Ⓓ Ⓔ
28. Ⓐ Ⓑ Ⓒ Ⓓ Ⓔ
29. Ⓐ Ⓑ Ⓒ Ⓓ Ⓔ
30. Ⓐ Ⓑ Ⓒ Ⓓ Ⓔ
31. Ⓐ Ⓑ Ⓒ Ⓓ Ⓔ
32. Ⓐ Ⓑ Ⓒ Ⓓ Ⓔ
33. Ⓐ Ⓑ Ⓒ Ⓓ Ⓔ
34. Ⓐ Ⓑ Ⓒ Ⓓ Ⓔ
35. Ⓐ Ⓑ Ⓒ Ⓓ Ⓔ
36. Ⓐ Ⓑ Ⓒ Ⓓ Ⓔ
37. Ⓐ Ⓑ Ⓒ Ⓓ Ⓔ
38. Ⓐ Ⓑ Ⓒ Ⓓ Ⓔ
39. Ⓐ Ⓑ Ⓒ Ⓓ Ⓔ
40. Ⓐ Ⓑ Ⓒ Ⓓ Ⓔ
41. Ⓐ Ⓑ Ⓒ Ⓓ Ⓔ
42. Ⓐ Ⓑ Ⓒ Ⓓ Ⓔ
43. Ⓐ Ⓑ Ⓒ Ⓓ Ⓔ
44. Ⓐ Ⓑ Ⓒ Ⓓ Ⓔ
45. Ⓐ Ⓑ Ⓒ Ⓓ Ⓔ
46. Ⓐ Ⓑ Ⓒ Ⓓ Ⓔ
47. Ⓐ Ⓑ Ⓒ Ⓓ Ⓔ
48. Ⓐ Ⓑ Ⓒ Ⓓ Ⓔ
49. Ⓐ Ⓑ Ⓒ Ⓓ Ⓔ
50. Ⓐ Ⓑ Ⓒ Ⓓ Ⓔ

51. Ⓐ Ⓑ Ⓒ Ⓓ Ⓔ
52. Ⓐ Ⓑ Ⓒ Ⓓ Ⓔ
53. Ⓐ Ⓑ Ⓒ Ⓓ Ⓔ
54. Ⓐ Ⓑ Ⓒ Ⓓ Ⓔ
55. Ⓐ Ⓑ Ⓒ Ⓓ Ⓔ
56. Ⓐ Ⓑ Ⓒ Ⓓ Ⓔ
57. Ⓐ Ⓑ Ⓒ Ⓓ Ⓔ
58. Ⓐ Ⓑ Ⓒ Ⓓ Ⓔ
59. Ⓐ Ⓑ Ⓒ Ⓓ Ⓔ
60. Ⓐ Ⓑ Ⓒ Ⓓ Ⓔ
61. Ⓐ Ⓑ Ⓒ Ⓓ Ⓔ
62. Ⓐ Ⓑ Ⓒ Ⓓ Ⓔ
63. Ⓐ Ⓑ Ⓒ Ⓓ Ⓔ
64. Ⓐ Ⓑ Ⓒ Ⓓ Ⓔ
65. Ⓐ Ⓑ Ⓒ Ⓓ Ⓔ
66. Ⓐ Ⓑ Ⓒ Ⓓ Ⓔ
67. Ⓐ Ⓑ Ⓒ Ⓓ Ⓔ
68. Ⓐ Ⓑ Ⓒ Ⓓ Ⓔ
69. Ⓐ Ⓑ Ⓒ Ⓓ Ⓔ
70. Ⓐ Ⓑ Ⓒ Ⓓ Ⓔ
71. Ⓐ Ⓑ Ⓒ Ⓓ Ⓔ
72. Ⓐ Ⓑ Ⓒ Ⓓ Ⓔ
73. Ⓐ Ⓑ Ⓒ Ⓓ Ⓔ
74. Ⓐ Ⓑ Ⓒ Ⓓ Ⓔ
75. Ⓐ Ⓑ Ⓒ Ⓓ Ⓔ

AP CHEMISTRY
EXAM 3 – PART II

AP CHEMISTRY
EXAM 3 – PART II

Advanced Placement Examination in
CHEMISTRY
Exam 4

1. Ⓐ Ⓑ Ⓒ Ⓓ Ⓔ
2. Ⓐ Ⓑ Ⓒ Ⓓ Ⓔ
3. Ⓐ Ⓑ Ⓒ Ⓓ Ⓔ
4. Ⓐ Ⓑ Ⓒ Ⓓ Ⓔ
5. Ⓐ Ⓑ Ⓒ Ⓓ Ⓔ
6. Ⓐ Ⓑ Ⓒ Ⓓ Ⓔ
7. Ⓐ Ⓑ Ⓒ Ⓓ Ⓔ
8. Ⓐ Ⓑ Ⓒ Ⓓ Ⓔ
9. Ⓐ Ⓑ Ⓒ Ⓓ Ⓔ
10. Ⓐ Ⓑ Ⓒ Ⓓ Ⓔ
11. Ⓐ Ⓑ Ⓒ Ⓓ Ⓔ
12. Ⓐ Ⓑ Ⓒ Ⓓ Ⓔ
13. Ⓐ Ⓑ Ⓒ Ⓓ Ⓔ
14. Ⓐ Ⓑ Ⓒ Ⓓ Ⓔ
15. Ⓐ Ⓑ Ⓒ Ⓓ Ⓔ
16. Ⓐ Ⓑ Ⓒ Ⓓ Ⓔ
17. Ⓐ Ⓑ Ⓒ Ⓓ Ⓔ
18. Ⓐ Ⓑ Ⓒ Ⓓ Ⓔ
19. Ⓐ Ⓑ Ⓒ Ⓓ Ⓔ
20. Ⓐ Ⓑ Ⓒ Ⓓ Ⓔ
21. Ⓐ Ⓑ Ⓒ Ⓓ Ⓔ
22. Ⓐ Ⓑ Ⓒ Ⓓ Ⓔ
23. Ⓐ Ⓑ Ⓒ Ⓓ Ⓔ
24. Ⓐ Ⓑ Ⓒ Ⓓ Ⓔ
25. Ⓐ Ⓑ Ⓒ Ⓓ Ⓔ

26. Ⓐ Ⓑ Ⓒ Ⓓ Ⓔ
27. Ⓐ Ⓑ Ⓒ Ⓓ Ⓔ
28. Ⓐ Ⓑ Ⓒ Ⓓ Ⓔ
29. Ⓐ Ⓑ Ⓒ Ⓓ Ⓔ
30. Ⓐ Ⓑ Ⓒ Ⓓ Ⓔ
31. Ⓐ Ⓑ Ⓒ Ⓓ Ⓔ
32. Ⓐ Ⓑ Ⓒ Ⓓ Ⓔ
33. Ⓐ Ⓑ Ⓒ Ⓓ Ⓔ
34. Ⓐ Ⓑ Ⓒ Ⓓ Ⓔ
35. Ⓐ Ⓑ Ⓒ Ⓓ Ⓔ
36. Ⓐ Ⓑ Ⓒ Ⓓ Ⓔ
37. Ⓐ Ⓑ Ⓒ Ⓓ Ⓔ
38. Ⓐ Ⓑ Ⓒ Ⓓ Ⓔ
39. Ⓐ Ⓑ Ⓒ Ⓓ Ⓔ
40. Ⓐ Ⓑ Ⓒ Ⓓ Ⓔ
41. Ⓐ Ⓑ Ⓒ Ⓓ Ⓔ
42. Ⓐ Ⓑ Ⓒ Ⓓ Ⓔ
43. Ⓐ Ⓑ Ⓒ Ⓓ Ⓔ
44. Ⓐ Ⓑ Ⓒ Ⓓ Ⓔ
45. Ⓐ Ⓑ Ⓒ Ⓓ Ⓔ
46. Ⓐ Ⓑ Ⓒ Ⓓ Ⓔ
47. Ⓐ Ⓑ Ⓒ Ⓓ Ⓔ
48. Ⓐ Ⓑ Ⓒ Ⓓ Ⓔ
49. Ⓐ Ⓑ Ⓒ Ⓓ Ⓔ
50. Ⓐ Ⓑ Ⓒ Ⓓ Ⓔ

51. Ⓐ Ⓑ Ⓒ Ⓓ Ⓔ
52. Ⓐ Ⓑ Ⓒ Ⓓ Ⓔ
53. Ⓐ Ⓑ Ⓒ Ⓓ Ⓔ
54. Ⓐ Ⓑ Ⓒ Ⓓ Ⓔ
55. Ⓐ Ⓑ Ⓒ Ⓓ Ⓔ
56. Ⓐ Ⓑ Ⓒ Ⓓ Ⓔ
57. Ⓐ Ⓑ Ⓒ Ⓓ Ⓔ
58. Ⓐ Ⓑ Ⓒ Ⓓ Ⓔ
59. Ⓐ Ⓑ Ⓒ Ⓓ Ⓔ
60. Ⓐ Ⓑ Ⓒ Ⓓ Ⓔ
61. Ⓐ Ⓑ Ⓒ Ⓓ Ⓔ
62. Ⓐ Ⓑ Ⓒ Ⓓ Ⓔ
63. Ⓐ Ⓑ Ⓒ Ⓓ Ⓔ
64. Ⓐ Ⓑ Ⓒ Ⓓ Ⓔ
65. Ⓐ Ⓑ Ⓒ Ⓓ Ⓔ
66. Ⓐ Ⓑ Ⓒ Ⓓ Ⓔ
67. Ⓐ Ⓑ Ⓒ Ⓓ Ⓔ
68. Ⓐ Ⓑ Ⓒ Ⓓ Ⓔ
69. Ⓐ Ⓑ Ⓒ Ⓓ Ⓔ
70. Ⓐ Ⓑ Ⓒ Ⓓ Ⓔ
71. Ⓐ Ⓑ Ⓒ Ⓓ Ⓔ
72. Ⓐ Ⓑ Ⓒ Ⓓ Ⓔ
73. Ⓐ Ⓑ Ⓒ Ⓓ Ⓔ
74. Ⓐ Ⓑ Ⓒ Ⓓ Ⓔ
75. Ⓐ Ⓑ Ⓒ Ⓓ Ⓔ

AP CHEMISTRY
EXAM 4 – PART II

AP CHEMISTRY
EXAM 4 – PART II

Advanced Placement Examination in
CHEMISTRY
Exam 5

1. Ⓐ Ⓑ Ⓒ Ⓓ Ⓔ   26. Ⓐ Ⓑ Ⓒ Ⓓ Ⓔ   51. Ⓐ Ⓑ Ⓒ Ⓓ Ⓔ
2. Ⓐ Ⓑ Ⓒ Ⓓ Ⓔ   27. Ⓐ Ⓑ Ⓒ Ⓓ Ⓔ   52. Ⓐ Ⓑ Ⓒ Ⓓ Ⓔ
3. Ⓐ Ⓑ Ⓒ Ⓓ Ⓔ   28. Ⓐ Ⓑ Ⓒ Ⓓ Ⓔ   53. Ⓐ Ⓑ Ⓒ Ⓓ Ⓔ
4. Ⓐ Ⓑ Ⓒ Ⓓ Ⓔ   29. Ⓐ Ⓑ Ⓒ Ⓓ Ⓔ   54. Ⓐ Ⓑ Ⓒ Ⓓ Ⓔ
5. Ⓐ Ⓑ Ⓒ Ⓓ Ⓔ   30. Ⓐ Ⓑ Ⓒ Ⓓ Ⓔ   55. Ⓐ Ⓑ Ⓒ Ⓓ Ⓔ
6. Ⓐ Ⓑ Ⓒ Ⓓ Ⓔ   31. Ⓐ Ⓑ Ⓒ Ⓓ Ⓔ   56. Ⓐ Ⓑ Ⓒ Ⓓ Ⓔ
7. Ⓐ Ⓑ Ⓒ Ⓓ Ⓔ   32. Ⓐ Ⓑ Ⓒ Ⓓ Ⓔ   57. Ⓐ Ⓑ Ⓒ Ⓓ Ⓔ
8. Ⓐ Ⓑ Ⓒ Ⓓ Ⓔ   33. Ⓐ Ⓑ Ⓒ Ⓓ Ⓔ   58. Ⓐ Ⓑ Ⓒ Ⓓ Ⓔ
9. Ⓐ Ⓑ Ⓒ Ⓓ Ⓔ   34. Ⓐ Ⓑ Ⓒ Ⓓ Ⓔ   59. Ⓐ Ⓑ Ⓒ Ⓓ Ⓔ
10. Ⓐ Ⓑ Ⓒ Ⓓ Ⓔ   35. Ⓐ Ⓑ Ⓒ Ⓓ Ⓔ   60. Ⓐ Ⓑ Ⓒ Ⓓ Ⓔ
11. Ⓐ Ⓑ Ⓒ Ⓓ Ⓔ   36. Ⓐ Ⓑ Ⓒ Ⓓ Ⓔ   61. Ⓐ Ⓑ Ⓒ Ⓓ Ⓔ
12. Ⓐ Ⓑ Ⓒ Ⓓ Ⓔ   37. Ⓐ Ⓑ Ⓒ Ⓓ Ⓔ   62. Ⓐ Ⓑ Ⓒ Ⓓ Ⓔ
13. Ⓐ Ⓑ Ⓒ Ⓓ Ⓔ   38. Ⓐ Ⓑ Ⓒ Ⓓ Ⓔ   63. Ⓐ Ⓑ Ⓒ Ⓓ Ⓔ
14. Ⓐ Ⓑ Ⓒ Ⓓ Ⓔ   39. Ⓐ Ⓑ Ⓒ Ⓓ Ⓔ   64. Ⓐ Ⓑ Ⓒ Ⓓ Ⓔ
15. Ⓐ Ⓑ Ⓒ Ⓓ Ⓔ   40. Ⓐ Ⓑ Ⓒ Ⓓ Ⓔ   65. Ⓐ Ⓑ Ⓒ Ⓓ Ⓔ
16. Ⓐ Ⓑ Ⓒ Ⓓ Ⓔ   41. Ⓐ Ⓑ Ⓒ Ⓓ Ⓔ   66. Ⓐ Ⓑ Ⓒ Ⓓ Ⓔ
17. Ⓐ Ⓑ Ⓒ Ⓓ Ⓔ   42. Ⓐ Ⓑ Ⓒ Ⓓ Ⓔ   67. Ⓐ Ⓑ Ⓒ Ⓓ Ⓔ
18. Ⓐ Ⓑ Ⓒ Ⓓ Ⓔ   43. Ⓐ Ⓑ Ⓒ Ⓓ Ⓔ   68. Ⓐ Ⓑ Ⓒ Ⓓ Ⓔ
19. Ⓐ Ⓑ Ⓒ Ⓓ Ⓔ   44. Ⓐ Ⓑ Ⓒ Ⓓ Ⓔ   69. Ⓐ Ⓑ Ⓒ Ⓓ Ⓔ
20. Ⓐ Ⓑ Ⓒ Ⓓ Ⓔ   45. Ⓐ Ⓑ Ⓒ Ⓓ Ⓔ   70. Ⓐ Ⓑ Ⓒ Ⓓ Ⓔ
21. Ⓐ Ⓑ Ⓒ Ⓓ Ⓔ   46. Ⓐ Ⓑ Ⓒ Ⓓ Ⓔ   71. Ⓐ Ⓑ Ⓒ Ⓓ Ⓔ
22. Ⓐ Ⓑ Ⓒ Ⓓ Ⓔ   47. Ⓐ Ⓑ Ⓒ Ⓓ Ⓔ   72. Ⓐ Ⓑ Ⓒ Ⓓ Ⓔ
23. Ⓐ Ⓑ Ⓒ Ⓓ Ⓔ   48. Ⓐ Ⓑ Ⓒ Ⓓ Ⓔ   73. Ⓐ Ⓑ Ⓒ Ⓓ Ⓔ
24. Ⓐ Ⓑ Ⓒ Ⓓ Ⓔ   49. Ⓐ Ⓑ Ⓒ Ⓓ Ⓔ   74. Ⓐ Ⓑ Ⓒ Ⓓ Ⓔ
25. Ⓐ Ⓑ Ⓒ Ⓓ Ⓔ   50. Ⓐ Ⓑ Ⓒ Ⓓ Ⓔ   75. Ⓐ Ⓑ Ⓒ Ⓓ Ⓔ

AP CHEMISTRY
EXAM 5 – PART II

AP CHEMISTRY
EXAM 5 – PART II

Advanced Placement Examination in
CHEMISTRY
Exam 6

1. Ⓐ Ⓑ Ⓒ Ⓓ Ⓔ
2. Ⓐ Ⓑ Ⓒ Ⓓ Ⓔ
3. Ⓐ Ⓑ Ⓒ Ⓓ Ⓔ
4. Ⓐ Ⓑ Ⓒ Ⓓ Ⓔ
5. Ⓐ Ⓑ Ⓒ Ⓓ Ⓔ
6. Ⓐ Ⓑ Ⓒ Ⓓ Ⓔ
7. Ⓐ Ⓑ Ⓒ Ⓓ Ⓔ
8. Ⓐ Ⓑ Ⓒ Ⓓ Ⓔ
9. Ⓐ Ⓑ Ⓒ Ⓓ Ⓔ
10. Ⓐ Ⓑ Ⓒ Ⓓ Ⓔ
11. Ⓐ Ⓑ Ⓒ Ⓓ Ⓔ
12. Ⓐ Ⓑ Ⓒ Ⓓ Ⓔ
13. Ⓐ Ⓑ Ⓒ Ⓓ Ⓔ
14. Ⓐ Ⓑ Ⓒ Ⓓ Ⓔ
15. Ⓐ Ⓑ Ⓒ Ⓓ Ⓔ
16. Ⓐ Ⓑ Ⓒ Ⓓ Ⓔ
17. Ⓐ Ⓑ Ⓒ Ⓓ Ⓔ
18. Ⓐ Ⓑ Ⓒ Ⓓ Ⓔ
19. Ⓐ Ⓑ Ⓒ Ⓓ Ⓔ
20. Ⓐ Ⓑ Ⓒ Ⓓ Ⓔ
21. Ⓐ Ⓑ Ⓒ Ⓓ Ⓔ
22. Ⓐ Ⓑ Ⓒ Ⓓ Ⓔ
23. Ⓐ Ⓑ Ⓒ Ⓓ Ⓔ
24. Ⓐ Ⓑ Ⓒ Ⓓ Ⓔ
25. Ⓐ Ⓑ Ⓒ Ⓓ Ⓔ

26. Ⓐ Ⓑ Ⓒ Ⓓ Ⓔ
27. Ⓐ Ⓑ Ⓒ Ⓓ Ⓔ
28. Ⓐ Ⓑ Ⓒ Ⓓ Ⓔ
29. Ⓐ Ⓑ Ⓒ Ⓓ Ⓔ
30. Ⓐ Ⓑ Ⓒ Ⓓ Ⓔ
31. Ⓐ Ⓑ Ⓒ Ⓓ Ⓔ
32. Ⓐ Ⓑ Ⓒ Ⓓ Ⓔ
33. Ⓐ Ⓑ Ⓒ Ⓓ Ⓔ
34. Ⓐ Ⓑ Ⓒ Ⓓ Ⓔ
35. Ⓐ Ⓑ Ⓒ Ⓓ Ⓔ
36. Ⓐ Ⓑ Ⓒ Ⓓ Ⓔ
37. Ⓐ Ⓑ Ⓒ Ⓓ Ⓔ
38. Ⓐ Ⓑ Ⓒ Ⓓ Ⓔ
39. Ⓐ Ⓑ Ⓒ Ⓓ Ⓔ
40. Ⓐ Ⓑ Ⓒ Ⓓ Ⓔ
41. Ⓐ Ⓑ Ⓒ Ⓓ Ⓔ
42. Ⓐ Ⓑ Ⓒ Ⓓ Ⓔ
43. Ⓐ Ⓑ Ⓒ Ⓓ Ⓔ
44. Ⓐ Ⓑ Ⓒ Ⓓ Ⓔ
45. Ⓐ Ⓑ Ⓒ Ⓓ Ⓔ
46. Ⓐ Ⓑ Ⓒ Ⓓ Ⓔ
47. Ⓐ Ⓑ Ⓒ Ⓓ Ⓔ
48. Ⓐ Ⓑ Ⓒ Ⓓ Ⓔ
49. Ⓐ Ⓑ Ⓒ Ⓓ Ⓔ
50. Ⓐ Ⓑ Ⓒ Ⓓ Ⓔ

51. Ⓐ Ⓑ Ⓒ Ⓓ Ⓔ
52. Ⓐ Ⓑ Ⓒ Ⓓ Ⓔ
53. Ⓐ Ⓑ Ⓒ Ⓓ Ⓔ
54. Ⓐ Ⓑ Ⓒ Ⓓ Ⓔ
55. Ⓐ Ⓑ Ⓒ Ⓓ Ⓔ
56. Ⓐ Ⓑ Ⓒ Ⓓ Ⓔ
57. Ⓐ Ⓑ Ⓒ Ⓓ Ⓔ
58. Ⓐ Ⓑ Ⓒ Ⓓ Ⓔ
59. Ⓐ Ⓑ Ⓒ Ⓓ Ⓔ
60. Ⓐ Ⓑ Ⓒ Ⓓ Ⓔ
61. Ⓐ Ⓑ Ⓒ Ⓓ Ⓔ
62. Ⓐ Ⓑ Ⓒ Ⓓ Ⓔ
63. Ⓐ Ⓑ Ⓒ Ⓓ Ⓔ
64. Ⓐ Ⓑ Ⓒ Ⓓ Ⓔ
65. Ⓐ Ⓑ Ⓒ Ⓓ Ⓔ
66. Ⓐ Ⓑ Ⓒ Ⓓ Ⓔ
67. Ⓐ Ⓑ Ⓒ Ⓓ Ⓔ
68. Ⓐ Ⓑ Ⓒ Ⓓ Ⓔ
69. Ⓐ Ⓑ Ⓒ Ⓓ Ⓔ
70. Ⓐ Ⓑ Ⓒ Ⓓ Ⓔ
71. Ⓐ Ⓑ Ⓒ Ⓓ Ⓔ
72. Ⓐ Ⓑ Ⓒ Ⓓ Ⓔ
73. Ⓐ Ⓑ Ⓒ Ⓓ Ⓔ
74. Ⓐ Ⓑ Ⓒ Ⓓ Ⓔ
75. Ⓐ Ⓑ Ⓒ Ⓓ Ⓔ

AP CHEMISTRY
EXAM 6 – PART II

AP CHEMISTRY
EXAM 6 – PART II

AP Chemistry Equations & Constants

ATOMIC STRUCTURE

$$E = hv \qquad c = \lambda v$$

$$\lambda = \frac{h}{mv} \qquad p = mv$$

$$E_n = \frac{-2.178 \times 10^{-18}}{n^2} \text{ joule}$$

EQUILIBRIUM

$$K_a = \frac{[H^+][A^-]}{[HA]}$$

$$K_b = \frac{[OH^-][HB^+]}{[B]}$$

$$K_w = [OH^-][H^+] = 1.0 \times 10^{-14} \text{ @ } 25°C$$

$$= K_a \times K_b$$

$$pH = -\log[H^+], \quad pOH = -\log[OH^-]$$

$$14 = pH + pOH$$

$$pH = pK_a + \log\frac{[A^-]}{[HA]}$$

$$pOH = pK_b + \log\frac{[HB^+]}{[B]}$$

$$pK_a = -\log K_a, \quad pK_b = -\log K_b$$

$$K_p = K_c(RT)^{\Delta n},$$

where Δn = moles product gas − moles reactant gas

THERMOCHEMISTRY/KINETICS

$$\Delta S° = \sum S° \text{ products} - \sum S° \text{ reactants}$$

$$\Delta H° = \sum \Delta H_f° \text{ products} - \sum \Delta H_f° \text{ reactants}$$

$$\Delta G° = \sum \Delta G_f° \text{ products} - \sum \Delta G_f° \text{ reactants}$$

$$\Delta G° = \Delta H° - T\Delta S°$$

$$= -RT \ln K = -2.303 \, RT \log K$$

$$= -n\mathcal{F}E°$$

$$\Delta G = \Delta G° + RT \ln Q = \Delta G° + 2.303 \, RT \log Q$$

$$q = mc\Delta T$$

$$C_p = \frac{\Delta H}{\Delta T}$$

$$\ln[A]_t - \ln[A]_0 = -kt$$

$$\frac{1}{[A]_t} - \frac{1}{[A]_0} = kt$$

$$\ln k = \frac{-E_a}{R}\left(\frac{1}{T}\right) + \ln A$$

E = energy v = velocity
v = frequency n = principal quantum number
λ = wavelength m = mass
p = momentum

Speed of light, $c = 3.0 \times 10^8 \text{ m s}^{-1}$

Planck's constant, $h = 6.63 \times 10^{-34} \text{ J s}$

Boltzmann's constant, $k = 1.38 \times 10^{-23} \text{ J K}^{-1}$

Avogadro's number $= 6.022 \times 10^{23} \text{ mol}^{-1}$

Electron charge, $e = -1.602 \times 10^{-19} \text{ coulomb}$

1 electron volt per atom $= 96.5 \text{ kJ mol}^{-1}$

Equilibrium Constants

K_a (weak acid)

K_b (weak base)

K_w (water)

K_p (gas pressure)

K_c (molar concentrations)

$S°$ = standard entropy

$H°$ = standard enthalpy

$G°$ = standard free energy

$E°$ = standard reduction potential

T = temperature

n = moles

m = mass

q = heat

c = specific heat capacity

C_p = molar heat capacity at constant pressure

E_a = activation energy

k = rate constant

A = frequency factor

Faraday's constant, $\mathcal{F}$ = 96,500 coulombs per mole of electrons

Gas constant, $R = 8.31 \text{ J mol}^{-1} \text{ K}^{-1}$

$$= 0.0821 \text{ L atm mol}^{-1} \text{ K}^{-1}$$

$$= 8.31 \text{ volt coulomb mol}^{-1} \text{ K}^{-1}$$

AP Chemistry Equations & Constants

GASES, LIQUIDS, AND SOLUTIONS

$$PV = nRT$$

$$\left(P + \frac{n^2a}{V^2} \right)(V - nb) = nRT$$

$$P_A = P_{total} \times X_A, \text{ where } X_A = \frac{\text{moles A}}{\text{total moles}}$$

$$P_{total} = P_A + P_B + P_C + ...$$

$$n = \frac{m}{M}$$

$$K = {}^{\circ}C + 273$$

$$\frac{P_1V_1}{T_1} = \frac{P_2V_2}{T_2}$$

$$D = \frac{m}{V}$$

$$u_{rms} = \sqrt{\frac{3kT}{m}} = \sqrt{\frac{3RT}{M}}$$

$$KE \text{ per molecule} = \frac{1}{2}mv^2$$

$$KE \text{ per mole} = \frac{3}{2}RT$$

$$\frac{r_1}{r_2} = \sqrt{\frac{M_2}{M_1}}$$

molarity, M = moles solute per liter solution

molality = moles solute per kilogram solvent

$$\Delta T_f = iK_f \times \text{molality}$$

$$\Delta T_b = iK_b \times \text{molality}$$

$$\pi = iMRT$$

$$A = abc$$

OXIDATION-REDUCTION; ELECTROCHEMISTRY

$$Q = \frac{[C]^c\,[D]^d}{[A]^a\,[B]^b}, \text{ where } a\,A + b\,B \rightarrow c\,C + d\,D$$

$$I = \frac{q}{t}$$

$$E_{cell} = E^{\circ}_{cell} - \frac{RT}{n\mathscr{F}}\ln Q = E^{\circ}_{cell} - \frac{0.0592}{n}\log Q \text{ @ 25}^{\circ}C$$

$$\log K = \frac{nE^{\circ}}{0.0592}$$

P = pressure
V = volume
T = temperature
n = number of moles
D = density
m = mass
v = velocity

u_{rms} = root-mean-square speed
KE = kinetic energy
r = rate of effusion
M = molar mass
π = osmotic pressure
i = van't Hoff factor
K_f = molal freezing-point depression constant
K_b = molal boiling-point elevation constant
A = absorbance
a = molar absorptivity
b = path length
c = concentration
Q = reaction quotient
I = current (amperes)
q = charge (coulombs)
t = time (seconds)
E° = standard reduction potential
K = equilibrium constant

Gas constant, R = 8.31 J mol^{-1} K^{-1}

 = 0.0821 L atm mol^{-1} K^{-1}

 = 8.31 volt coulomb mol^{-1} K^{-1}

Boltzmann's constant, k = 1.38 × 10^{-23} J K^{-1}

K_f for H_2O = 1.86 K kg mol^{-1}

K_b for H_2O = 0.512 K kg mol^{-1}

1 atm = 760 mm Hg

 = 760 torr

STP = 0.000°C and 1.000 atm

Faraday's constant, $\mathscr{F}$ = 96,500 coulombs per mole
of electrons

THE PERIODIC TABLE

METALS — NONMETALS

KEY

22	← Atomic Number
IVA / IVB	← Group Classification
Ti	← Symbol
47.88	← Atomic Weight

( ) indicates most stable or best known isotope

TRANSITIONAL METALS

Alkali Metals · Alkaline Earth Metals · Halogens · Noble Gases

1 IA/IA	2 IIA/IIA	3 IIIA/IIIB	4 IVA/IVB	5 VA/VB	6 VIA/VIB	7 VIIA/VIIB	8 VIIIA/VIII	9 VIIIA/VIII	10 VIIIA/VIII	11 IB/IB	12 IIB/IIB	13 IIIB/IIIA	14 IVB/IVA	15 VB/VA	16 VIB/VIA	17 VIIB/VIIA	18 VIII/0
1 H 1.008																	2 He 4.003
3 Li 6.941	4 Be 9.012											5 B 10.811	6 C 12.011	7 N 14.007	8 O 15.999	9 F 18.998	10 Ne 20.180
11 Na 22.990	12 Mg 24.305											13 Al 26.982	14 Si 28.086	15 P 30.974	16 S 32.066	17 Cl 35.453	18 Ar 39.948
19 K 39.098	20 Ca 40.078	21 Sc 44.956	22 Ti 47.88	23 V 50.942	24 Cr 51.996	25 Mn 54.938	26 Fe 55.847	27 Co 58.933	28 Ni 58.693	29 Cu 63.546	30 Zn 65.39	31 Ga 69.723	32 Ge 72.61	33 As 74.922	34 Se 78.96	35 Br 79.904	36 Kr 83.8
37 Rb 85.468	38 Sr 87.62	39 Y 88.906	40 Zr 91.224	41 Nb 92.906	42 Mo 95.94	43 Tc (97.907)	44 Ru 101.07	45 Rh 102.906	46 Pd 106.4	47 Ag 107.868	48 Cd 112.411	49 In 114.818	50 Sn 118.710	51 Sb 121.757	52 Te 127.60	53 I 126.905	54 Xe 131.29
55 Cs 132.905	56 Ba 137.327	57 La 138.906	72 Hf 178.49	73 Ta 180.948	74 W 183.84	75 Re 186.207	76 Os 190.23	77 Ir 192.22	78 Pt 195.08	79 Au 196.967	80 Hg 200.59	81 Tl 204.383	82 Pb 207.2	83 Bi 208.980	84 Po (208.982)	85 At (209.982)	86 Rn (222.018)
87 Fr (223.020)	88 Ra (226.025)	89 Ac (227.028)	104 Unq (261.11)	105 Unp (262.114)	106 Unh (263.118)	107 Uns (262.12)	108 Uno (265)	109 Une (266)	110 Uun (269)	111 Uuu (272.153)	112 Uub (277)						

LANTHANIDE SERIES

58 Ce 140.115	59 Pr 140.908	60 Nd 144.24	61 Pm (144.913)	62 Sm 150.36	63 Eu 151.965	64 Gd 157.25	65 Tb 158.925	66 Dy 162.50	67 Ho 164.930	68 Er 167.26	69 Tm 168.934	70 Yb 173.04	71 Lu 174.967

ACTINIDE SERIES

90 Th 232.038	91 Pa 231.036	92 U 238.029	93 Np (237.048)	94 Pu (244.064)	95 Am (243.061)	96 Cm (247.070)	97 Bk (247.070)	98 Cf (251.080)	99 Es (252.083)	100 Fm (257.095)	101 Md (258.1)	102 No (259.101)	103 Lr (262.11)